SOUL EATER

11

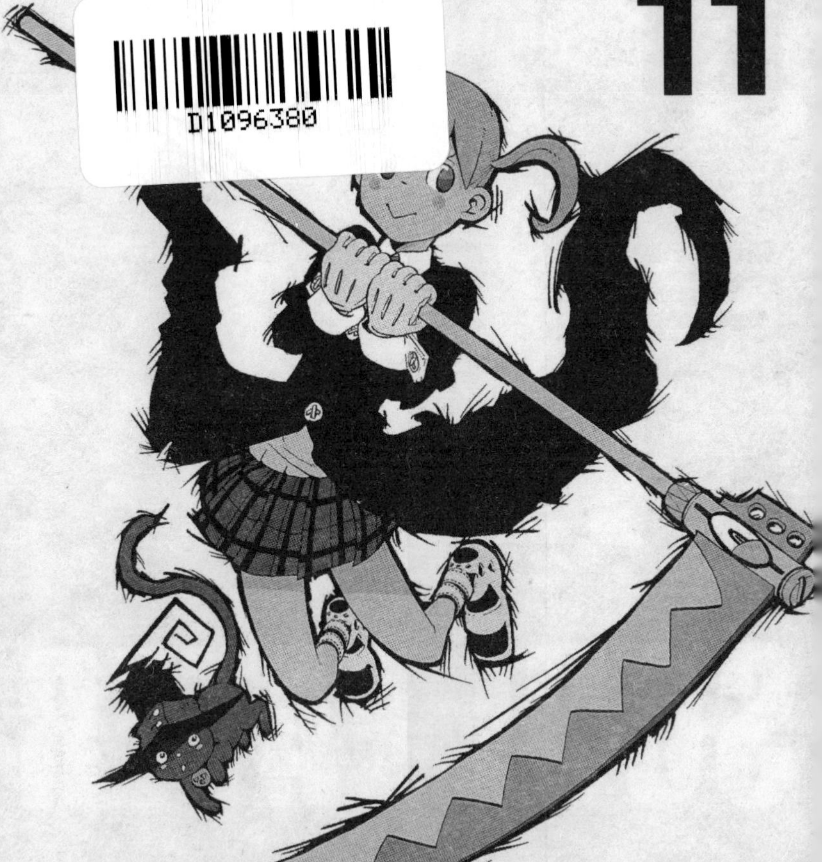

ATSUSHI OHKUBO

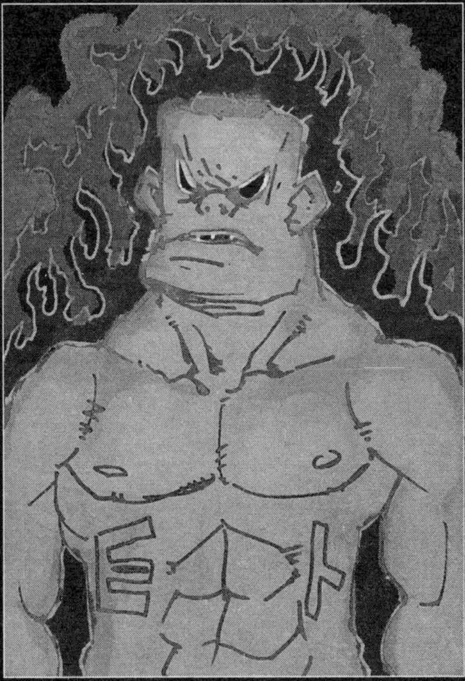
モト

SOUL EATE

vol. 11

by ATSUSHI OHKUBO

FACE UP!
EYES HIGH!
BLAZE YOUR
SOULS!

SOUL EATER 11

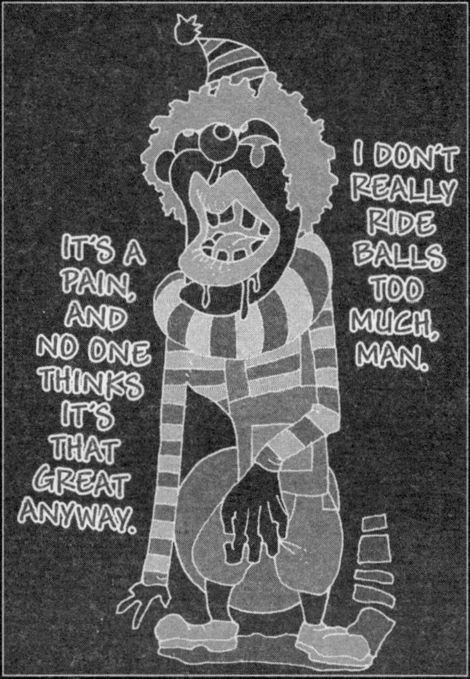
I DON'T REALLY RIDE BALLS TOO MUCH, MAN.
IT'S A PAIN, AND NO ONE THINKS IT'S THAT GREAT ANYWAY.

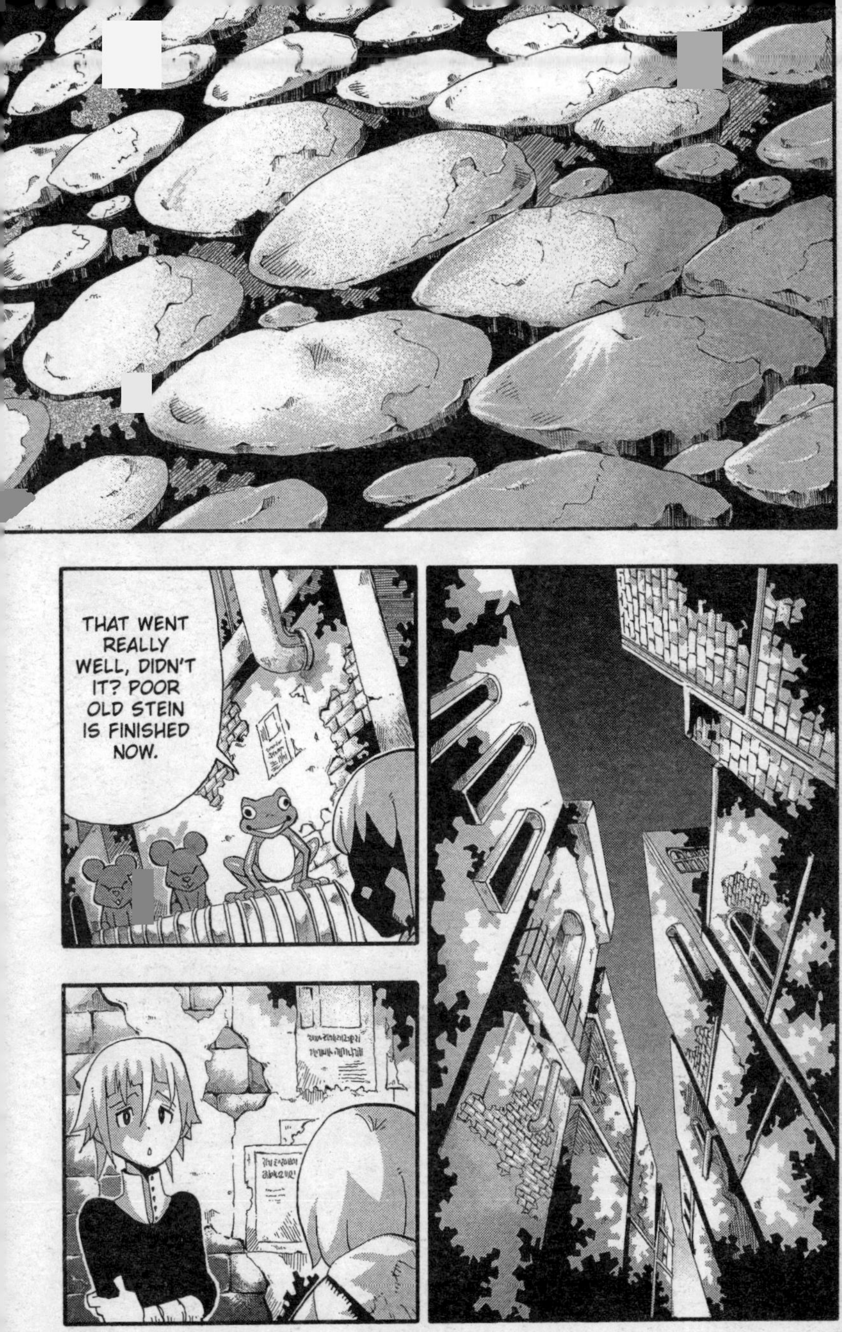
THAT WENT REALLY WELL, DIDN'T IT? POOR OLD STEIN IS FINISHED NOW.

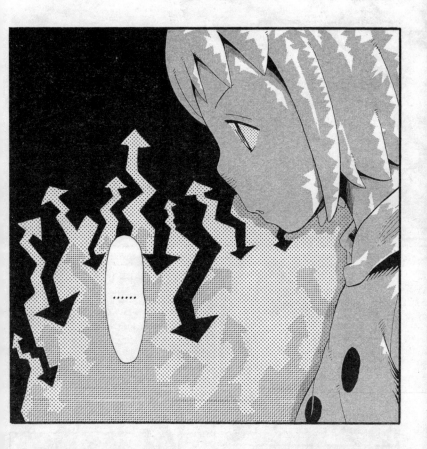

SOUL EATER

CHAPTER 40: RESOLVE

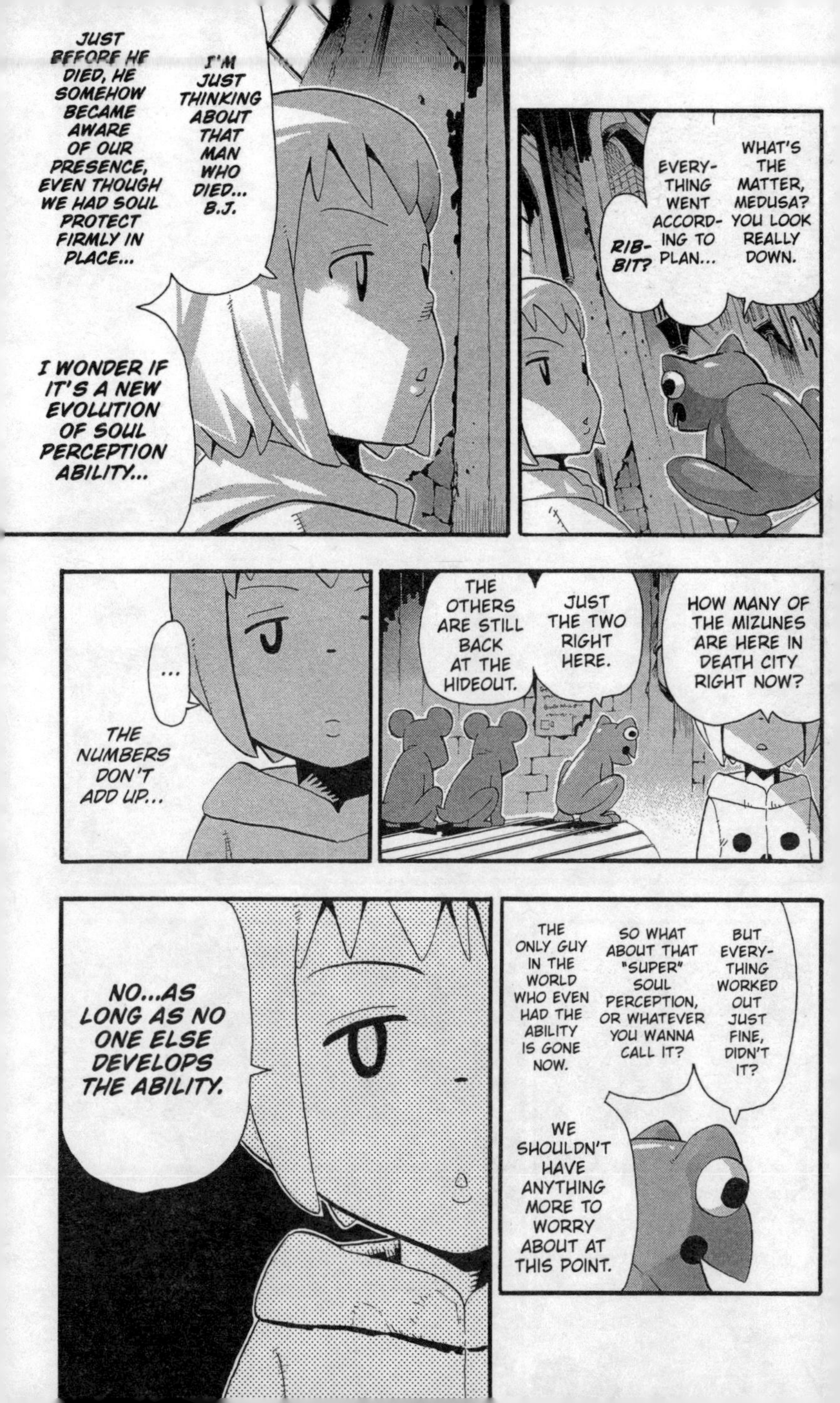
WHAT'S THE MATTER, MEDUSA? YOU LOOK REALLY DOWN.
EVERYTHING WENT ACCORDING TO PLAN...
RIBBIT?
I'M JUST THINKING ABOUT THAT MAN WHO DIED... B.J.
JUST BEFORE HE DIED, HE SOMEHOW BECAME AWARE OF OUR PRESENCE, EVEN THOUGH WE HAD SOUL PROTECT FIRMLY IN PLACE...
I WONDER IF IT'S A NEW EVOLUTION OF SOUL PERCEPTION ABILITY...
HOW MANY OF THE MIZUNES ARE HERE IN DEATH CITY RIGHT NOW?
JUST THE TWO RIGHT HERE.
THE OTHERS ARE STILL BACK AT THE HIDEOUT.
...
THE NUMBERS DON'T ADD UP...
BUT EVERYTHING WORKED OUT JUST FINE, DIDN'T IT?
SO WHAT ABOUT THAT "SUPER" SOUL PERCEPTION, OR WHATEVER YOU WANNA CALL IT?
THE ONLY GUY IN THE WORLD WHO EVEN HAD THE ABILITY IS GONE NOW.
WE SHOULDN'T HAVE ANYTHING MORE TO WORRY ABOUT AT THIS POINT.
NO...AS LONG AS NO ONE ELSE DEVELOPS THE ABILITY.

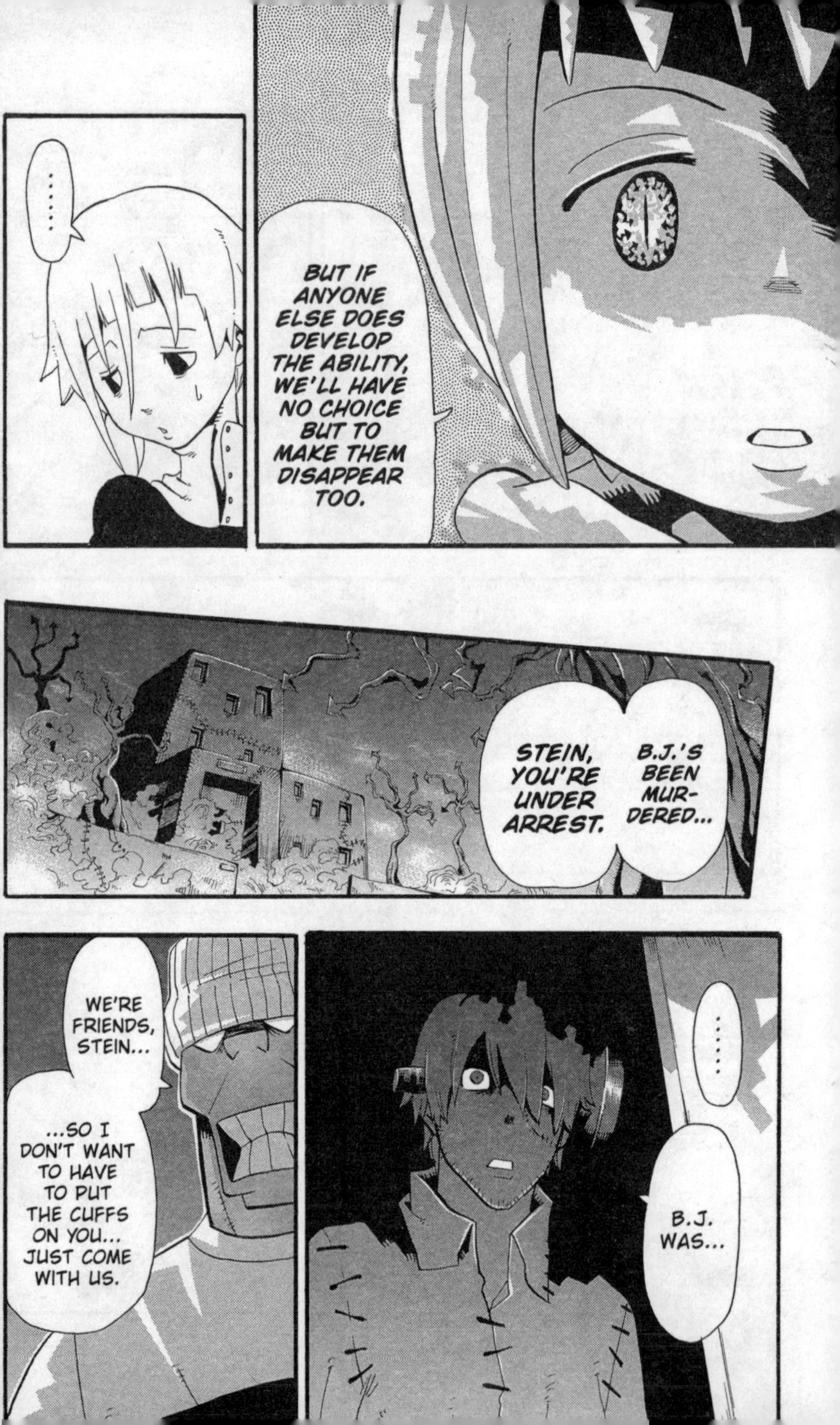
BUT IF ANYONE ELSE DOES DEVELOP THE ABILITY, WE'LL HAVE NO CHOICE BUT TO MAKE THEM DISAPPEAR TOO.
......
B.J.'S BEEN MURDERED...
STEIN, YOU'RE UNDER ARREST.
......
B.J. WAS...
WE'RE FRIENDS, STEIN...
...SO I DON'T WANT TO HAVE TO PUT THE CUFFS ON YOU... JUST COME WITH US.

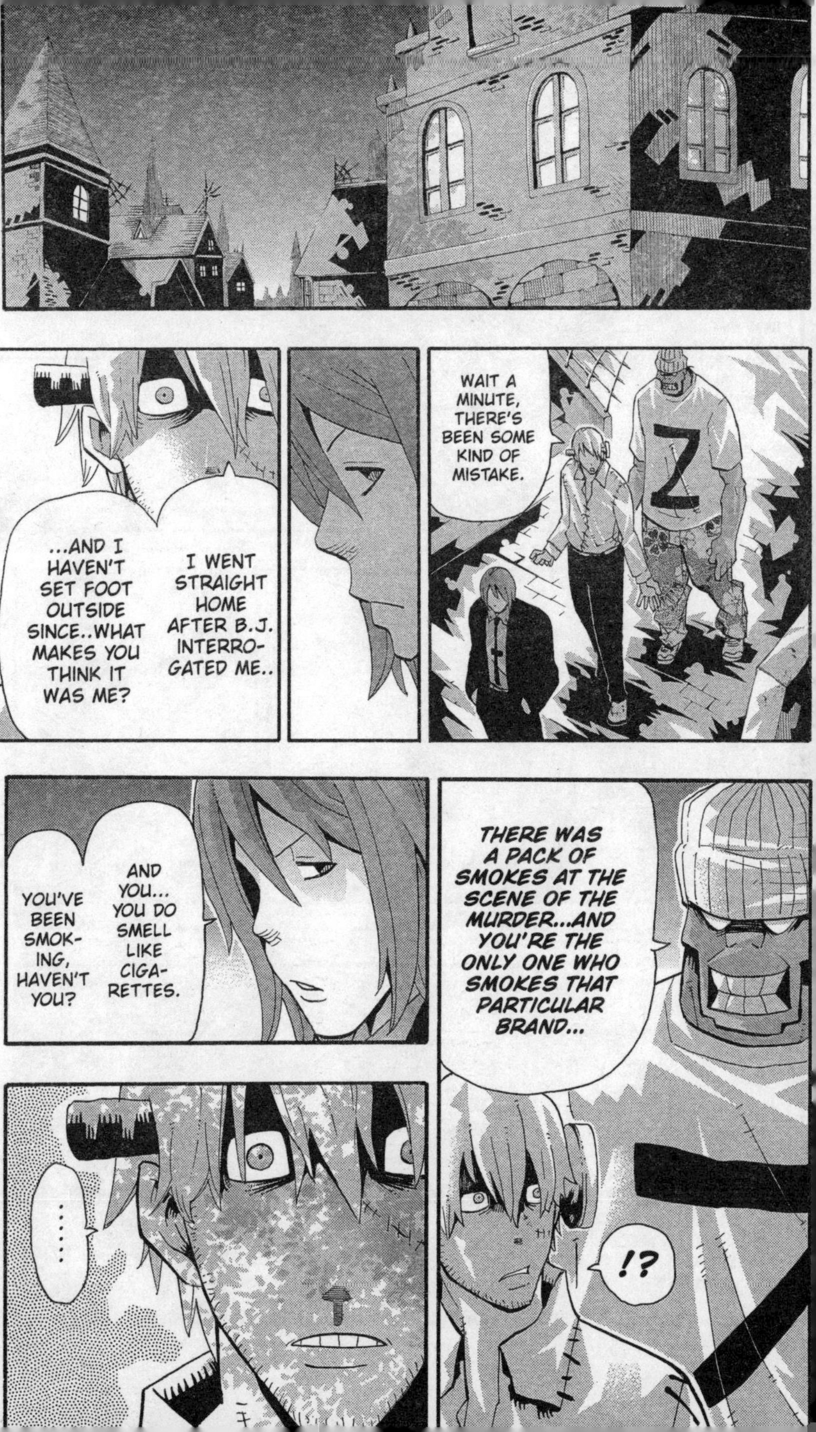
WAIT A MINUTE, THERE'S BEEN SOME KIND OF MISTAKE.
I WENT STRAIGHT HOME AFTER B.J. INTERROGATED ME..
...AND I HAVEN'T SET FOOT OUTSIDE SINCE..WHAT MAKES YOU THINK IT WAS ME?
THERE WAS A PACK OF SMOKES AT THE SCENE OF THE MURDER...AND YOU'RE THE ONLY ONE WHO SMOKES THAT PARTICULAR BRAND...
!?
AND YOU... YOU DO SMELL LIKE CIGA-RETTES.
YOU'VE BEEN SMOK-ING, HAVEN'T YOU?
......

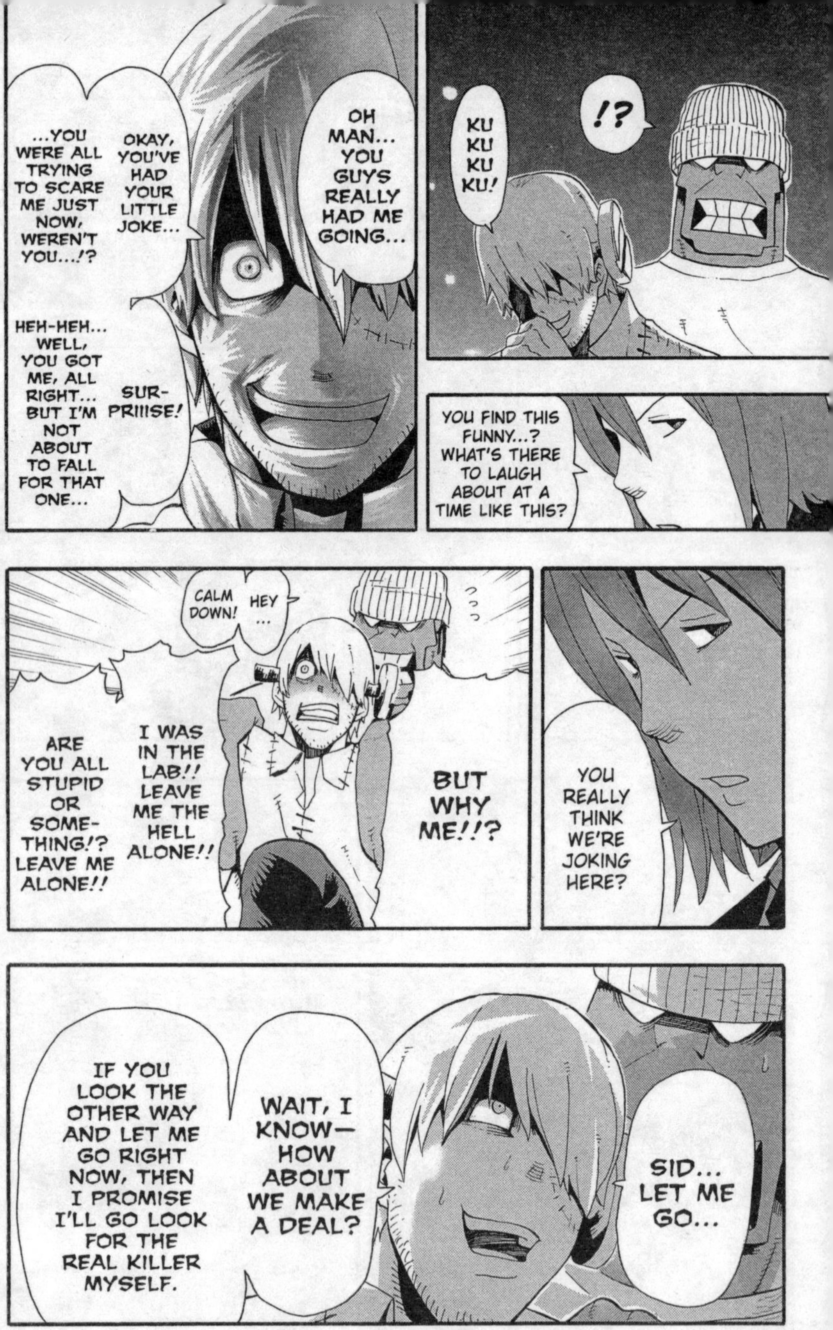
!?
KU KU KU KU!
YOU FIND THIS FUNNY...? WHAT'S THERE TO LAUGH ABOUT AT A TIME LIKE THIS?
OH MAN... YOU GUYS REALLY HAD ME GOING...
OKAY, YOU'VE HAD YOUR LITTLE JOKE...
...YOU WERE ALL TRYING TO SCARE ME JUST NOW, WEREN'T YOU...!?
SUR-PRIIISE!
HEH-HEH... WELL, YOU GOT ME, ALL RIGHT... BUT I'M NOT ABOUT TO FALL FOR THAT ONE...
YOU REALLY THINK WE'RE JOKING HERE?
HEY...
CALM DOWN!
BUT WHY ME!!?
I WAS IN THE LAB!! LEAVE ME THE HELL ALONE!!
ARE YOU ALL STUPID OR SOME-THING!? LEAVE ME ALONE!!
SID... LET ME GO...
WAIT, I KNOW— HOW ABOUT WE MAKE A DEAL?
IF YOU LOOK THE OTHER WAY AND LET ME GO RIGHT NOW, THEN I PROMISE I'LL GO LOOK FOR THE REAL KILLER MYSELF.

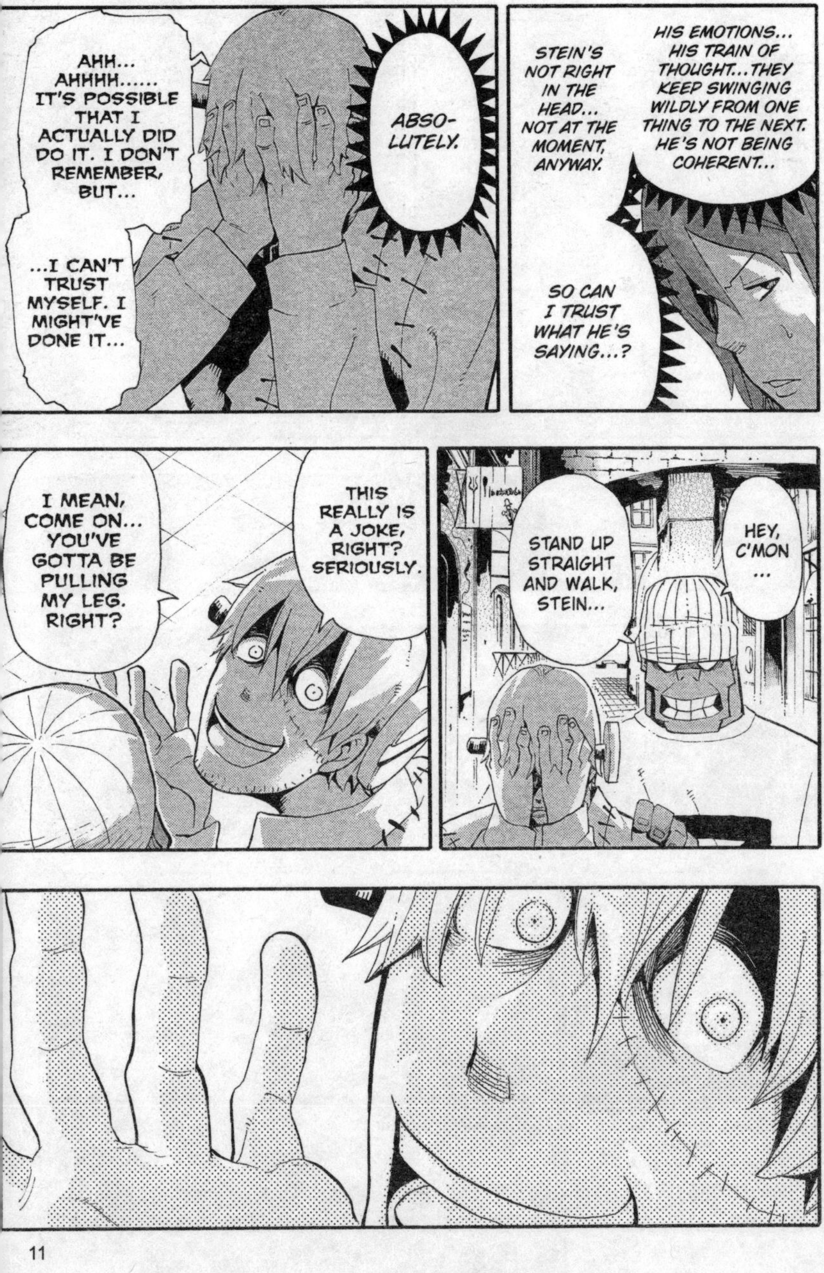
HIS EMOTIONS... HIS TRAIN OF THOUGHT...THEY KEEP SWINGING WILDLY FROM ONE THING TO THE NEXT. HE'S NOT BEING COHERENT...
STEIN'S NOT RIGHT IN THE HEAD... NOT AT THE MOMENT, ANYWAY.
SO CAN I TRUST WHAT HE'S SAYING...?
ABSO-LUTELY.
AHH... AHHHH...... IT'S POSSIBLE THAT I ACTUALLY DID DO IT. I DON'T REMEMBER, BUT...
...I CAN'T TRUST MYSELF. I MIGHT'VE DONE IT...
HEY, C'MON ...
STAND UP STRAIGHT AND WALK, STEIN...
THIS REALLY IS A JOKE, RIGHT? SERIOUSLY.
I MEAN, COME ON... YOU'VE GOTTA BE PULLING MY LEG. RIGHT?

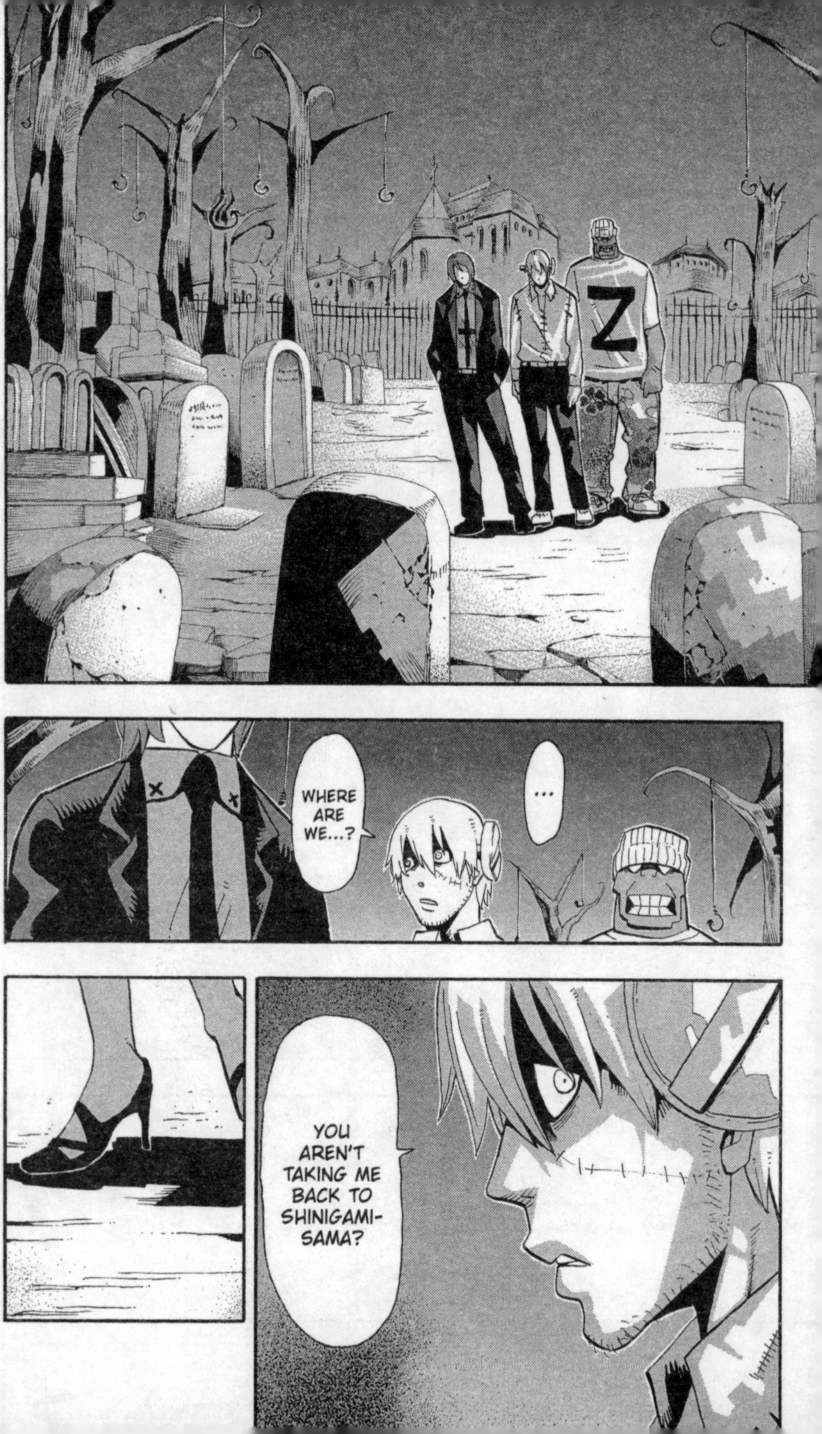
...
WHERE ARE WE...?
YOU AREN'T TAKING ME BACK TO SHINIGAMI-SAMA?

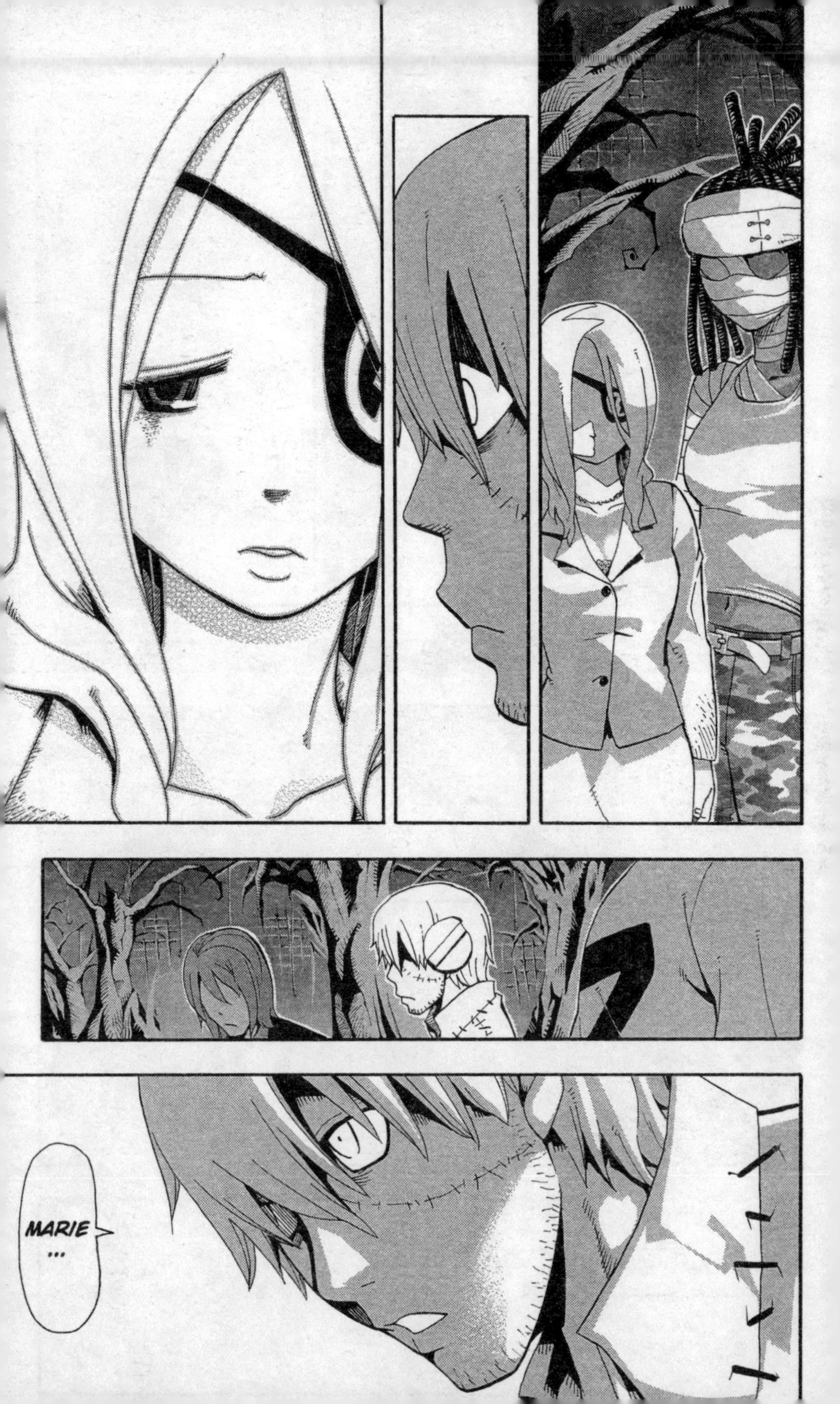
MARIE ...

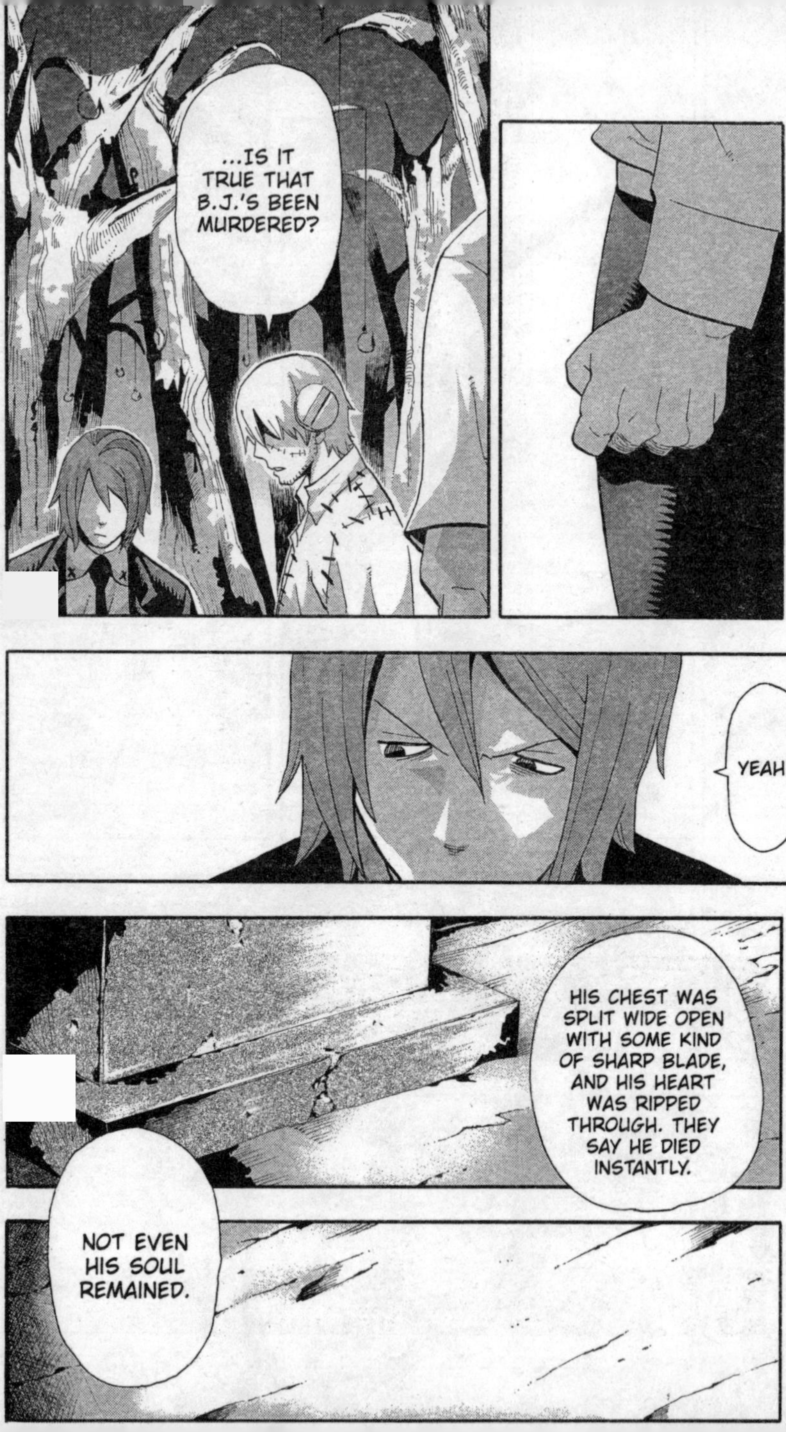
...IS IT TRUE THAT B.J.'S BEEN MURDERED?
YEAH.
HIS CHEST WAS SPLIT WIDE OPEN WITH SOME KIND OF SHARP BLADE, AND HIS HEART WAS RIPPED THROUGH. THEY SAY HE DIED INSTANTLY.
NOT EVEN HIS SOUL REMAINED.

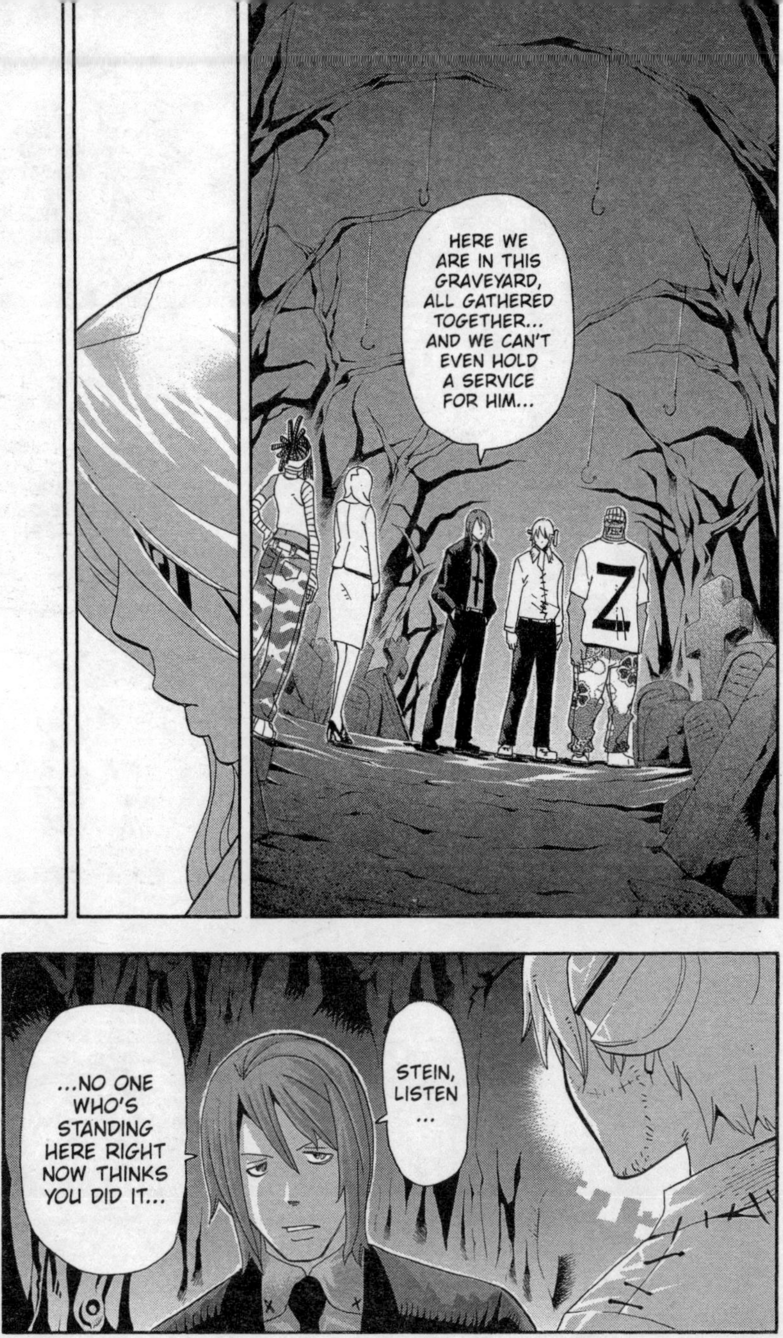
HERE WE ARE IN THIS GRAVEYARD, ALL GATHERED TOGETHER... AND WE CAN'T EVEN HOLD A SERVICE FOR HIM...
Z
STEIN, LISTEN...
...NO ONE WHO'S STANDING HERE RIGHT NOW THINKS YOU DID IT...

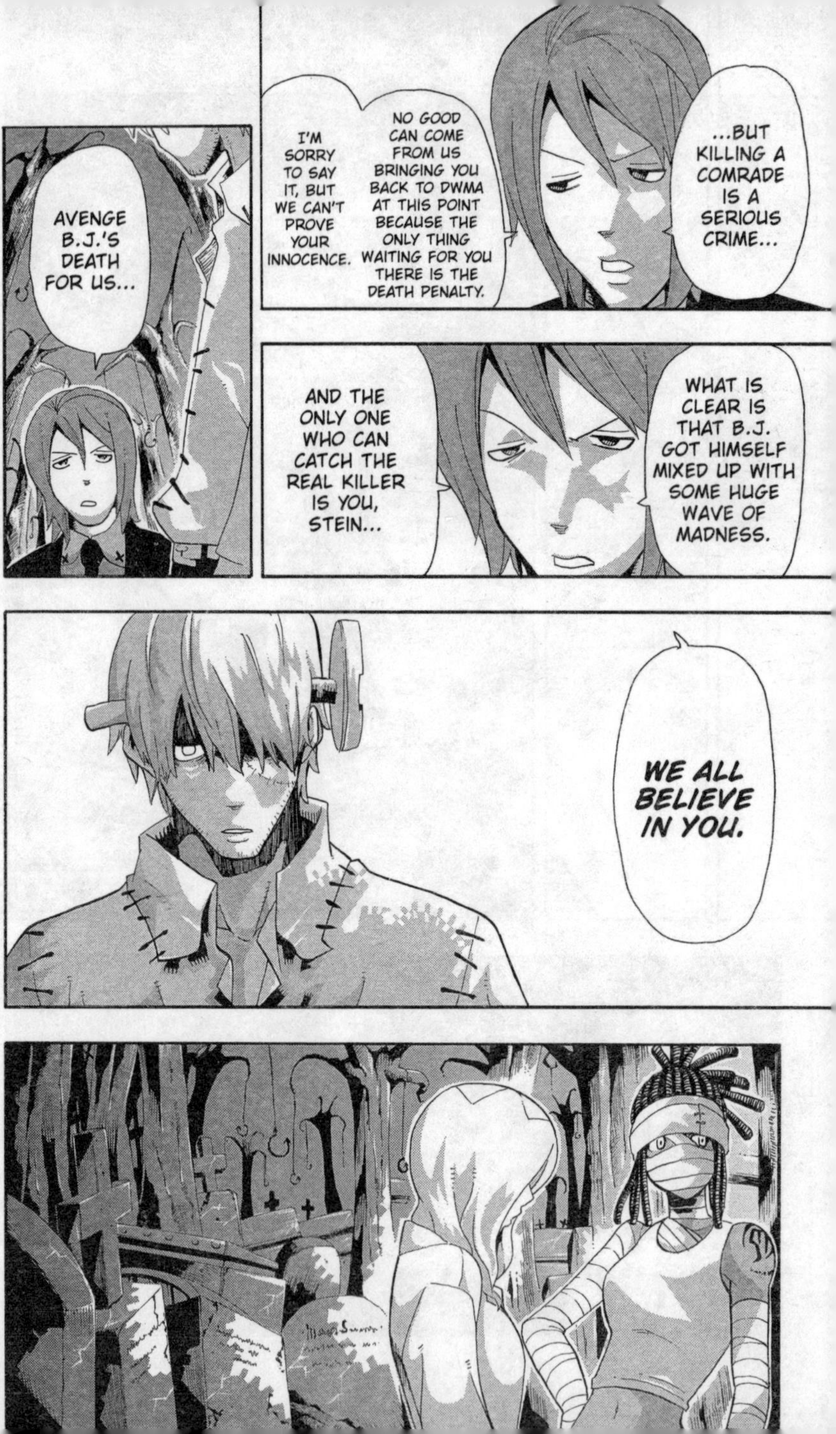
...BUT KILLING A COMRADE IS A SERIOUS CRIME...
NO GOOD CAN COME FROM US BRINGING YOU BACK TO DWMA AT THIS POINT BECAUSE THE ONLY THING WAITING FOR YOU THERE IS THE DEATH PENALTY.
I'M SORRY TO SAY IT, BUT WE CAN'T PROVE YOUR INNOCENCE.
WHAT IS CLEAR IS THAT B.J. GOT HIMSELF MIXED UP WITH SOME HUGE WAVE OF MADNESS.
AND THE ONLY ONE WHO CAN CATCH THE REAL KILLER IS YOU, STEIN...
AVENGE B.J.'S DEATH FOR US...
WE ALL BELIEVE IN YOU.

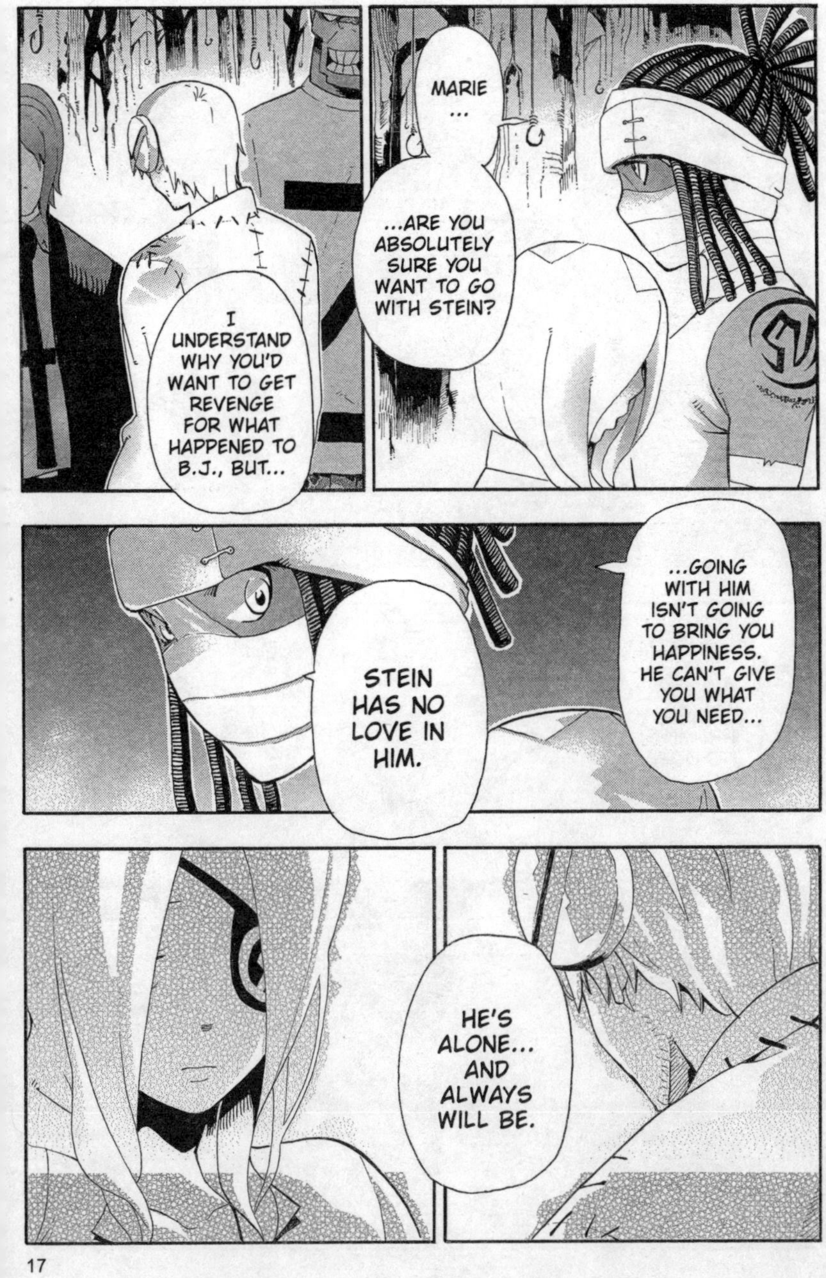
MARIE ...
...ARE YOU ABSOLUTELY SURE YOU WANT TO GO WITH STEIN?
I UNDERSTAND WHY YOU'D WANT TO GET REVENGE FOR WHAT HAPPENED TO B.J., BUT...
...GOING WITH HIM ISN'T GOING TO BRING YOU HAPPINESS. HE CAN'T GIVE YOU WHAT YOU NEED...
STEIN HAS NO LOVE IN HIM.
HE'S ALONE... AND ALWAYS WILL BE.

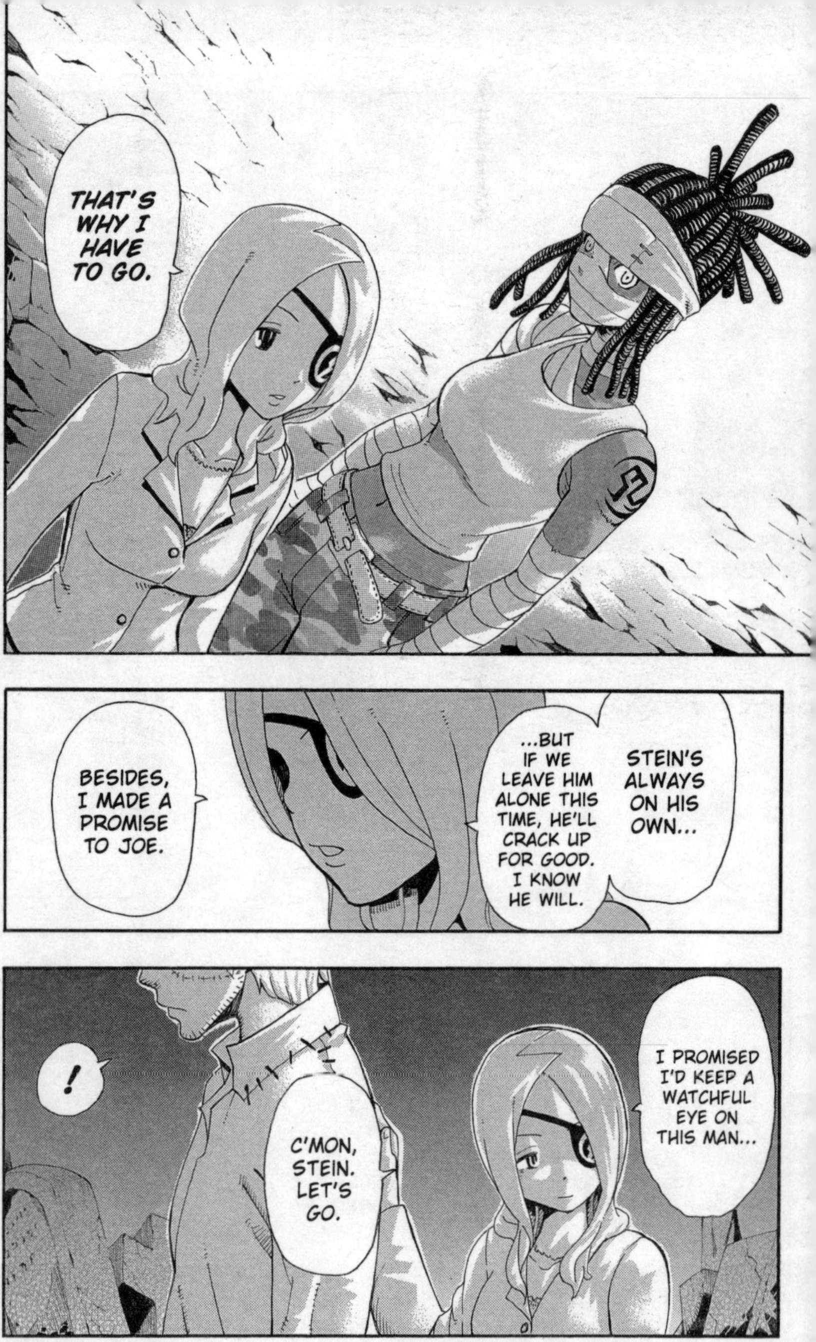
THAT'S WHY I HAVE TO GO.
STEIN'S ALWAYS ON HIS OWN...
...BUT IF WE LEAVE HIM ALONE THIS TIME, HE'LL CRACK UP FOR GOOD. I KNOW HE WILL.
BESIDES, I MADE A PROMISE TO JOE.
I PROMISED I'D KEEP A WATCHFUL EYE ON THIS MAN...
C'MON, STEIN. LET'S GO.
!

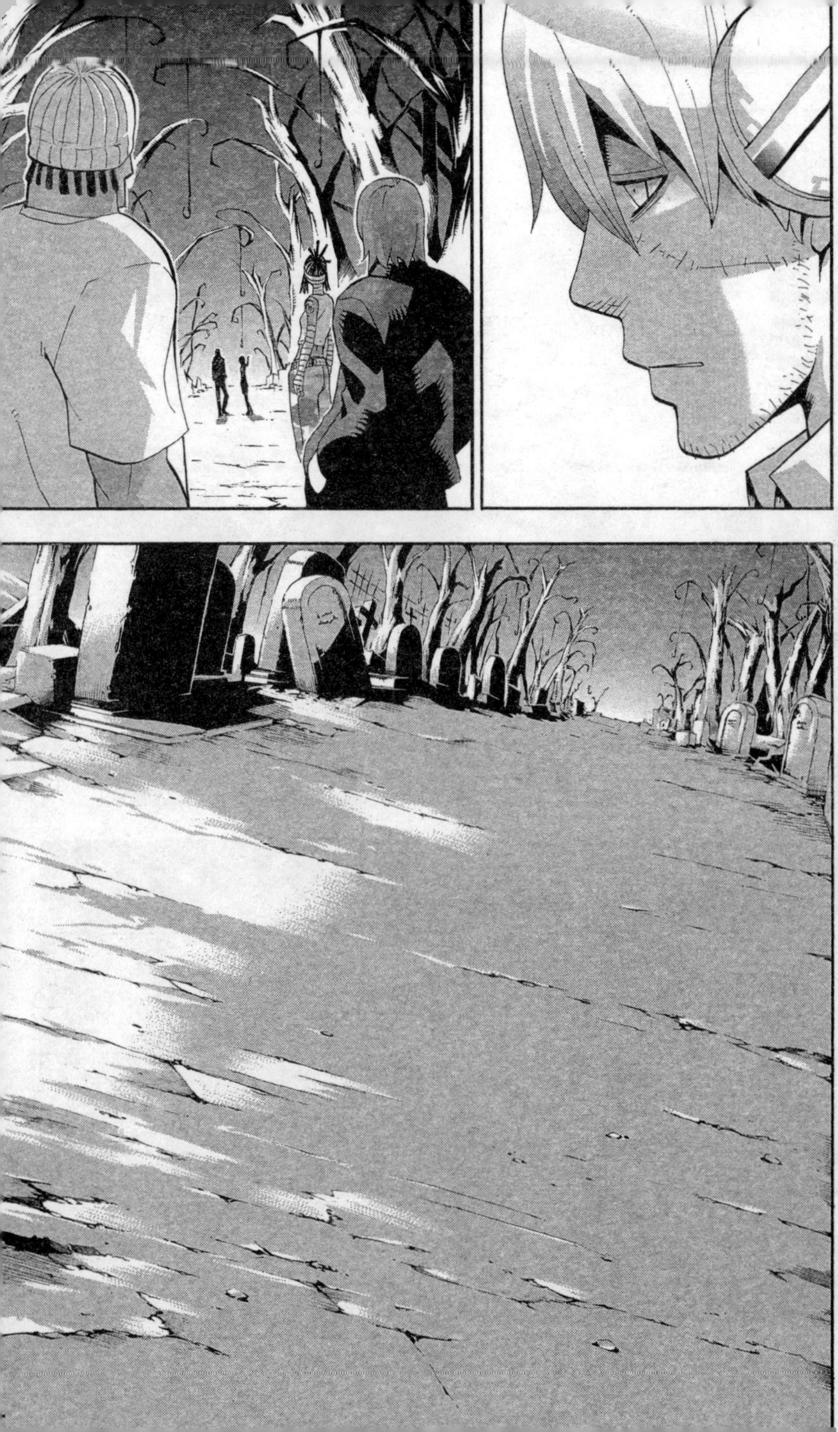

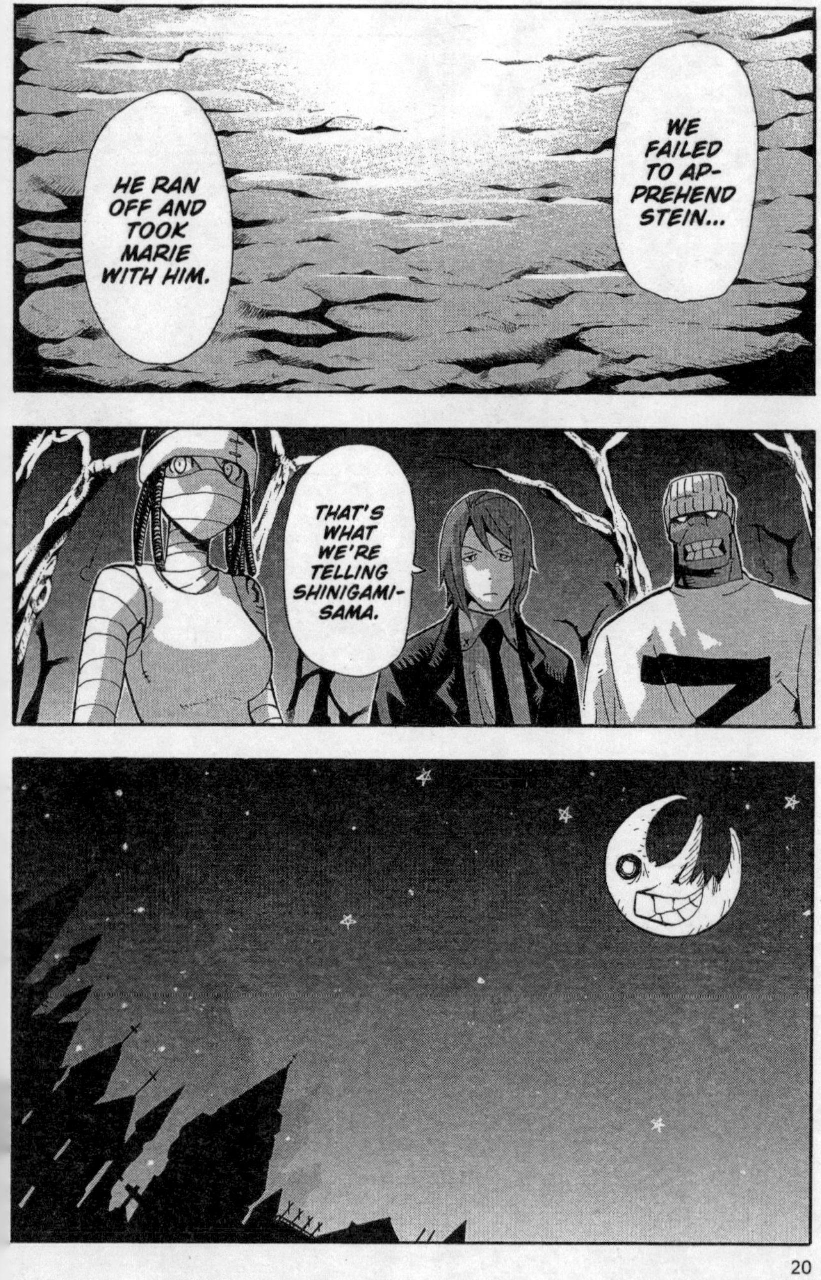
WE FAILED TO APPREHEND STEIN...
HE RAN OFF AND TOOK MARIE WITH HIM.
THAT'S WHAT WE'RE TELLING SHINIGAMI-SAMA.

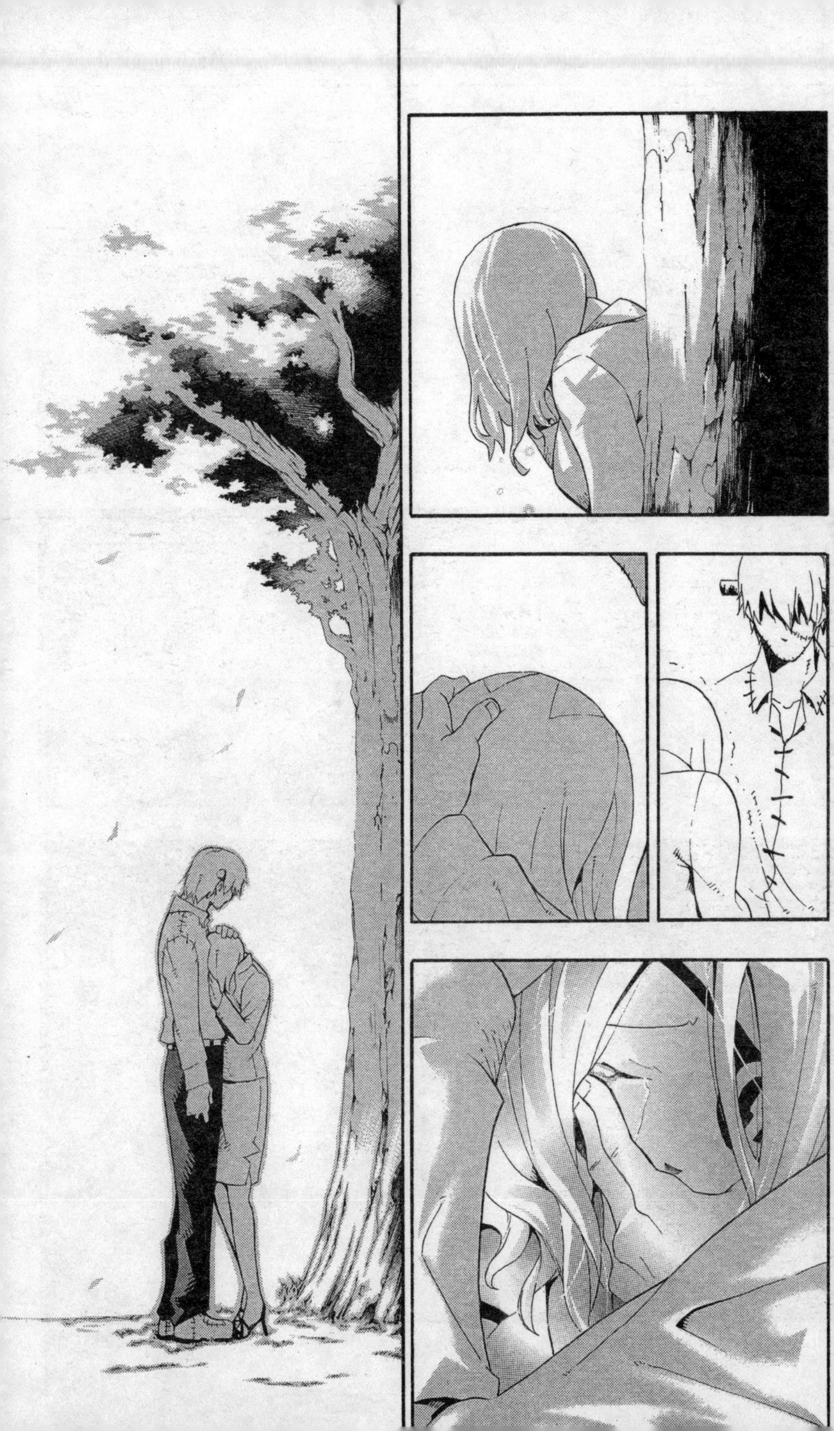

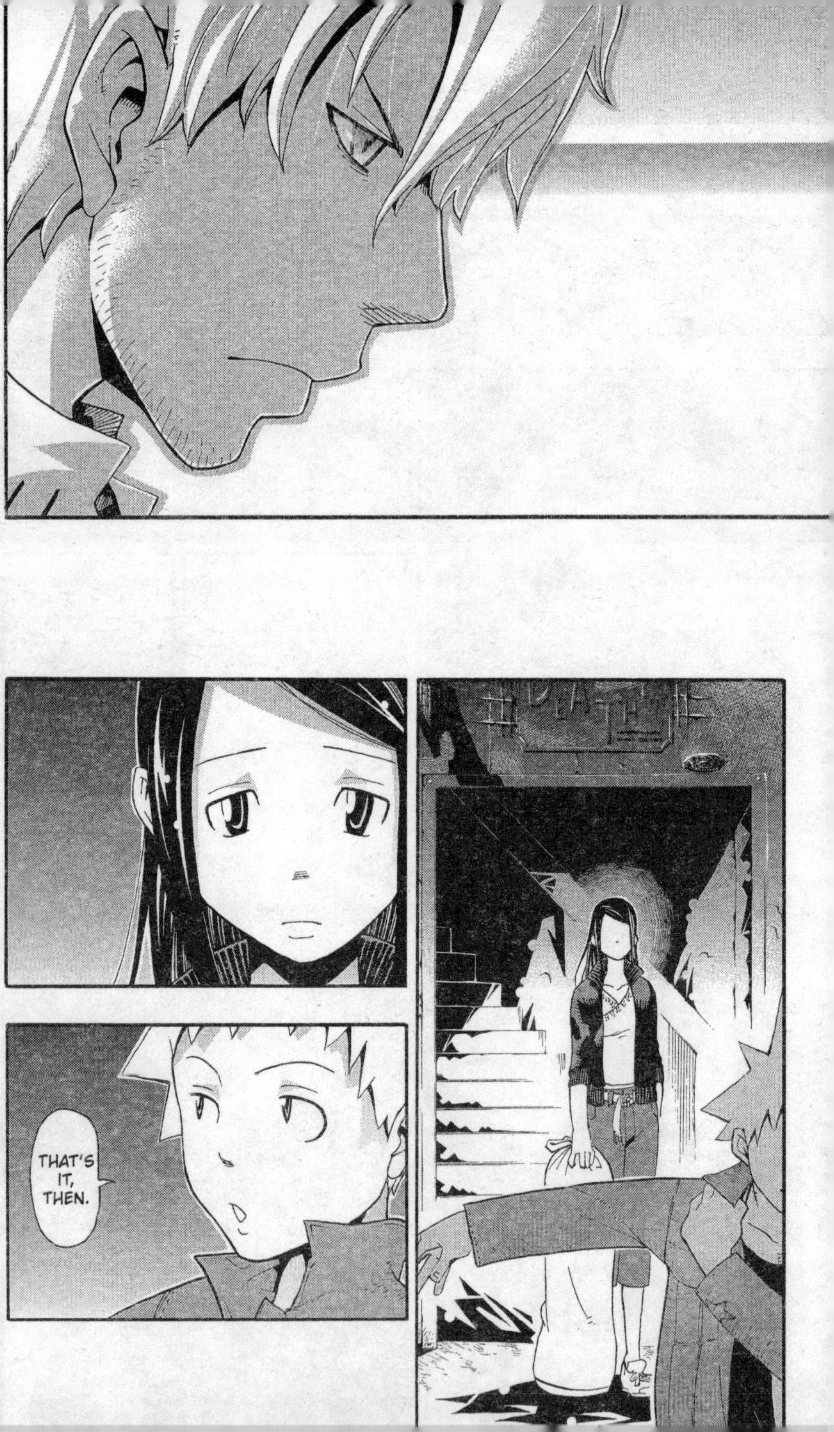
THAT'S IT, THEN.

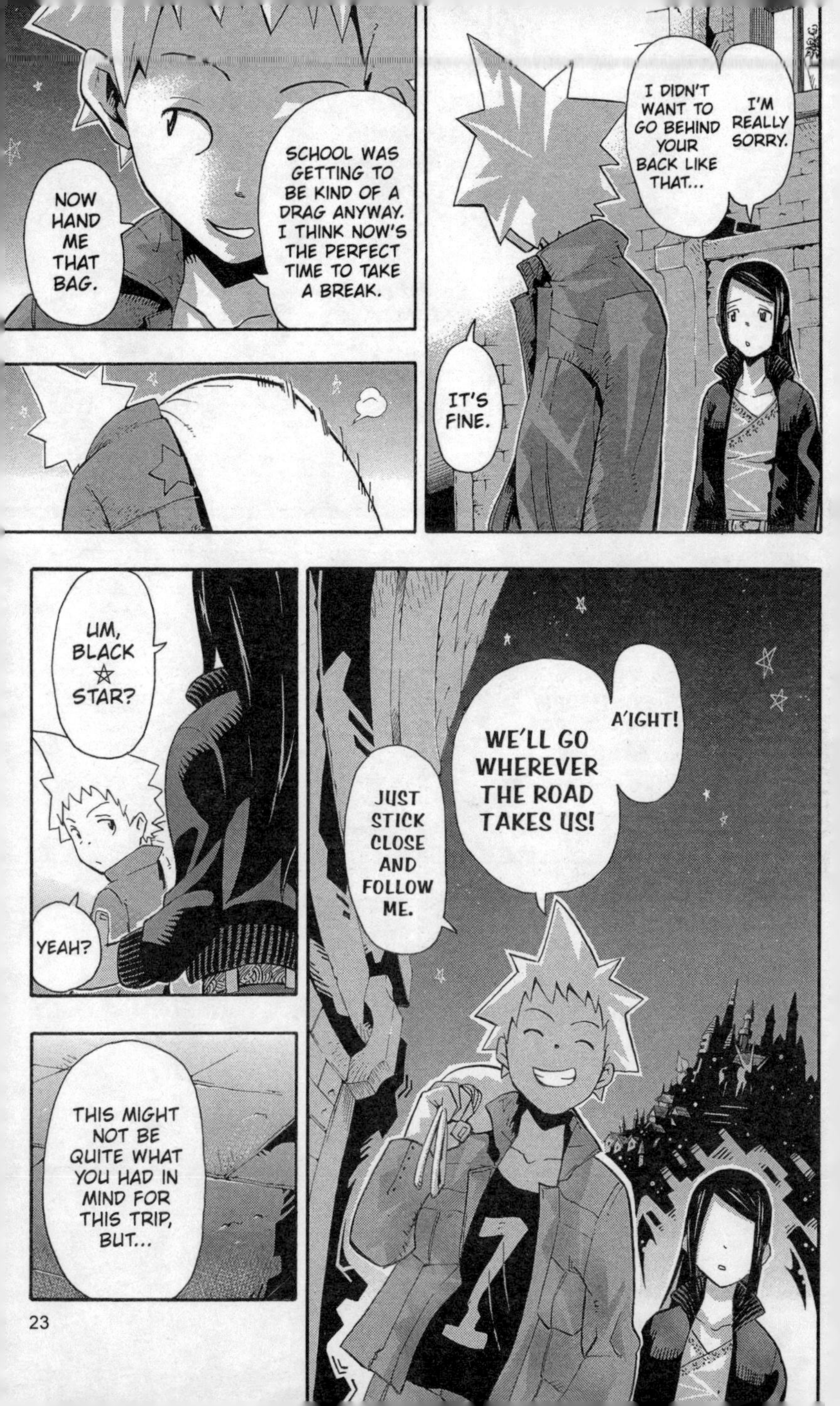

I'M REALLY SORRY.
I DIDN'T WANT TO GO BEHIND YOUR BACK LIKE THAT...
IT'S FINE.
SCHOOL WAS GETTING TO BE KIND OF A DRAG ANYWAY. I THINK NOW'S THE PERFECT TIME TO TAKE A BREAK.
NOW HAND ME THAT BAG.
A'IGHT!
WE'LL GO WHEREVER THE ROAD TAKES US!
JUST STICK CLOSE AND FOLLOW ME.
UM, BLACK☆STAR?
YEAH?
THIS MIGHT NOT BE QUITE WHAT YOU HAD IN MIND FOR THIS TRIP, BUT...

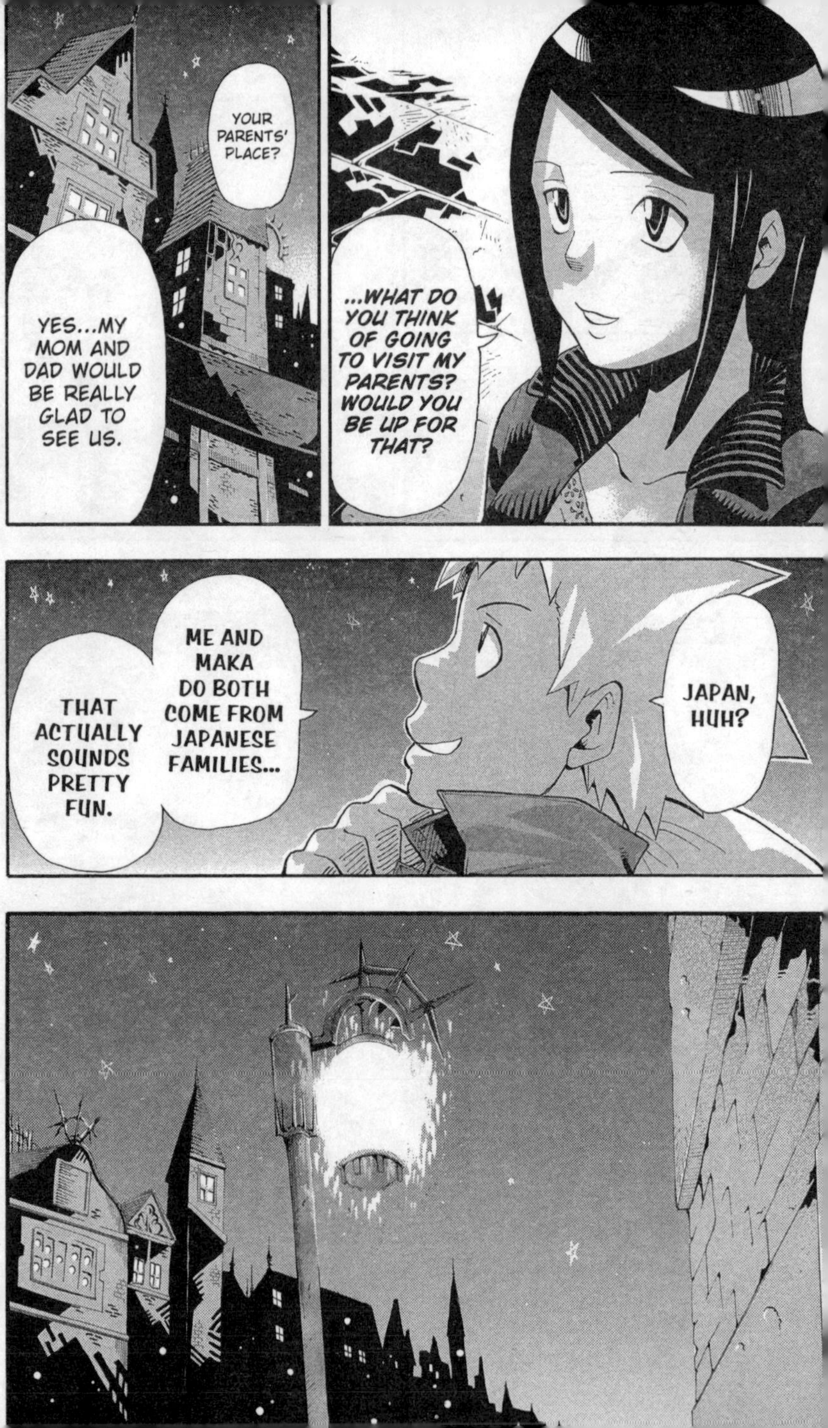
...WHAT DO YOU THINK OF GOING TO VISIT MY PARENTS? WOULD YOU BE UP FOR THAT?
YOUR PARENTS' PLACE?
YES...MY MOM AND DAD WOULD BE REALLY GLAD TO SEE US.
JAPAN, HUH?
ME AND MAKA DO BOTH COME FROM JAPANESE FAMILIES...
THAT ACTUALLY SOUNDS PRETTY FUN.

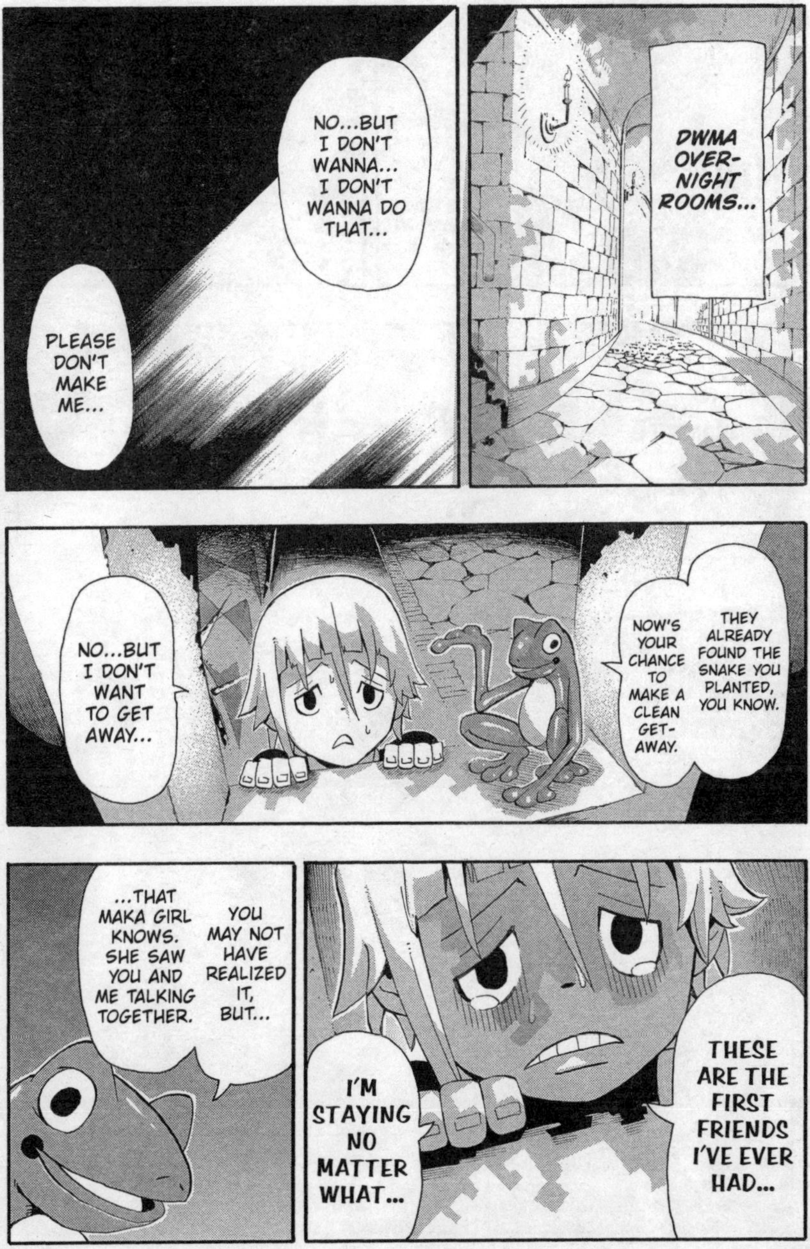
DWMA OVER-NIGHT ROOMS...
NO...BUT I DON'T WANNA... I DON'T WANNA DO THAT...
PLEASE DON'T MAKE ME...
THEY ALREADY FOUND THE SNAKE YOU PLANTED, YOU KNOW.
NOW'S YOUR CHANCE TO MAKE A CLEAN GET-AWAY.
NO...BUT I DON'T WANT TO GET AWAY...
THESE ARE THE FIRST FRIENDS I'VE EVER HAD...
I'M STAYING NO MATTER WHAT...
YOU MAY NOT HAVE REALIZED IT, BUT...
...THAT MAKA GIRL KNOWS. SHE SAW YOU AND ME TALKING TOGETHER.

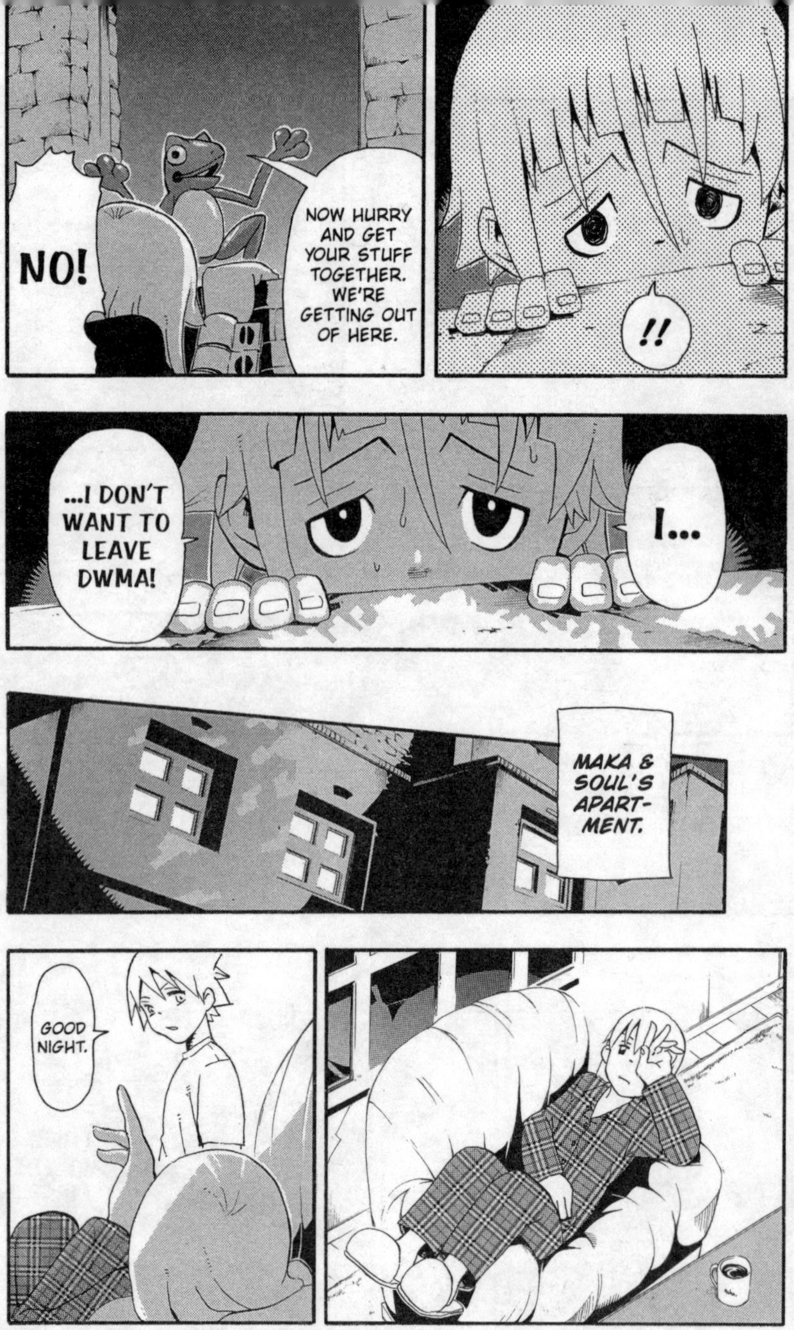
!!
NOW HURRY AND GET YOUR STUFF TOGETHER. WE'RE GETTING OUT OF HERE.
NO!
I...
...I DON'T WANT TO LEAVE DWMA!
MAKA & SOUL'S APARTMENT.
GOOD NIGHT.

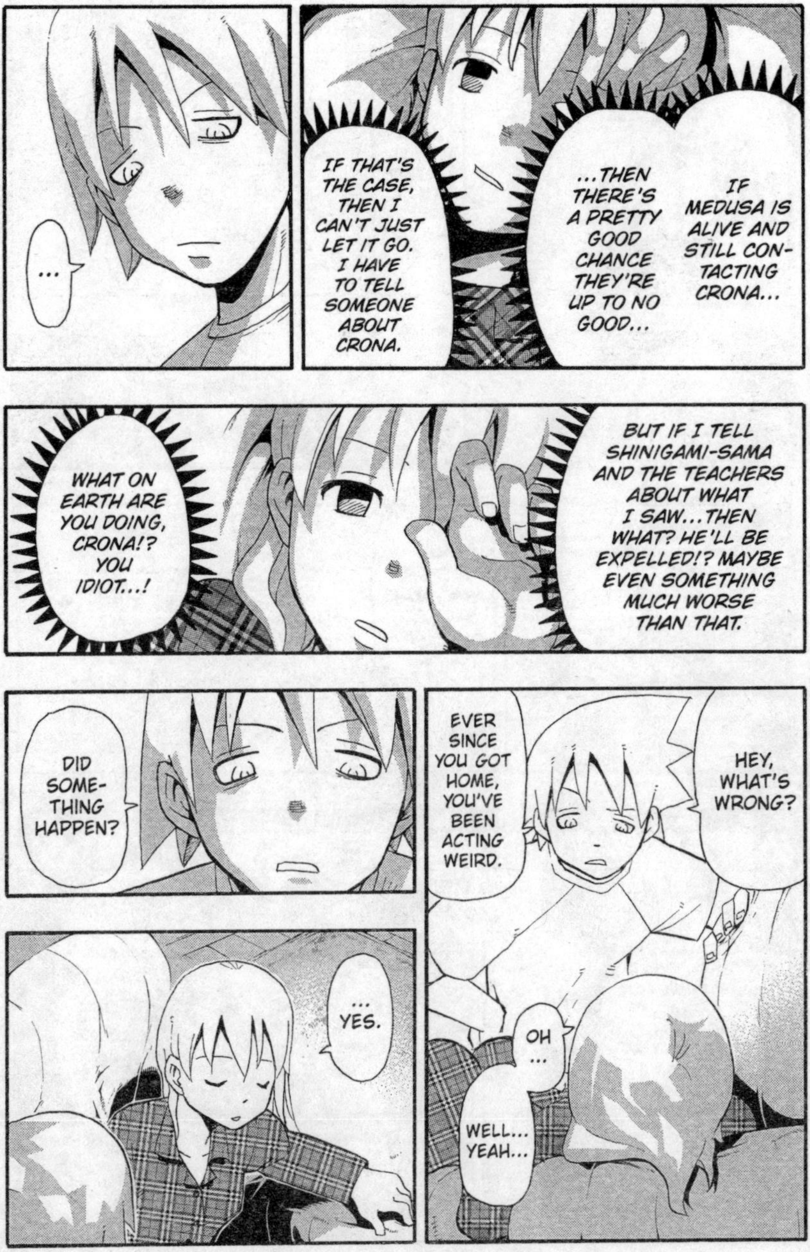
IF MEDUSA IS ALIVE AND STILL CON-TACTING CRONA...
...THEN THERE'S A PRETTY GOOD CHANCE THEY'RE UP TO NO GOOD...
IF THAT'S THE CASE, THEN I CAN'T JUST LET IT GO. I HAVE TO TELL SOMEONE ABOUT CRONA.
...
BUT IF I TELL SHINIGAMI-SAMA AND THE TEACHERS ABOUT WHAT I SAW...THEN WHAT? HE'LL BE EXPELLED!? MAYBE EVEN SOMETHING MUCH WORSE THAN THAT.
WHAT ON EARTH ARE YOU DOING, CRONA!? YOU IDIOT...!
HEY, WHAT'S WRONG?
EVER SINCE YOU GOT HOME, YOU'VE BEEN ACTING WEIRD.
OH ...
WELL... YEAH...
DID SOME-THING HAPPEN?
... YES.

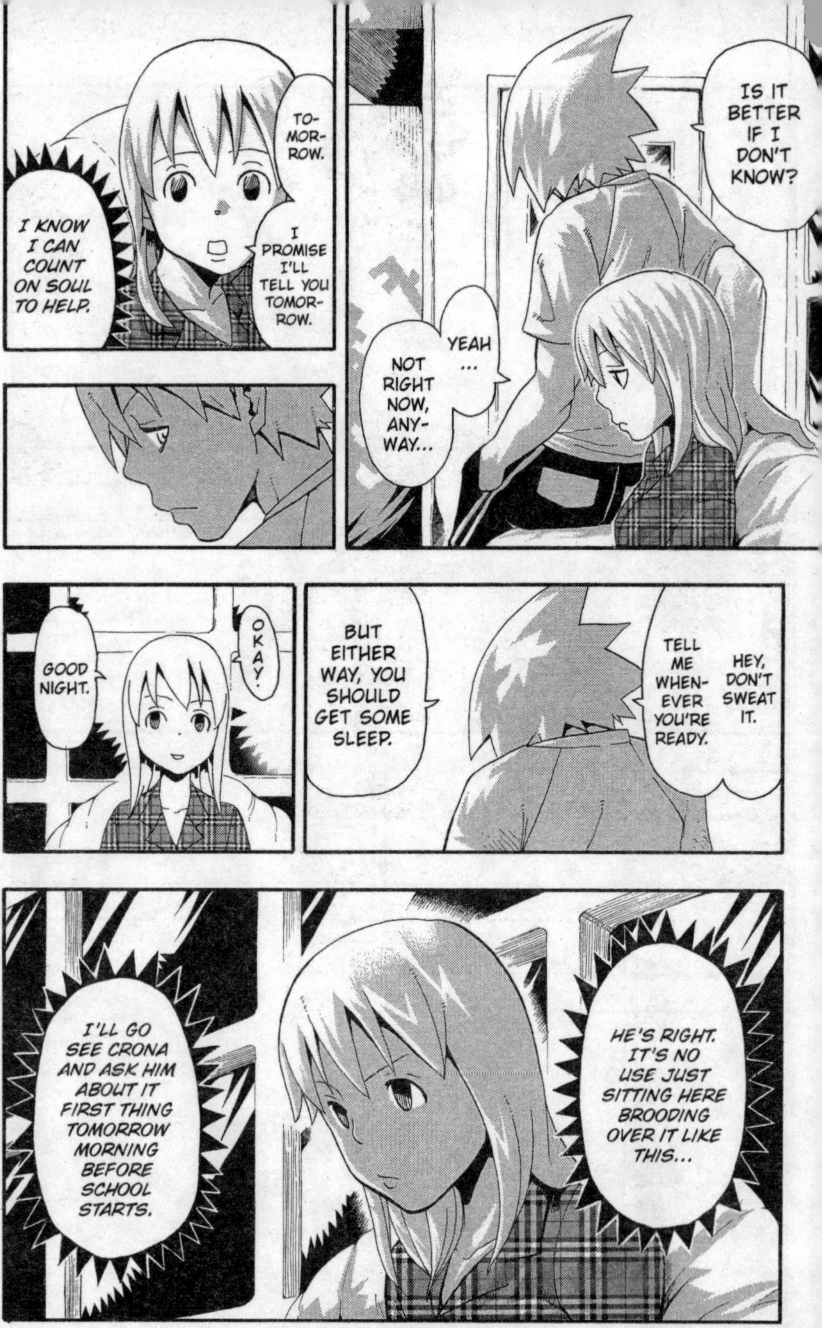
IS IT BETTER IF I DON'T KNOW?
YEAH ...
NOT RIGHT NOW, ANY-WAY...
TO-MOR-ROW.
I PROMISE I'LL TELL YOU TOMOR-ROW.
I KNOW I CAN COUNT ON SOUL TO HELP.
HEY, DON'T SWEAT IT.
TELL ME WHEN-EVER YOU'RE READY.
BUT EITHER WAY, YOU SHOULD GET SOME SLEEP.
OKAY.
GOOD NIGHT.
HE'S RIGHT. IT'S NO USE JUST SITTING HERE BROODING OVER IT LIKE THIS...
I'LL GO SEE CRONA AND ASK HIM ABOUT IT FIRST THING TOMORROW MORNING BEFORE SCHOOL STARTS.

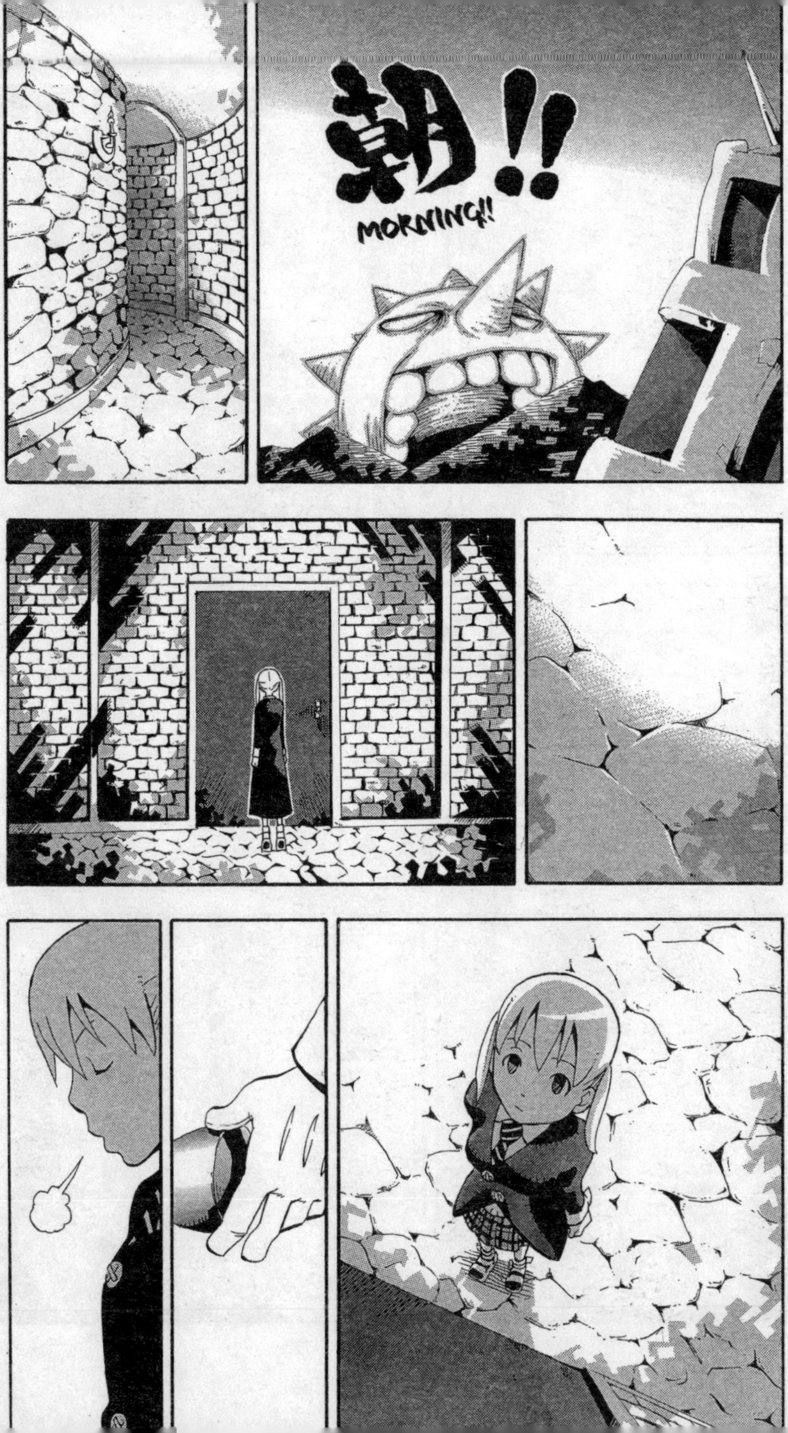
朝!!
MORNING!!

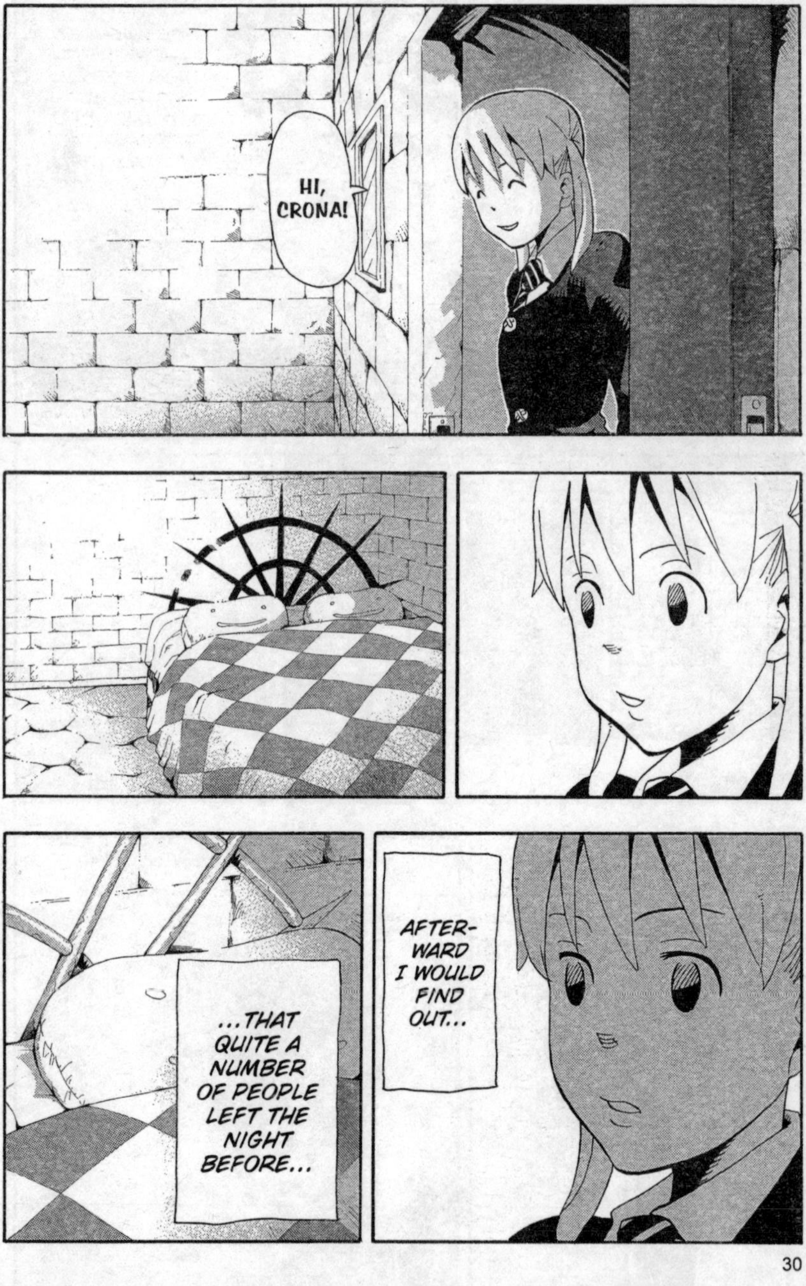
HI, CRONA!
AFTER-WARD I WOULD FIND OUT...
...THAT QUITE A NUMBER OF PEOPLE LEFT THE NIGHT BEFORE...

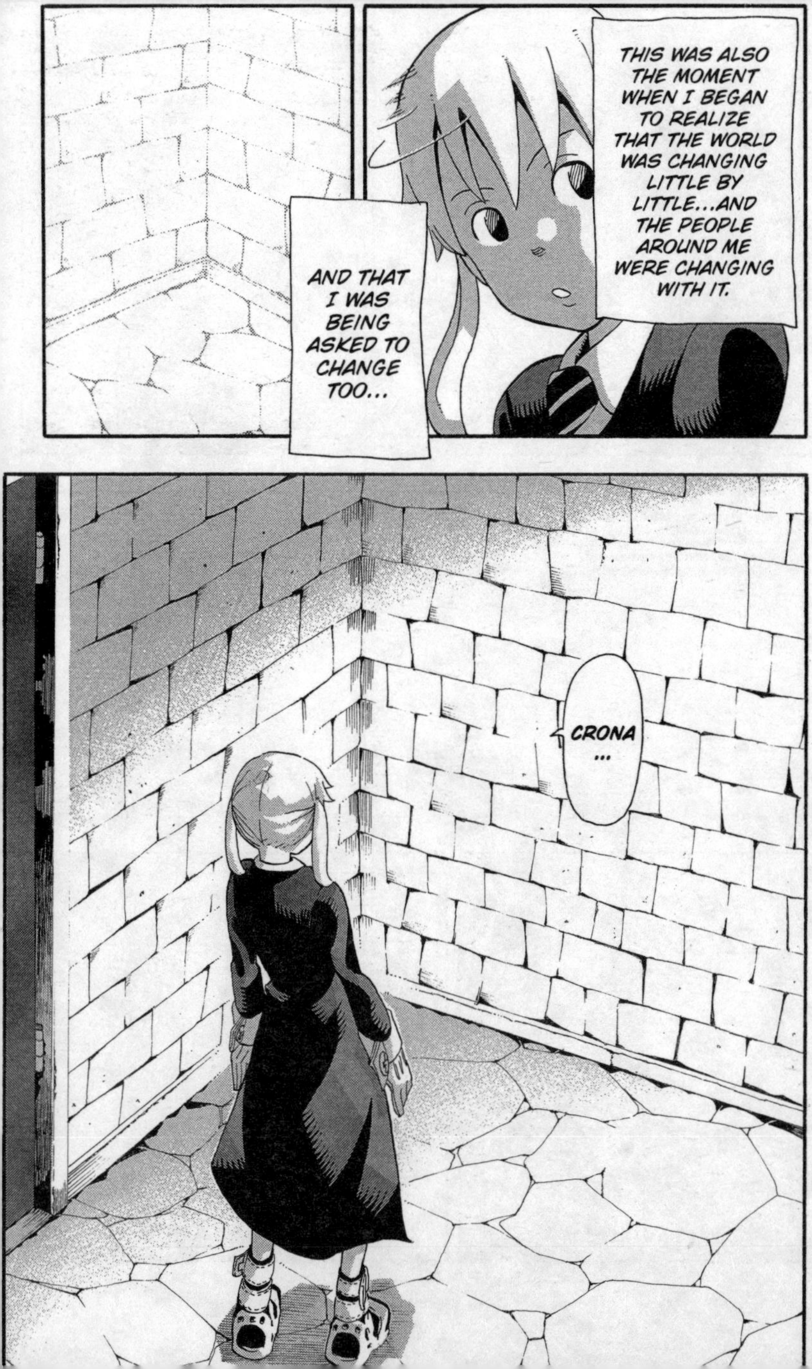
THIS WAS ALSO THE MOMENT WHEN I BEGAN TO REALIZE THAT THE WORLD WAS CHANGING LITTLE BY LITTLE...AND THE PEOPLE AROUND ME WERE CHANGING WITH IT.
AND THAT I WAS BEING ASKED TO CHANGE TOO...
CRONA ...

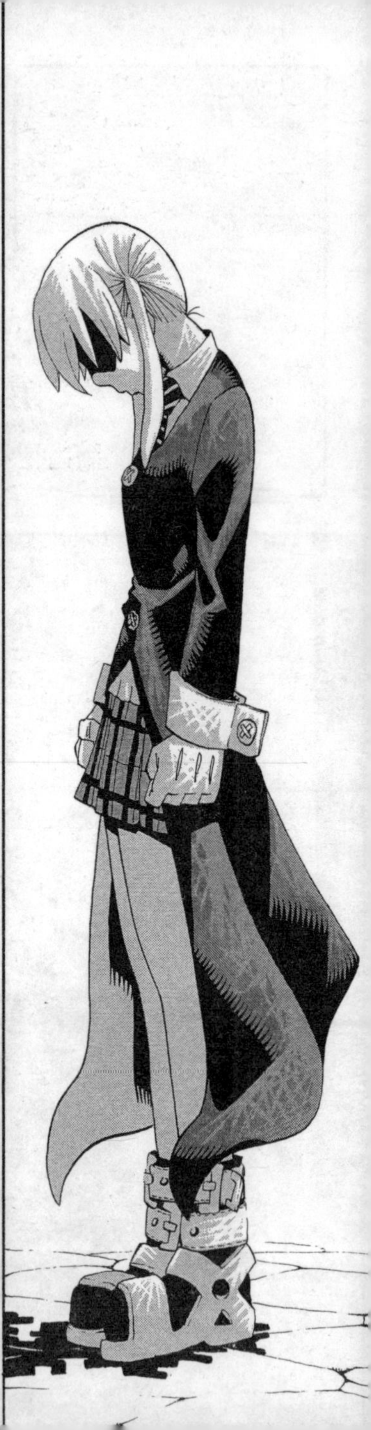

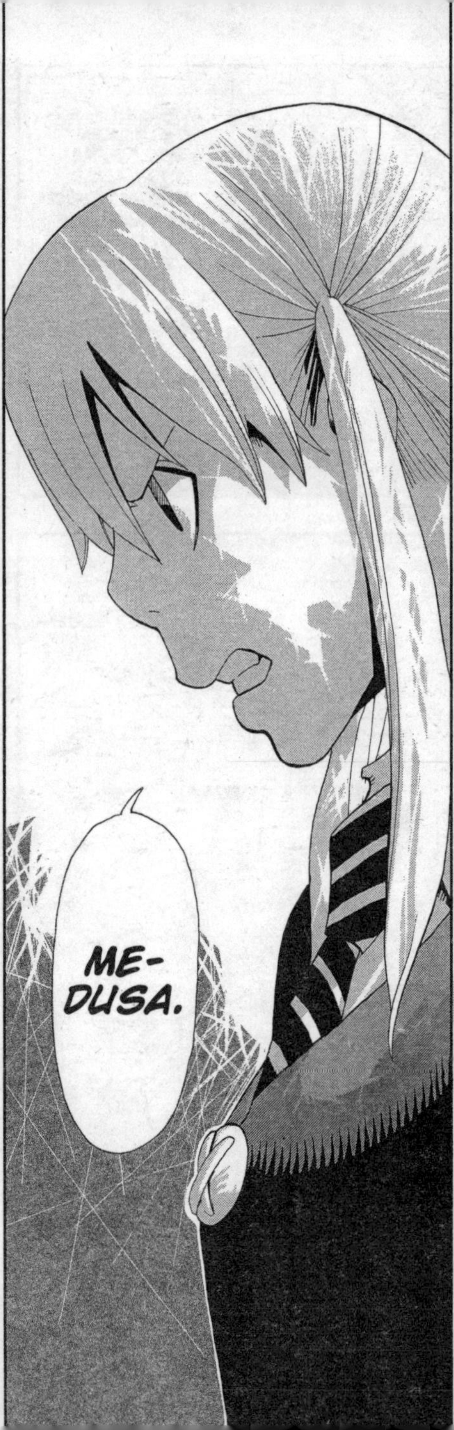
ME-
DUSA.

SOUL EATER

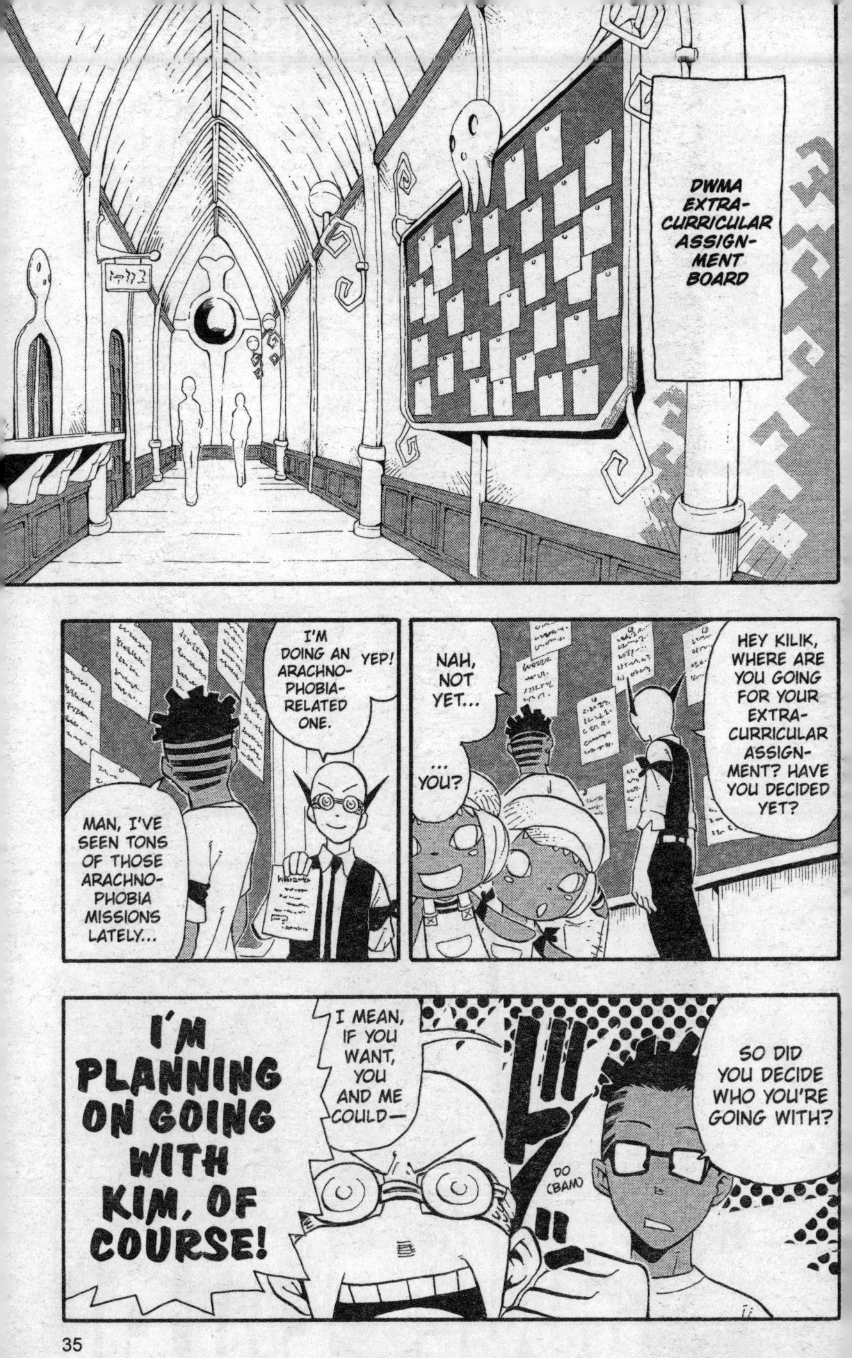
DWMA EXTRA-CURRICULAR ASSIGNMENT BOARD
HEY KILIK, WHERE ARE YOU GOING FOR YOUR EXTRA-CURRICULAR ASSIGNMENT? HAVE YOU DECIDED YET?
NAH, NOT YET...
...YOU?
YEP!
I'M DOING AN ARACHNOPHOBIA-RELATED ONE.
MAN, I'VE SEEN TONS OF THOSE ARACHNOPHOBIA MISSIONS LATELY...
SO DID YOU DECIDE WHO YOU'RE GOING WITH?
DO (BAM)
I MEAN, IF YOU WANT, YOU AND ME COULD—
I'M PLANNING ON GOING WITH KIM, OF COURSE!

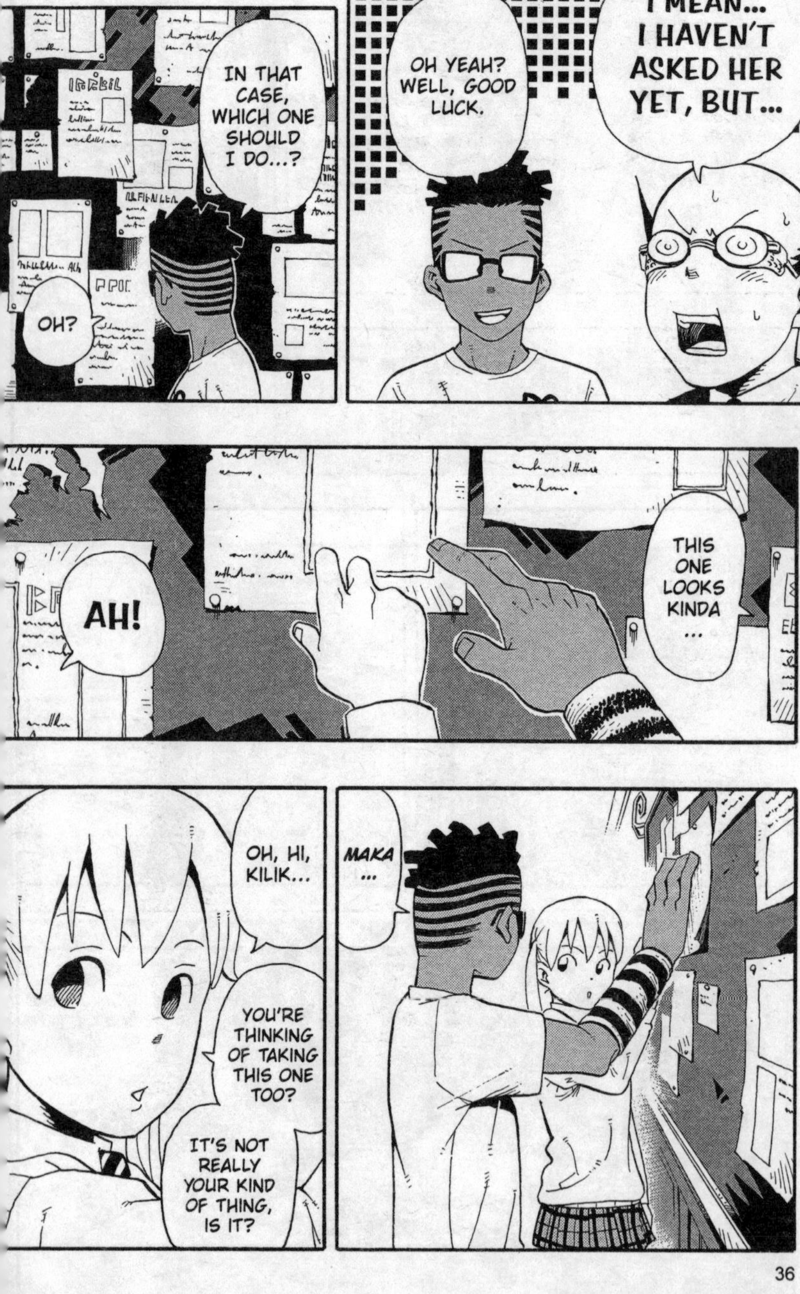
I MEAN... I HAVEN'T ASKED HER YET, BUT...
OH YEAH? WELL, GOOD LUCK.
IN THAT CASE, WHICH ONE SHOULD I DO...?
OH?
THIS ONE LOOKS KINDA ...
AH!
MAKA ...
OH, HI, KILIK...
YOU'RE THINKING OF TAKING THIS ONE TOO?
IT'S NOT REALLY YOUR KIND OF THING, IS IT?

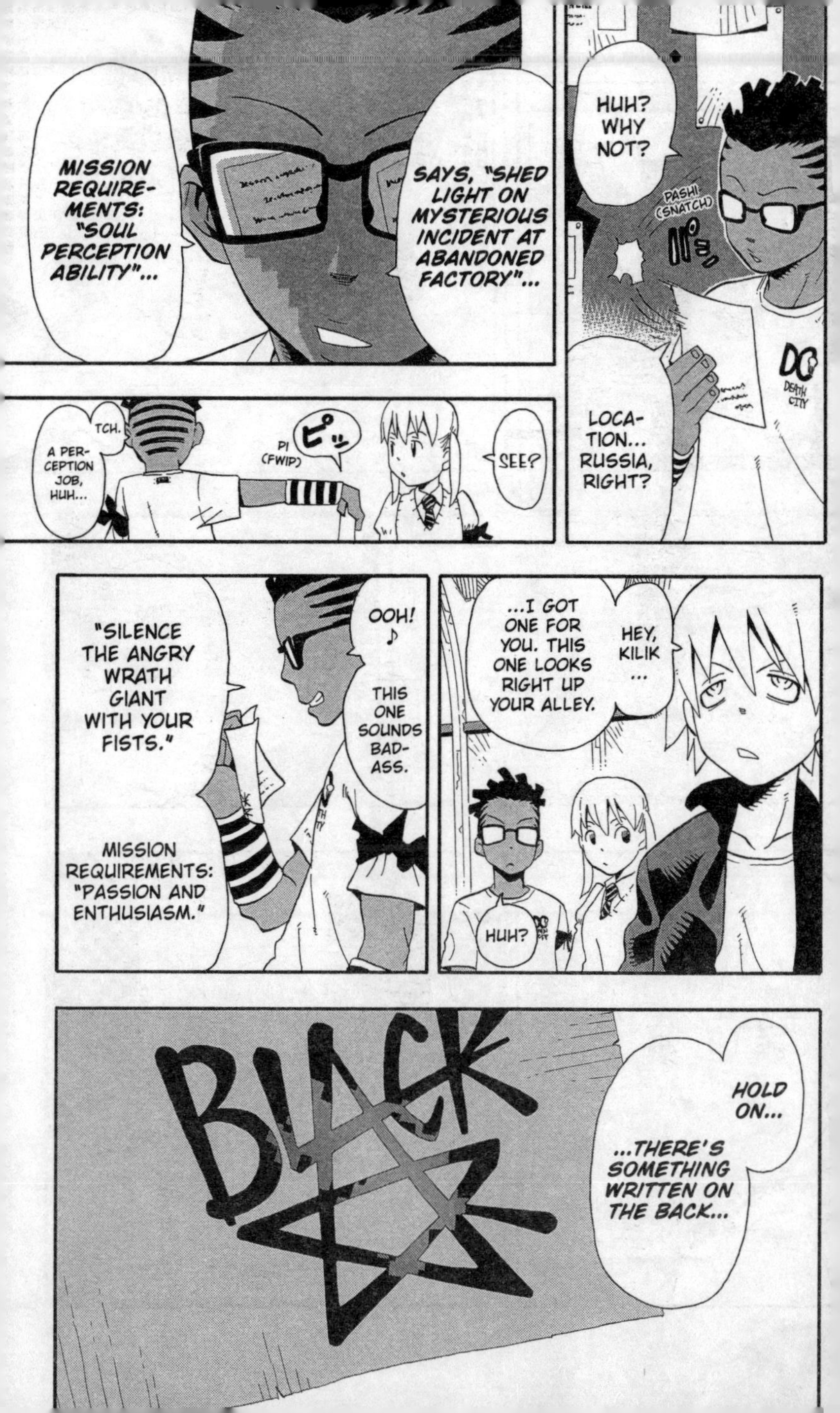

HUH? WHY NOT?
PASHI (SNATCH)
LOCA-TION... RUSSIA, RIGHT?
DC DEATH CITY
SAYS, "SHED LIGHT ON MYSTERIOUS INCIDENT AT ABANDONED FACTORY"...
MISSION REQUIRE-MENTS: "SOUL PERCEPTION ABILITY"...
SEE?
PI (FWIP)
TCH.
A PER-CEPTION JOB, HUH...
HEY, KILIK ...
...I GOT ONE FOR YOU. THIS ONE LOOKS RIGHT UP YOUR ALLEY.
HUH?
OOH! ♪
THIS ONE SOUNDS BAD-ASS.
"SILENCE THE ANGRY WRATH GIANT WITH YOUR FISTS."
MISSION REQUIREMENTS: "PASSION AND ENTHUSIASM."
HOLD ON...
...THERE'S SOMETHING WRITTEN ON THE BACK...
BLACK

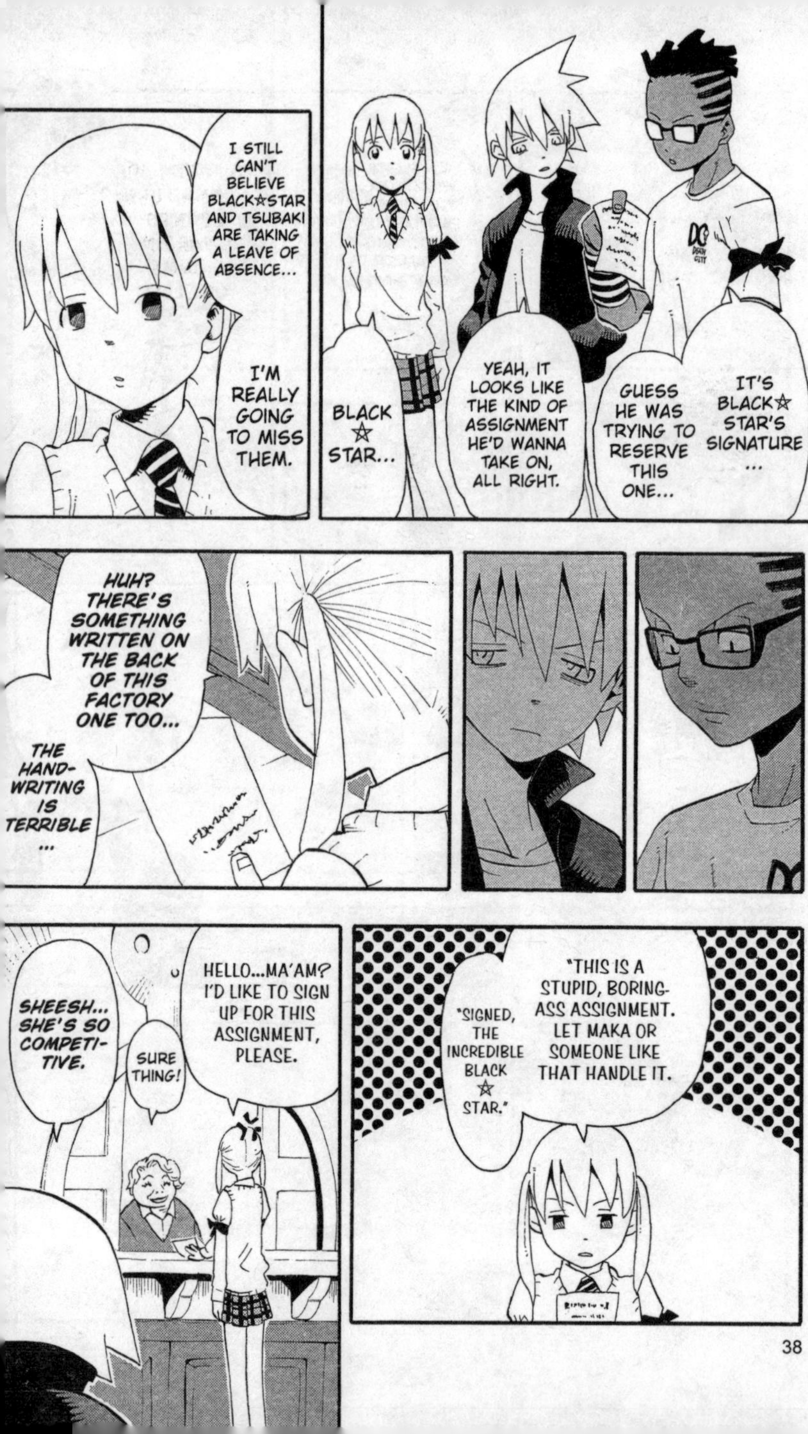
IT'S BLACK☆STAR'S SIGNATURE...
GUESS HE WAS TRYING TO RESERVE THIS ONE...
YEAH, IT LOOKS LIKE THE KIND OF ASSIGNMENT HE'D WANNA TAKE ON, ALL RIGHT.
BLACK☆STAR...
I STILL CAN'T BELIEVE BLACK☆STAR AND TSUBAKI ARE TAKING A LEAVE OF ABSENCE...
I'M REALLY GOING TO MISS THEM.
HUH? THERE'S SOMETHING WRITTEN ON THE BACK OF THIS FACTORY ONE TOO...
THE HANDWRITING IS TERRIBLE...
"THIS IS A STUPID, BORING-ASS ASSIGNMENT. LET MAKA OR SOMEONE LIKE THAT HANDLE IT.
"SIGNED, THE INCREDIBLE BLACK☆STAR."
HELLO...MA'AM? I'D LIKE TO SIGN UP FOR THIS ASSIGNMENT, PLEASE.
SURE THING!
SHEESH... SHE'S SO COMPETITIVE.

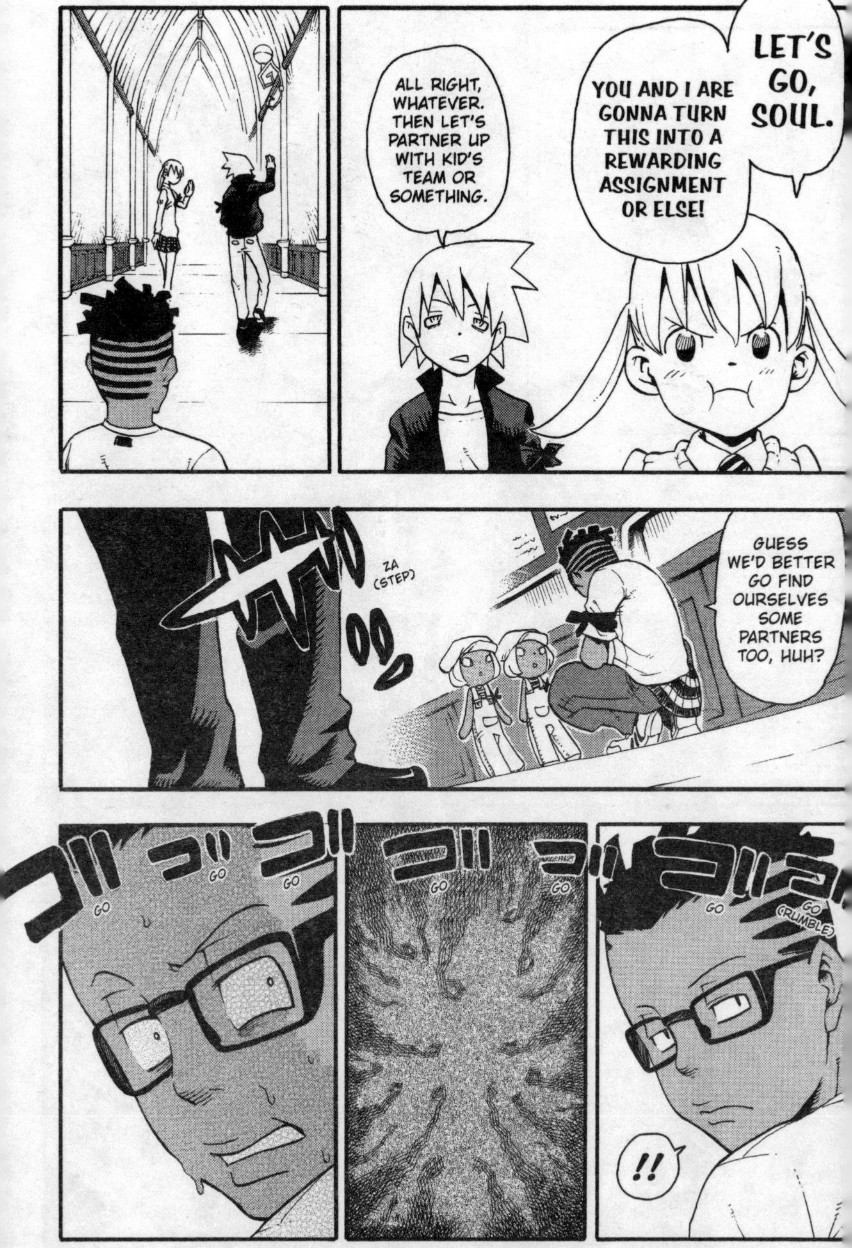
LET'S GO, SOUL.
YOU AND I ARE GONNA TURN THIS INTO A REWARDING ASSIGNMENT OR ELSE!
ALL RIGHT, WHATEVER. THEN LET'S PARTNER UP WITH KID'S TEAM OR SOMETHING.
GUESS WE'D BETTER GO FIND OURSELVES SOME PARTNERS TOO, HUH?
ZA (STEP)
GO (RUMBLE)
GO
!!
GO
GO
GO
GO
GO

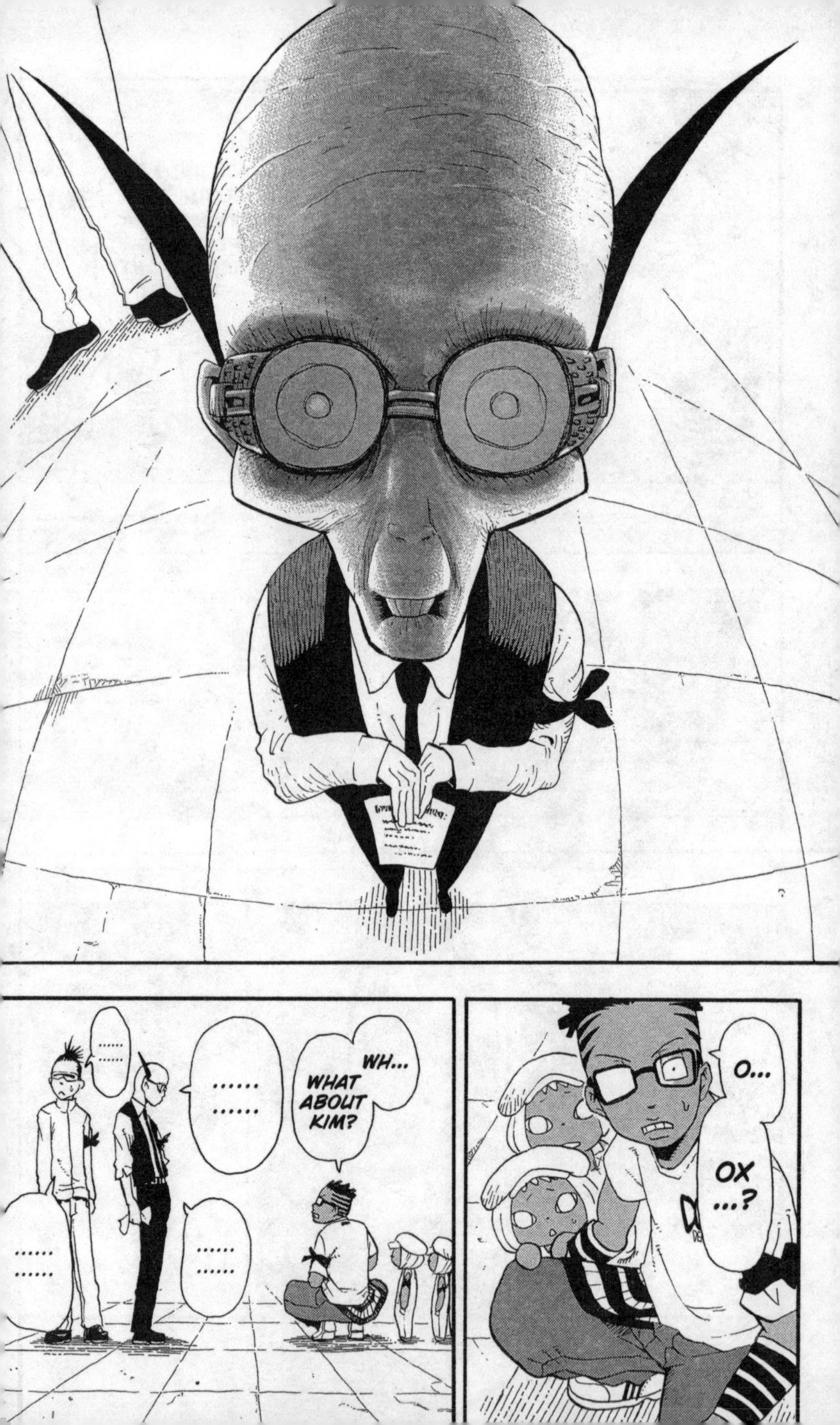
O...
OX ...?
WH... WHAT ABOUT KIM?
....
....
....
....

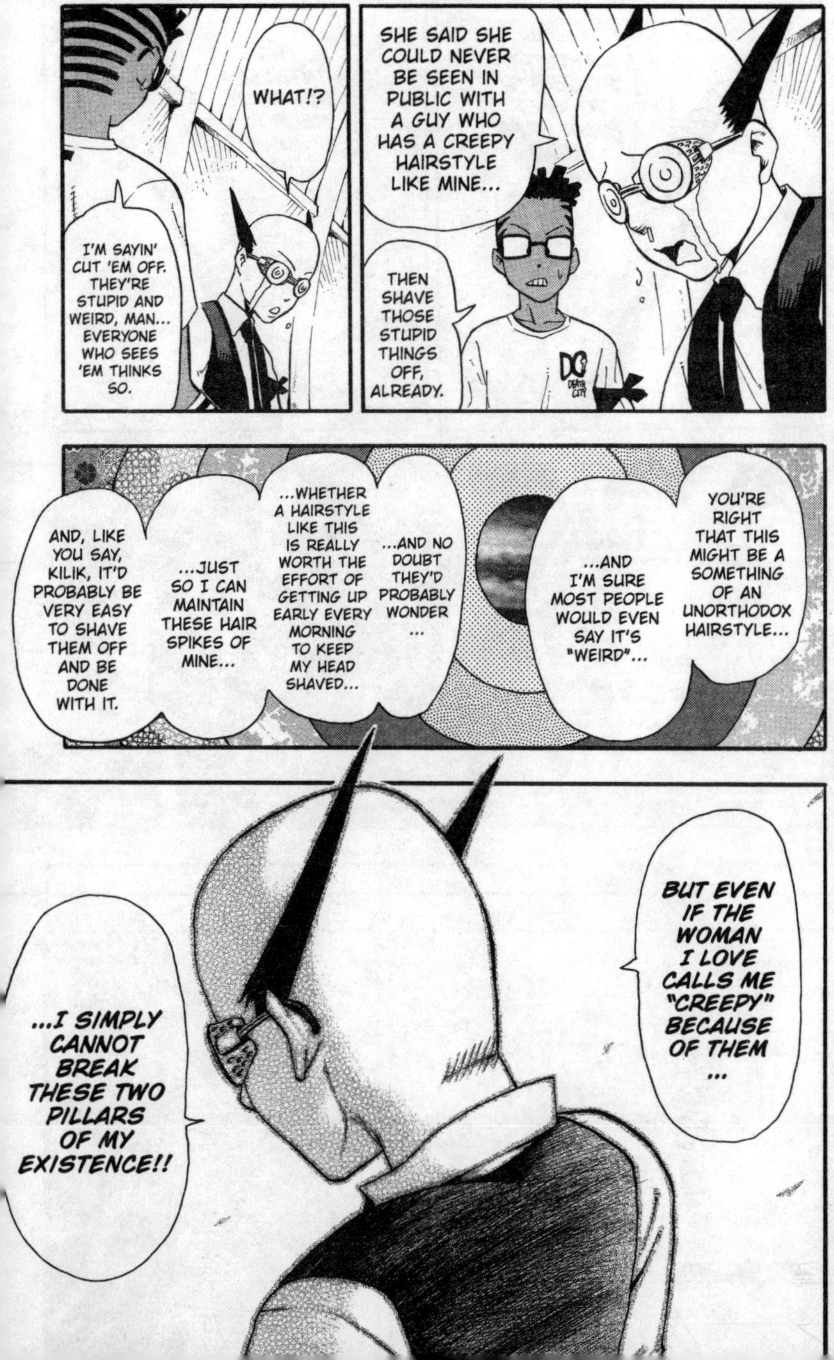
SHE SAID SHE COULD NEVER BE SEEN IN PUBLIC WITH A GUY WHO HAS A CREEPY HAIRSTYLE LIKE MINE...
THEN SHAVE THOSE STUPID THINGS OFF, ALREADY.
WHAT!?
I'M SAYIN' CUT 'EM OFF. THEY'RE STUPID AND WEIRD, MAN... EVERYONE WHO SEES 'EM THINKS SO.
YOU'RE RIGHT THAT THIS MIGHT BE A SOMETHING OF AN UNORTHODOX HAIRSTYLE...
...AND I'M SURE MOST PEOPLE WOULD EVEN SAY IT'S "WEIRD"...
...AND NO DOUBT THEY'D PROBABLY WONDER...
...WHETHER A HAIRSTYLE LIKE THIS IS REALLY WORTH THE EFFORT OF GETTING UP EARLY EVERY MORNING TO KEEP MY HEAD SHAVED...
...JUST SO I CAN MAINTAIN THESE HAIR SPIKES OF MINE...
AND, LIKE YOU SAY, KILIK, IT'D PROBABLY BE VERY EASY TO SHAVE THEM OFF AND BE DONE WITH IT.
BUT EVEN IF THE WOMAN I LOVE CALLS ME "CREEPY" BECAUSE OF THEM...
...I SIMPLY CANNOT BREAK THESE TWO PILLARS OF MY EXISTENCE!!

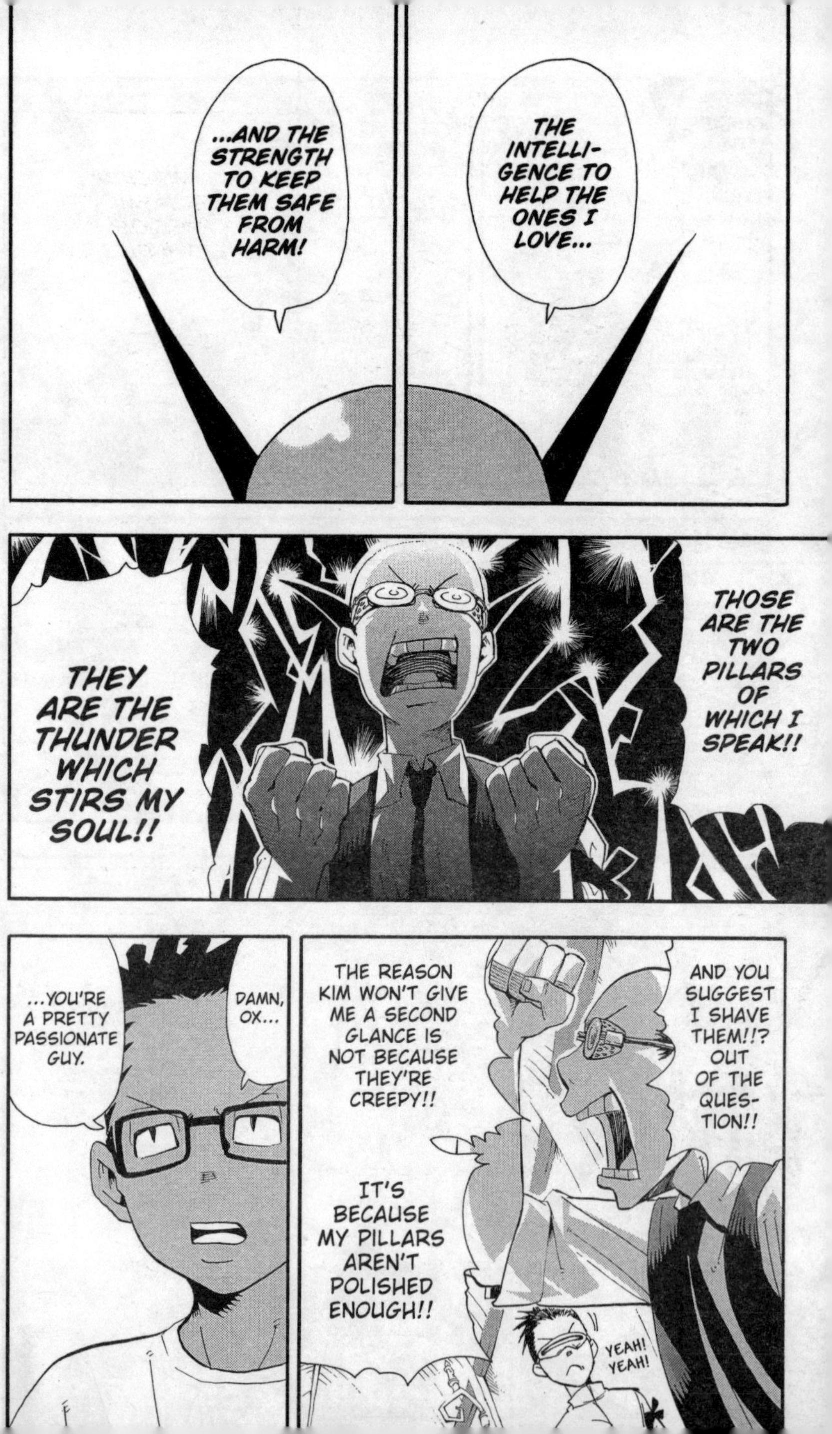
THE INTELLIGENCE TO HELP THE ONES I LOVE...
...AND THE STRENGTH TO KEEP THEM SAFE FROM HARM!
THOSE ARE THE TWO PILLARS OF WHICH I SPEAK!!
THEY ARE THE THUNDER WHICH STIRS MY SOUL!!
AND YOU SUGGEST I SHAVE THEM!!? OUT OF THE QUES-TION!!
THE REASON KIM WON'T GIVE ME A SECOND GLANCE IS NOT BECAUSE THEY'RE CREEPY!!
IT'S BECAUSE MY PILLARS AREN'T POLISHED ENOUGH!!
YEAH! YEAH!
DAMN, OX...
...YOU'RE A PRETTY PASSIONATE GUY.

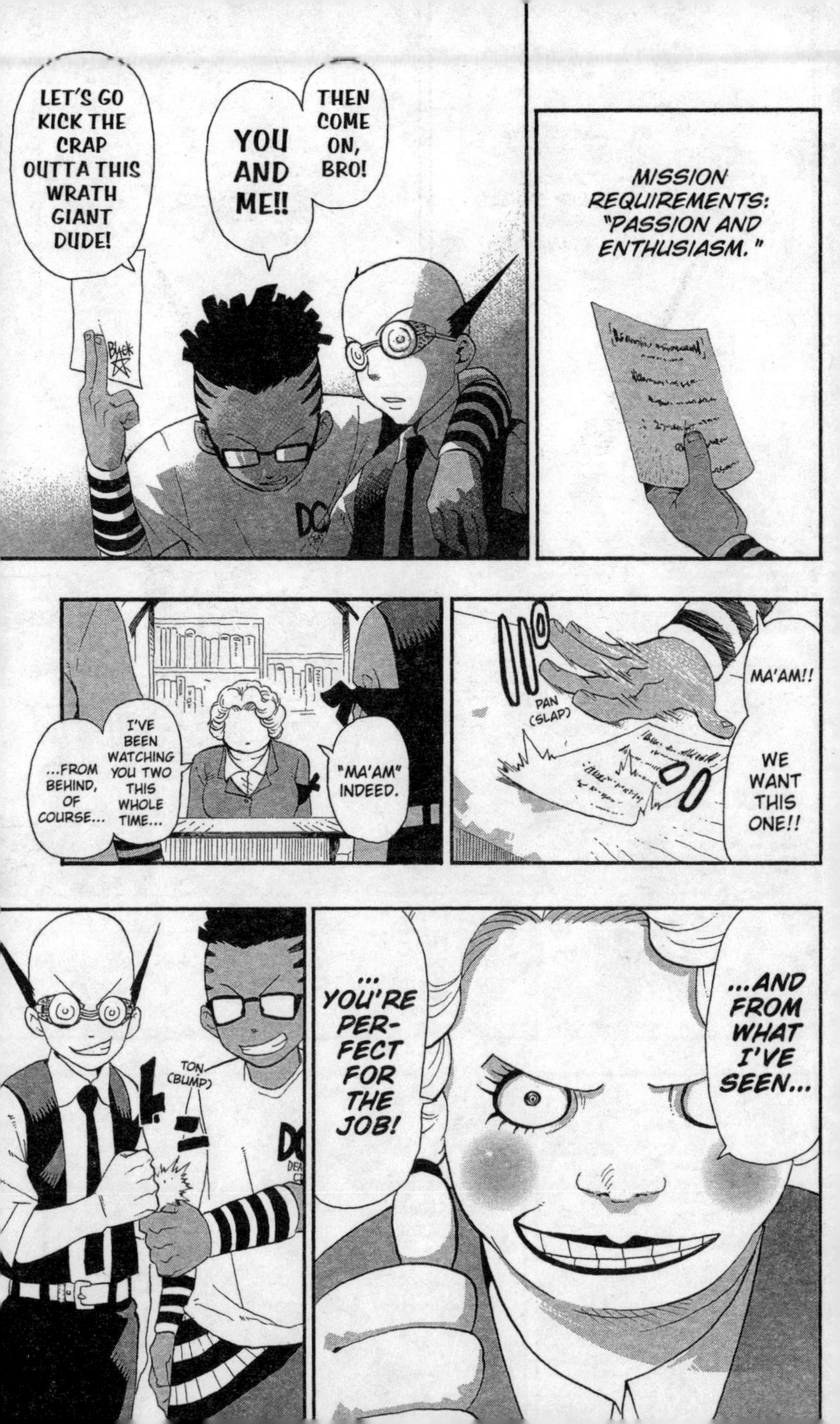
MISSION REQUIREMENTS: "PASSION AND ENTHUSIASM."
THEN COME ON, BRO!
YOU AND ME!!
LET'S GO KICK THE CRAP OUTTA THIS WRATH GIANT DUDE!
MA'AM!!
WE WANT THIS ONE!!
PAN (SLAP)
"MA'AM" INDEED.
I'VE BEEN WATCHING YOU TWO THIS WHOLE TIME...
...FROM BEHIND, OF COURSE...
...AND FROM WHAT I'VE SEEN...
...YOU'RE PER-FECT FOR THE JOB!
TON (BUMP)

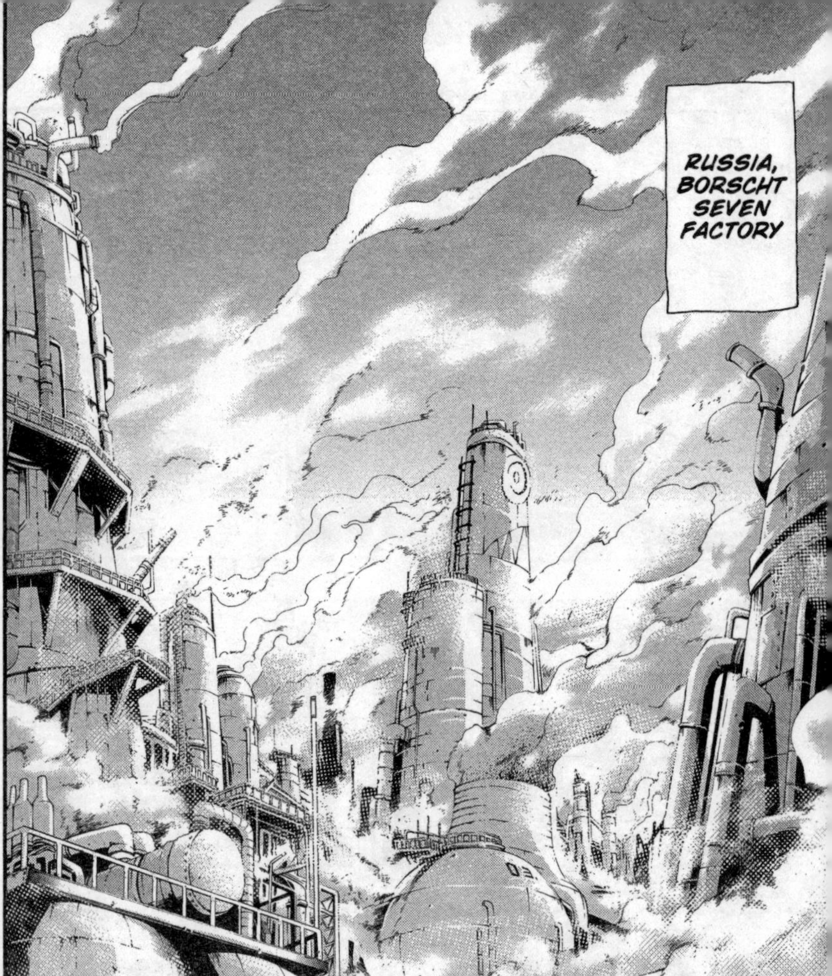
RUSSIA, BORSCHT SEVEN FACTORY

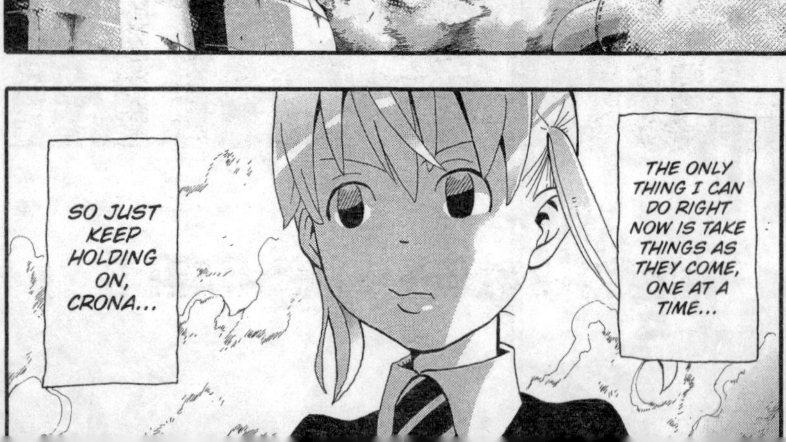
THE ONLY THING I CAN DO RIGHT NOW IS TAKE THINGS AS THEY COME, ONE AT A TIME...
SO JUST KEEP HOLDING ON, CRONA...

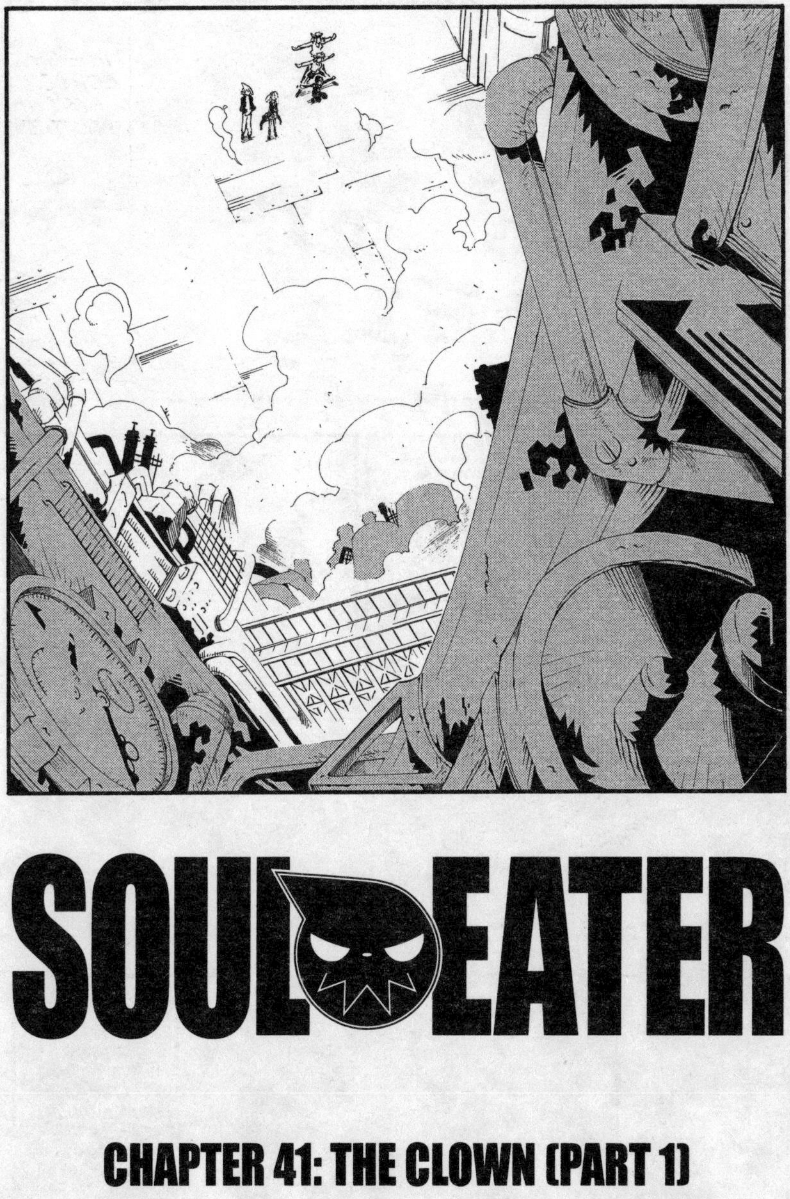

SOUL EATER

CHAPTER 41: THE CLOWN (PART 1)

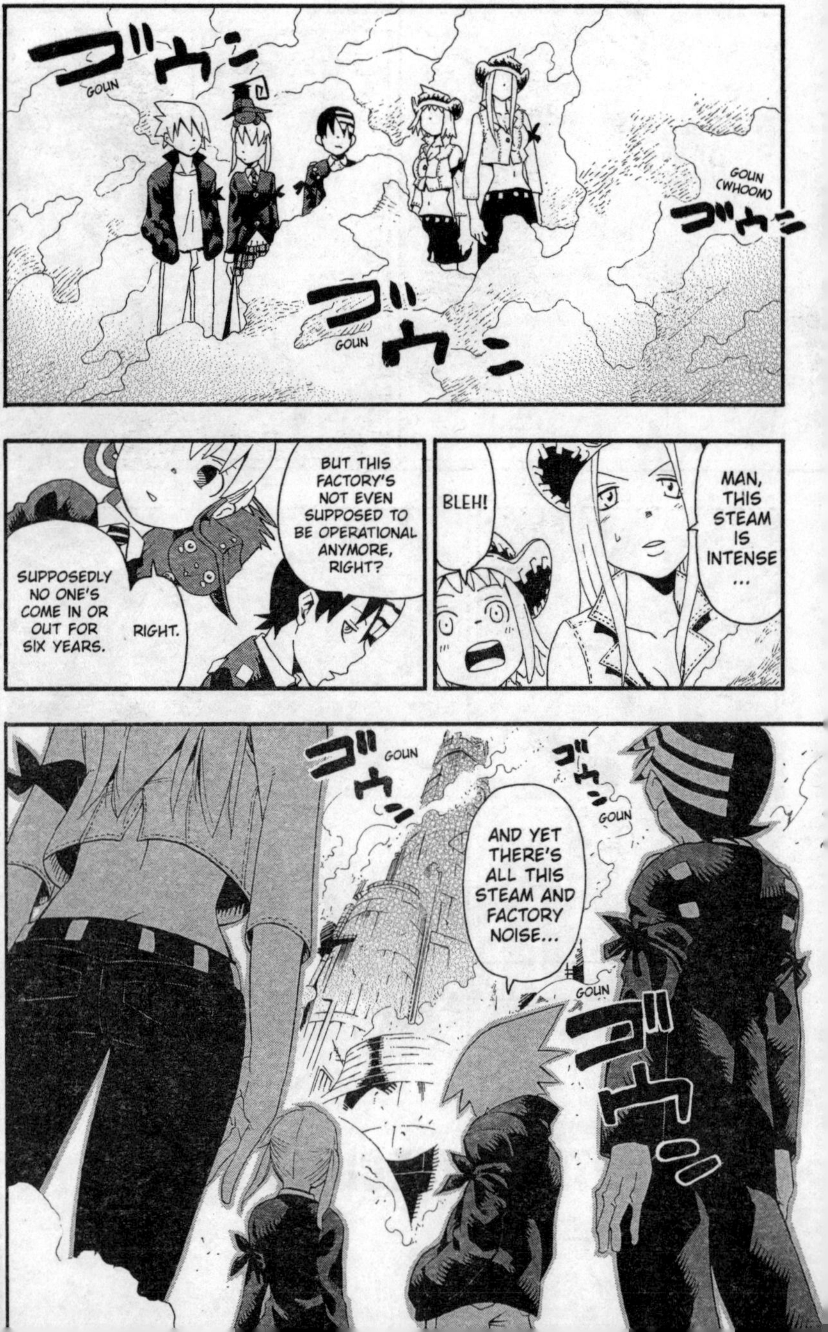
GOUN (WHOOM)
ゴウン
ゴウン
GOUN
ゴウン
GOUN
MAN, THIS STEAM IS INTENSE...
BLEH!
BUT THIS FACTORY'S NOT EVEN SUPPOSED TO BE OPERATIONAL ANYMORE, RIGHT?
RIGHT.
SUPPOSEDLY NO ONE'S COME IN OR OUT FOR SIX YEARS.
ゴウン
GOUN
ゴウン
GOUN
AND YET THERE'S ALL THIS STEAM AND FACTORY NOISE...
GOUN

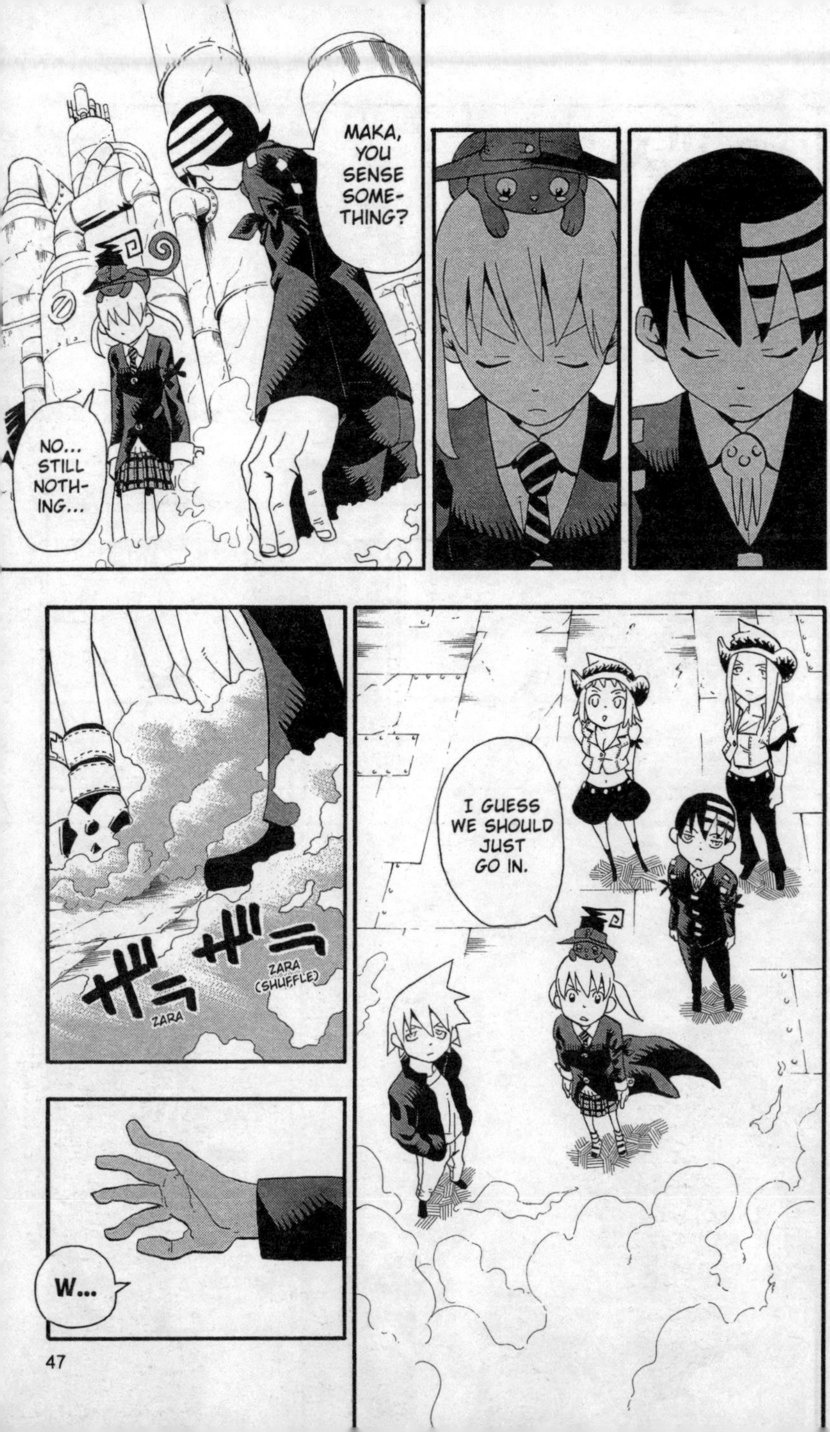
MAKA, YOU SENSE SOME-THING?
NO... STILL NOTH-ING...
I GUESS WE SHOULD JUST GO IN.
ZARA (SHUFFLE)
ZARA
W...

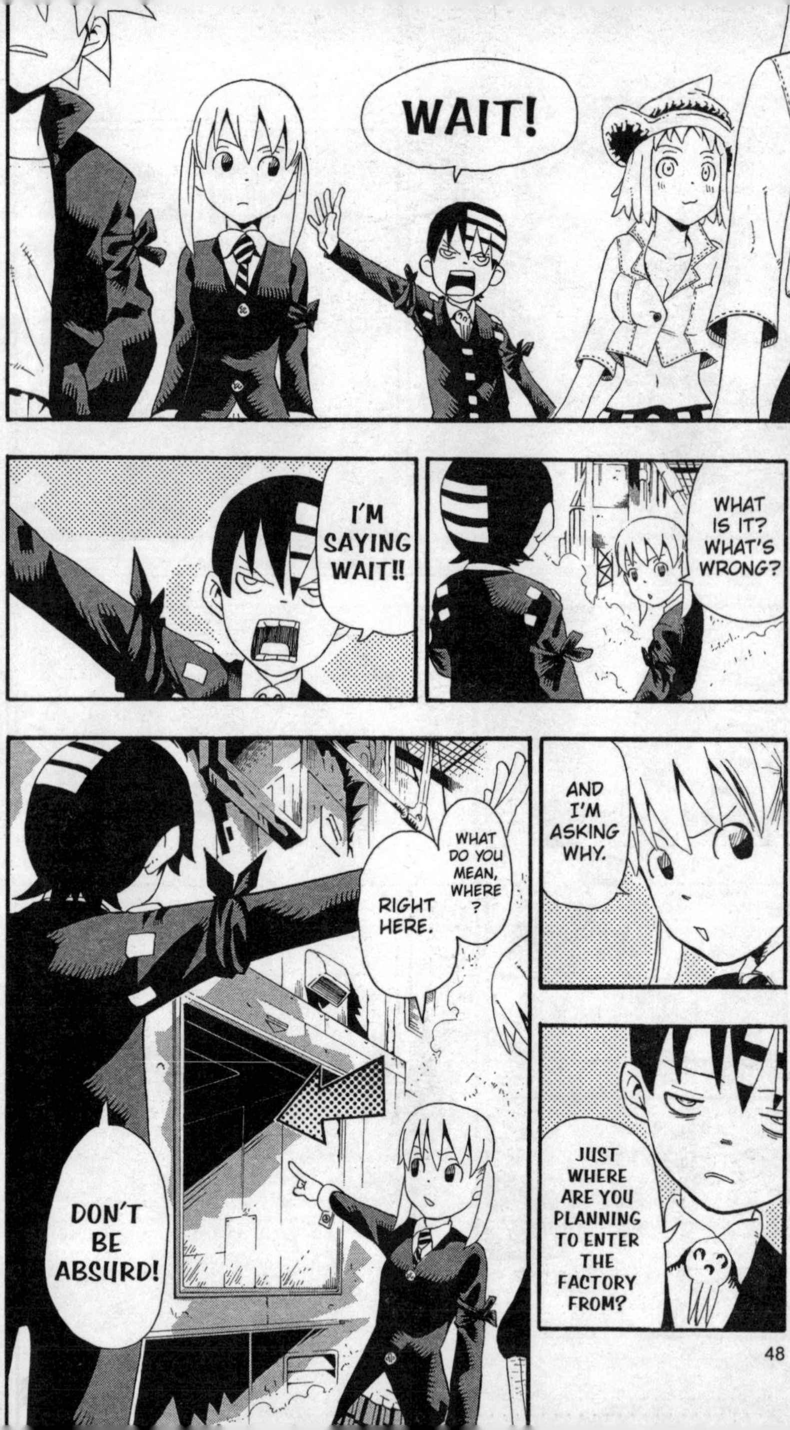
WAIT!
WHAT IS IT? WHAT'S WRONG?
I'M SAYING WAIT!!
AND I'M ASKING WHY.
JUST WHERE ARE YOU PLANNING TO ENTER THE FACTORY FROM?
WHAT DO YOU MEAN, WHERE?
RIGHT HERE.
DON'T BE ABSURD!

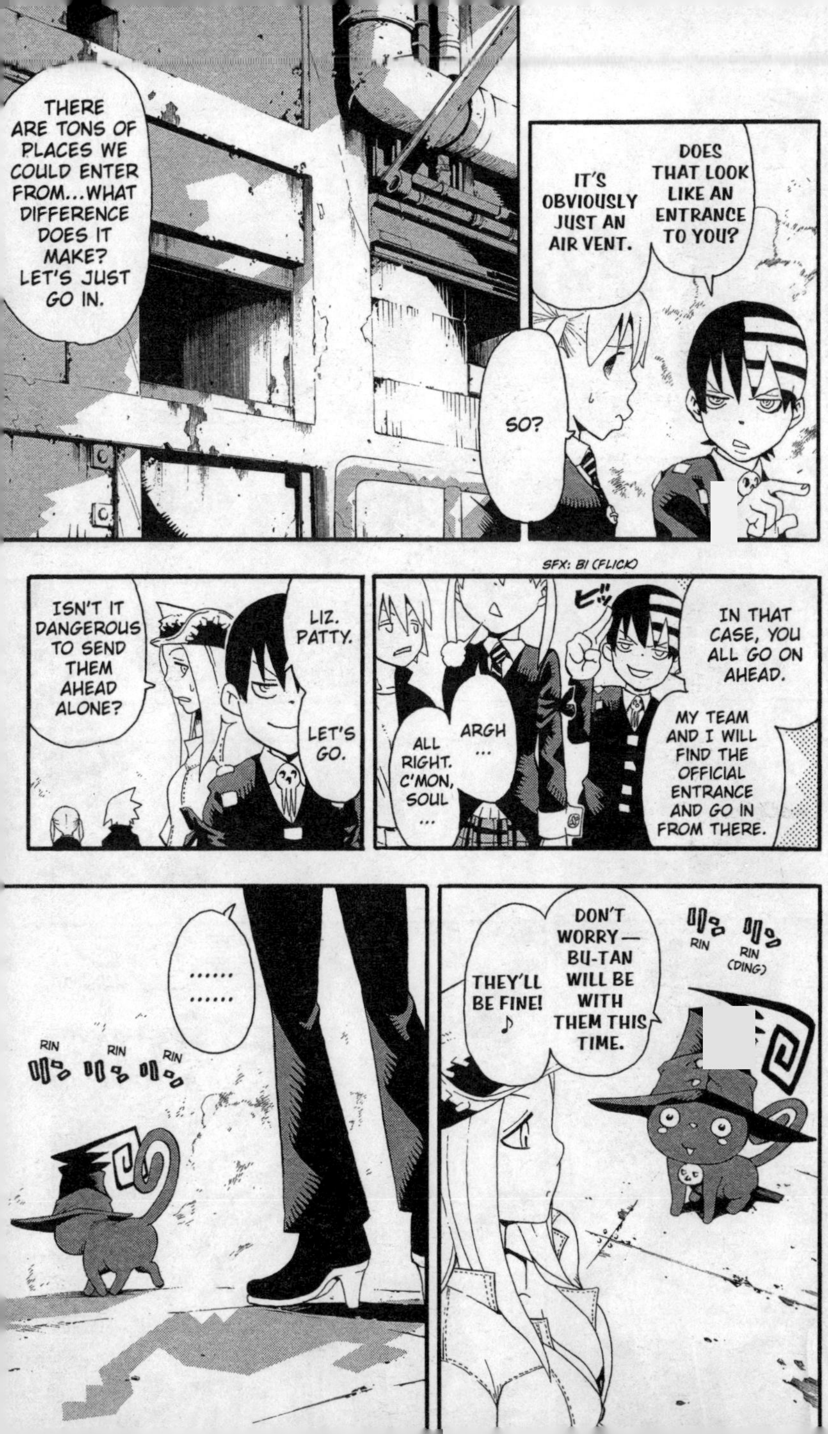
DOES THAT LOOK LIKE AN ENTRANCE TO YOU?
IT'S OBVIOUSLY JUST AN AIR VENT.
SO?
THERE ARE TONS OF PLACES WE COULD ENTER FROM...WHAT DIFFERENCE DOES IT MAKE? LET'S JUST GO IN.
SFX: BI (FLICK)
IN THAT CASE, YOU ALL GO ON AHEAD.
MY TEAM AND I WILL FIND THE OFFICIAL ENTRANCE AND GO IN FROM THERE.
ARGH ...
ALL RIGHT. C'MON, SOUL ...
LIZ. PATTY.
LET'S GO.
ISN'T IT DANGEROUS TO SEND THEM AHEAD ALONE?
DON'T WORRY— BU-TAN WILL BE WITH THEM THIS TIME.
THEY'LL BE FINE! ♪
RIN
RIN (DING)
......
......
RIN
RIN
RIN

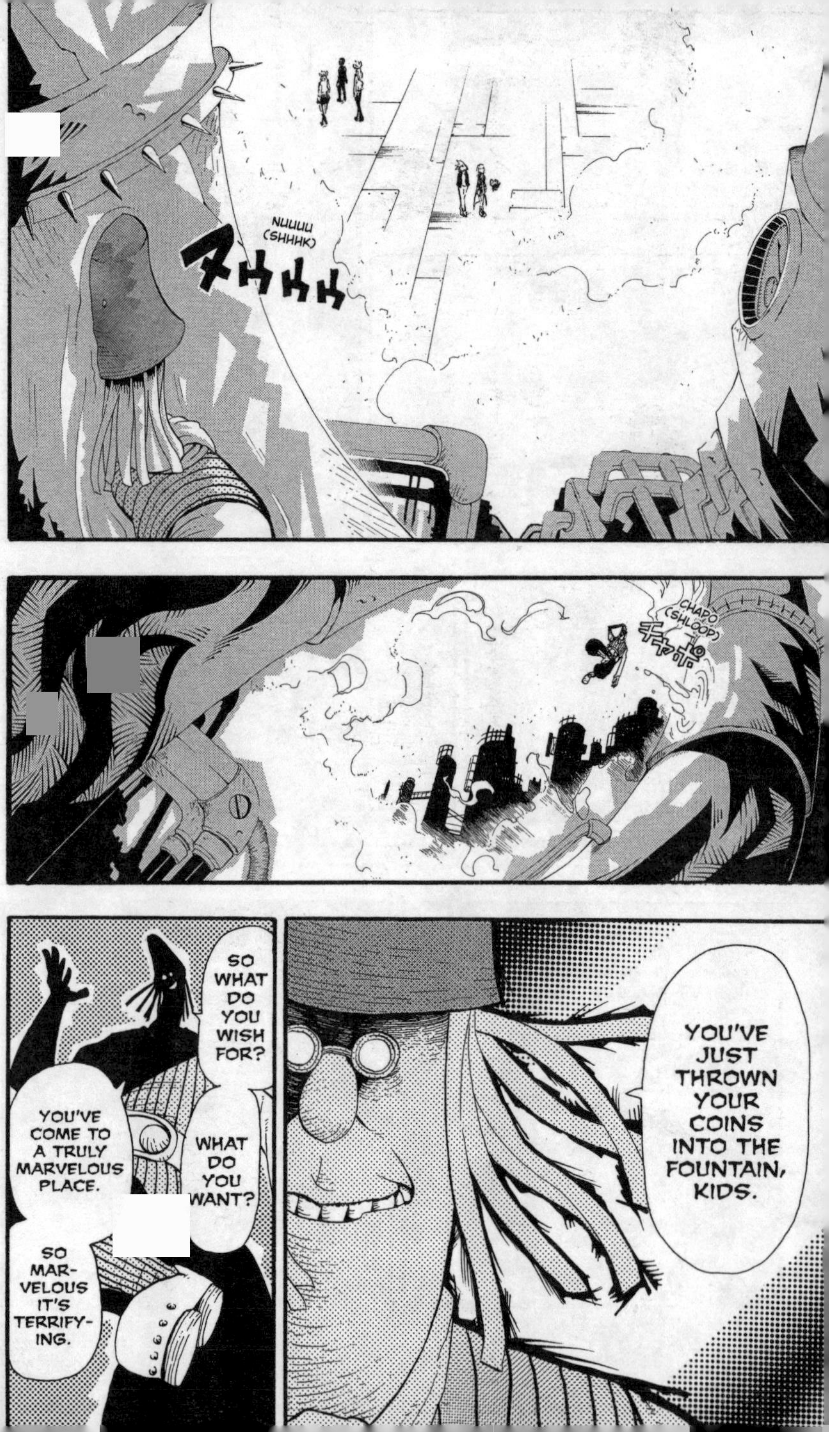

NUUUU (SHHHK)
ヌゥゥゥ
CHAPO (SHLOOP)
チャポ
YOU'VE JUST THROWN YOUR COINS INTO THE FOUNTAIN, KIDS.
SO WHAT DO YOU WISH FOR?
WHAT DO YOU WANT?
YOU'VE COME TO A TRULY MARVELOUS PLACE.
SO MAR-VELOUS IT'S TERRIFY-ING.

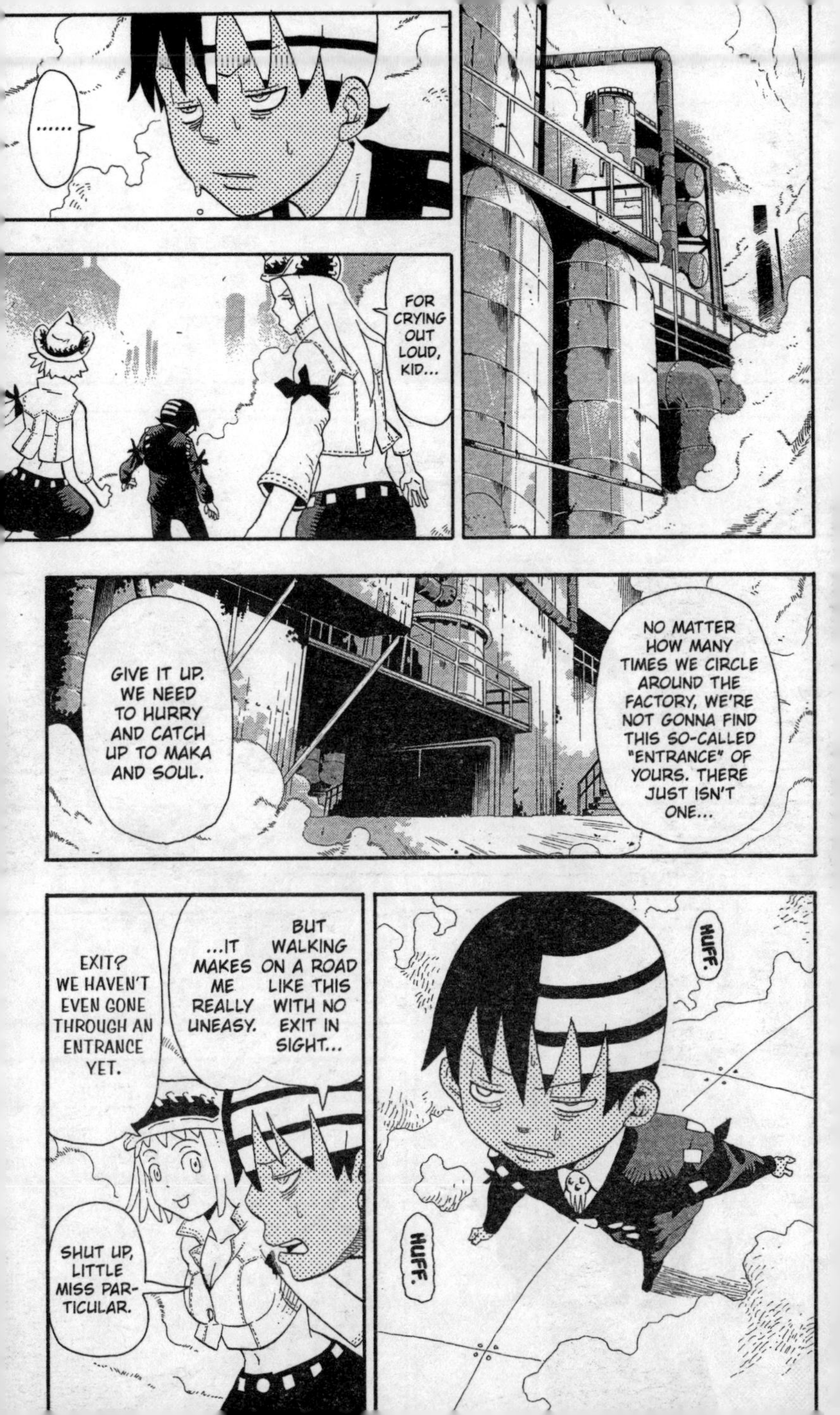
......
FOR CRYING OUT LOUD, KID...
NO MATTER HOW MANY TIMES WE CIRCLE AROUND THE FACTORY, WE'RE NOT GONNA FIND THIS SO-CALLED "ENTRANCE" OF YOURS. THERE JUST ISN'T ONE...
GIVE IT UP. WE NEED TO HURRY AND CATCH UP TO MAKA AND SOUL.
HUFF.
HUFF.
BUT WALKING ON A ROAD LIKE THIS WITH NO EXIT IN SIGHT...
...IT MAKES ME REALLY UNEASY.
EXIT? WE HAVEN'T EVEN GONE THROUGH AN ENTRANCE YET.
SHUT UP, LITTLE MISS PAR-TICULAR.

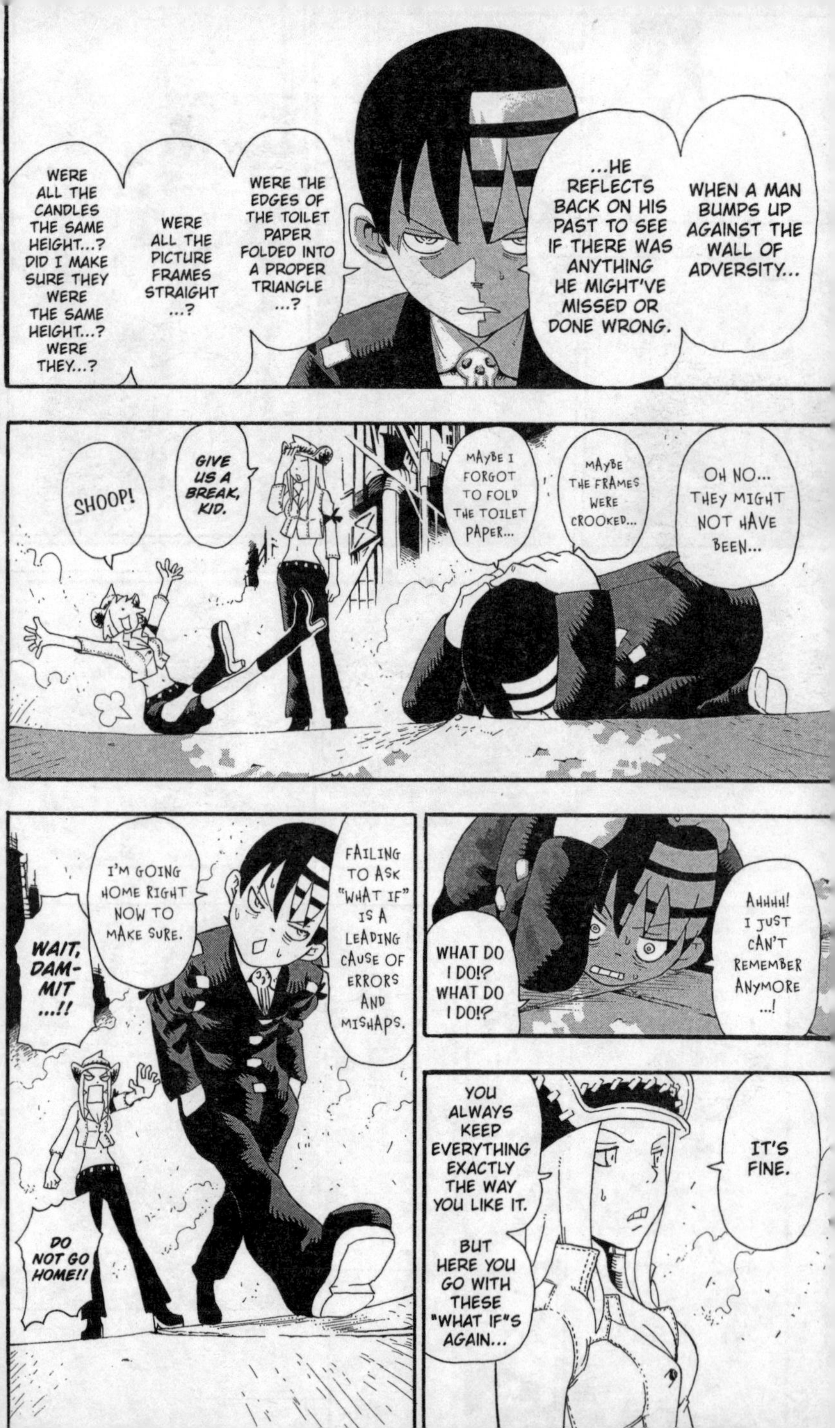
WHEN A MAN BUMPS UP AGAINST THE WALL OF ADVERSITY...
...HE REFLECTS BACK ON HIS PAST TO SEE IF THERE WAS ANYTHING HE MIGHT'VE MISSED OR DONE WRONG.
WERE THE EDGES OF THE TOILET PAPER FOLDED INTO A PROPER TRIANGLE ...?
WERE ALL THE PICTURE FRAMES STRAIGHT ...?
WERE ALL THE CANDLES THE SAME HEIGHT...? DID I MAKE SURE THEY WERE THE SAME HEIGHT...? WERE THEY...?
OH NO... THEY MIGHT NOT HAVE BEEN...
MAYBE THE FRAMES WERE CROOKED...
MAYBE I FORGOT TO FOLD THE TOILET PAPER...
GIVE US A BREAK, KID.
SHOOP!
AHHHH! I JUST CAN'T REMEMBER ANYMORE ...!
WHAT DO I DO!? WHAT DO I DO!?
IT'S FINE.
YOU ALWAYS KEEP EVERYTHING EXACTLY THE WAY YOU LIKE IT.
BUT HERE YOU GO WITH THESE "WHAT IF"S AGAIN...
FAILING TO ASK "WHAT IF" IS A LEADING CAUSE OF ERRORS AND MISHAPS.
I'M GOING HOME RIGHT NOW TO MAKE SURE.
WAIT, DAMMIT ...!!
DO NOT GO HOME!!

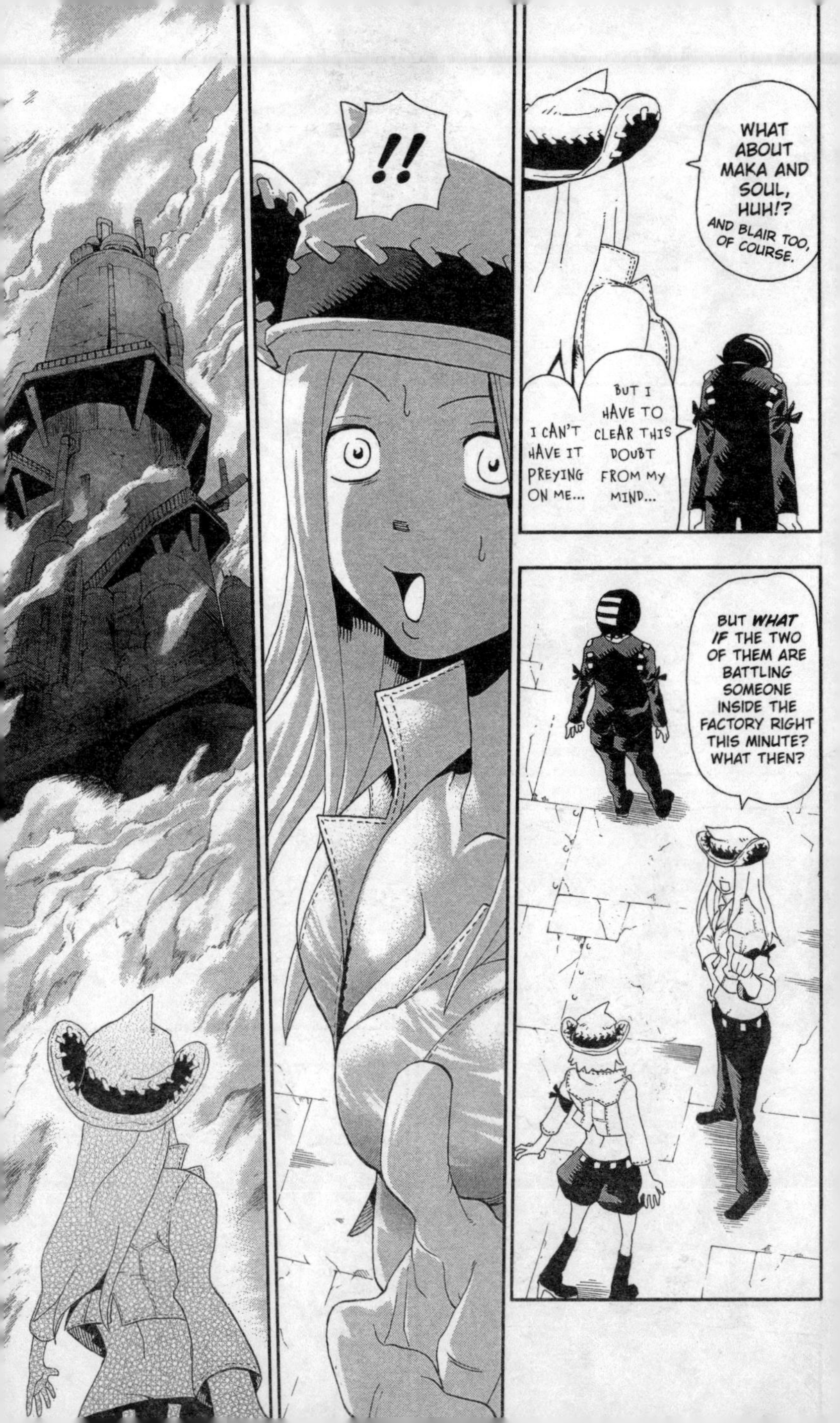
WHAT ABOUT MAKA AND SOUL, HUH!?
AND BLAIR TOO, OF COURSE.
BUT I HAVE TO CLEAR THIS DOUBT FROM MY MIND...
I CAN'T HAVE IT PREYING ON ME...
BUT *WHAT IF* THE TWO OF THEM ARE BATTLING SOMEONE INSIDE THE FACTORY RIGHT THIS MINUTE? WHAT THEN?
!!

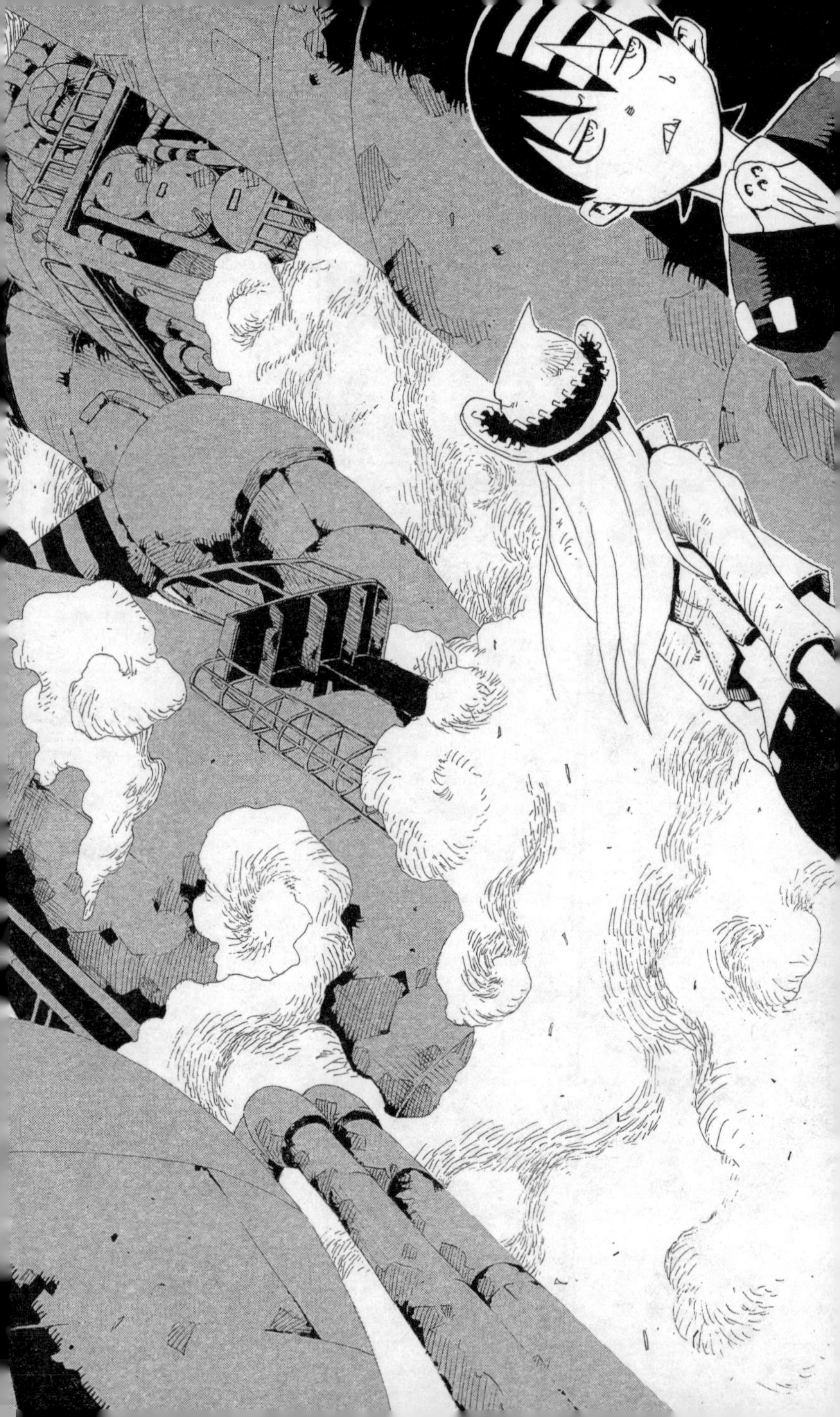

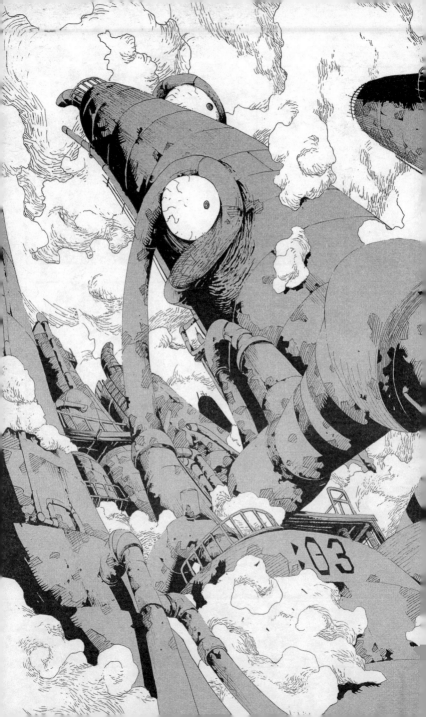

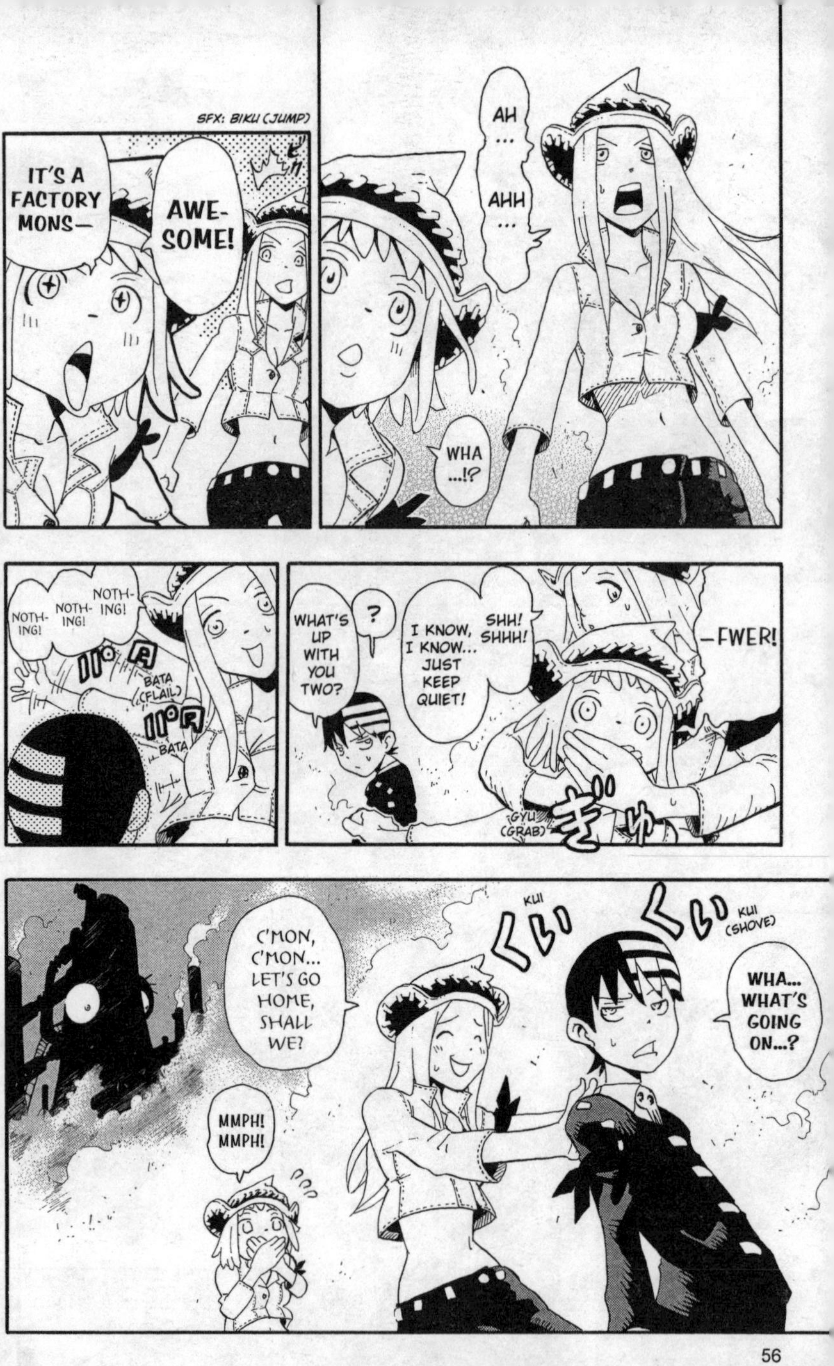
AH...
AHH...
WHA...!?
SFX: BIKU (JUMP)
AWE-SOME!
IT'S A FACTORY MONS—
—FWER!
SHH! SHHH!
I KNOW, I KNOW... JUST KEEP QUIET!
?
WHAT'S UP WITH YOU TWO?
GYU (GRAB)
NOTH-ING!
NOTH-ING!
NOTH-ING!
BATA (FLAIL)
BATA
KUI (SHOVE)
KUI
WHA... WHAT'S GOING ON...?
C'MON, C'MON... LET'S GO HOME, SHALL WE?
MMPH! MMPH!

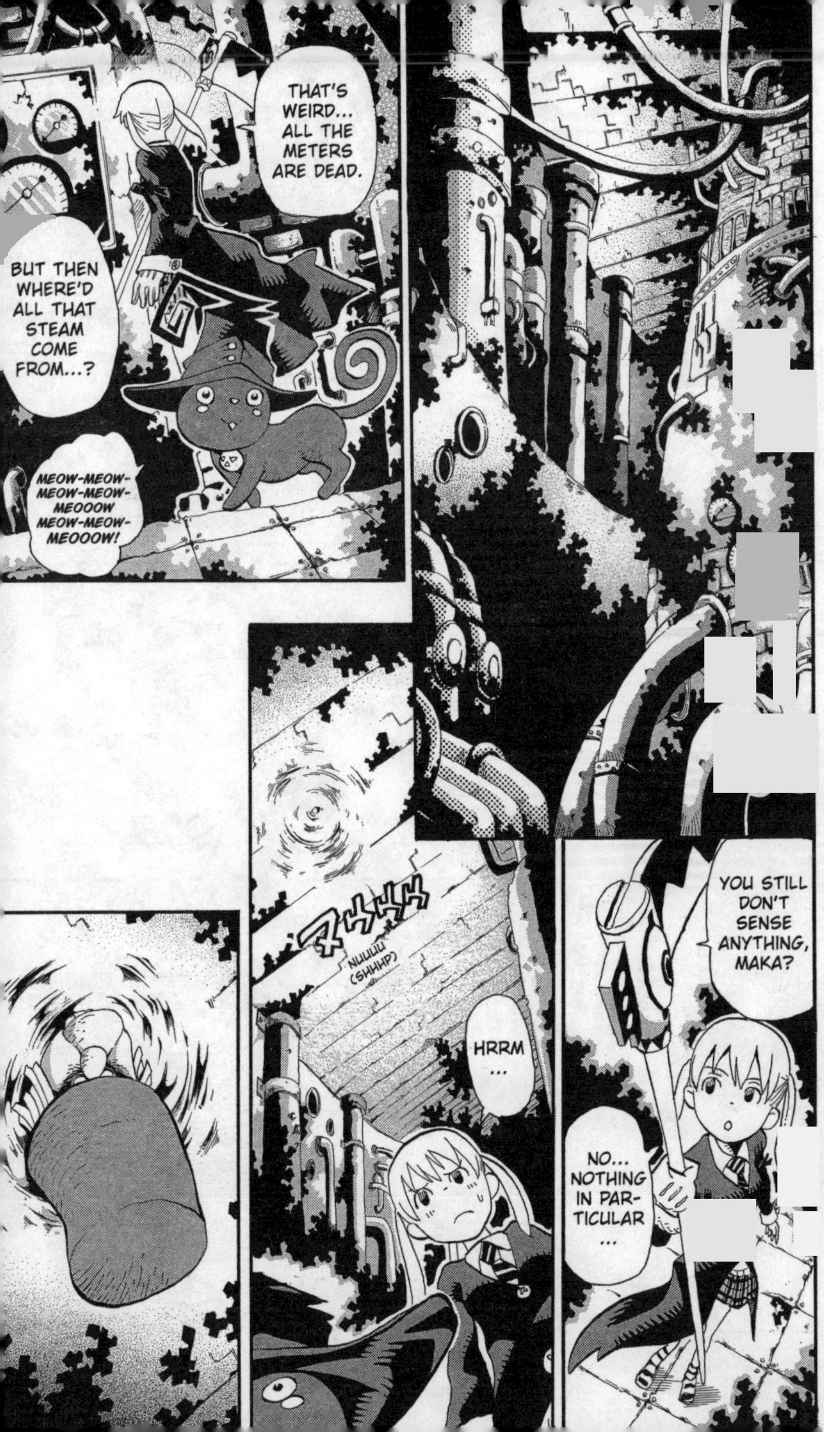
THAT'S WEIRD... ALL THE METERS ARE DEAD.
BUT THEN WHERE'D ALL THAT STEAM COME FROM...?
MEOW-MEOW-MEOW-MEOW-MEOOOW MEOW-MEOW-MEOOOW!
YOU STILL DON'T SENSE ANYTHING, MAKA?
NO... NOTHING IN PAR-TICULAR...
NUUUU (SHHHP)
HRRM...

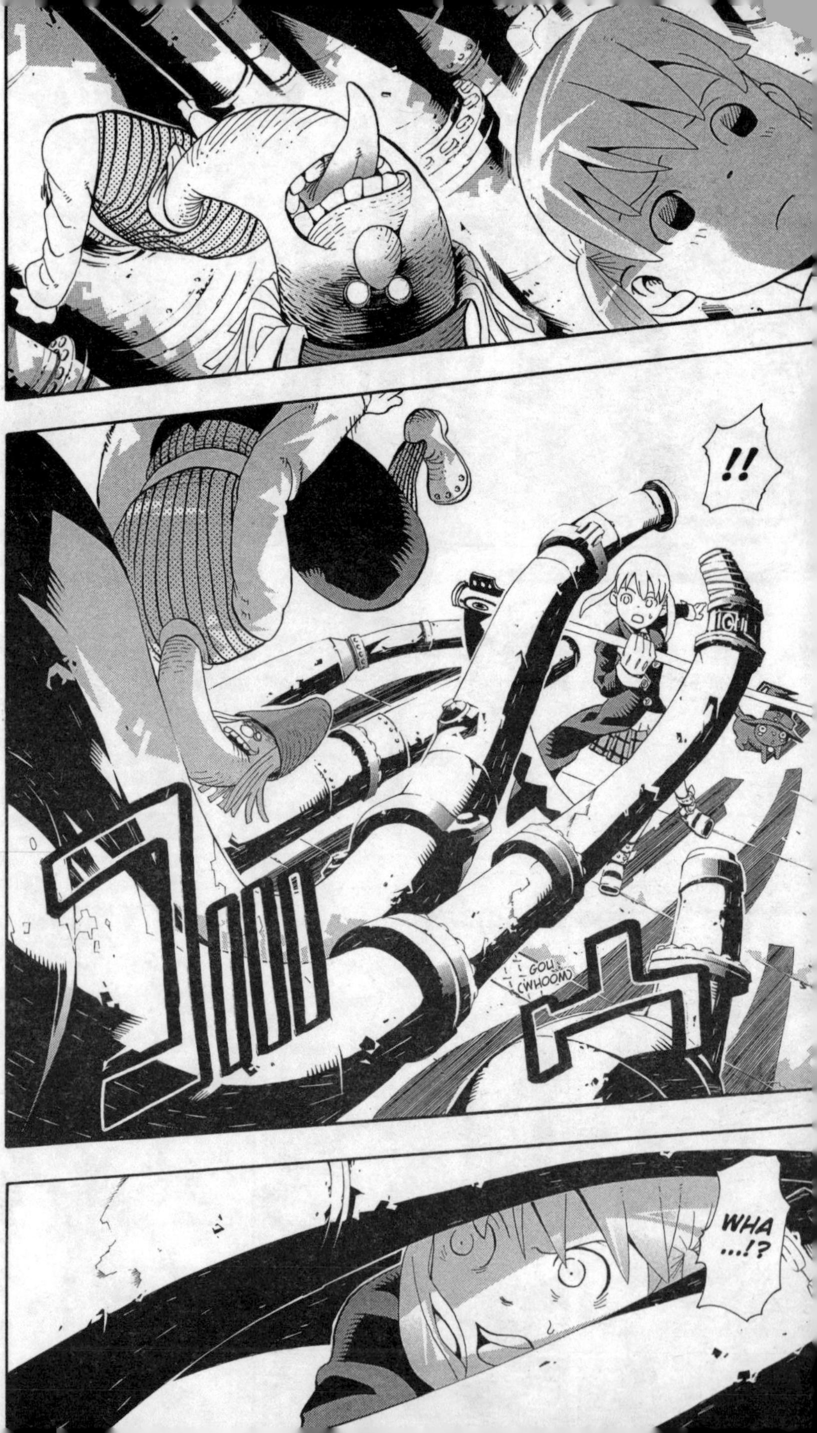
!!
GOU (WHOOM)
WHA ...!?

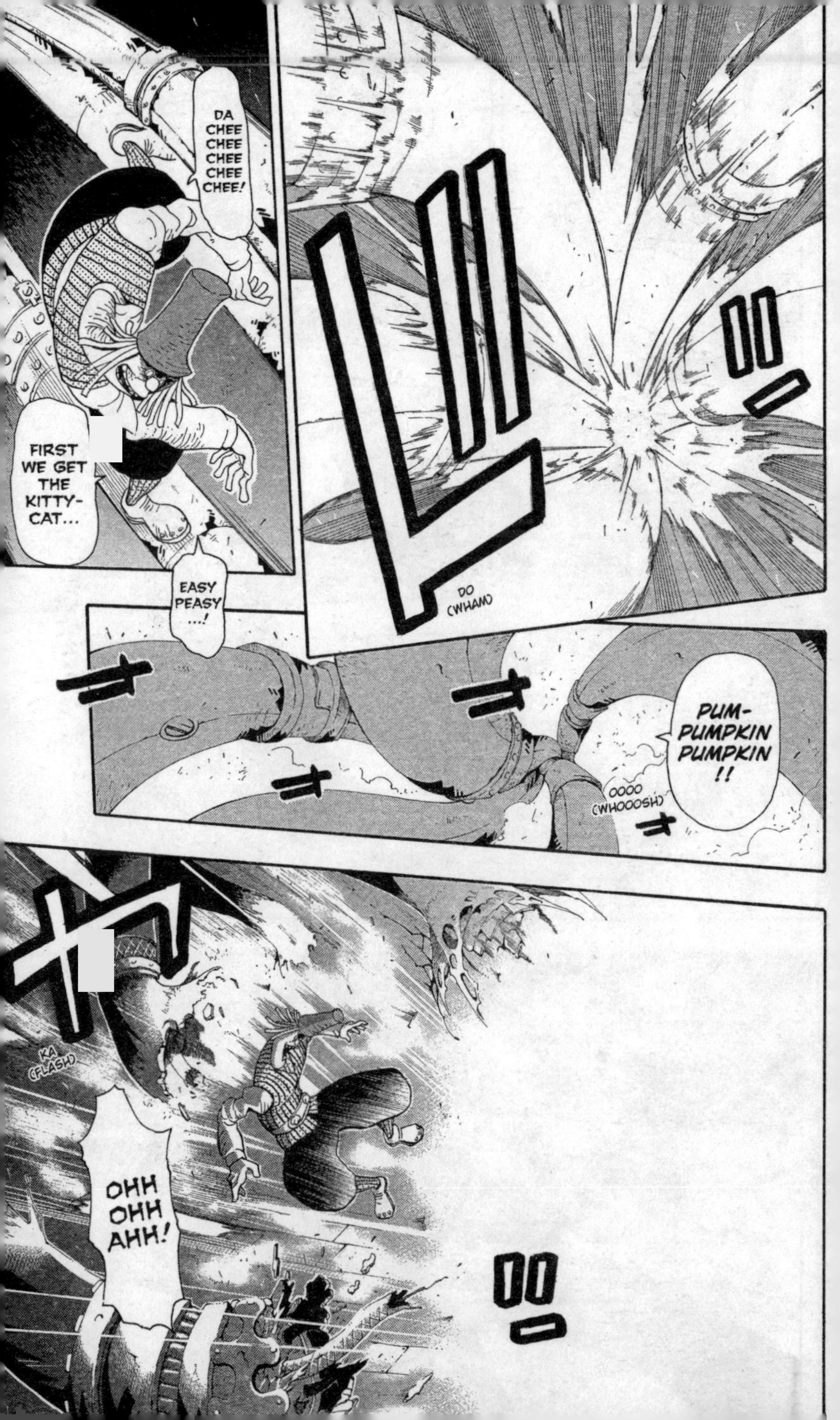
DO (WHAM)
DA CHEE CHEE CHEE CHEE CHEE!
FIRST WE GET THE KITTY-CAT...
EASY PEASY ...!
PUM-PUMPKIN PUMPKIN !!
OOOO (WHOOOSH)
KA (FLASH)
OHH OHH AHH!

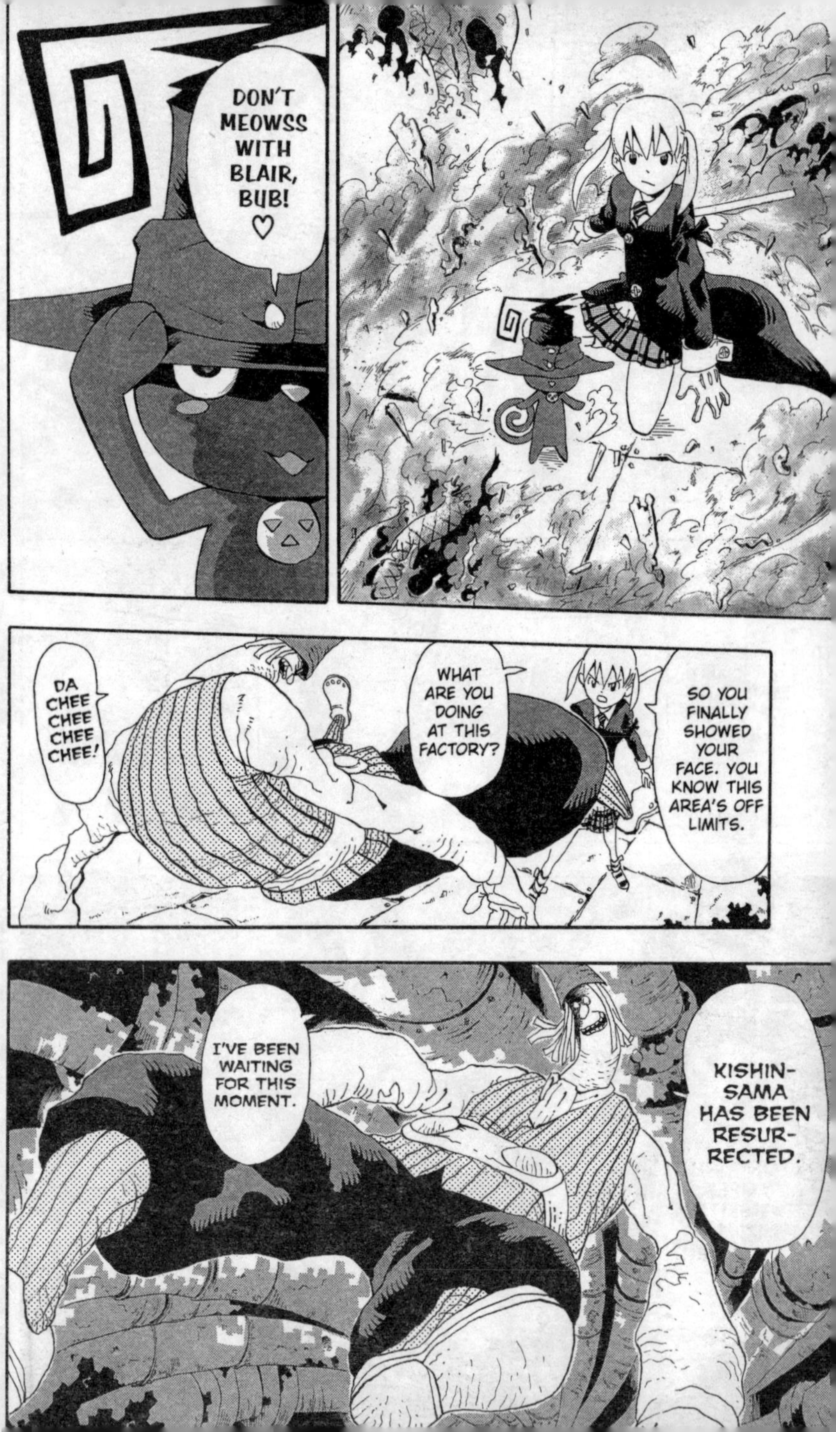
DON'T MEOWSS WITH BLAIR, BUB! ♡
SO YOU FINALLY SHOWED YOUR FACE. YOU KNOW THIS AREA'S OFF LIMITS.
WHAT ARE YOU DOING AT THIS FACTORY?
DA CHEE CHEE CHEE CHEE!
KISHIN-SAMA HAS BEEN RESURRECTED.
I'VE BEEN WAITING FOR THIS MOMENT.

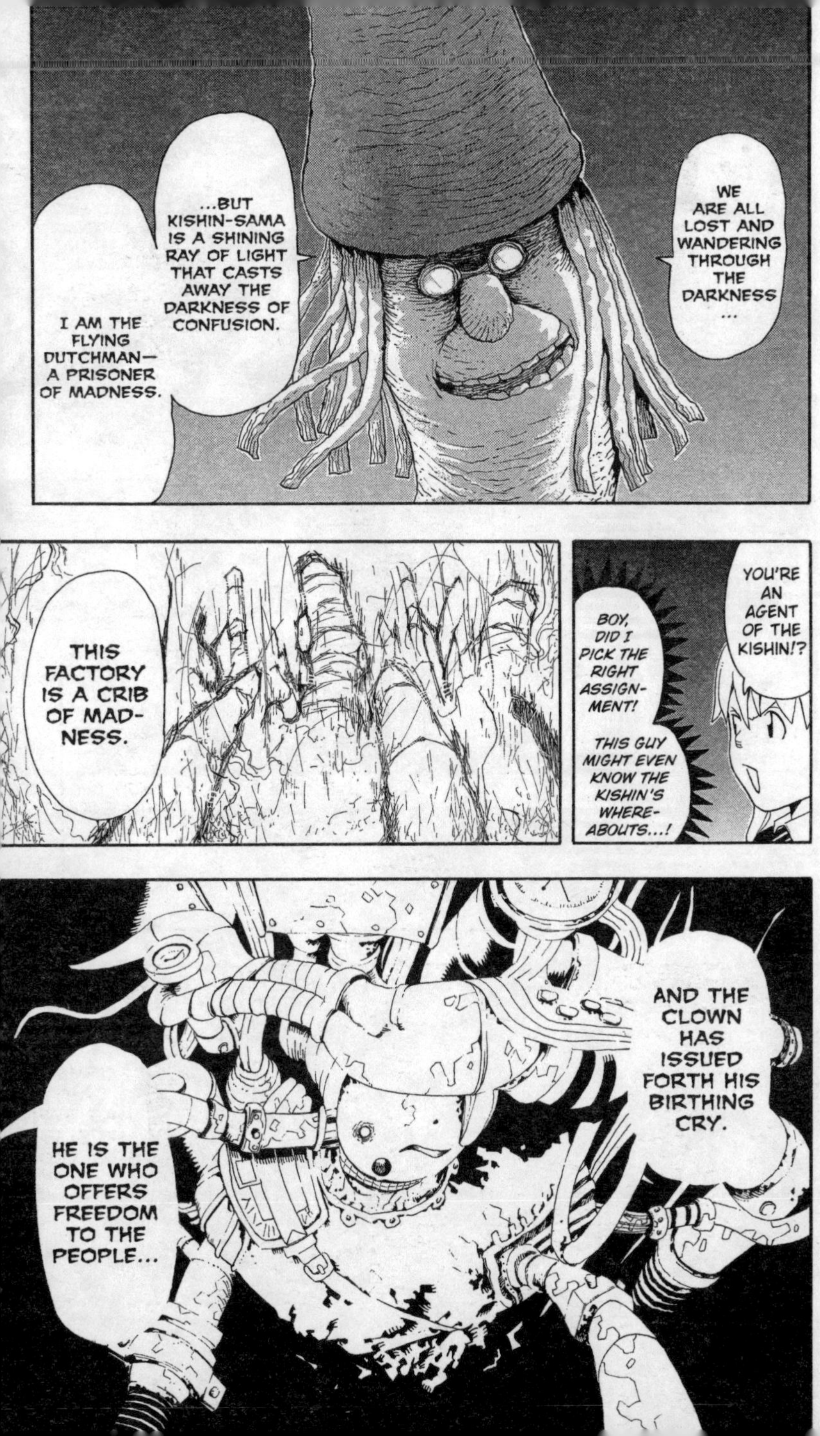
WE ARE ALL LOST AND WANDERING THROUGH THE DARKNESS ...
...BUT KISHIN-SAMA IS A SHINING RAY OF LIGHT THAT CASTS AWAY THE DARKNESS OF CONFUSION.
I AM THE FLYING DUTCHMAN— A PRISONER OF MADNESS.
YOU'RE AN AGENT OF THE KISHIN!?
BOY, DID I PICK THE RIGHT ASSIGN-MENT!
THIS GUY MIGHT EVEN KNOW THE KISHIN'S WHERE-ABOUTS...!
THIS FACTORY IS A CRIB OF MAD-NESS.
AND THE CLOWN HAS ISSUED FORTH HIS BIRTHING CRY.
HE IS THE ONE WHO OFFERS FREEDOM TO THE PEOPLE...

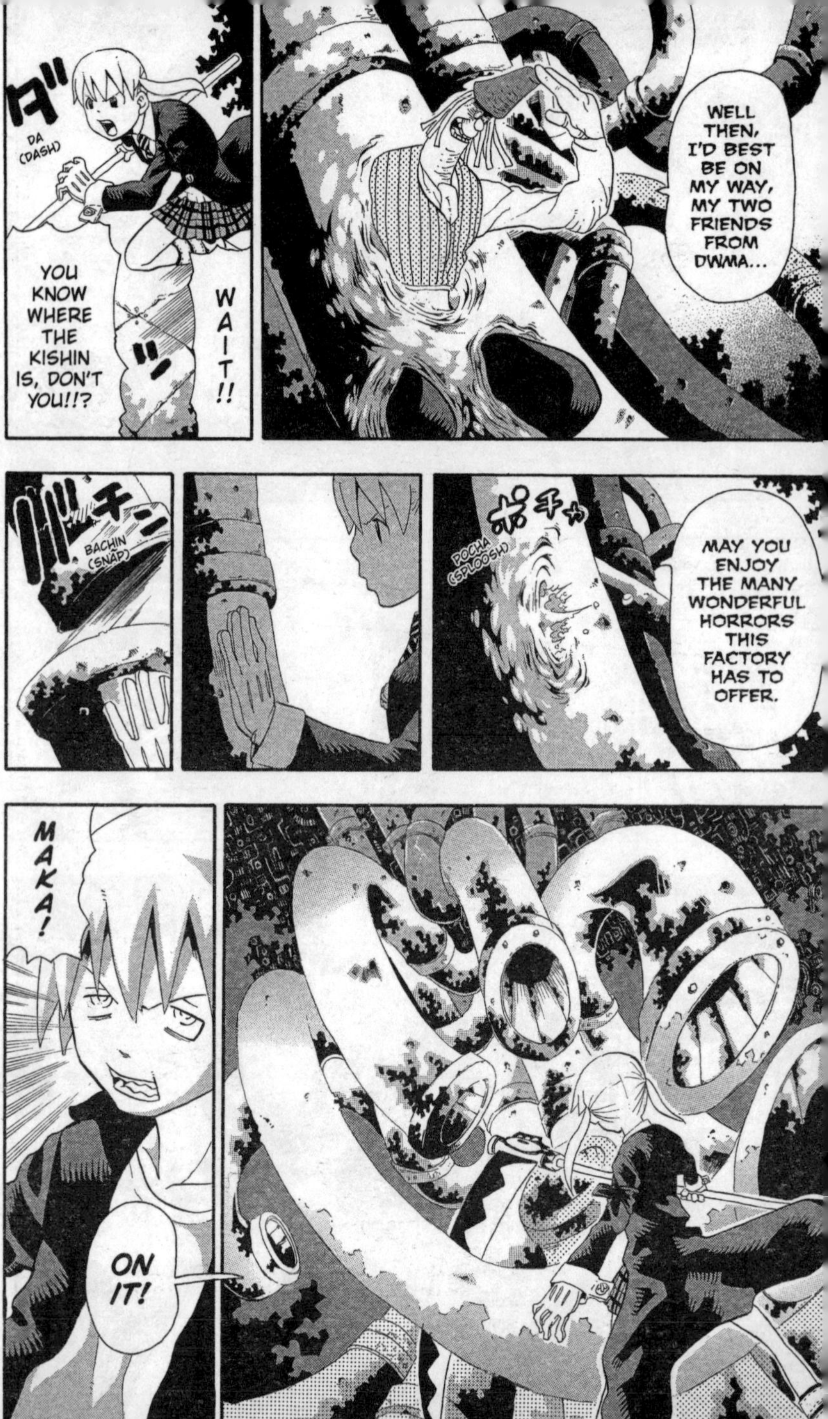
WELL THEN, I'D BEST BE ON MY WAY, MY TWO FRIENDS FROM DWMA...
ダ
DA (DASH)
WAIT!!
YOU KNOW WHERE THE KISHIN IS, DON'T YOU!!?
MAY YOU ENJOY THE MANY WONDERFUL HORRORS THIS FACTORY HAS TO OFFER.
ポチャ
POCHA (SPLOOSH)
バチン
BACHIN (SNAP)
MAKA!
ON IT!

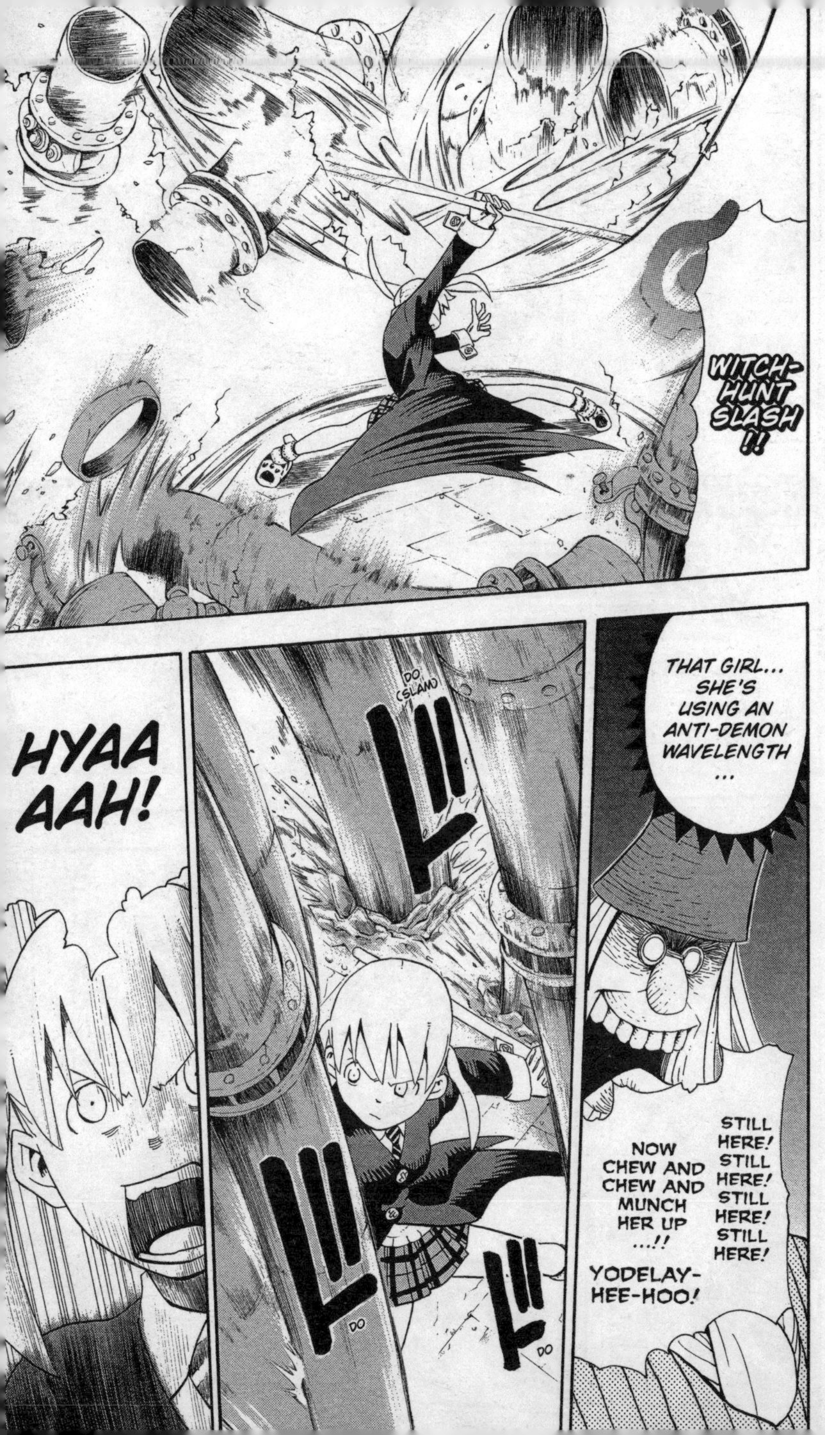
WITCH-HUNT SLASH!!
THAT GIRL... SHE'S USING AN ANTI-DEMON WAVELENGTH...
STILL HERE! STILL HERE! STILL HERE! STILL HERE!
NOW CHEW AND CHEW AND MUNCH HER UP...!!
YODELAY-HEE-HOO!
DO (SLAM)
DO
DO
HYAAAAH!

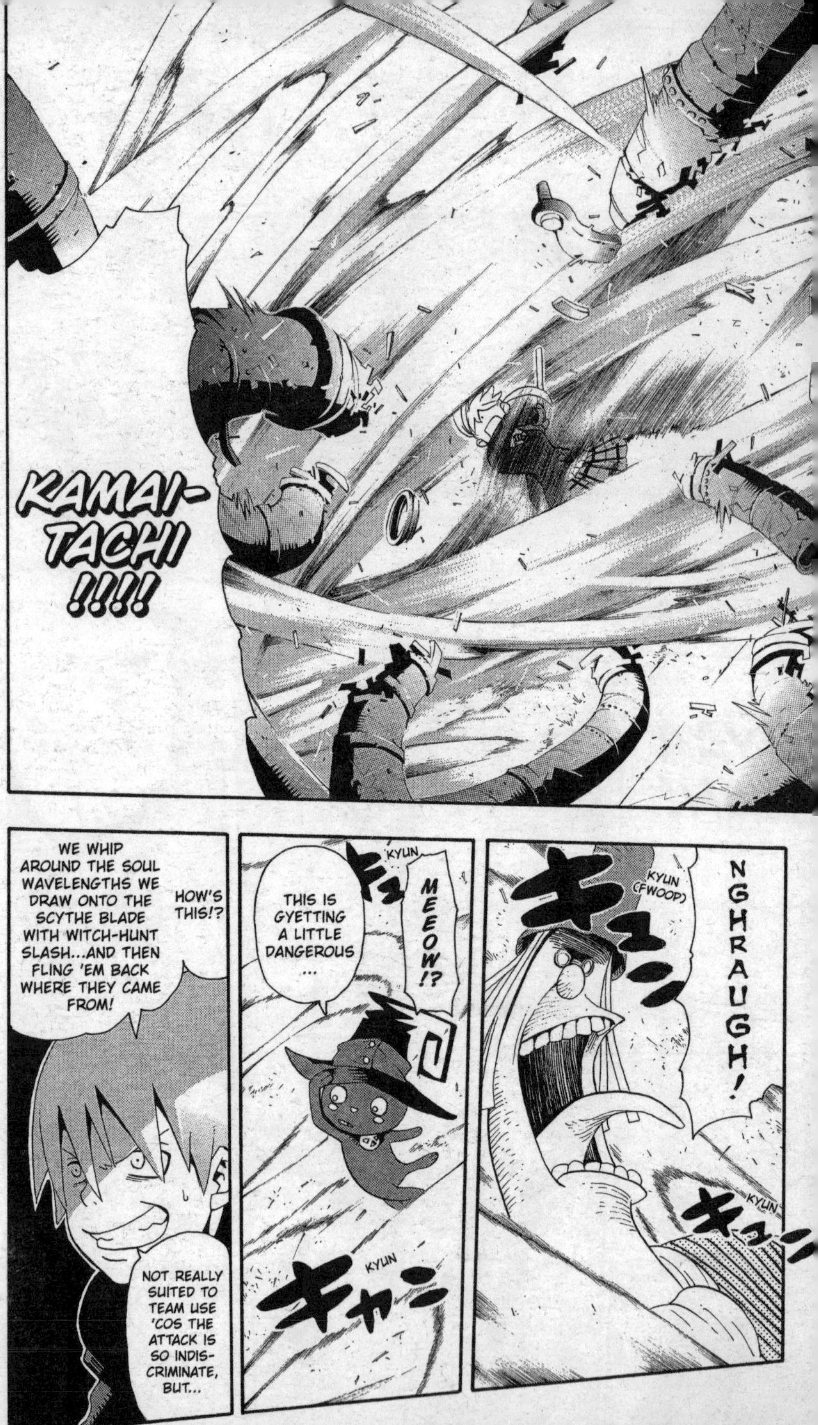
KAMAI-TACHI!!!!
KYUN (FWOOP)
NGHRAUGH!
KYUN
KYUN
MEEEOW!?
THIS IS GYETTING A LITTLE DANGEROUS...
KYUN
HOW'S THIS!?
WE WHIP AROUND THE SOUL WAVELENGTHS WE DRAW ONTO THE SCYTHE BLADE WITH WITCH-HUNT SLASH...AND THEN FLING 'EM BACK WHERE THEY CAME FROM!
NOT REALLY SUITED TO TEAM USE 'COS THE ATTACK IS SO INDIS-CRIMINATE, BUT...

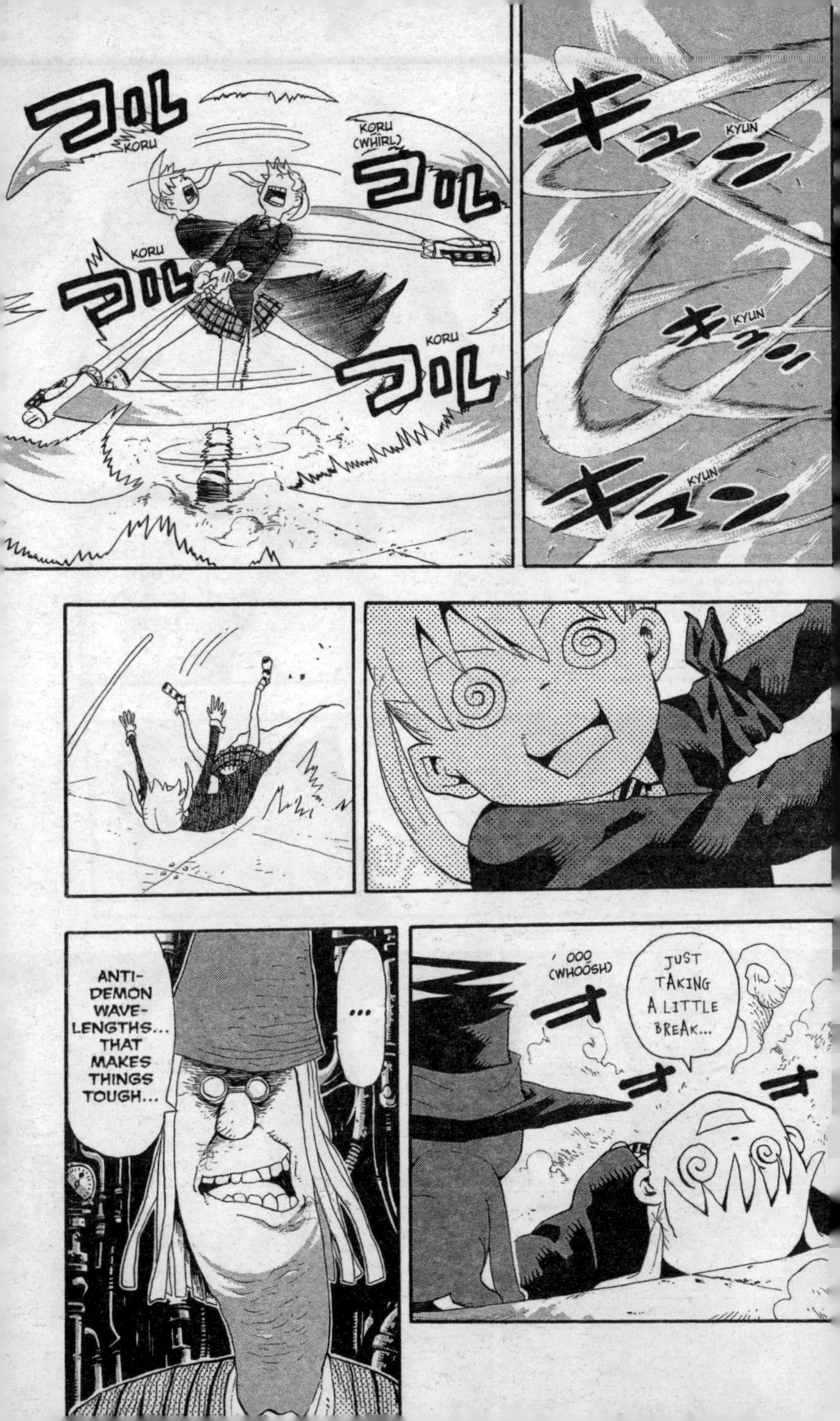
KYUN
KYUN
KYUN
KORU (WHIRL)
KORU
KORU
KORU
OOO (WHOOSH)
JUST TAKING A LITTLE BREAK...
...
ANTI-DEMON WAVE-LENGTHS... THAT MAKES THINGS TOUGH...

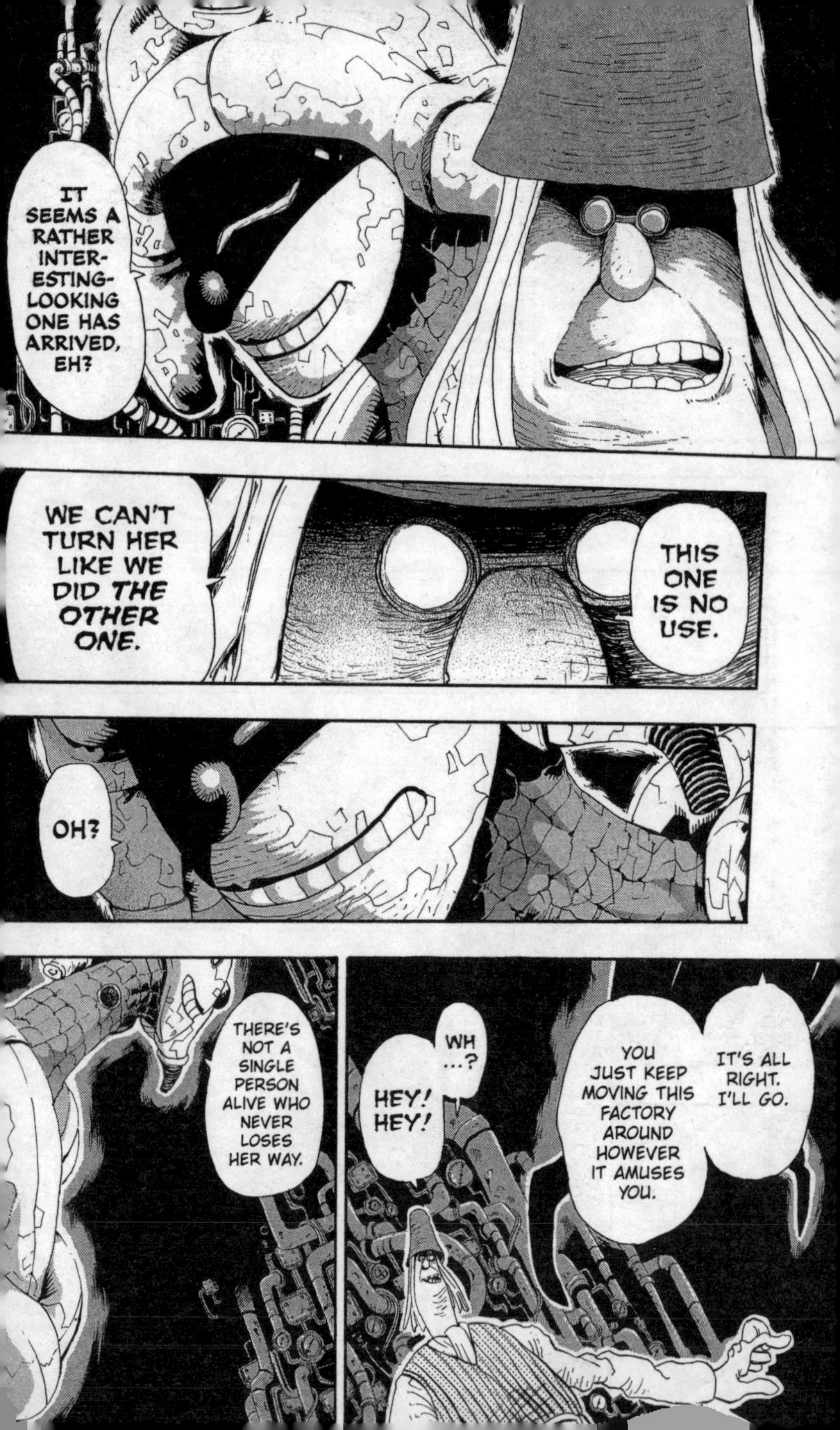
IT SEEMS A RATHER INTERESTING-LOOKING ONE HAS ARRIVED, EH?
THIS ONE IS NO USE.
WE CAN'T TURN HER LIKE WE DID *THE OTHER ONE*.
OH?
IT'S ALL RIGHT. I'LL GO.
YOU JUST KEEP MOVING THIS FACTORY AROUND HOWEVER IT AMUSES YOU.
WH...?
HEY! HEY!
THERE'S NOT A SINGLE PERSON ALIVE WHO NEVER LOSES HER WAY.

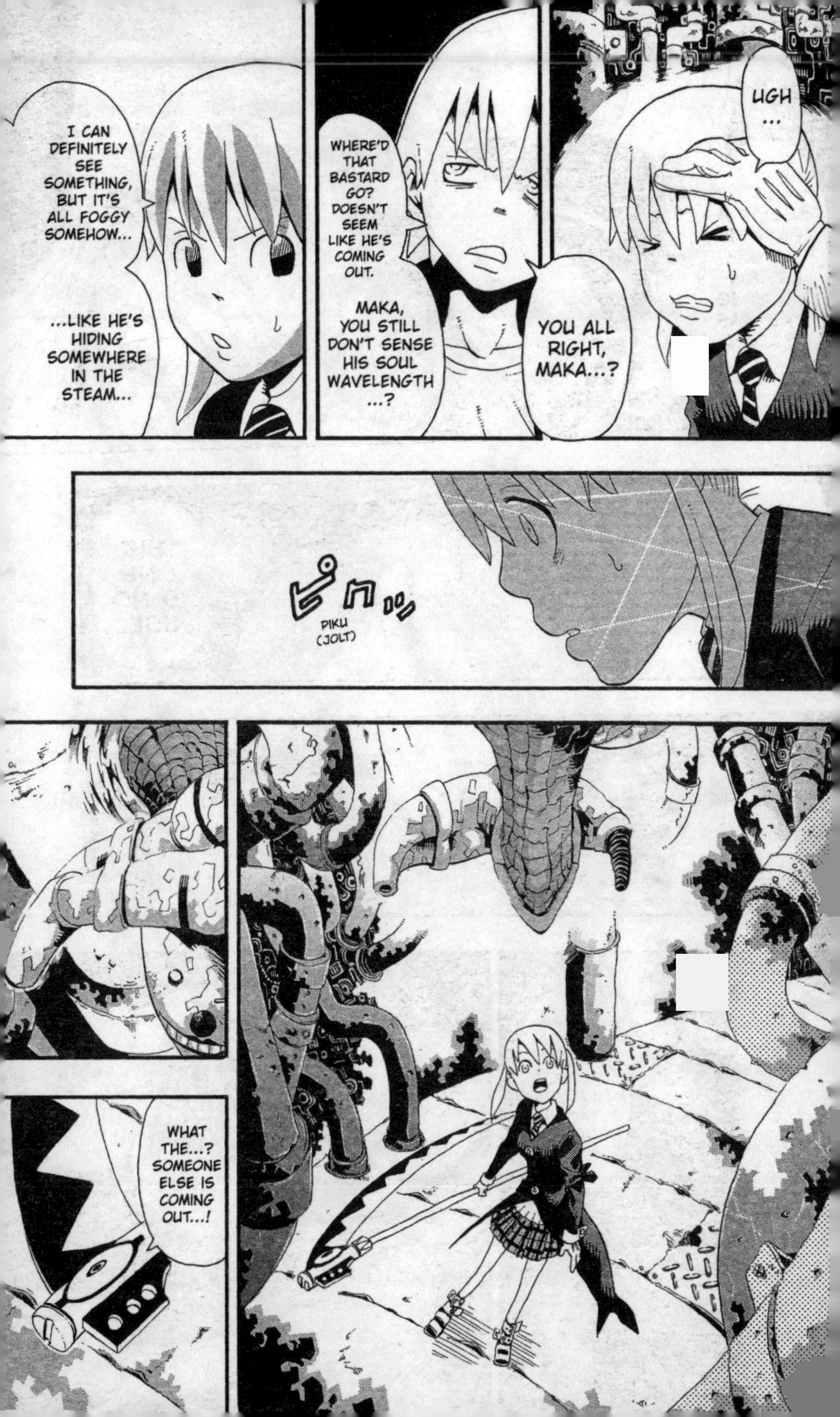
UGH ...
YOU ALL RIGHT, MAKA...?
WHERE'D THAT BASTARD GO? DOESN'T SEEM LIKE HE'S COMING OUT.
MAKA, YOU STILL DON'T SENSE HIS SOUL WAVELENGTH ...?
I CAN DEFINITELY SEE SOMETHING, BUT IT'S ALL FOGGY SOMEHOW...
...LIKE HE'S HIDING SOMEWHERE IN THE STEAM...
ピクッ
PIKU (JOLT)
WHAT THE...? SOMEONE ELSE IS COMING OUT...!

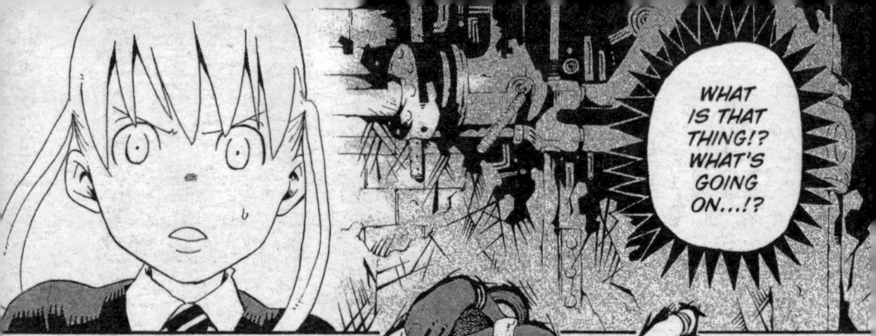
WHAT IS THAT THING!? WHAT'S GOING ON...!?

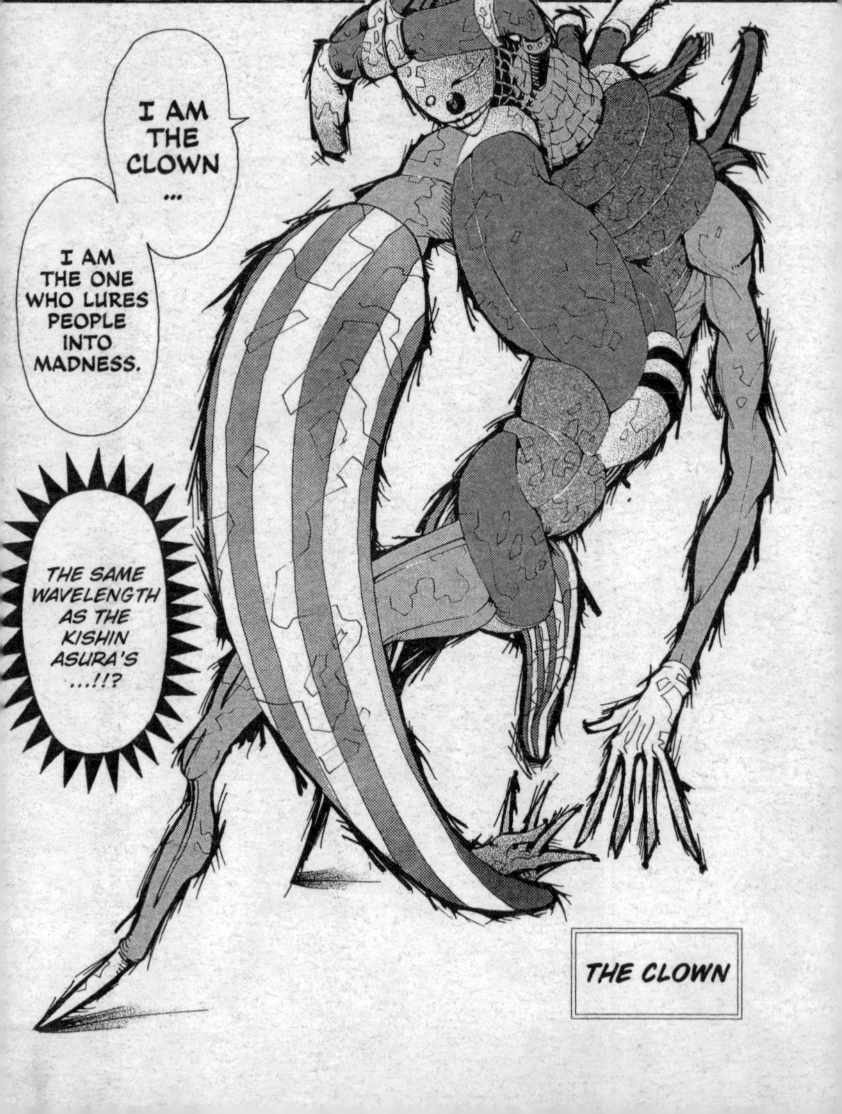
I AM THE CLOWN ...
I AM THE ONE WHO LURES PEOPLE INTO MADNESS.
THE SAME WAVELENGTH AS THE KISHIN ASURA'S ...!!?
THE CLOWN

SOUL EATER

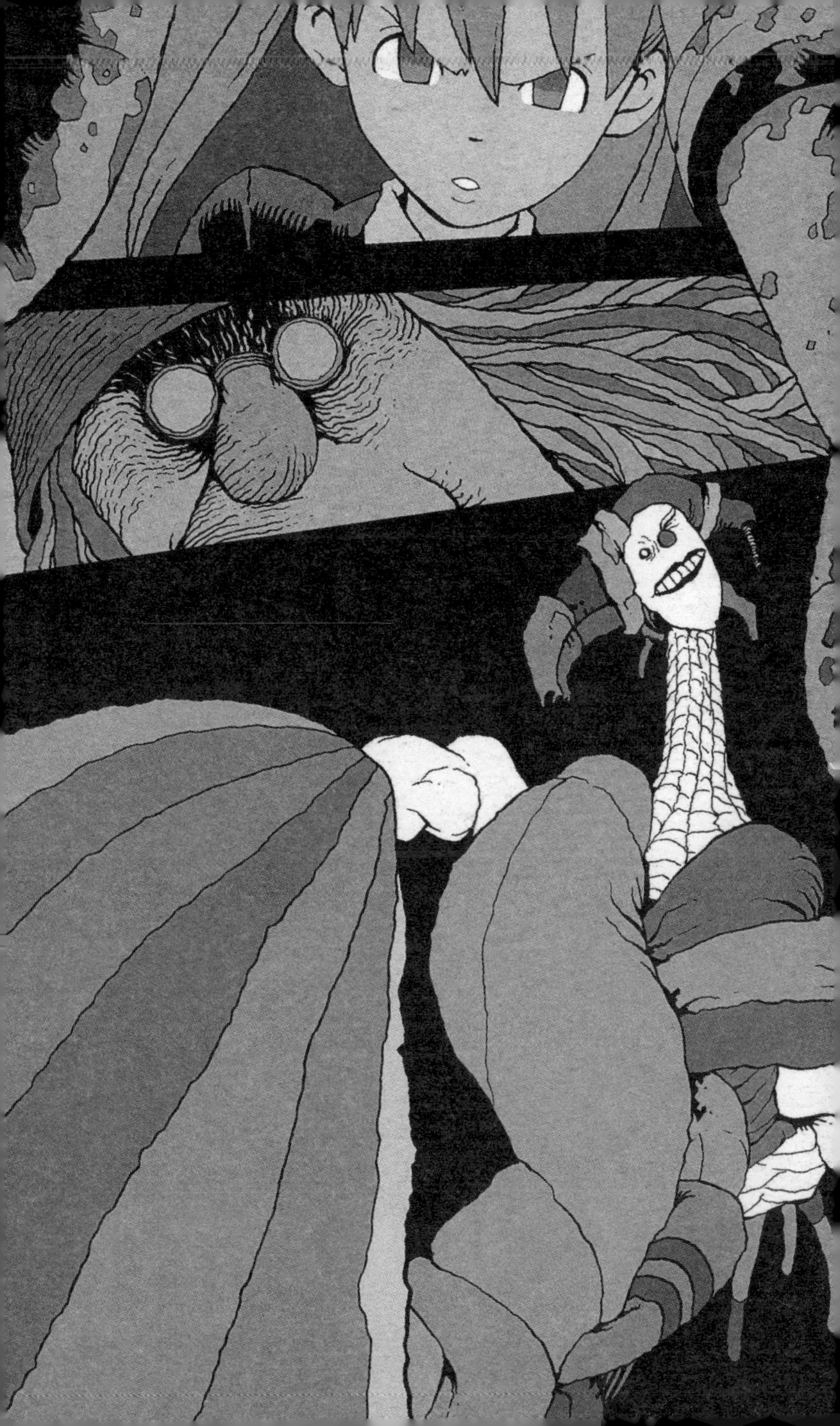

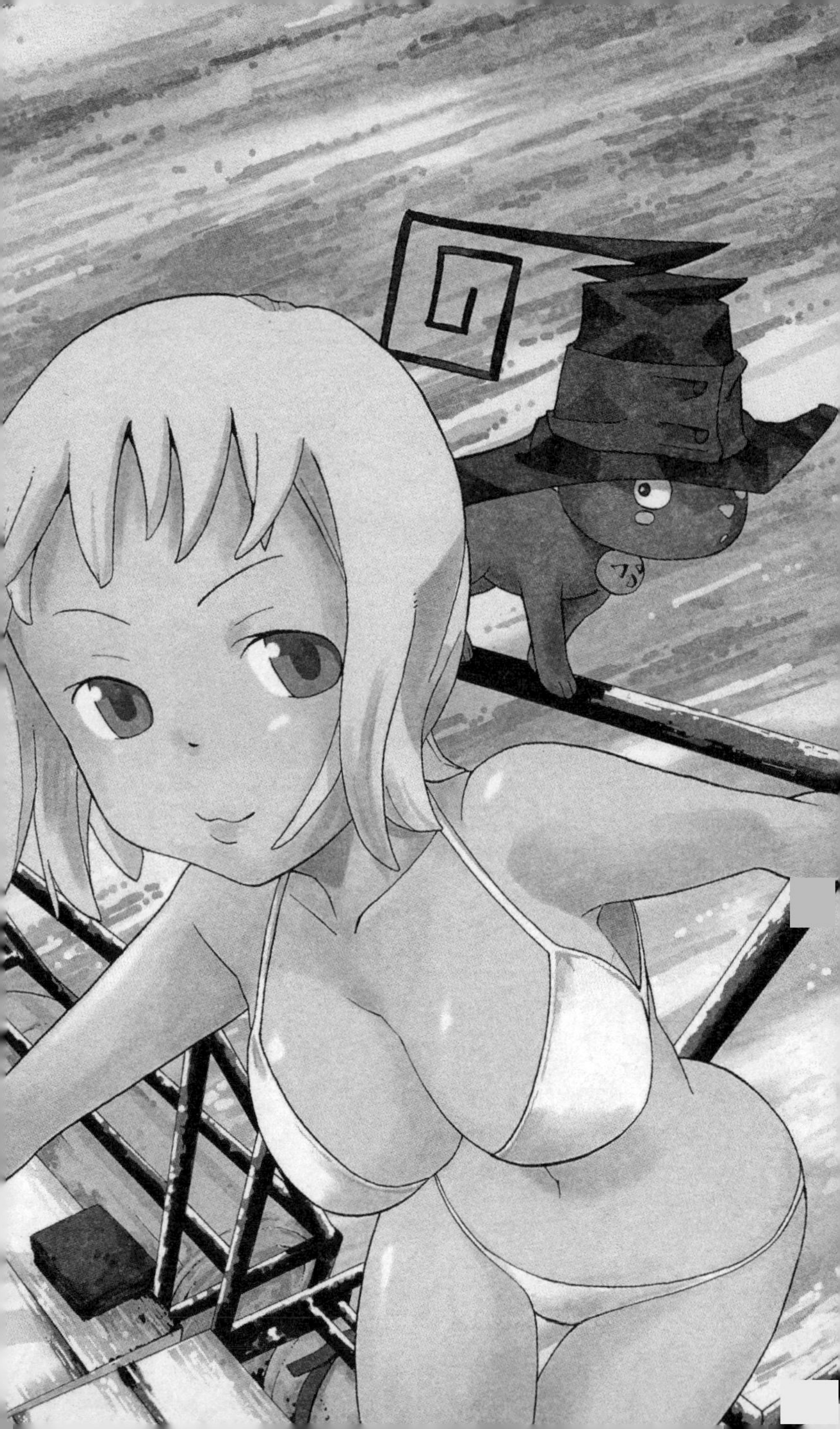

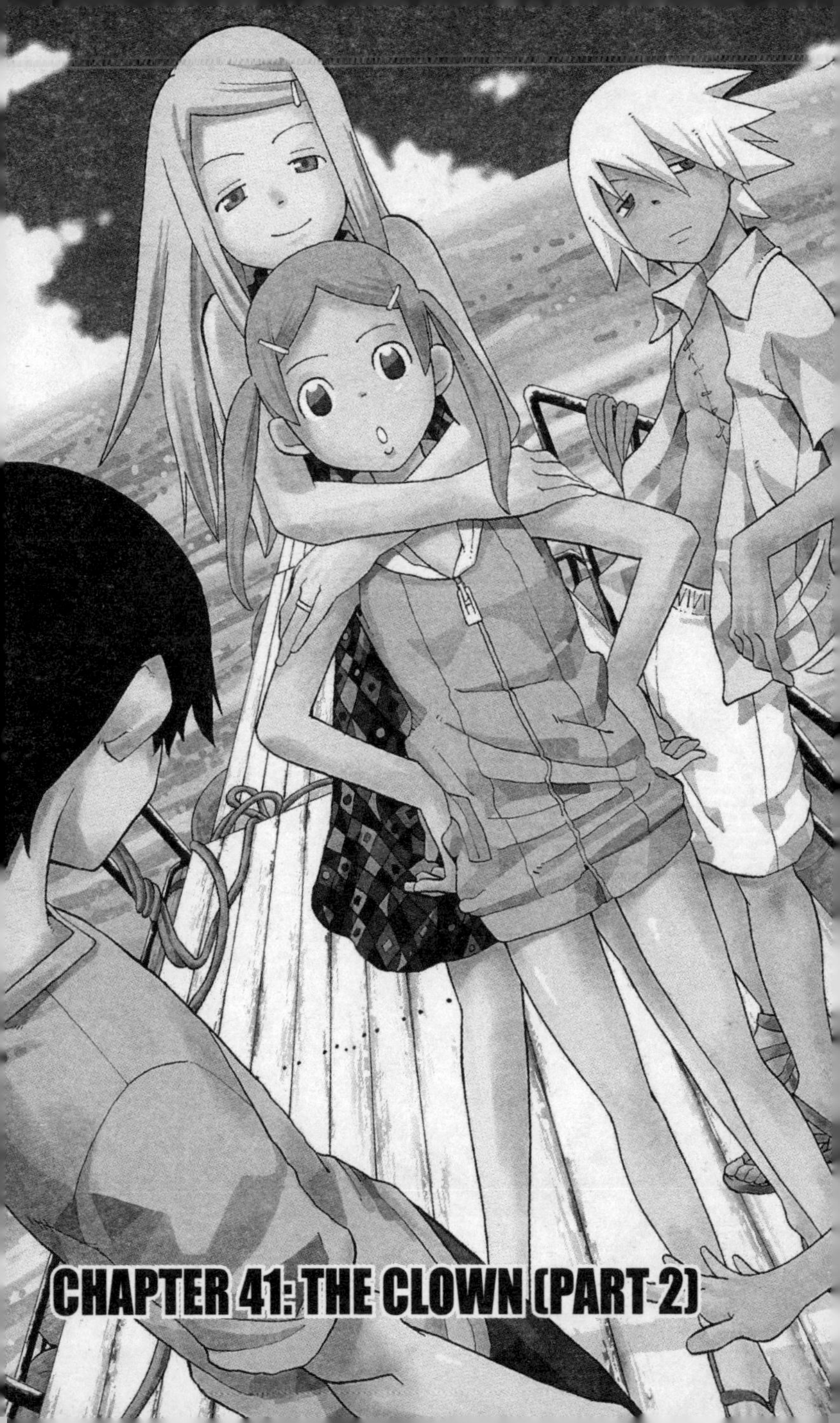
CHAPTER 41: THE CLOWN (PART 2)

SOUL EATER

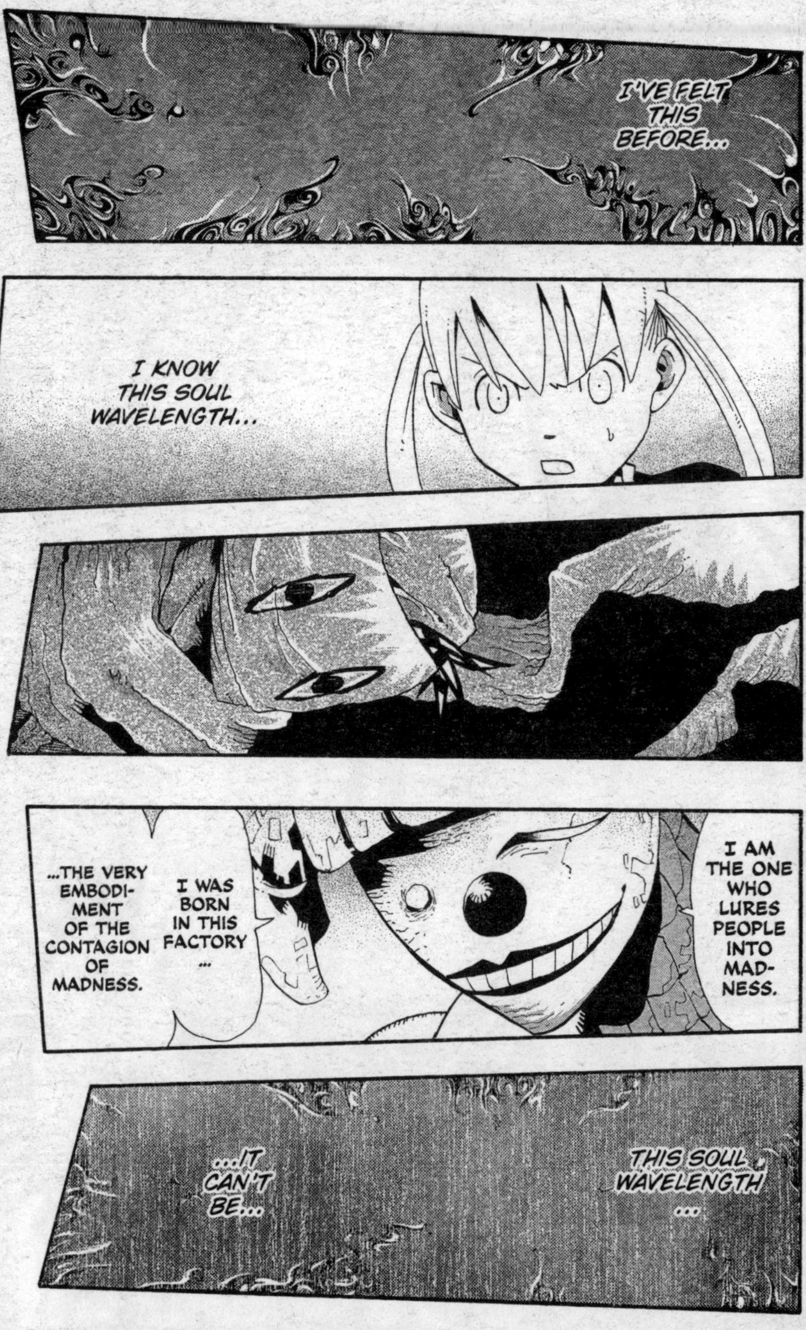
I'VE FELT THIS BEFORE...
I KNOW THIS SOUL WAVELENGTH...
I AM THE ONE WHO LURES PEOPLE INTO MAD-NESS.
I WAS BORN IN THIS FACTORY...
...THE VERY EMBODI-MENT OF THE CONTAGION OF MADNESS.
THIS SOUL WAVELENGTH...
...IT CAN'T BE...

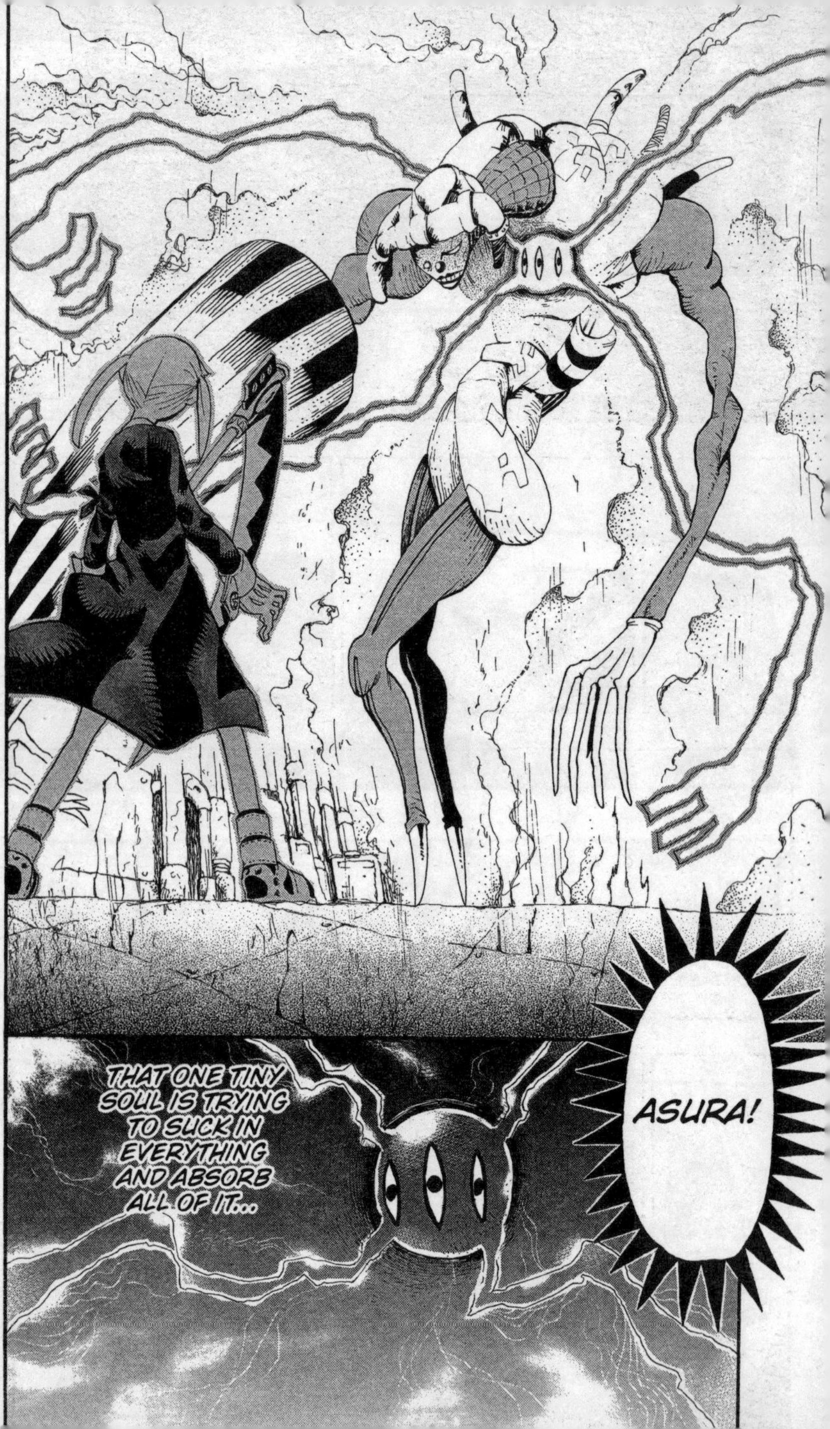
ASURA!
THAT ONE TINY SOUL IS TRYING TO SUCK IN EVERYTHING AND ABSORB ALL OF IT...

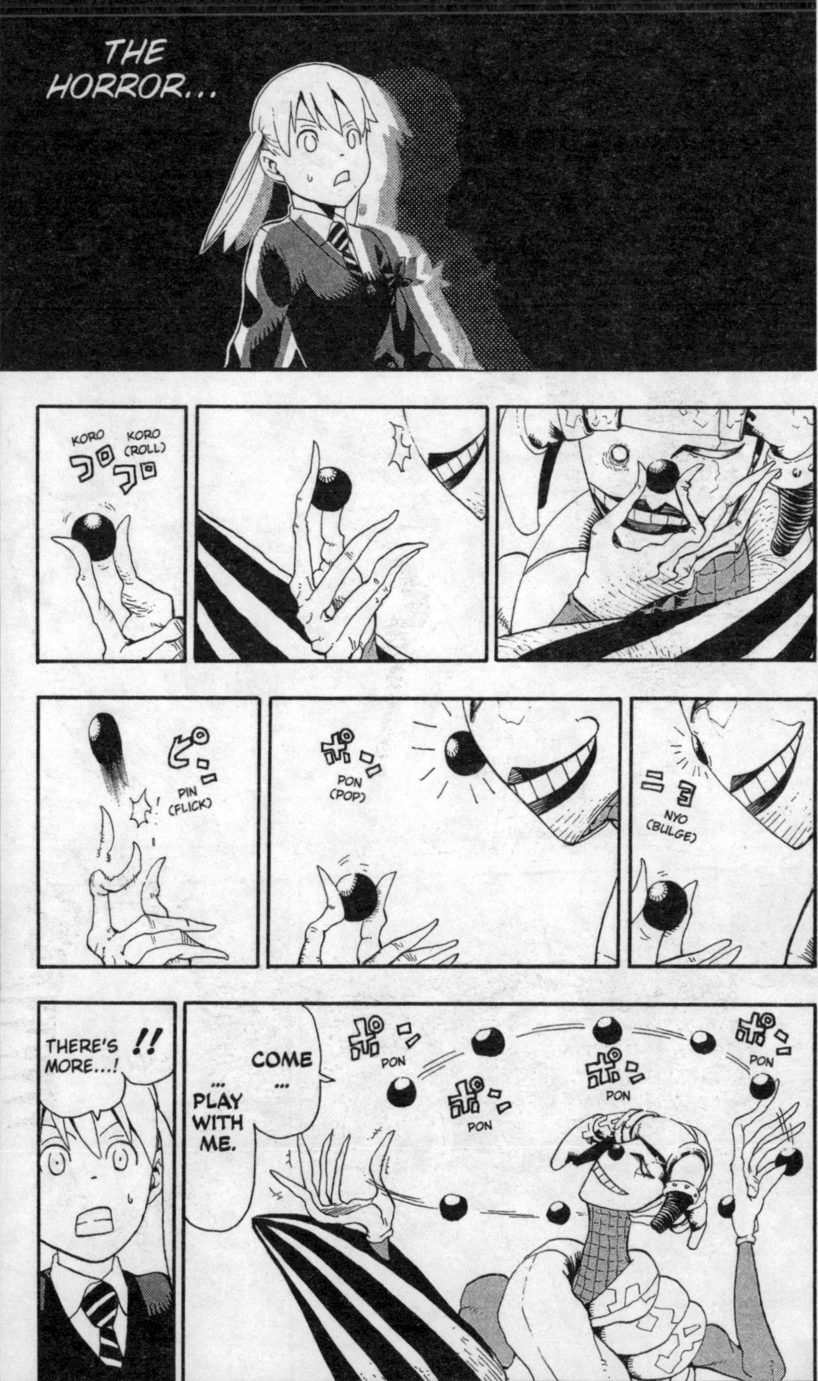
THE HORROR...
KORO KORO (ROLL)
NYO (BULGE)
PON (POP)
PIN (FLICK)
COME ...
... PLAY WITH ME.
PON
PON
PON
PON
THERE'S MORE...! !!

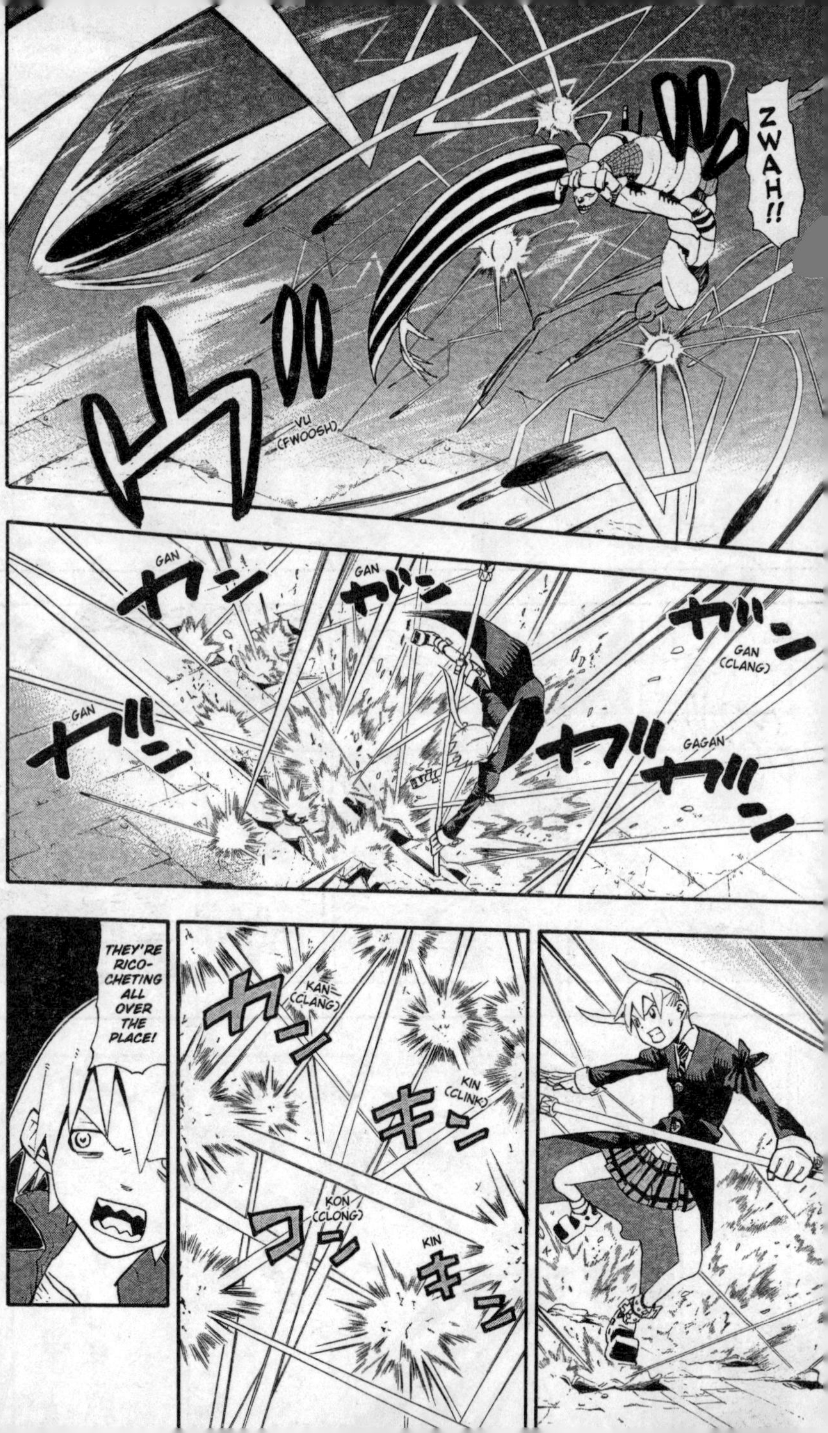
ZWAH!!
VU (FWOOSH)
GAN (CLANG)
GAN
GAN
GAGAN
GAN
KAN (CLANG)
KIN (CLINK)
KON (CLONG)
KIN
THEY'RE RICOCHETING ALL OVER THE PLACE!

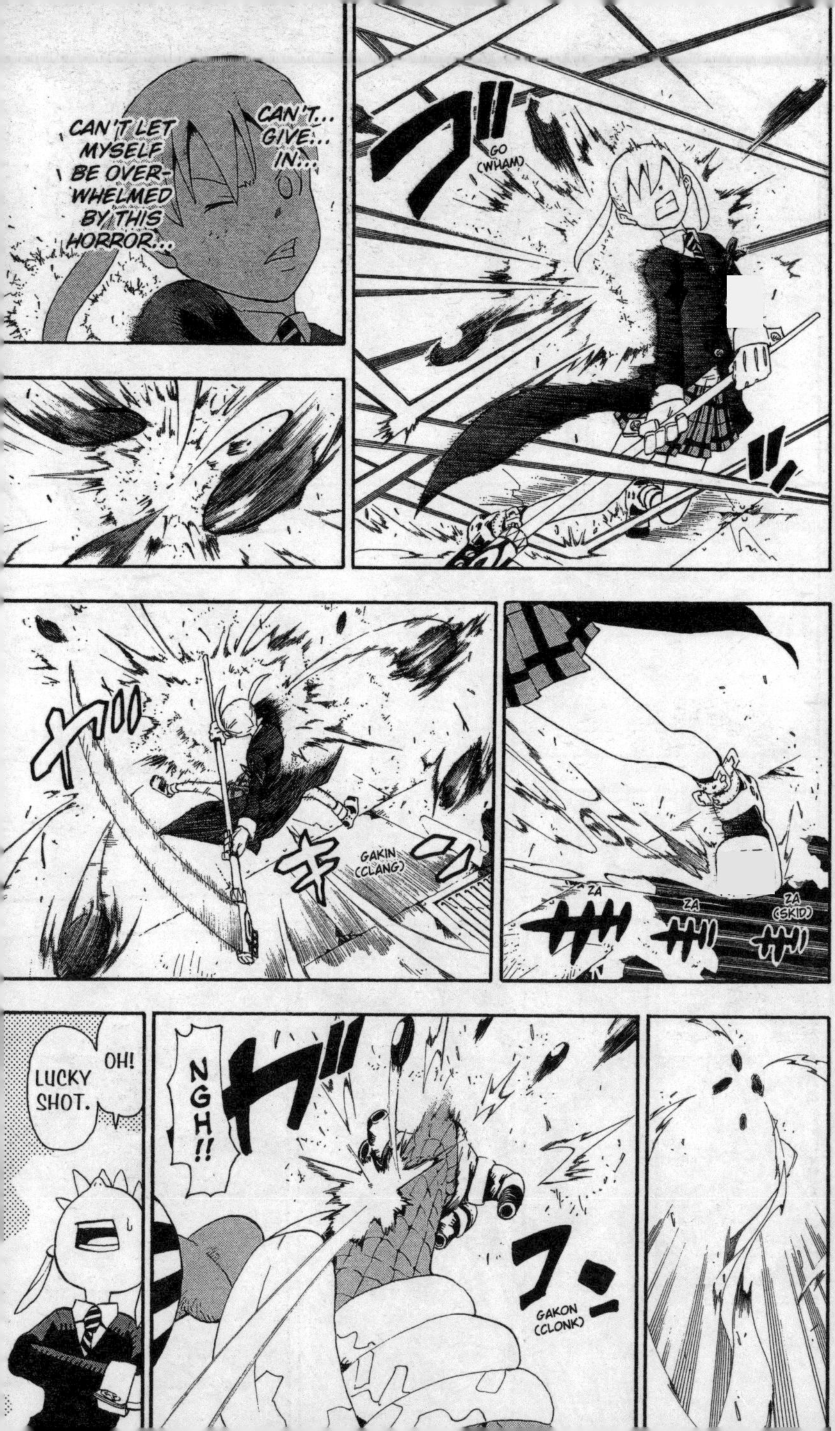
GO (WHAM)
CAN'T... GIVE... IN...
CAN'T LET MYSELF BE OVER-WHELMED BY THIS HORROR...
ZA
ZA
ZA (SKID)
GAKIN (CLANG)
NGH!!
GAKON (CLONK)
OH! LUCKY SHOT.

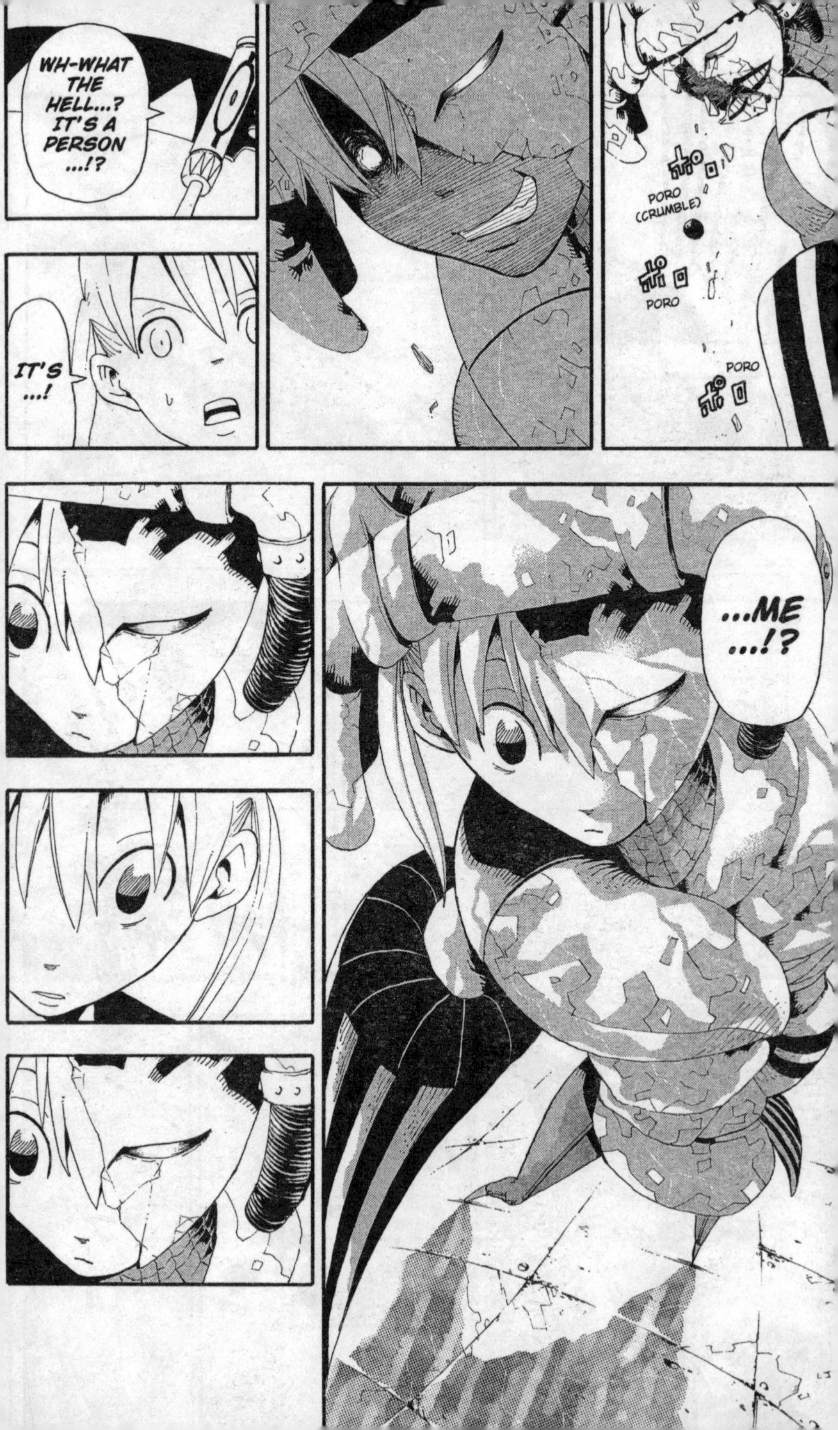
ポロ
PORO (CRUMBLE)
ポロ
PORO
PORO
ポロ
WH-WHAT THE HELL...? IT'S A PERSON ...!?
IT'S ...!
...ME ...!?

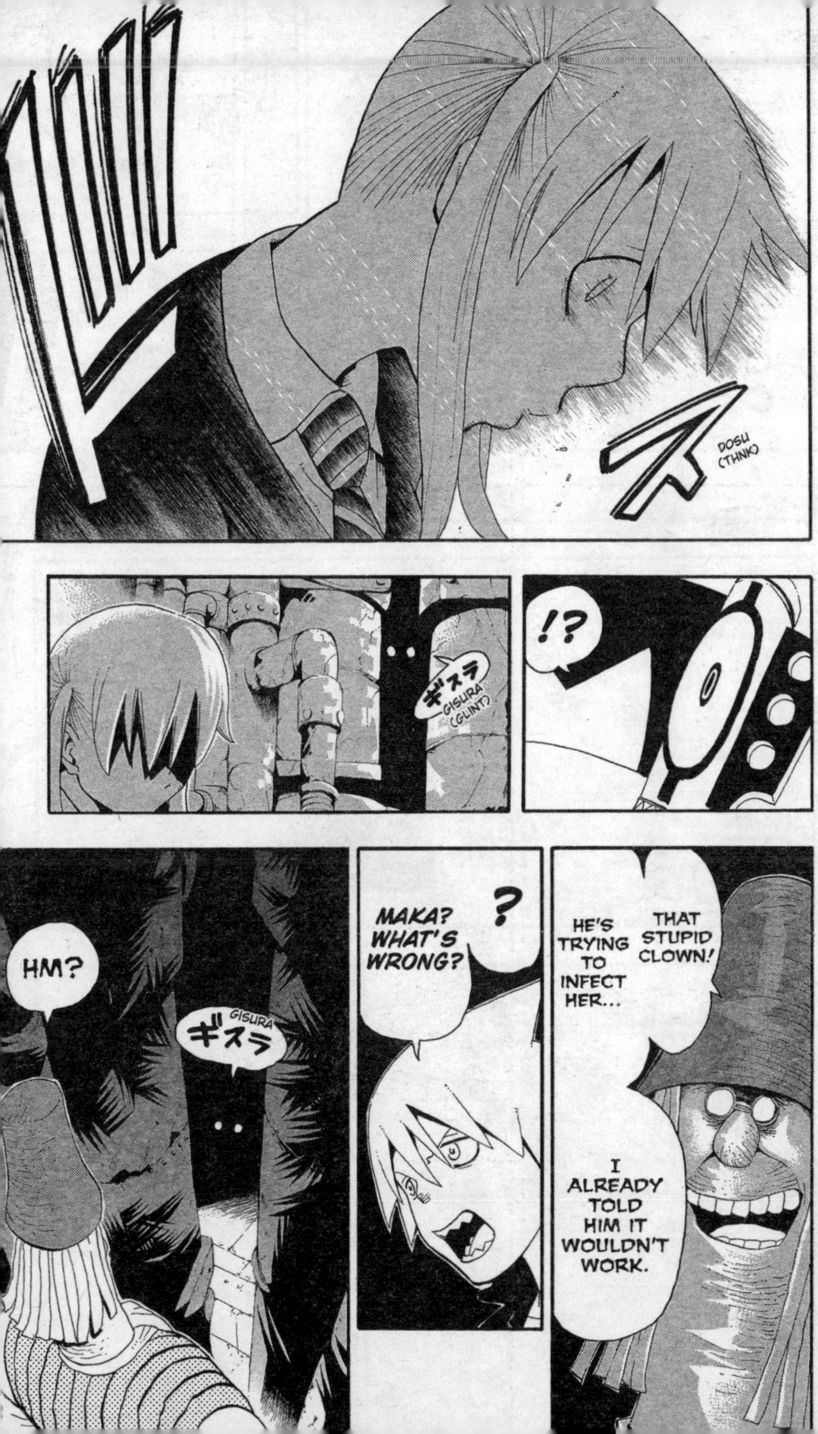
DOSU (THNK)
!?
ギスラ
GISURA (GLINT)
THAT STUPID CLOWN!
HE'S TRYING TO INFECT HER...
I ALREADY TOLD HIM IT WOULDN'T WORK.
?
MAKA? WHAT'S WRONG?
HM?
GISURA
ギスラ

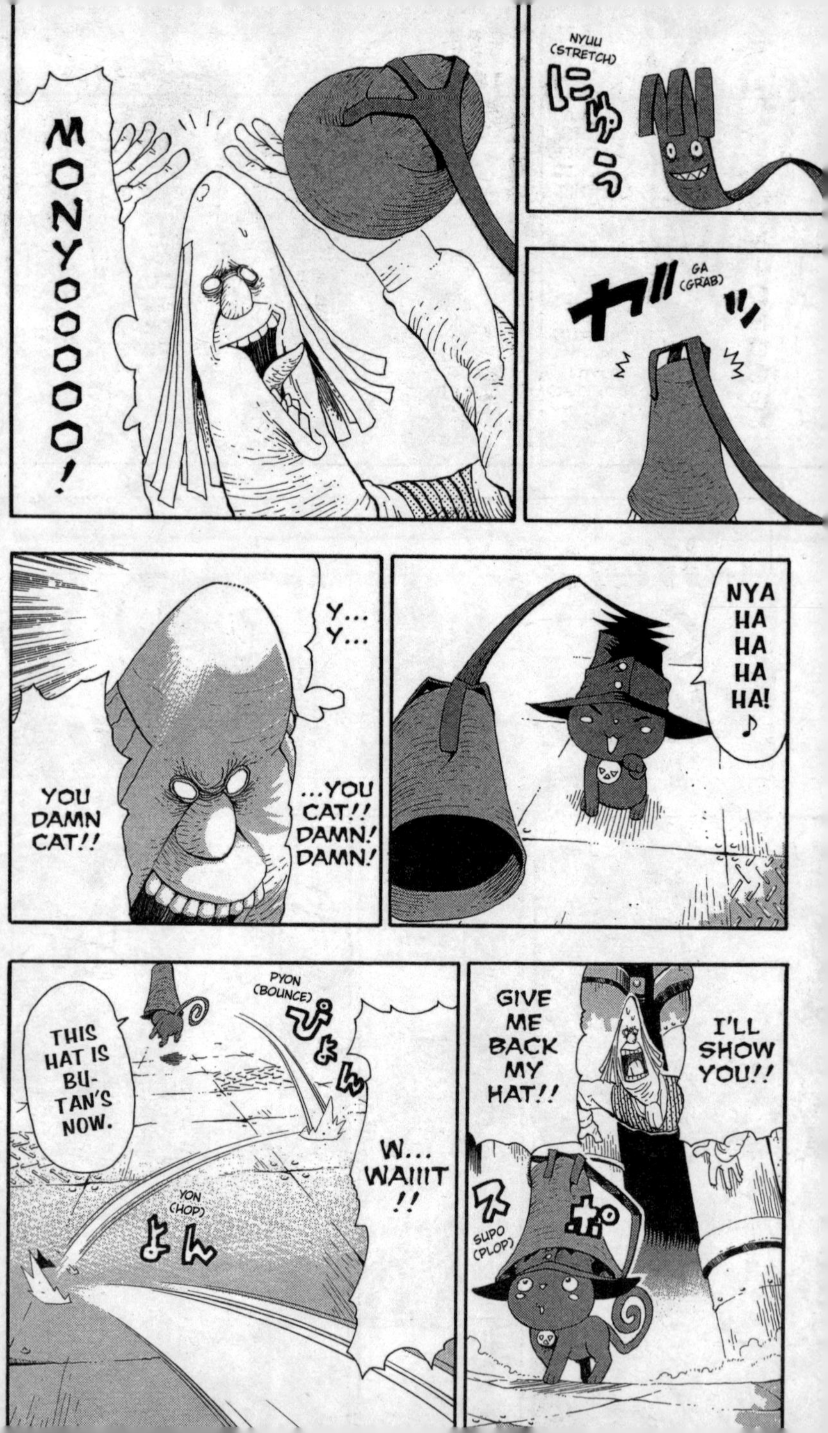
NYUU (STRETCH)
にゅっ
GA (GRAB)
ガッ
MONYOOOOOO!
NYA HA HA HA HA! ♪
Y... Y...
...YOU CAT!! DAMN! DAMN!
YOU DAMN CAT!!
I'LL SHOW YOU!!
GIVE ME BACK MY HAT!!
SUPO (PLOP)
W... WAIIIT!!
PYON (BOUNCE)
ぴょん
THIS HAT IS BU-TAN'S NOW.
YON (HOP)
よん

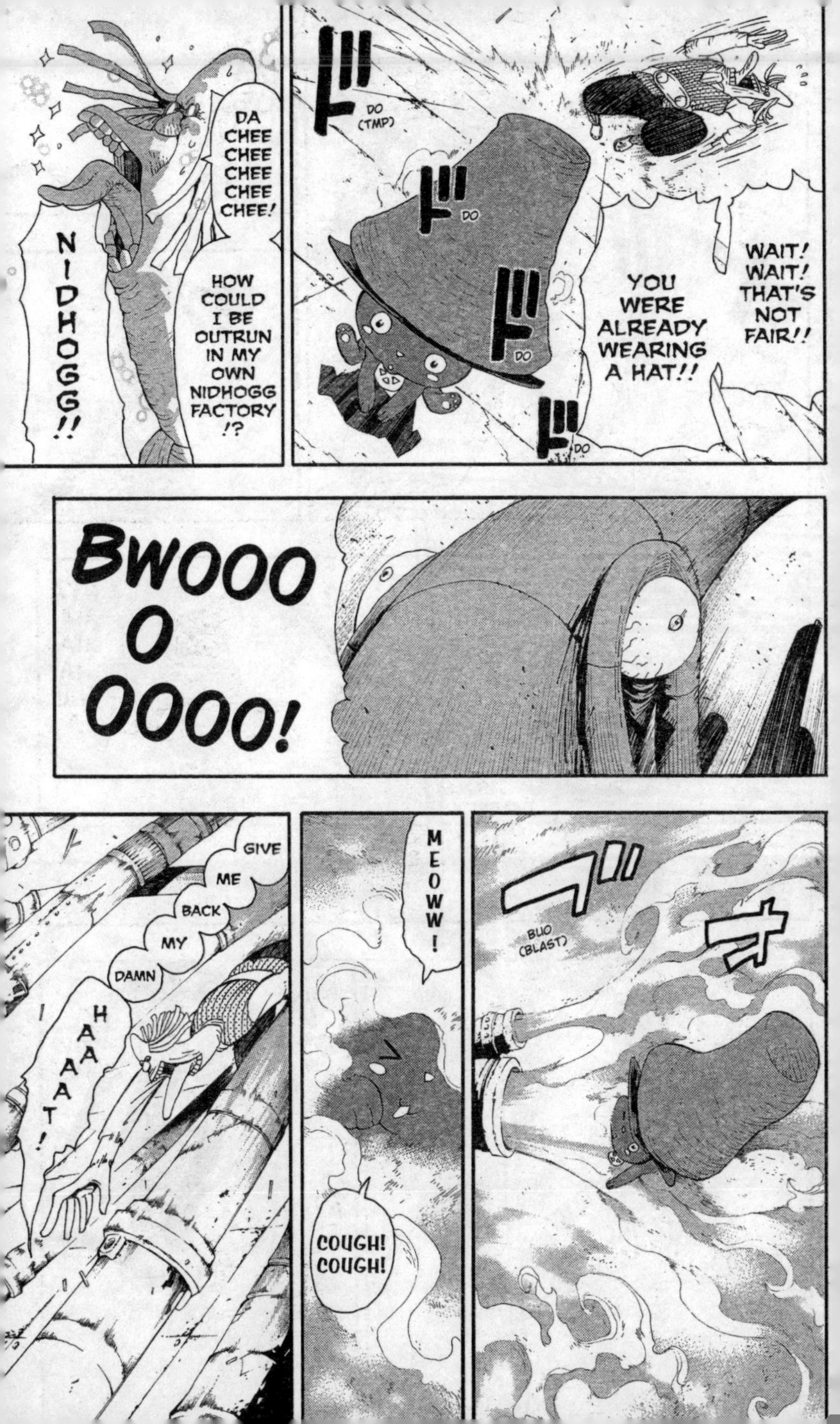
ド
DO (TMP)
ド
DO
ド
DO
ド
DO
WAIT! WAIT! THAT'S NOT FAIR!!
YOU WERE ALREADY WEARING A HAT!!
DA CHEE CHEE CHEE CHEE CHEE!
HOW COULD I BE OUTRUN IN MY OWN NIDHOGG FACTORY!?
NIDHOGG!!
BWOOOO O OOOO!
ブオ
BUO (BLAST)
MEOWW!
COUGH! COUGH!
GIVE ME BACK MY DAMN
HAAAAT!

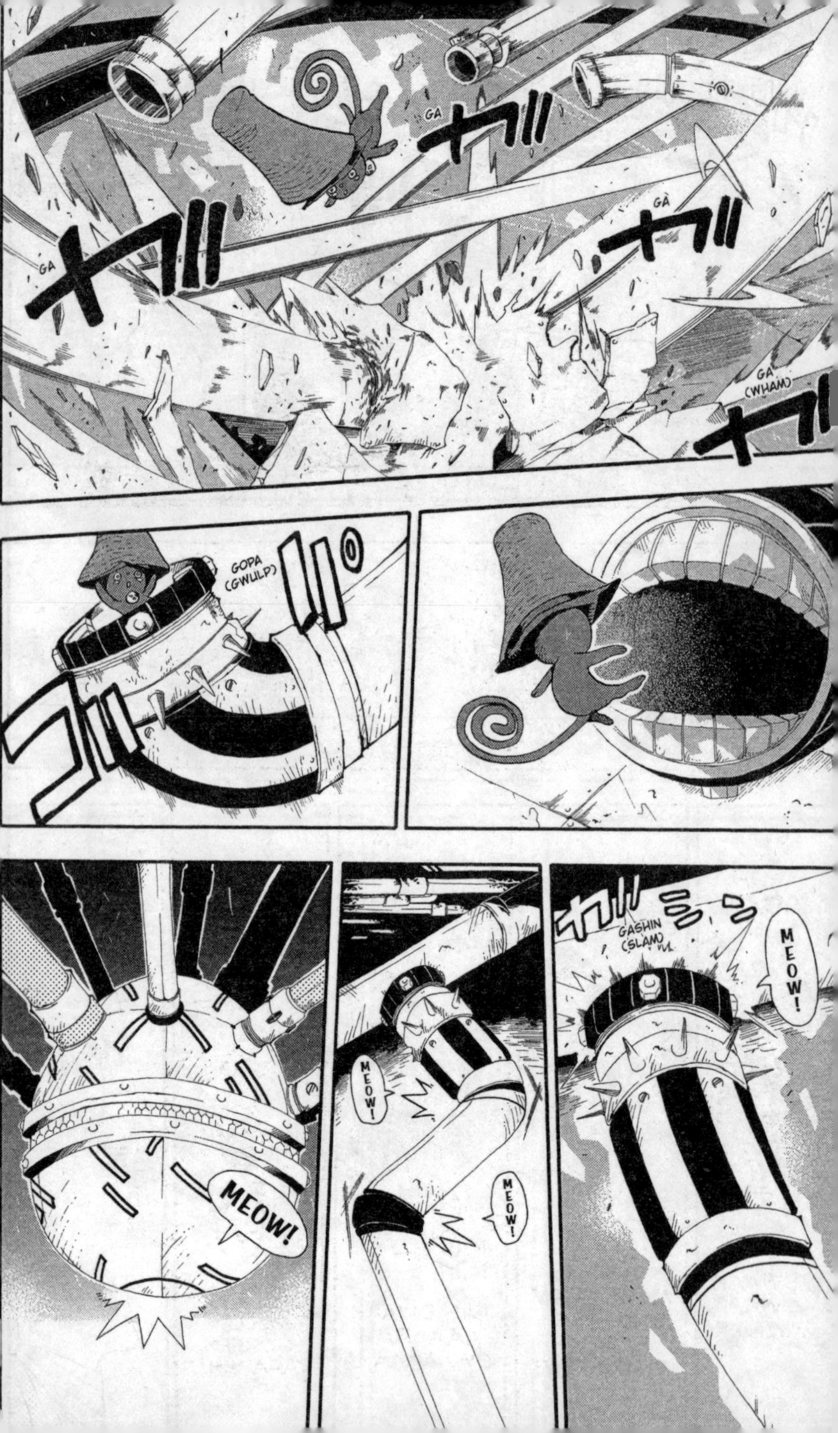
GA
GA
GA (WHAM)
GA
GOPA (GWULP)
GASHIN (SLAM)
MEOW!
MEOW!
MEOW!
MEOW!

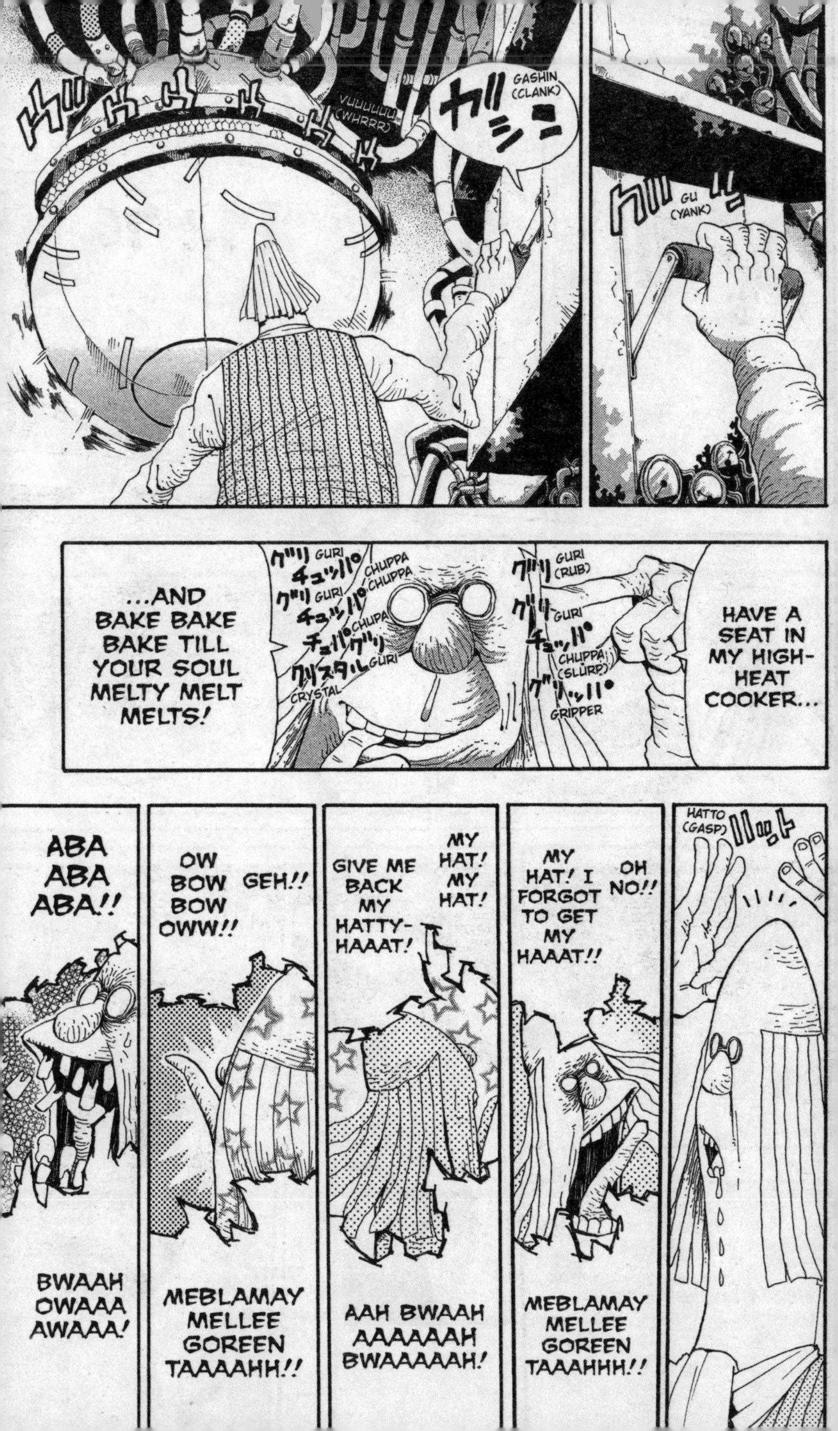
GU (YANK)
GASHIN (CLANK)
VUUUUUU (WHRRR)
HAVE A SEAT IN MY HIGH-HEAT COOKER...
GURI (RUB)
GURI
CHUPPA (SLURP)
GRIPPER
GURI
CHUPPA CHUPPA
GURI
CHUPPA
GURI
CRYSTAL
...AND BAKE BAKE BAKE TILL YOUR SOUL MELTY MELT MELTS!
HATTO (GASP)
OH NO!!
MY HAT! I FORGOT TO GET MY HAAAT!!
MEBLAMAY MELLEE GOREEN TAAAHHH!!
MY HAT! MY HAT!
GIVE ME BACK MY HATTY-HAAAT!
AAH BWAAH AAAAAAH BWAAAAAAH!
GEH!!
OW BOW BOW OWW!!
MEBLAMAY MELLEE GOREEN TAAAAHH!!
ABA ABA ABA!!
BWAAH OWAAA AWAAA!

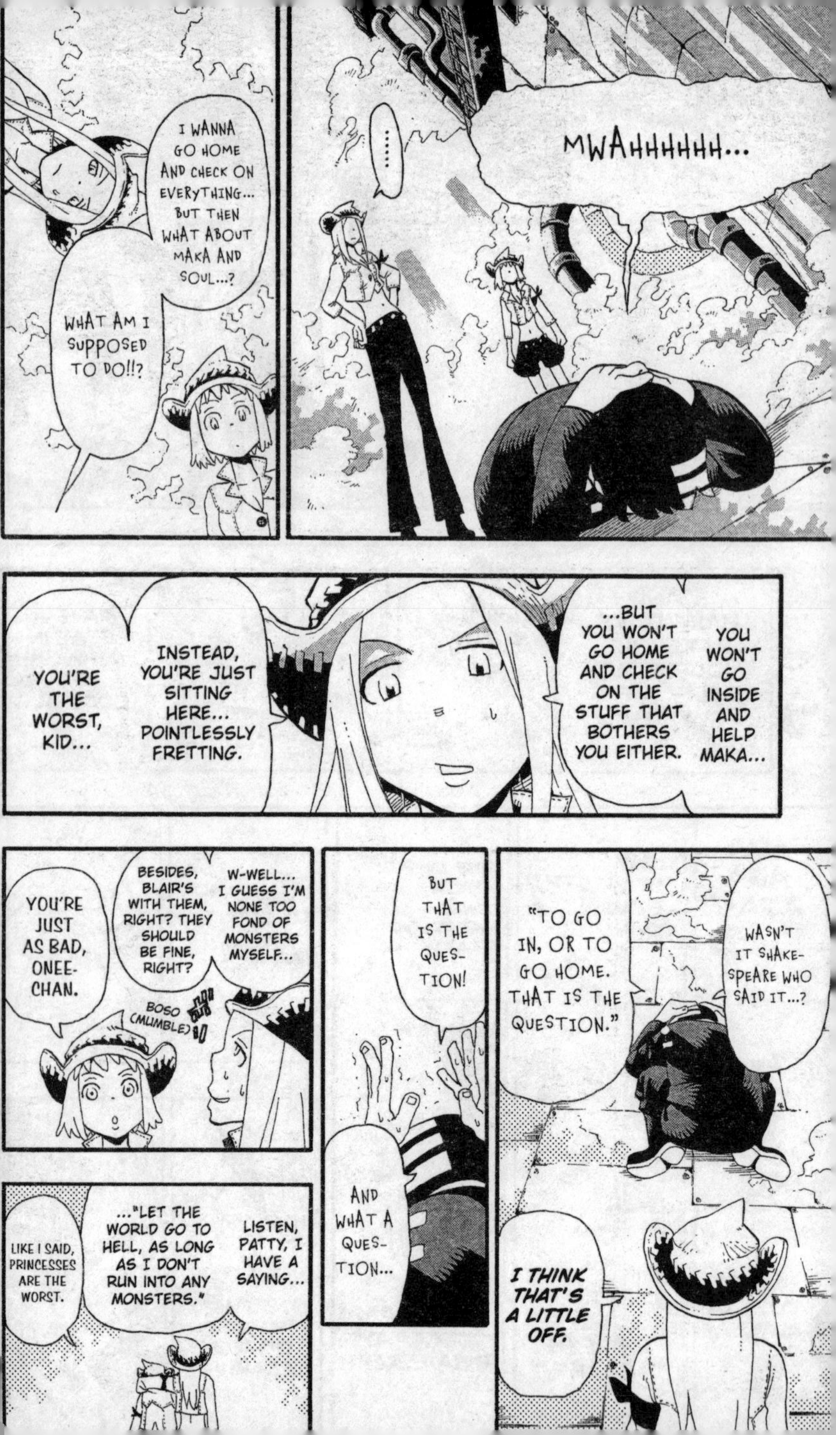
MWAHHHHHH...
......
I WANNA GO HOME AND CHECK ON EVERYTHING... BUT THEN WHAT ABOUT MAKA AND SOUL...?
WHAT AM I SUPPOSED TO DO!!?
YOU WON'T GO INSIDE AND HELP MAKA...
...BUT YOU WON'T GO HOME AND CHECK ON THE STUFF THAT BOTHERS YOU EITHER.
INSTEAD, YOU'RE JUST SITTING HERE... POINTLESSLY FRETTING.
YOU'RE THE WORST, KID...
WASN'T IT SHAKESPEARE WHO SAID IT...?
"TO GO IN, OR TO GO HOME. THAT IS THE QUESTION."
I THINK THAT'S A LITTLE OFF.
BUT THAT IS THE QUES-TION!
AND WHAT A QUES-TION...
W-WELL... I GUESS I'M NONE TOO FOND OF MONSTERS MYSELF...
BESIDES, BLAIR'S WITH THEM, RIGHT? THEY SHOULD BE FINE, RIGHT?
BOSO (MUMBLE)
YOU'RE JUST AS BAD, ONEE-CHAN.
LISTEN, PATTY, I HAVE A SAYING...
..."LET THE WORLD GO TO HELL, AS LONG AS I DON'T RUN INTO ANY MONSTERS."
LIKE I SAID, PRINCESSES ARE THE WORST.

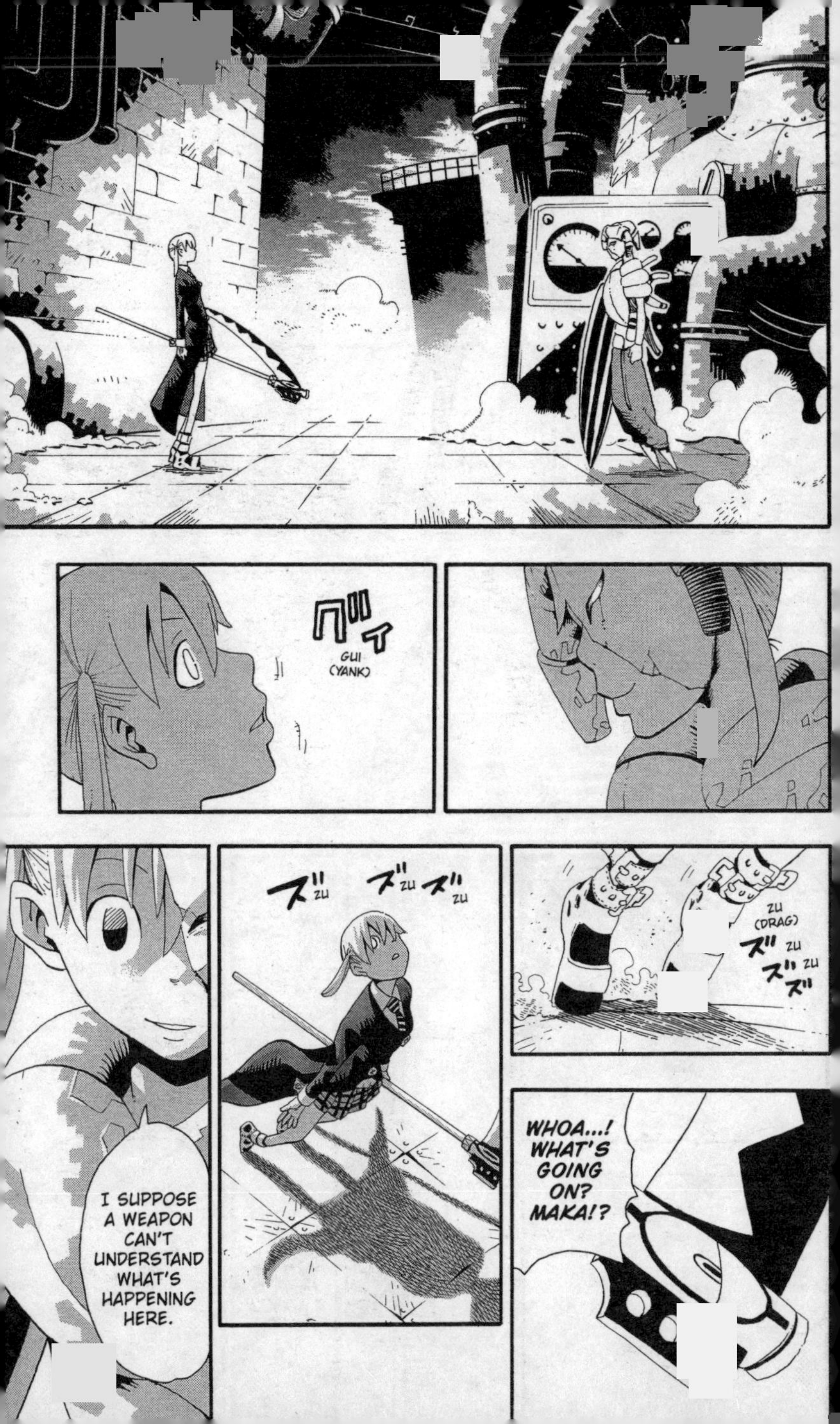
グイ
GUI (YANK)
ZU (DRAG)
ズ ZU ズ ZU ズ
WHOA...! WHAT'S GOING ON? MAKA!?
ズ ZU ズ ZU ズ ZU
I SUPPOSE A WEAPON CAN'T UNDERSTAND WHAT'S HAPPENING HERE.

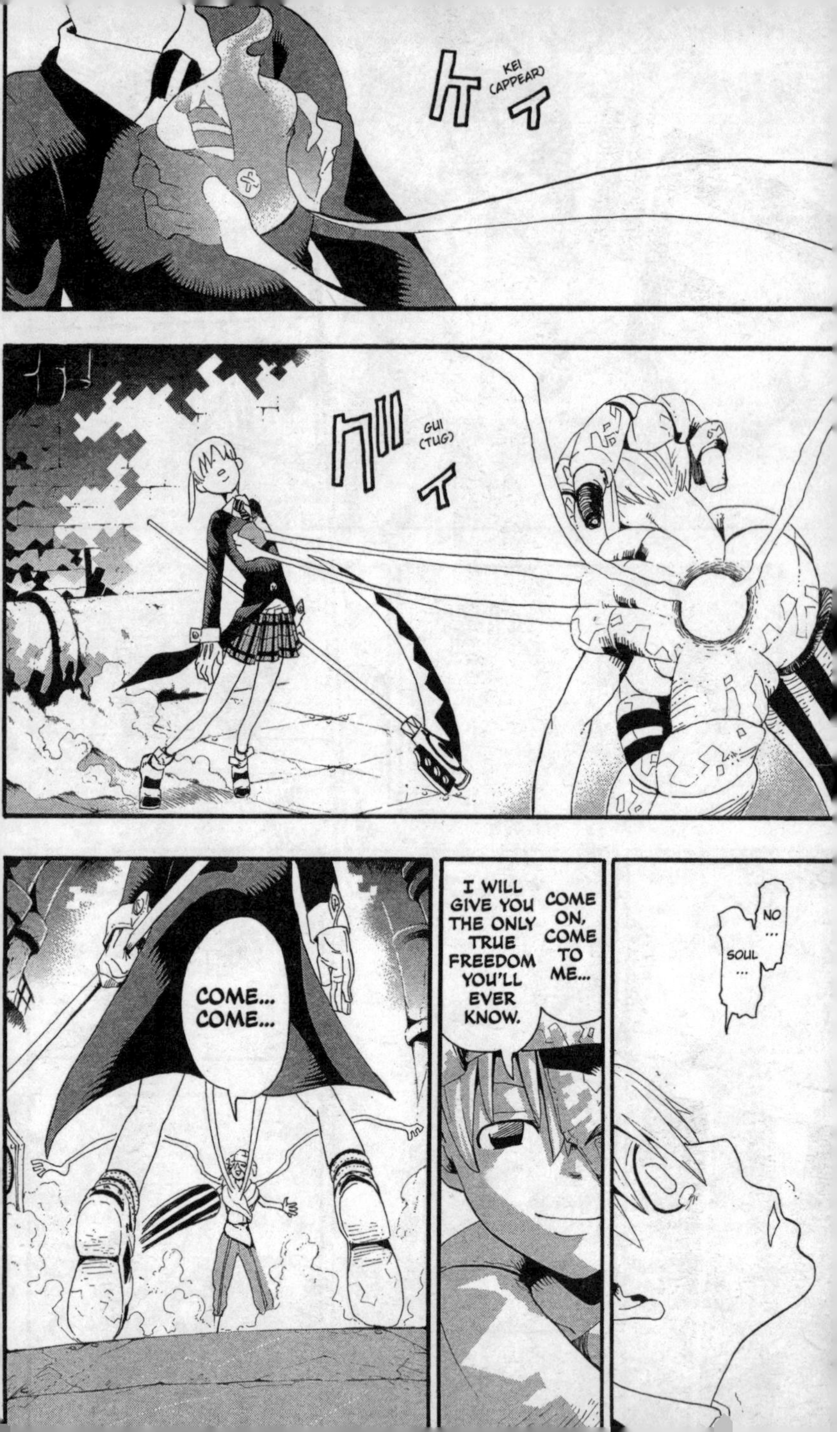

ケイ
KEI (APPEAR)
グイ
GUI (TUG)
NO... SOUL...
COME ON, COME TO ME...
I WILL GIVE YOU THE ONLY TRUE FREEDOM YOU'LL EVER KNOW.
COME... COME...

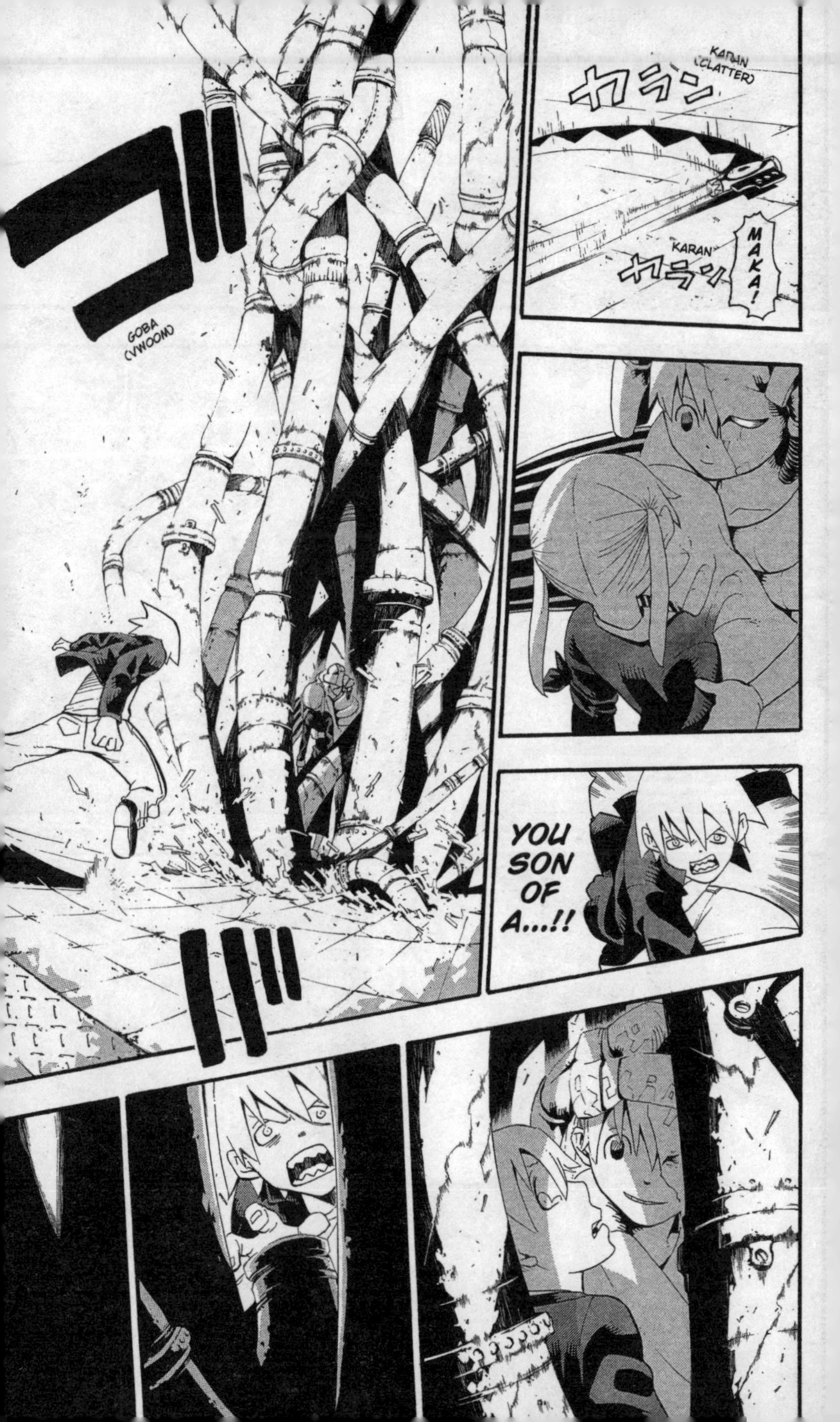

カラン
KARAN (CLATTER)
カラン
KARAN
MAKA!
YOU SON OF A...!!
GOBA (VWOOM)

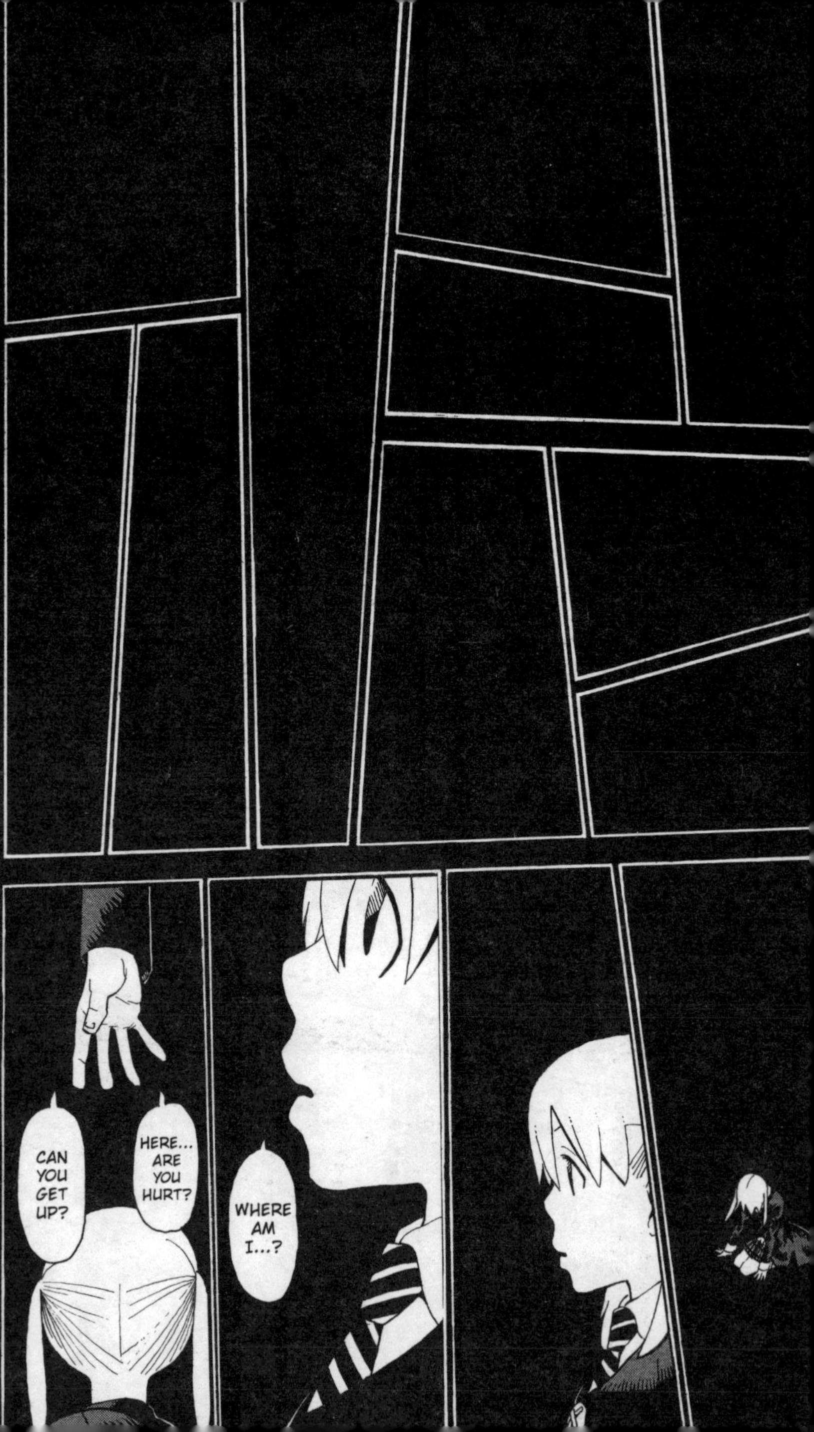
WHERE AM I...?
HERE... ARE YOU HURT?
CAN YOU GET UP?

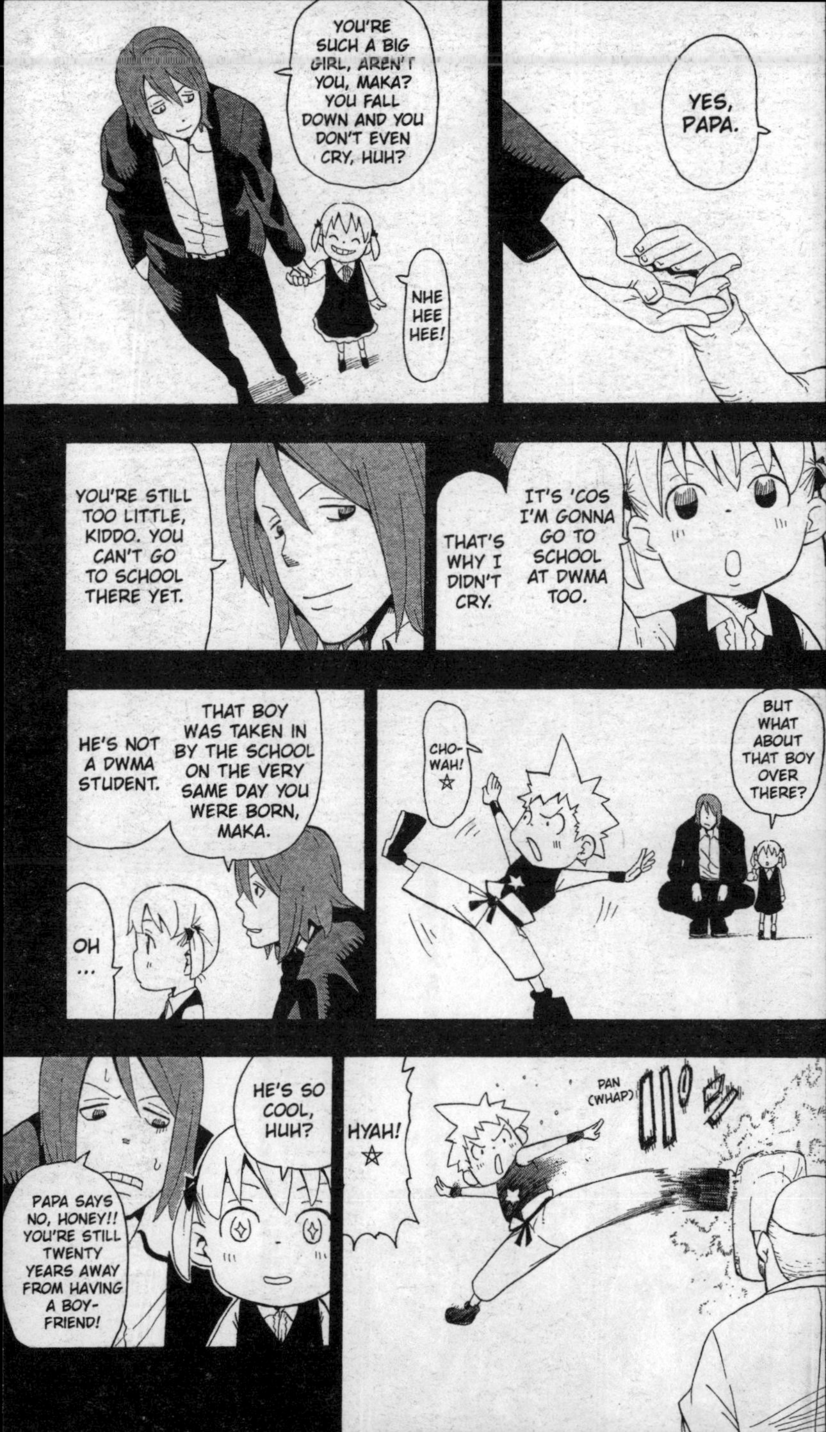
YES, PAPA.
YOU'RE SUCH A BIG GIRL, AREN'T YOU, MAKA? YOU FALL DOWN AND YOU DON'T EVEN CRY, HUH?
NHE HEE HEE!
IT'S 'COS I'M GONNA GO TO SCHOOL AT DWMA TOO.
THAT'S WHY I DIDN'T CRY.
YOU'RE STILL TOO LITTLE, KIDDO. YOU CAN'T GO TO SCHOOL THERE YET.
BUT WHAT ABOUT THAT BOY OVER THERE?
CHO-WAH! ☆
THAT BOY WAS TAKEN IN BY THE SCHOOL ON THE VERY SAME DAY YOU WERE BORN, MAKA.
HE'S NOT A DWMA STUDENT.
OH ...
HYAH! ☆
PAN (WHAP)
HE'S SO COOL, HUH?
PAPA SAYS NO, HONEY!! YOU'RE STILL TWENTY YEARS AWAY FROM HAVING A BOY-FRIEND!

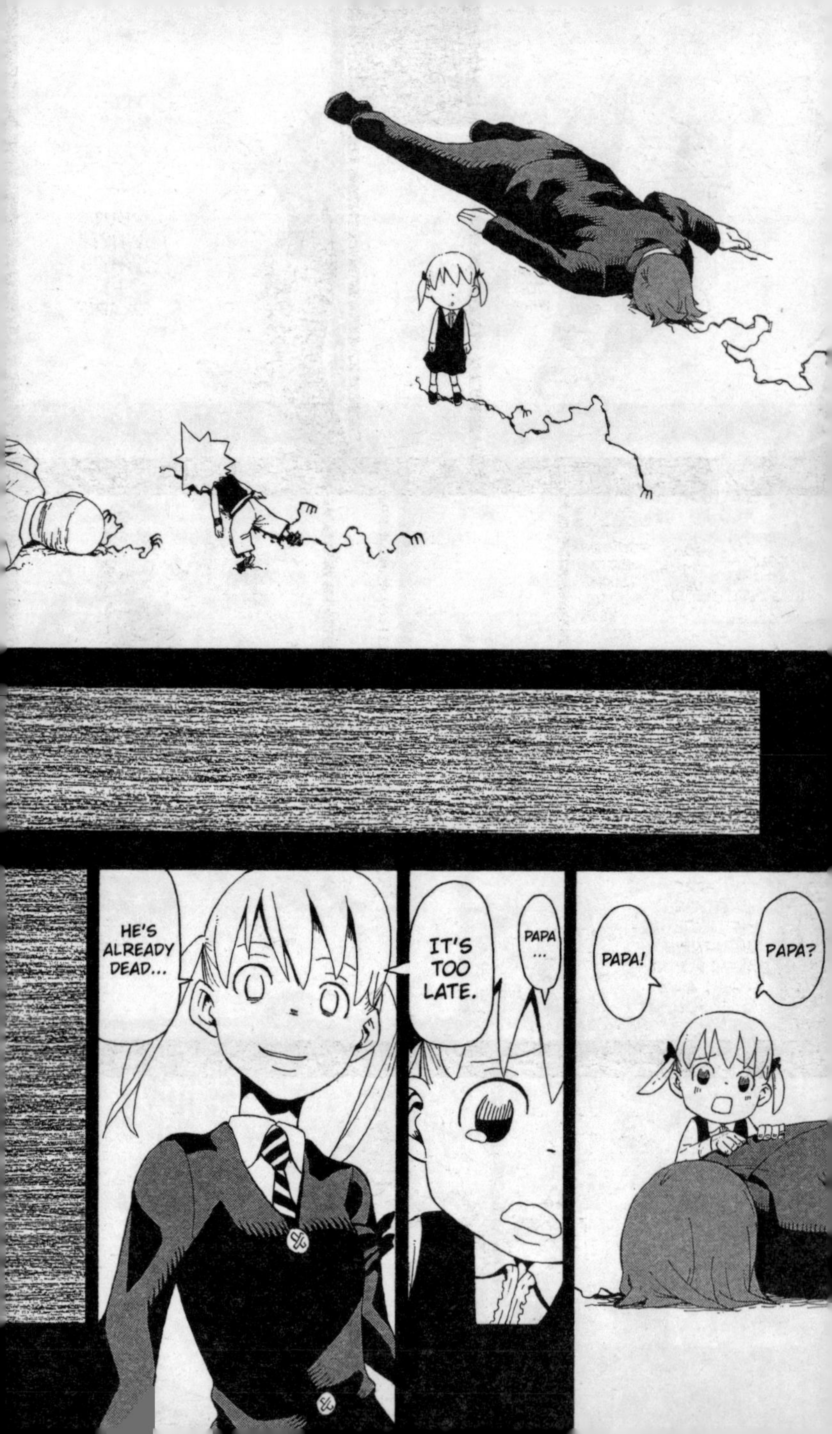
PAPA?
PAPA!
PAPA ...
IT'S TOO LATE.
HE'S ALREADY DEAD...

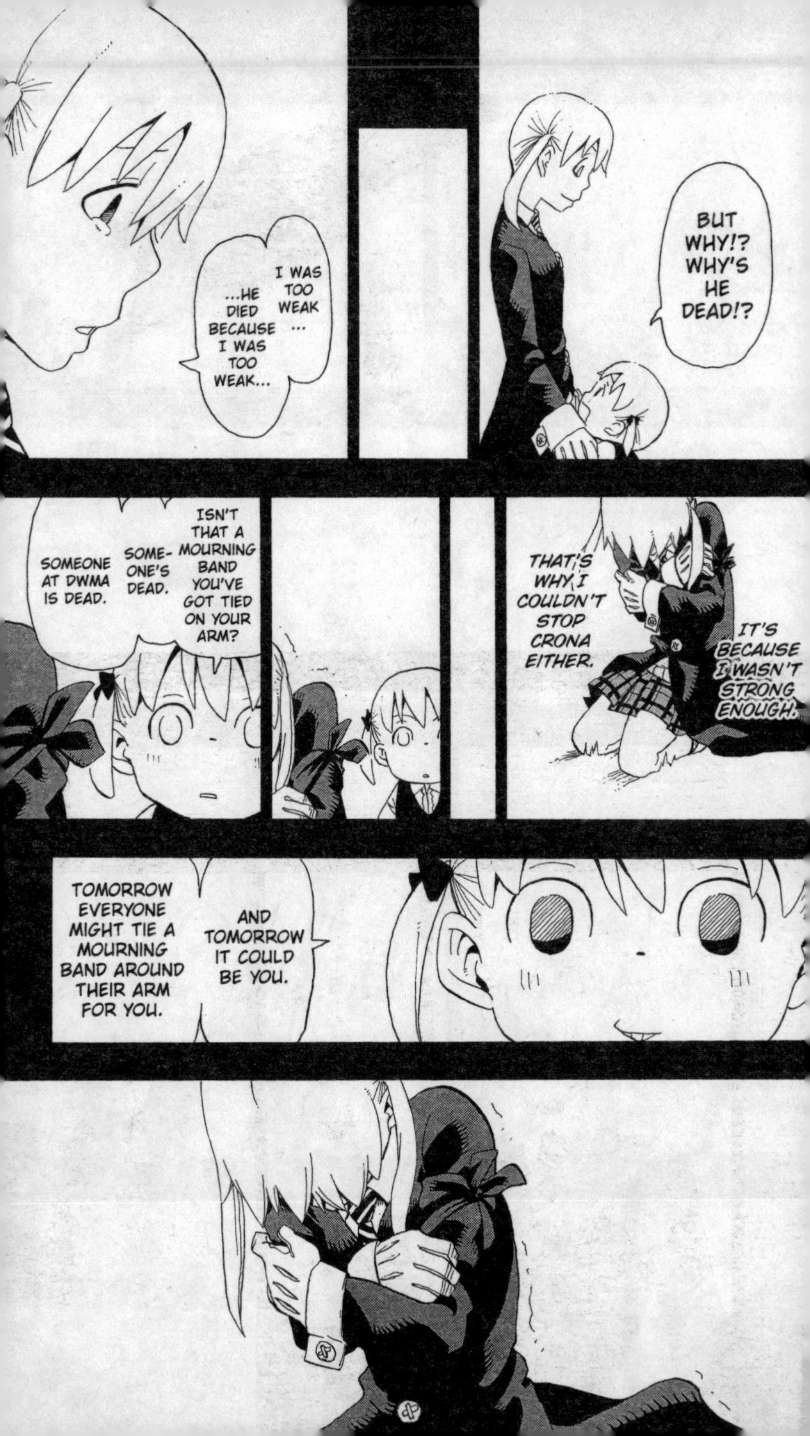
BUT WHY!? WHY'S HE DEAD!?
I WAS TOO WEAK ...
...HE DIED BECAUSE I WAS TOO WEAK...
IT'S BECAUSE I WASN'T STRONG ENOUGH.
THAT'S WHY I COULDN'T STOP CRONA EITHER.
ISN'T THAT A MOURNING BAND YOU'VE GOT TIED ON YOUR ARM?
SOME-ONE'S DEAD.
SOMEONE AT DWMA IS DEAD.
AND TOMORROW IT COULD BE YOU.
TOMORROW EVERYONE MIGHT TIE A MOURNING BAND AROUND THEIR ARM FOR YOU.

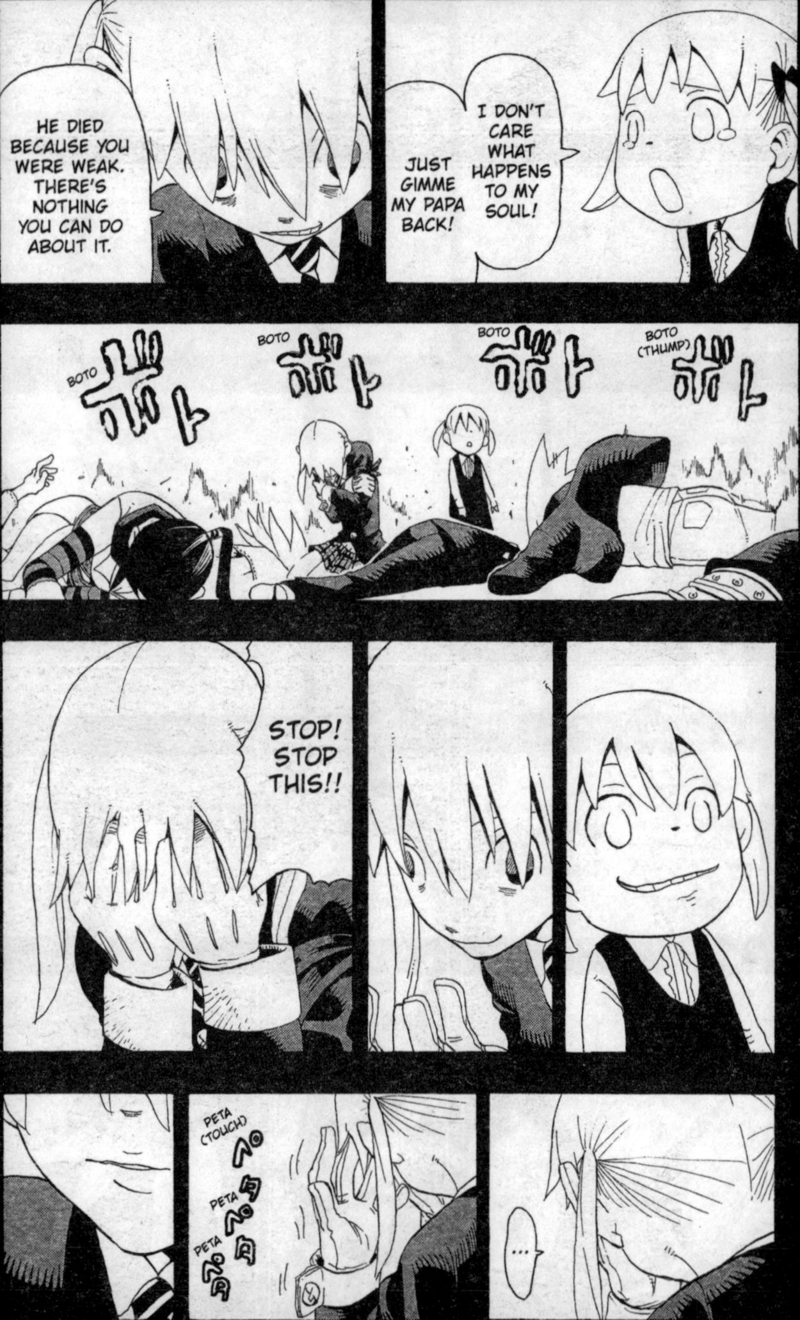
I DON'T CARE WHAT HAPPENS TO MY SOUL!
JUST GIMME MY PAPA BACK!
HE DIED BECAUSE YOU WERE WEAK. THERE'S NOTHING YOU CAN DO ABOUT IT.
BOTO (THUMP)
BOTO
BOTO
BOTO
STOP! STOP THIS!!
...
PETA (TOUCH)
PETA
PETA

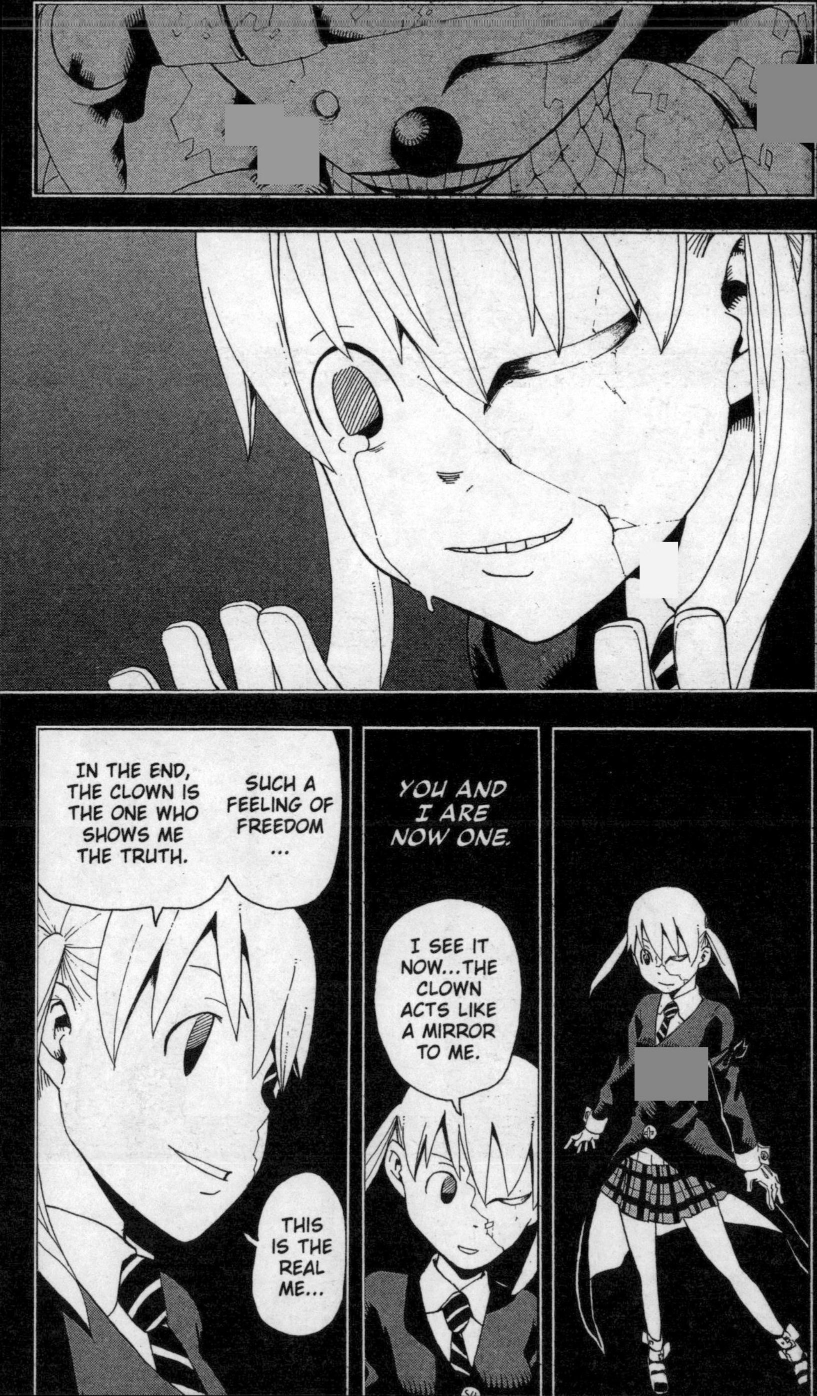
YOU AND I ARE NOW ONE.
I SEE IT NOW...THE CLOWN ACTS LIKE A MIRROR TO ME.
SUCH A FEELING OF FREEDOM...
IN THE END, THE CLOWN IS THE ONE WHO SHOWS ME THE TRUTH.
THIS IS THE REAL ME...

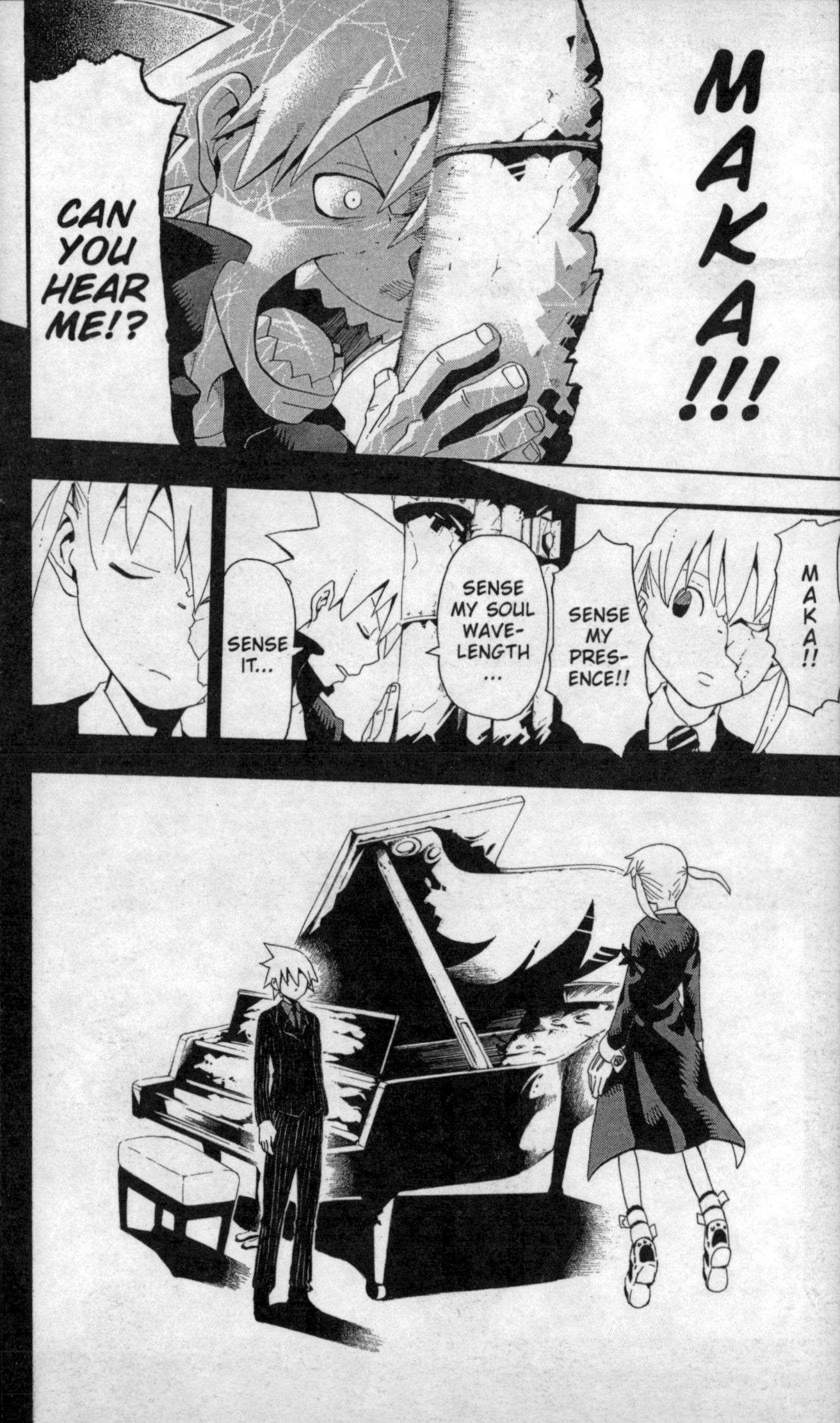
MAKA!!!
CAN YOU HEAR ME!?
MAKA!!
SENSE MY PRESENCE!!
SENSE MY SOUL WAVE-LENGTH ...
SENSE IT...

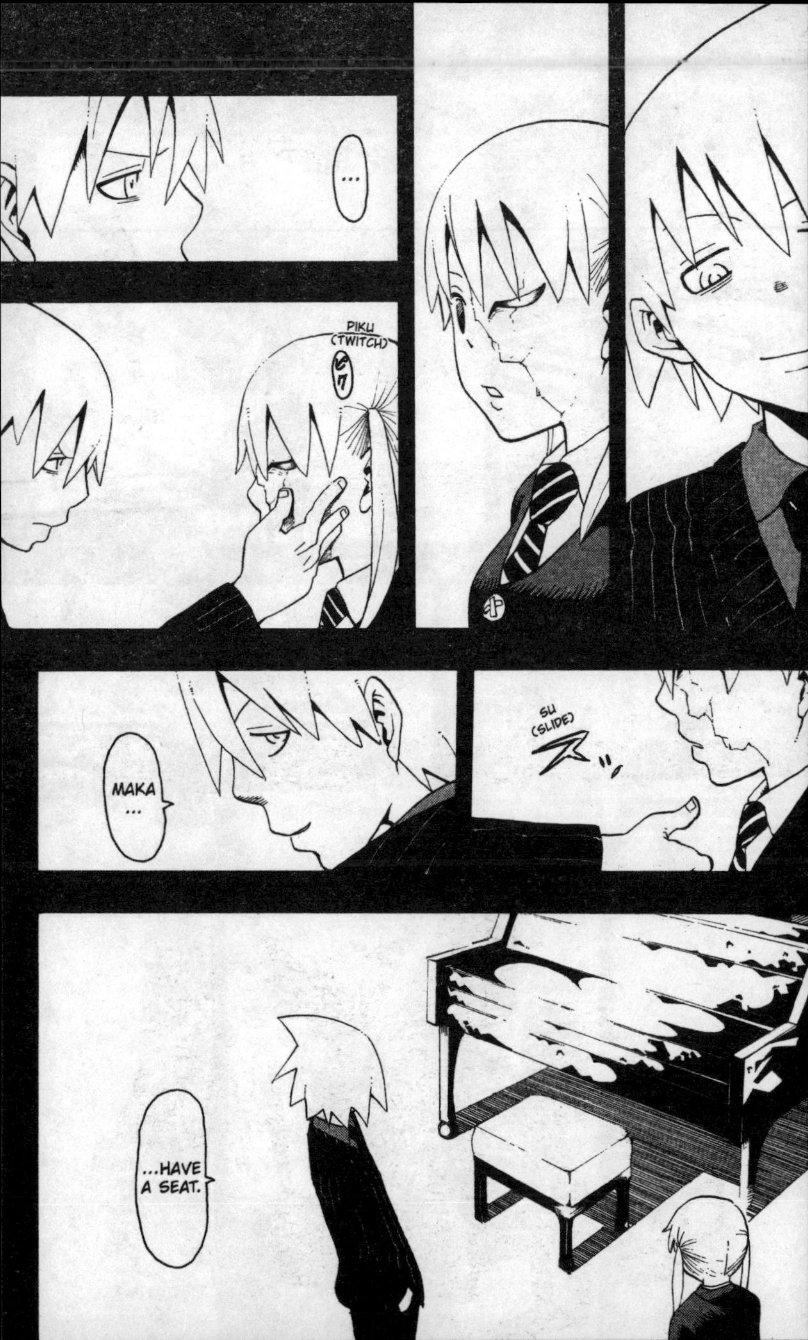
...
PIKU (TWITCH)
ピク
SU (SLIDE)
ス
MAKA ...
...HAVE A SEAT.

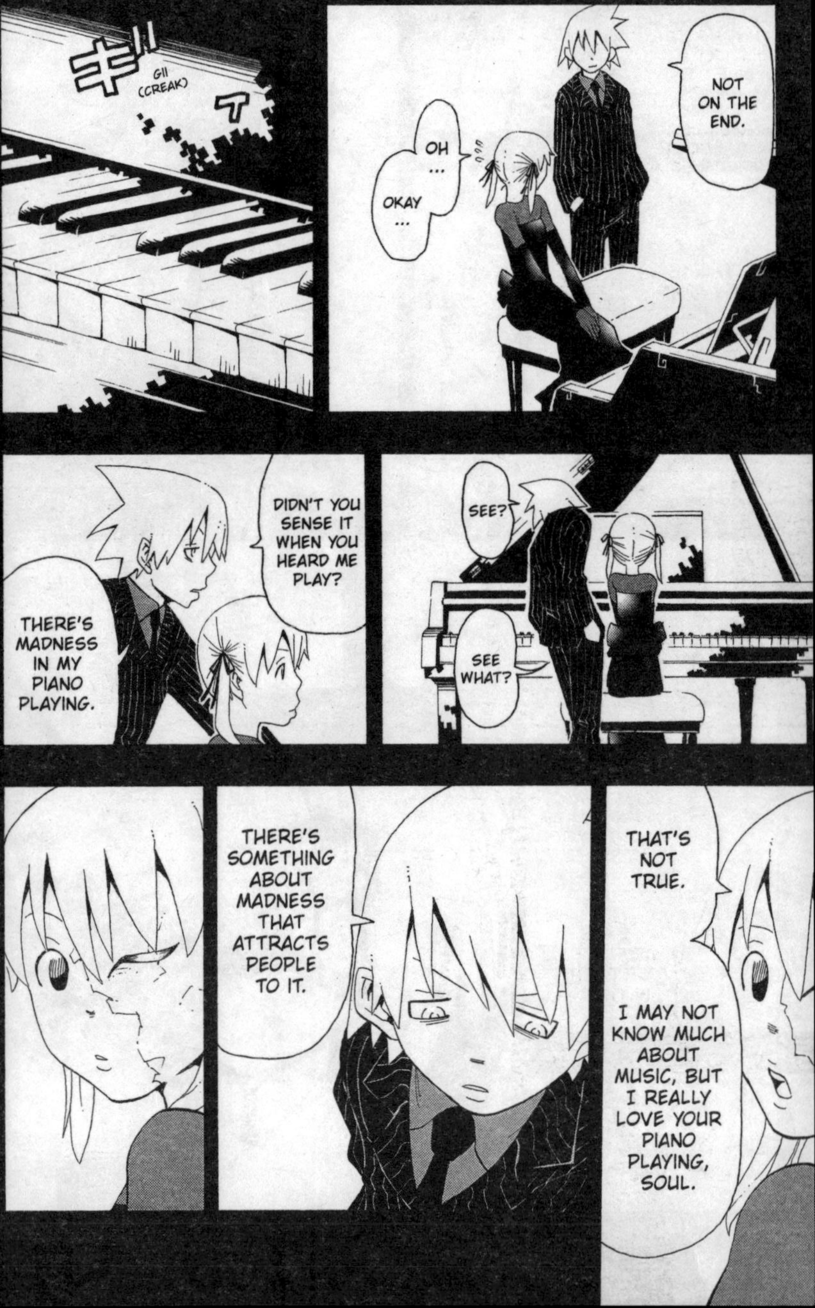
NOT ON THE END.
OH ...
OKAY ...
GII (CREAK)
SEE?
SEE WHAT?
DIDN'T YOU SENSE IT WHEN YOU HEARD ME PLAY?
THERE'S MADNESS IN MY PIANO PLAYING.
THAT'S NOT TRUE.
I MAY NOT KNOW MUCH ABOUT MUSIC, BUT I REALLY LOVE YOUR PIANO PLAYING, SOUL.
THERE'S SOMETHING ABOUT MADNESS THAT ATTRACTS PEOPLE TO IT.

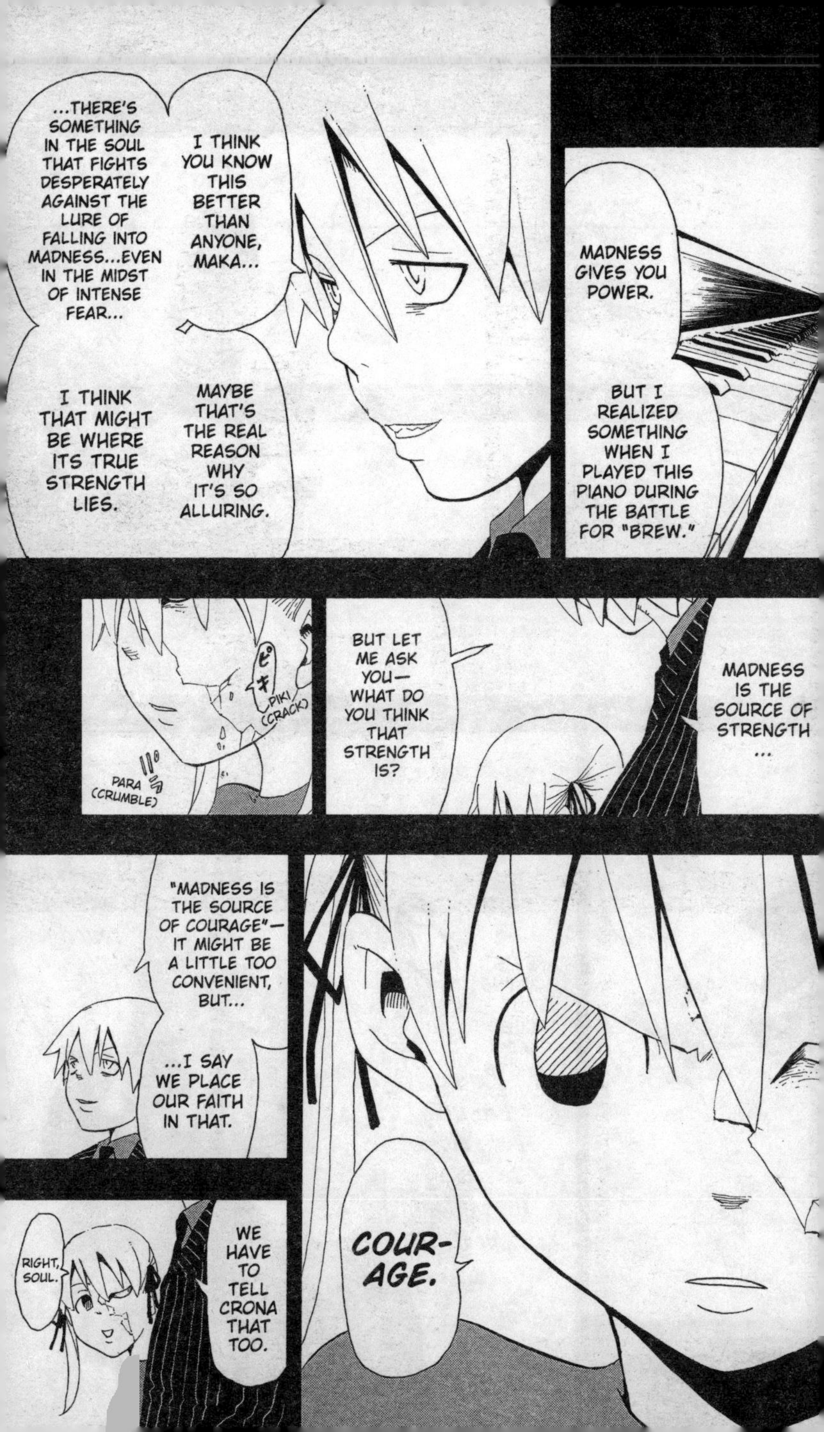
MADNESS GIVES YOU POWER.
BUT I REALIZED SOMETHING WHEN I PLAYED THIS PIANO DURING THE BATTLE FOR "BREW."
I THINK YOU KNOW THIS BETTER THAN ANYONE, MAKA...
...THERE'S SOMETHING IN THE SOUL THAT FIGHTS DESPERATELY AGAINST THE LURE OF FALLING INTO MADNESS...EVEN IN THE MIDST OF INTENSE FEAR...
MAYBE THAT'S THE REAL REASON WHY IT'S SO ALLURING.
I THINK THAT MIGHT BE WHERE ITS TRUE STRENGTH LIES.
MADNESS IS THE SOURCE OF STRENGTH...
BUT LET ME ASK YOU— WHAT DO YOU THINK THAT STRENGTH IS?
ピキ
PIKI (CRACK)
PARA (CRUMBLE)
COUR-AGE.
"MADNESS IS THE SOURCE OF COURAGE"— IT MIGHT BE A LITTLE TOO CONVENIENT, BUT...
...I SAY WE PLACE OUR FAITH IN THAT.
WE HAVE TO TELL CRONA THAT TOO.
RIGHT, SOUL.

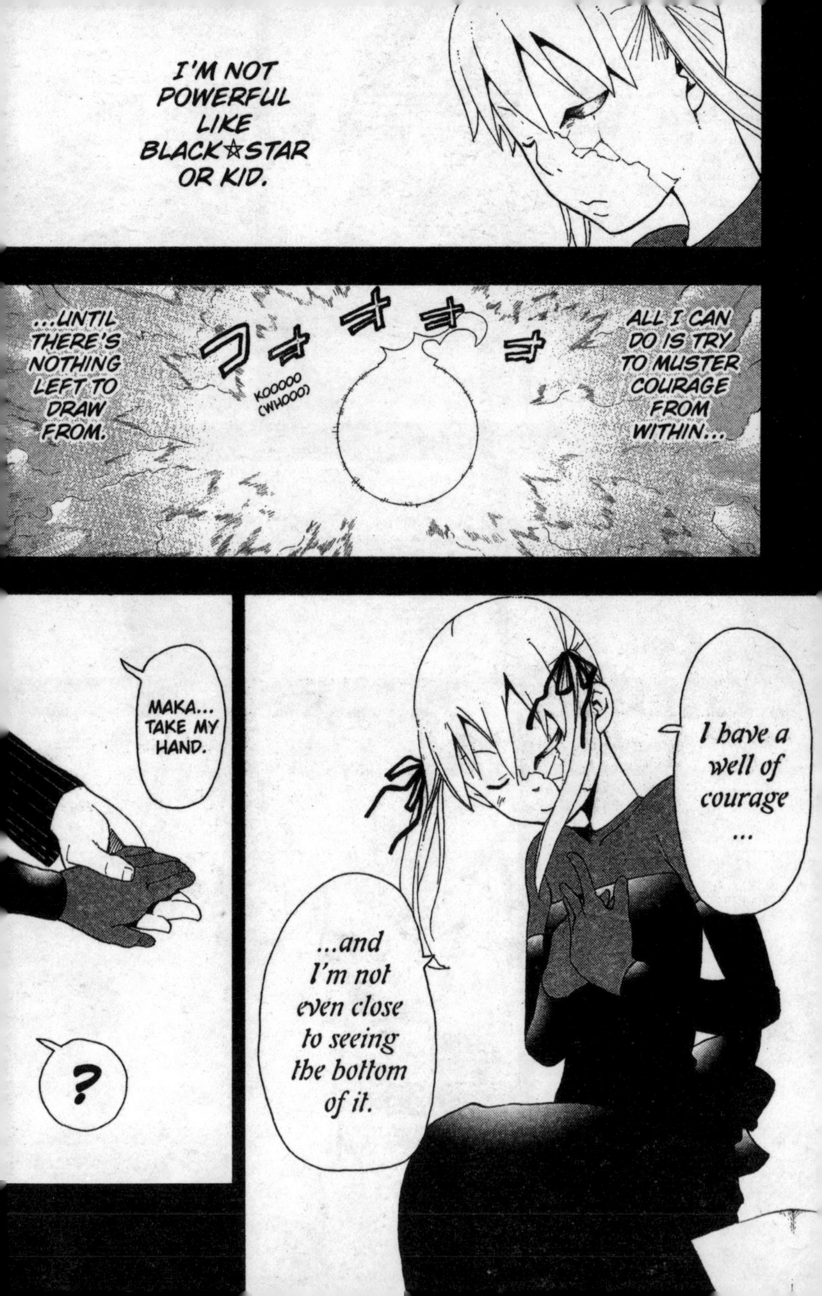
I'M NOT POWERFUL LIKE BLACK☆STAR OR KID.
ALL I CAN DO IS TRY TO MUSTER COURAGE FROM WITHIN...
KOOOOO (WHOOO)
...UNTIL THERE'S NOTHING LEFT TO DRAW FROM.
I have a well of courage ...
...and I'm not even close to seeing the bottom of it.
MAKA... TAKE MY HAND.
?

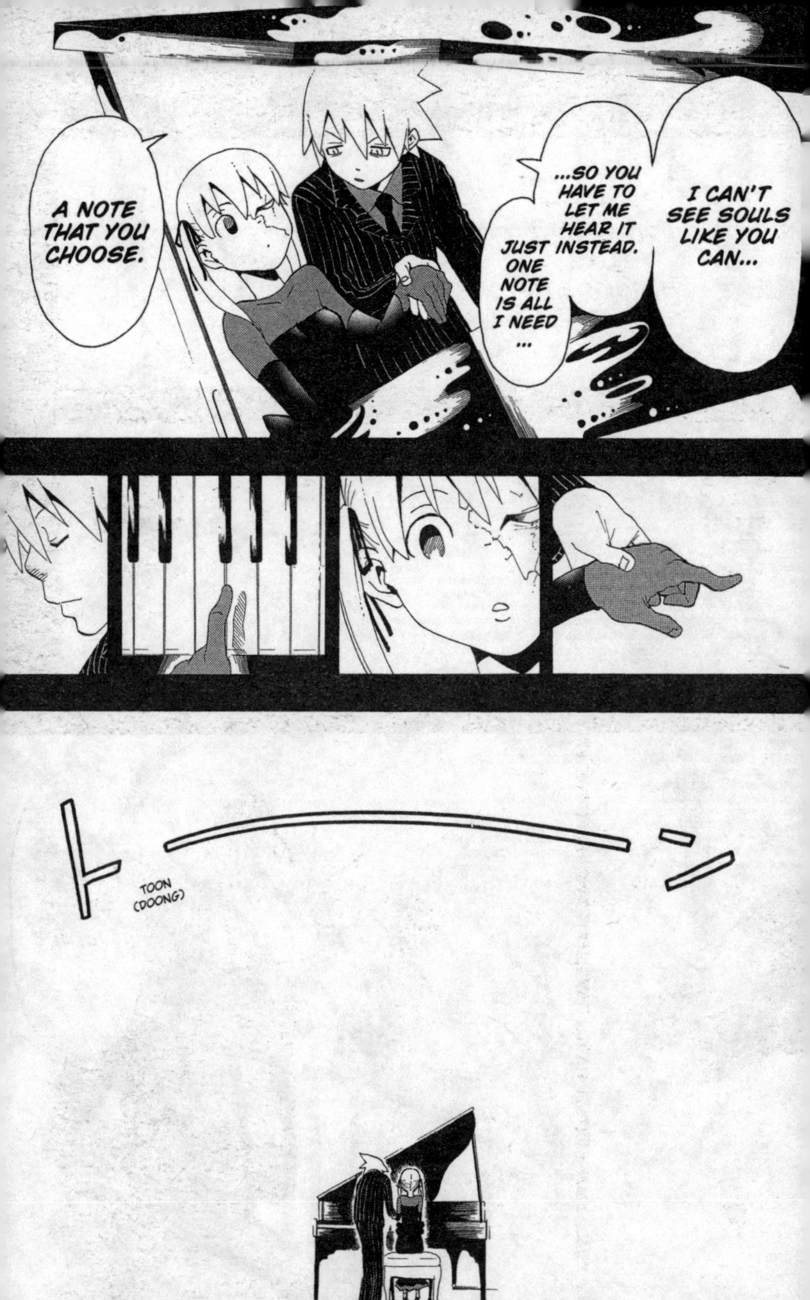
I CAN'T SEE SOULS LIKE YOU CAN...
...SO YOU HAVE TO LET ME HEAR IT INSTEAD.
JUST ONE NOTE IS ALL I NEED...
A NOTE THAT YOU CHOOSE.
TOON (DOONG)

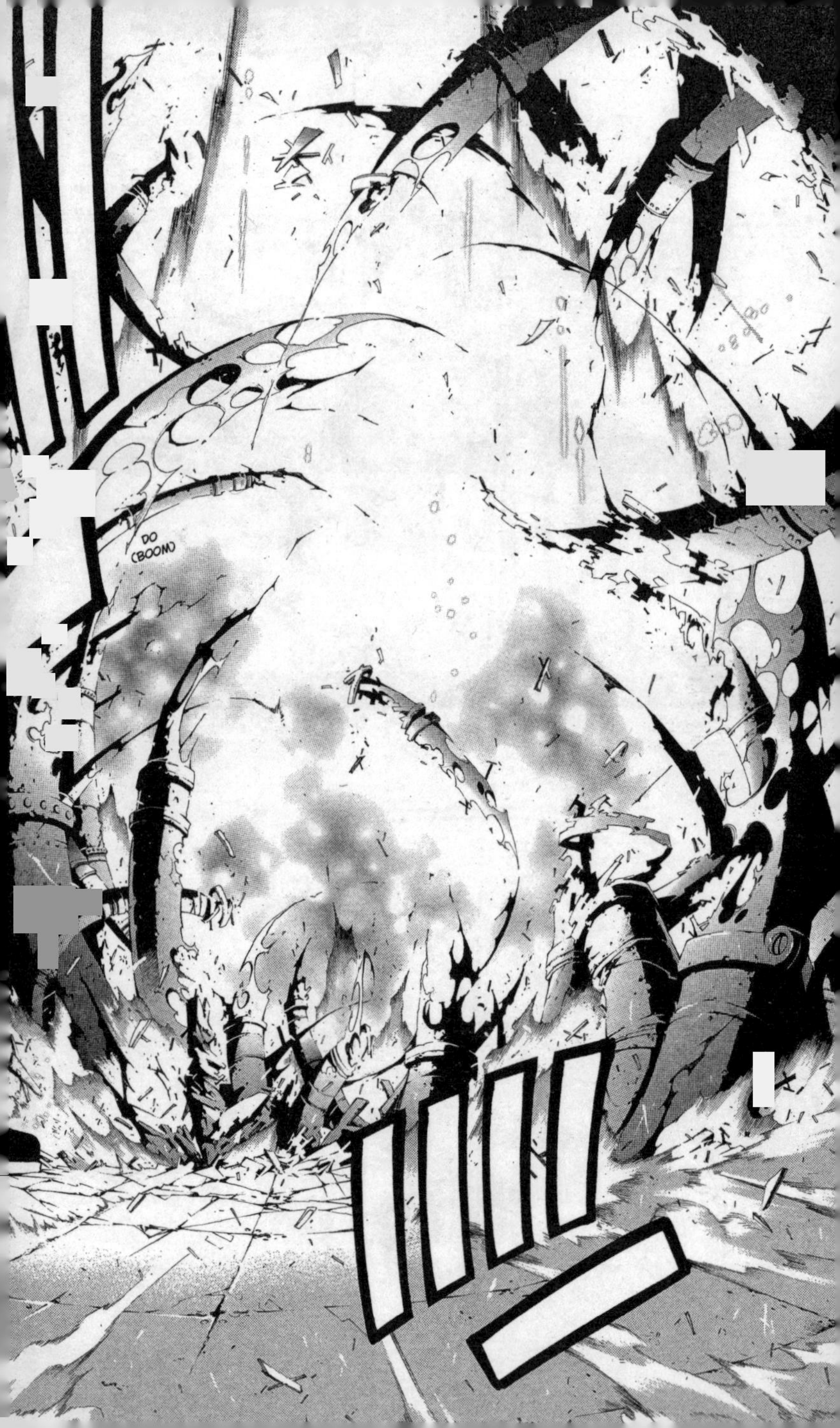
DO
(BOOM)

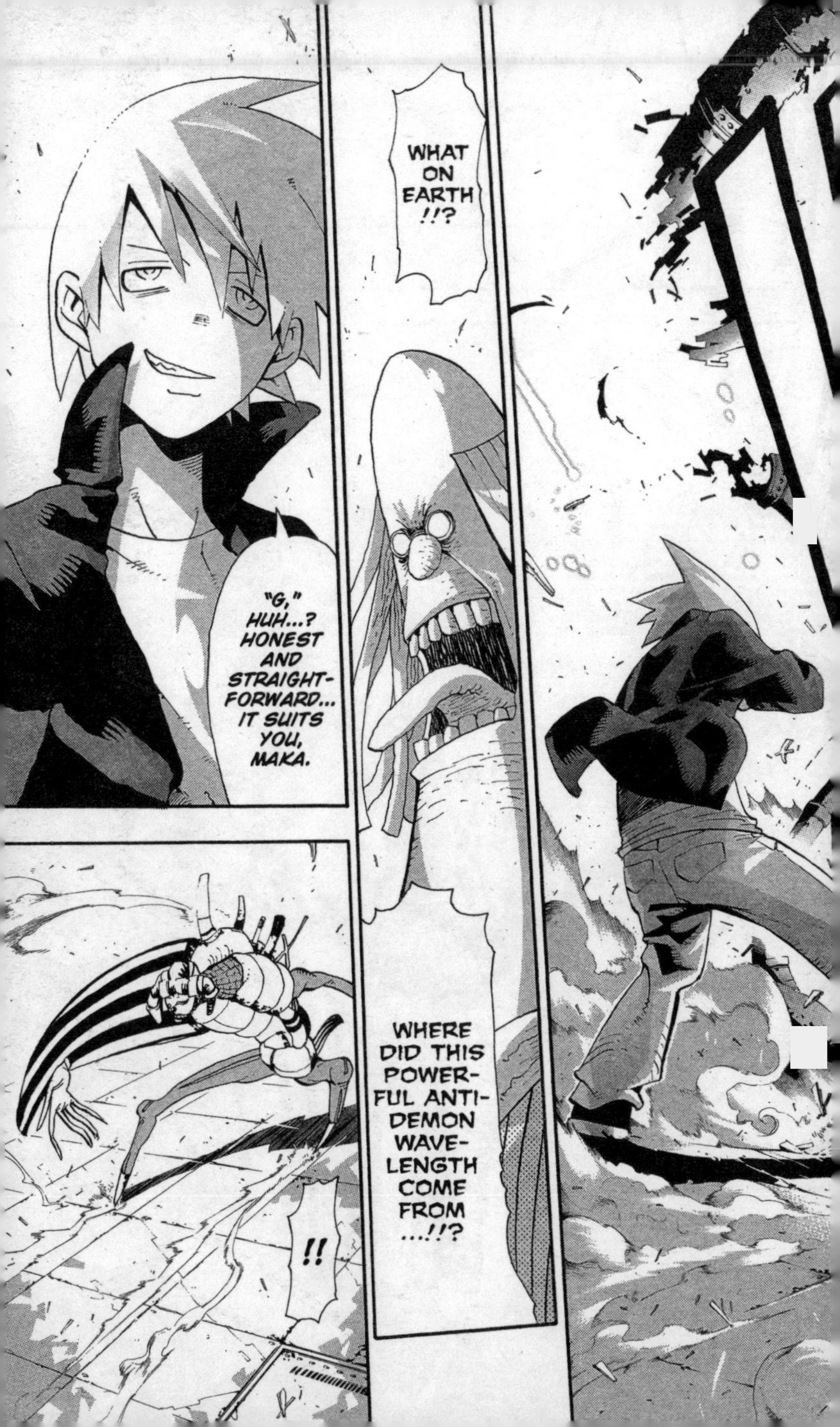
WHAT ON EARTH!!?
WHERE DID THIS POWERFUL ANTI-DEMON WAVELENGTH COME FROM...!!?
"G," HUH...? HONEST AND STRAIGHTFORWARD... IT SUITS YOU, MAKA.
!!

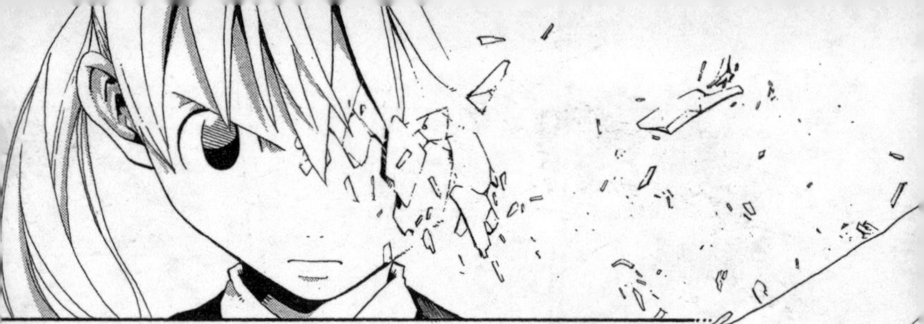
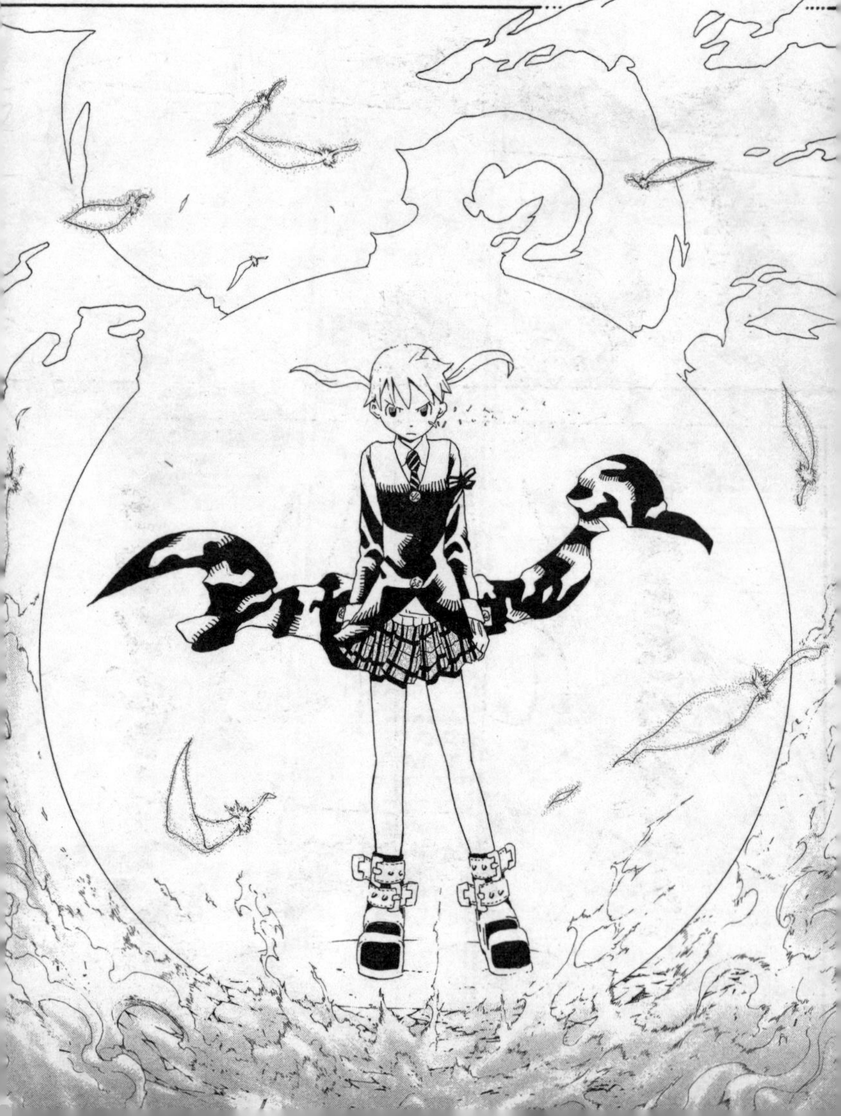

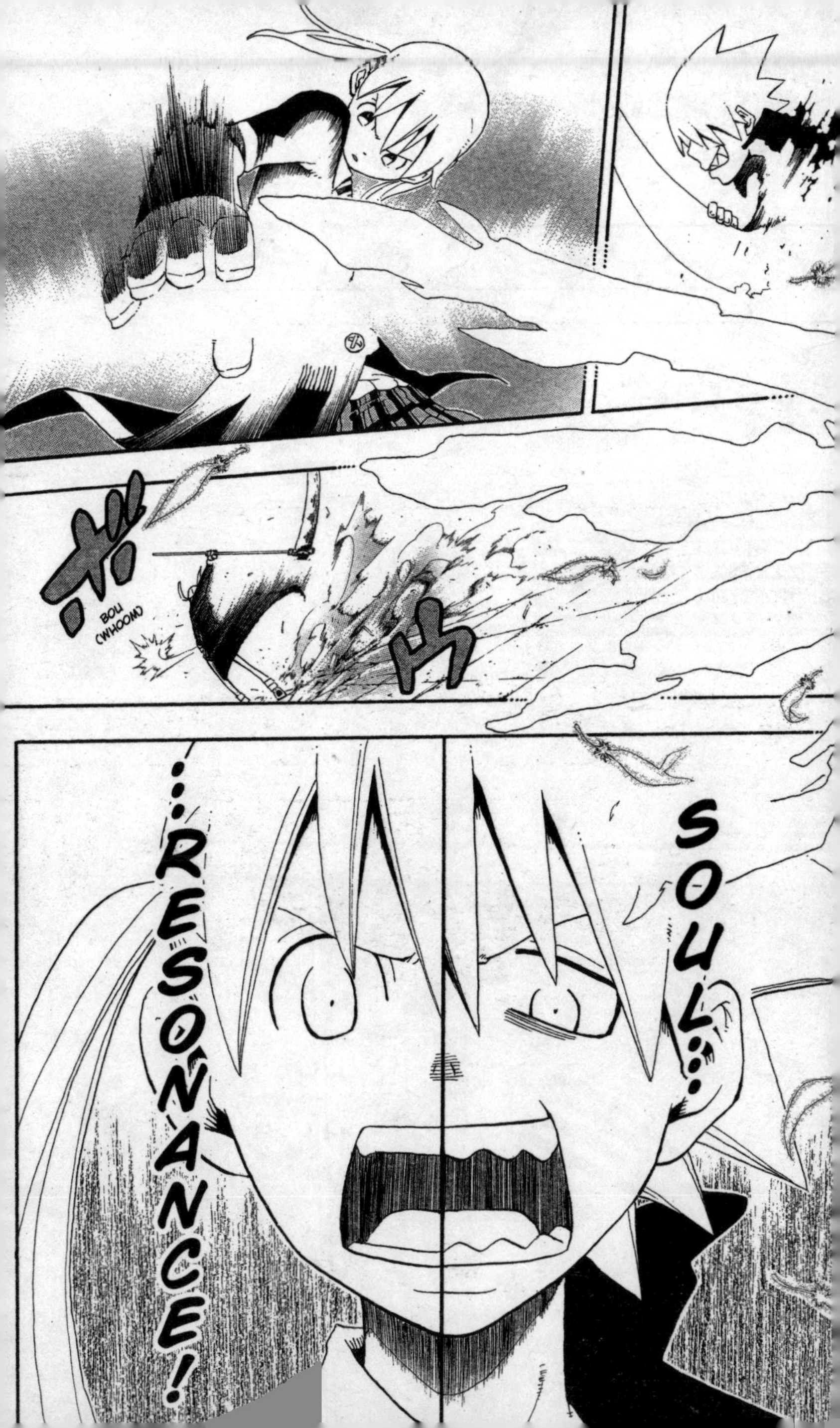
BOU (WHOOM)
...SOUL...
...RESONANCE!

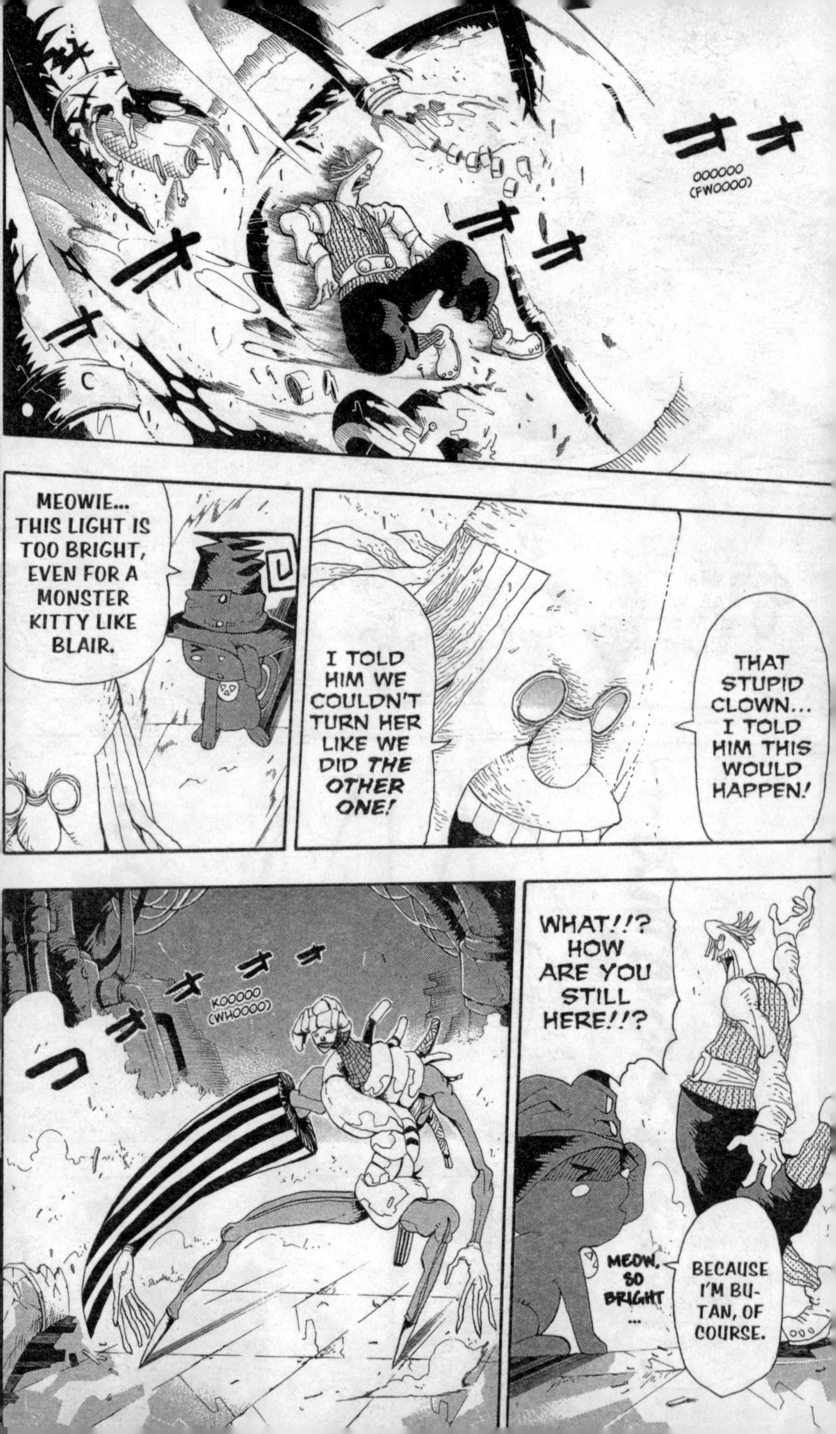
OOOOOO (FWOOOO)
THAT STUPID CLOWN... I TOLD HIM THIS WOULD HAPPEN!
I TOLD HIM WE COULDN'T TURN HER LIKE WE DID *THE OTHER ONE!*
MEOWIE... THIS LIGHT IS TOO BRIGHT, EVEN FOR A MONSTER KITTY LIKE BLAIR.
WHAT!!? HOW ARE YOU STILL HERE!!?
BECAUSE I'M BU-TAN, OF COURSE.
MEOW. SO BRIGHT ...
KOOOOO (WHOOOO)

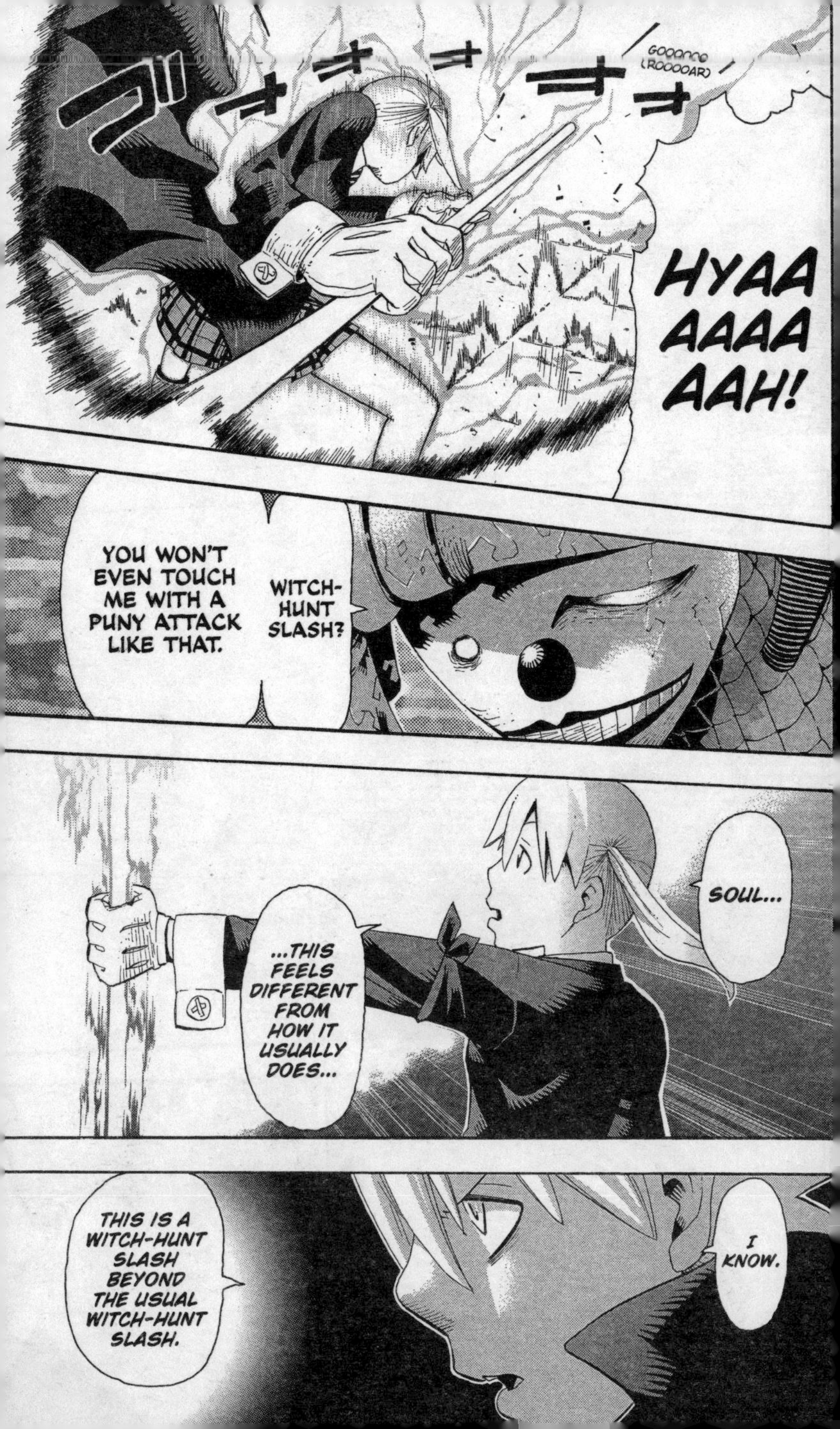
GOOOOOO (ROOOOAR)
HYAAAAAAAH!
WITCH-HUNT SLASH?
YOU WON'T EVEN TOUCH ME WITH A PUNY ATTACK LIKE THAT.
SOUL...
...THIS FEELS DIFFERENT FROM HOW IT USUALLY DOES...
I KNOW.
THIS IS A WITCH-HUNT SLASH BEYOND THE USUAL WITCH-HUNT SLASH.

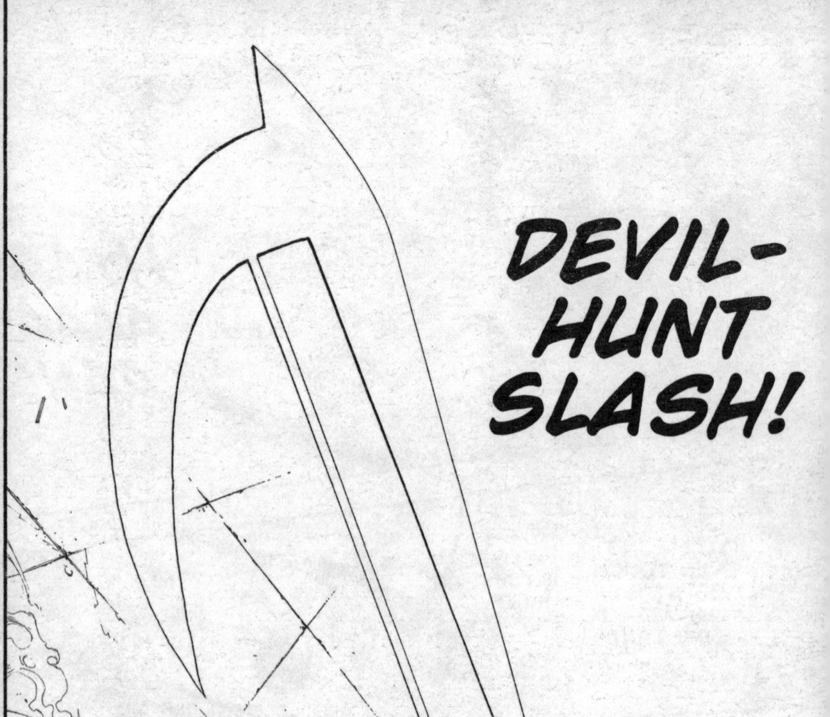
DEVIL-HUNT SLASH!
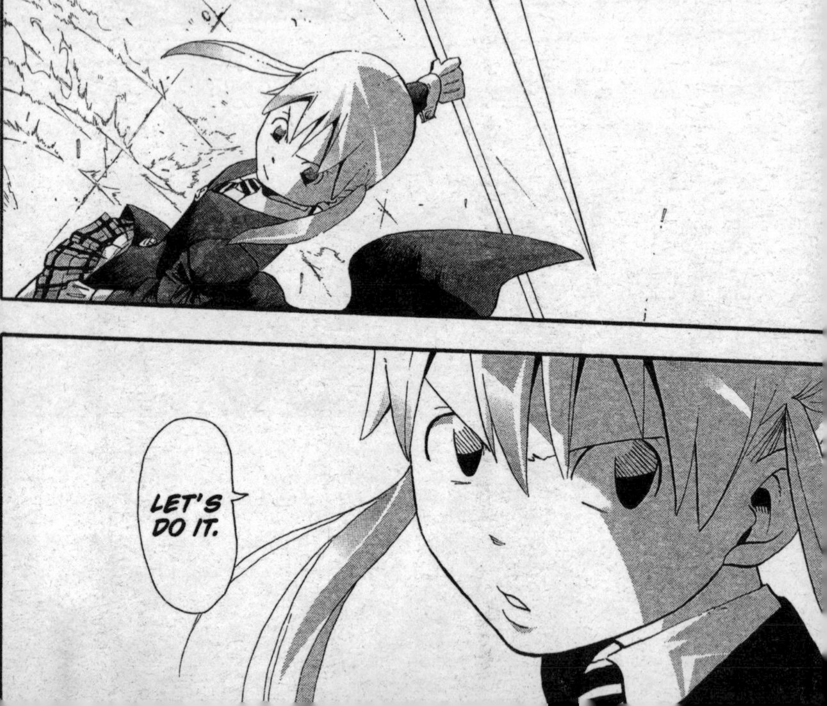
LET'S DO IT.

SOUL EATER

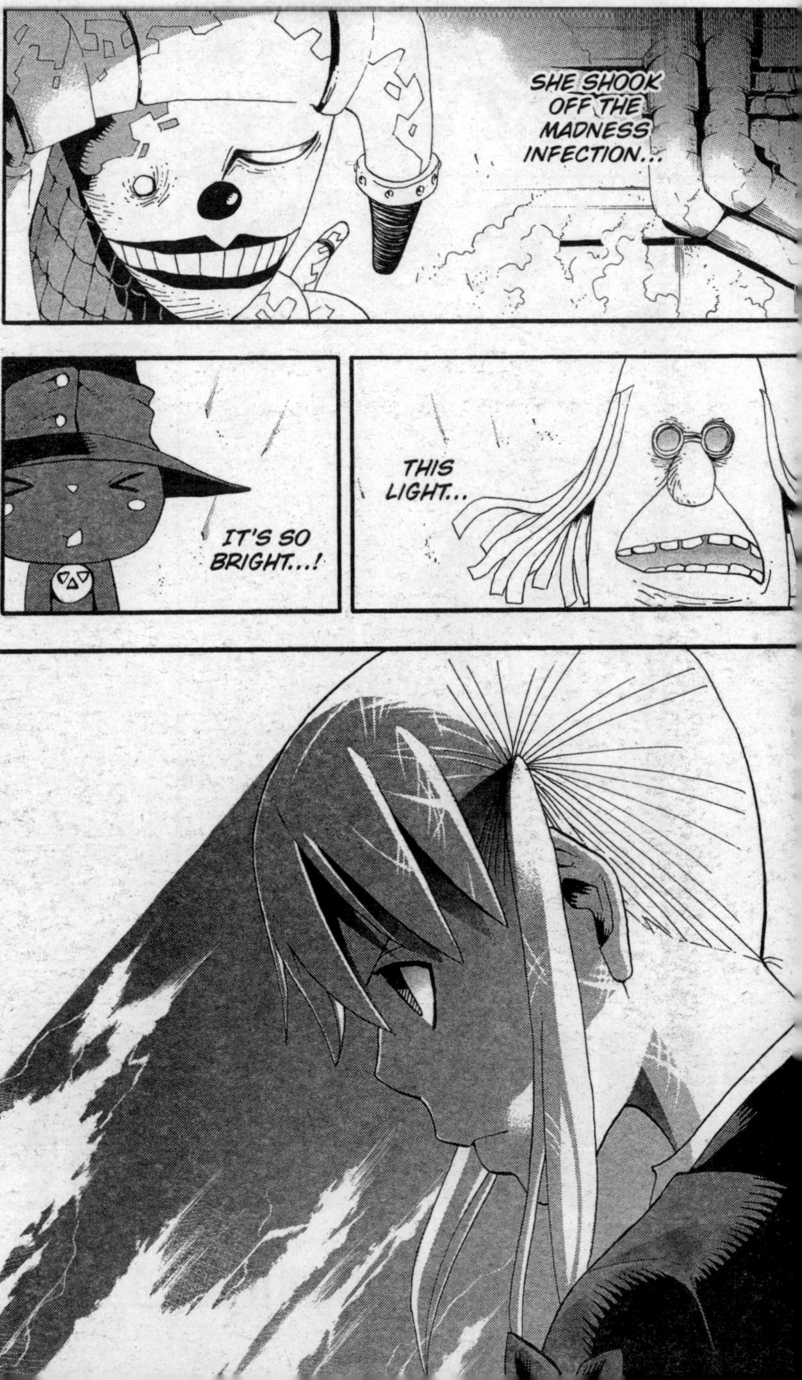
SHE SHOOK OFF THE MADNESS INFECTION...
THIS LIGHT...
IT'S SO BRIGHT...!

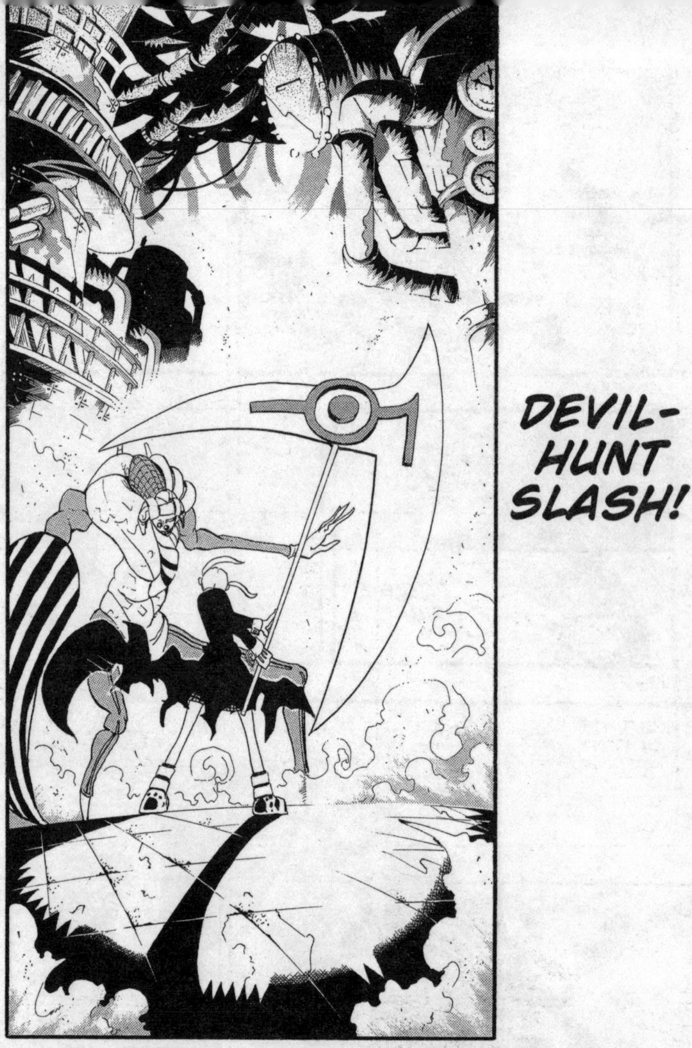
DEVIL-HUNT SLASH!

SOUL EATER

CHAPTER 43: THE CLOWN (PART 3)

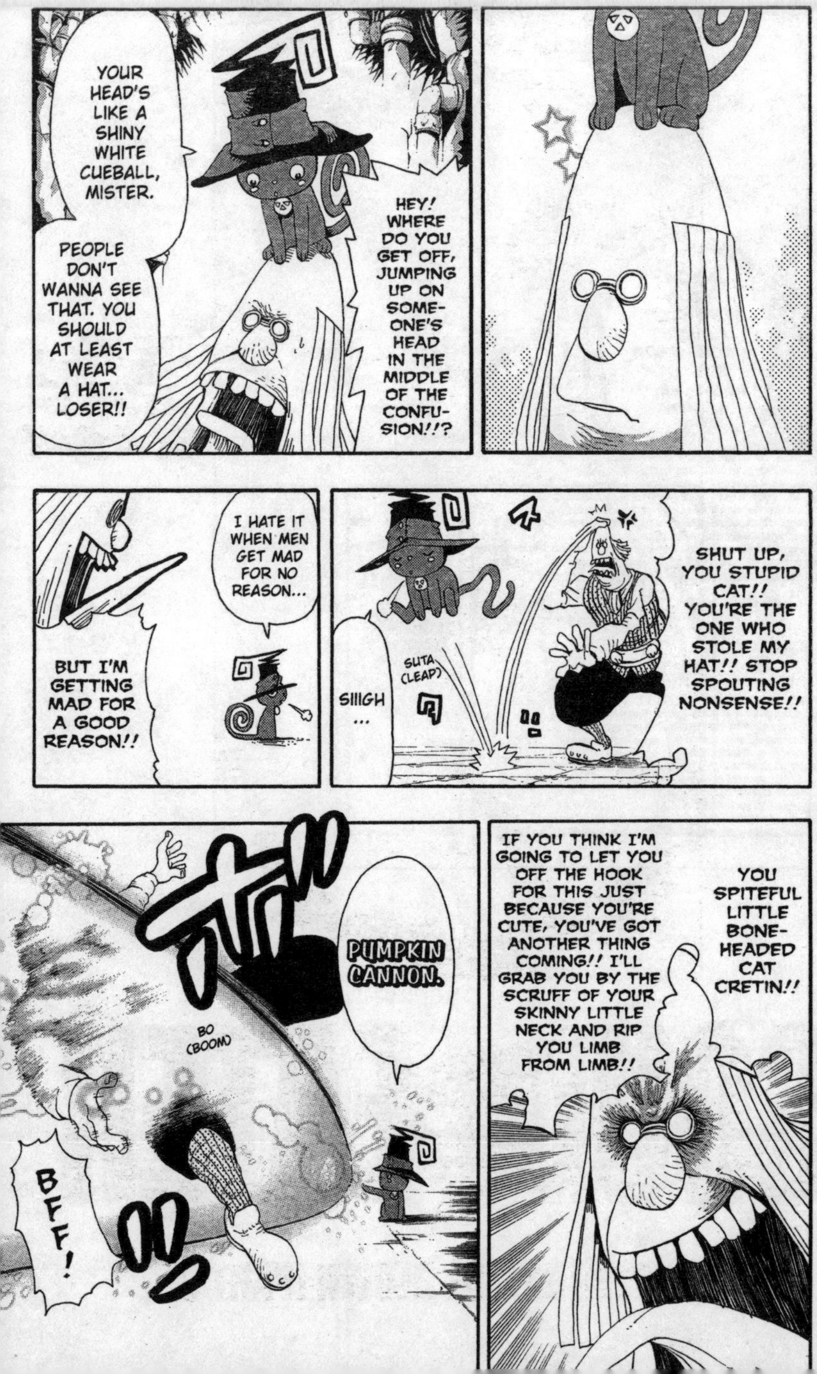
YOUR HEAD'S LIKE A SHINY WHITE CUEBALL, MISTER.
HEY! WHERE DO YOU GET OFF, JUMPING UP ON SOME-ONE'S HEAD IN THE MIDDLE OF THE CONFU-SION!!?
PEOPLE DON'T WANNA SEE THAT. YOU SHOULD AT LEAST WEAR A HAT... LOSER!!
SHUT UP, YOU STUPID CAT!! YOU'RE THE ONE WHO STOLE MY HAT!! STOP SPOUTING NONSENSE!!
SUTA (LEAP)
SIIIGH ...
I HATE IT WHEN MEN GET MAD FOR NO REASON...
BUT I'M GETTING MAD FOR A GOOD REASON!!
YOU SPITEFUL LITTLE BONE-HEADED CAT CRETIN!!
IF YOU THINK I'M GOING TO LET YOU OFF THE HOOK FOR THIS JUST BECAUSE YOU'RE CUTE, YOU'VE GOT ANOTHER THING COMING!! I'LL GRAB YOU BY THE SCRUFF OF YOUR SKINNY LITTLE NECK AND RIP YOU LIMB FROM LIMB!!
PUMPKIN CANNON.
BO (BOOM)
BFF!

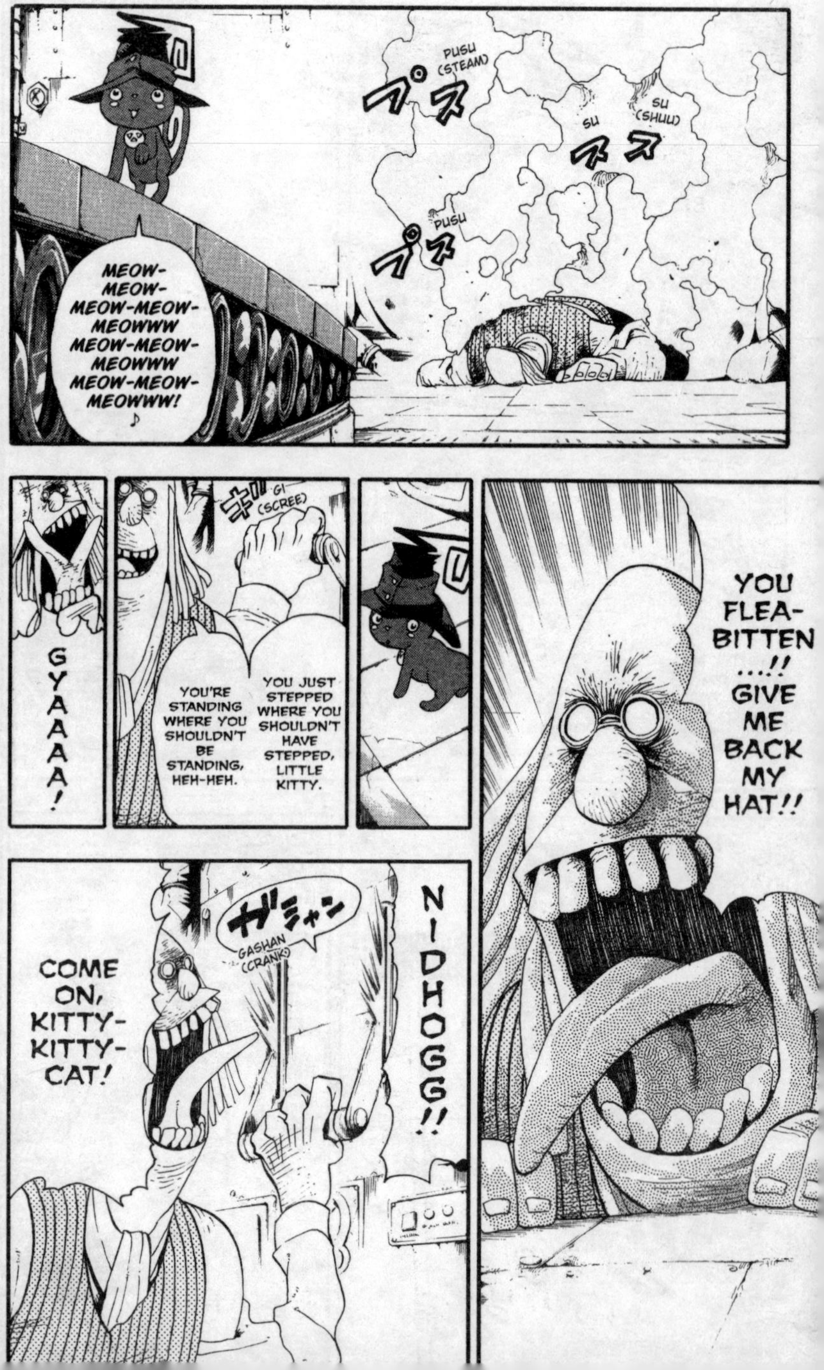
プス
PUSU (STEAM)
スス
SU (SHUU)
SU
プス
PUSU
MEOW-MEOW-MEOW-MEOW-MEOWWW MEOW-MEOW-MEOWWW MEOW-MEOW-MEOWWW! ♪
YOU FLEA-BITTEN...!! GIVE ME BACK MY HAT!!
ギッ
GI (SCREE)
YOU JUST STEPPED WHERE YOU SHOULDN'T HAVE STEPPED, LITTLE KITTY.
YOU'RE STANDING WHERE YOU SHOULDN'T BE STANDING, HEH-HEH.
GYAAAA!
NIDHOGG!!
ガシャン
GASHAN (CRANK)
COME ON, KITTY-KITTY-CAT!

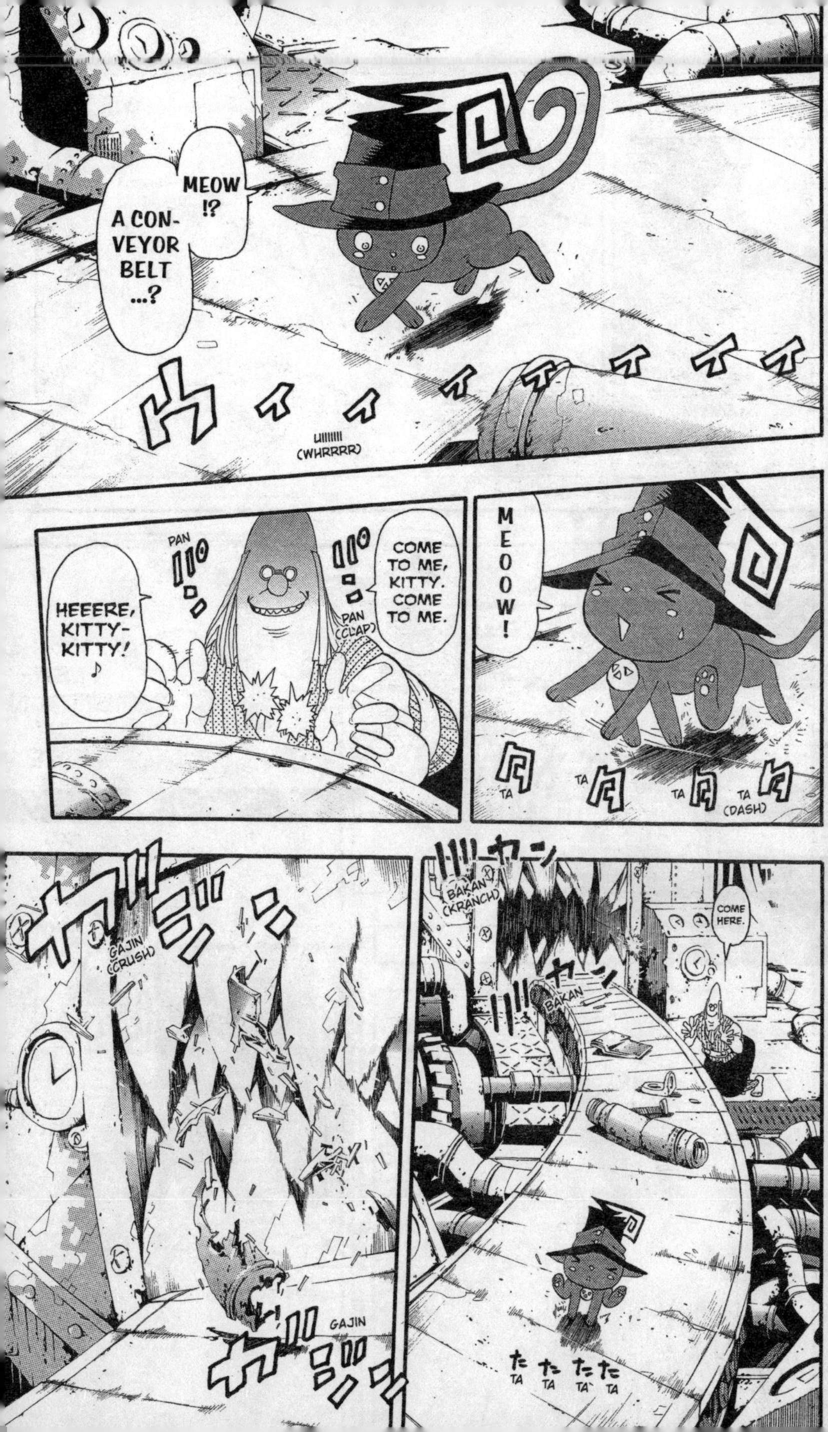
MEOW !?
A CON-VEYOR BELT ...?
UIIIIIII (WHRRRR)
MEOOOW!
TA TA TA TA (DASH)
COME TO ME, KITTY. COME TO ME.
PAN PAN (CLAP)
HEEERE, KITTY-KITTY! ♪
BAKAN (KRANCH)
COME HERE.
BAKAN
たた たた
TA TA TA TA
GAJIN (CRUSH)
GAJIN

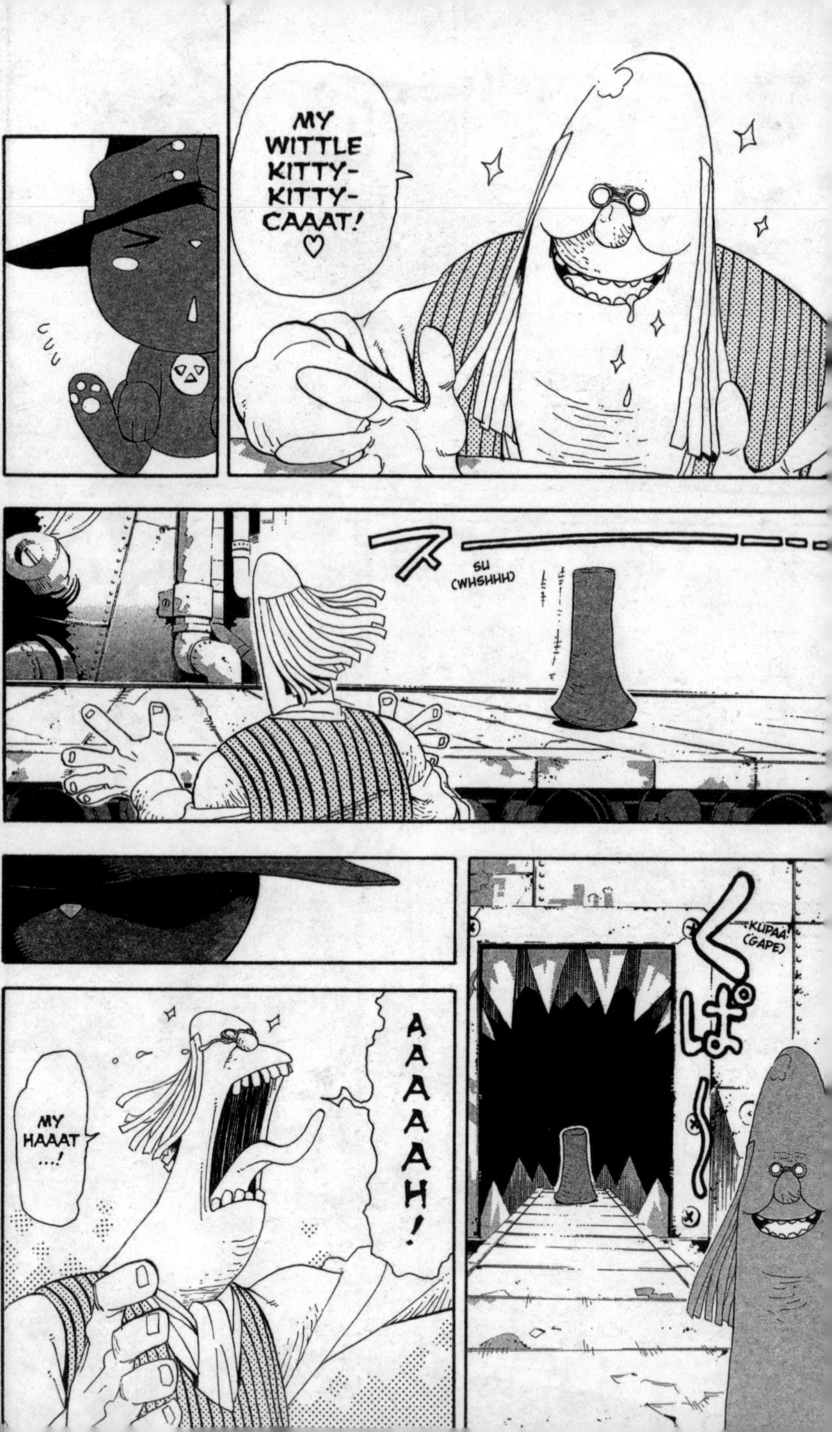
MY WITTLE KITTY-KITTY-CAAAT! ♡
ス
SU (WHSHHH)
KUPAA! (GAPE)
AAAAAH!
MY HAAAT...!

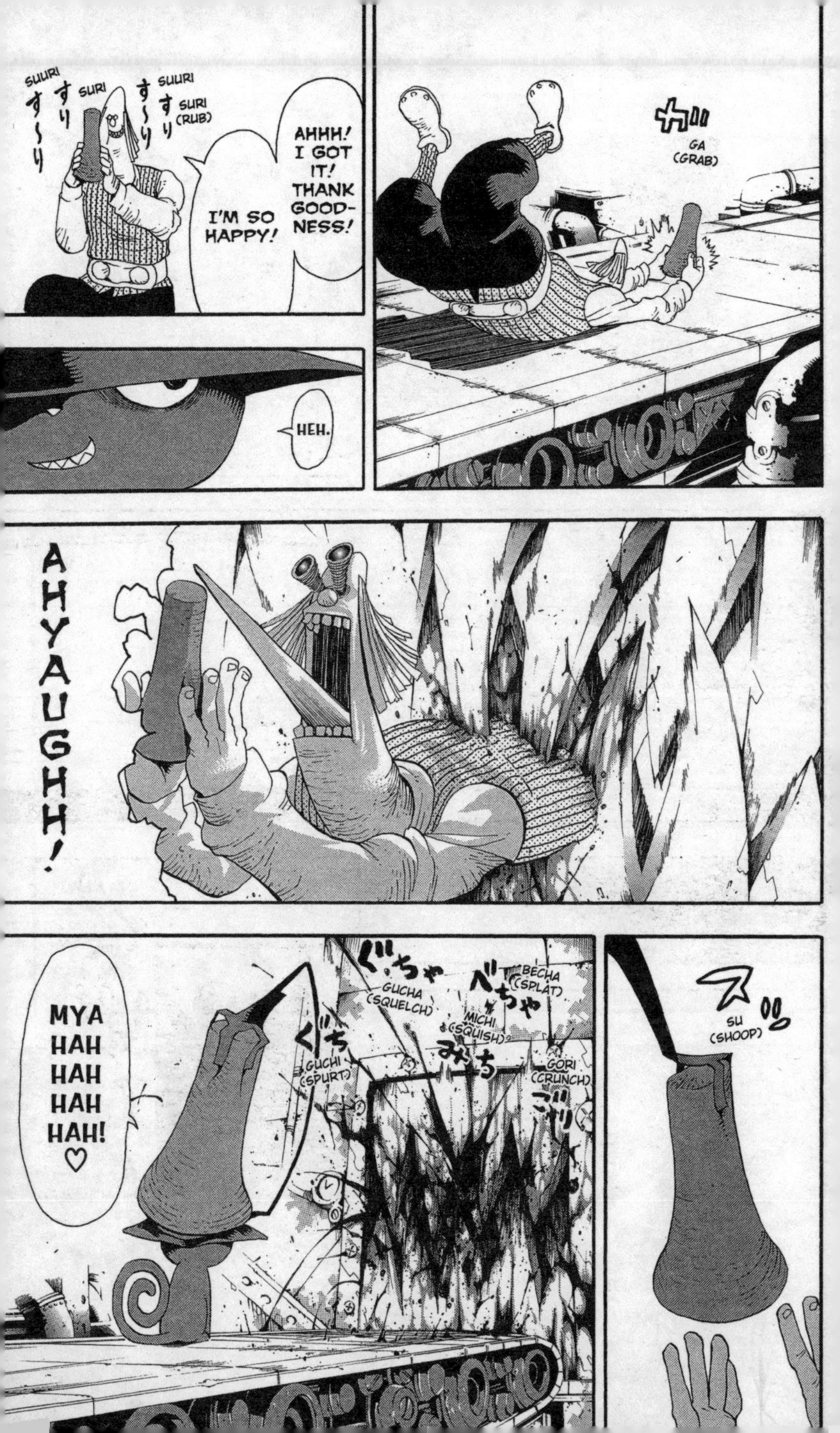

ガッ
GA (GRAB)
すり すり すり すり
SUURI SURI SUURI SURI (RUB)
AHHH! I GOT IT! THANK GOODNESS!
I'M SO HAPPY!
HEH.
AHYAUGHH!
ス
SU (SHOOP)
ぐちゃ
GUCHA (SQUELCH)
べちゃ
BECHA (SPLAT)
みち
MICHI (SQUISH)
ぐち
GUCHI (SPURT)
ごり
GORI (CRUNCH)
MYA HAH HAH HAH HAH! ♡

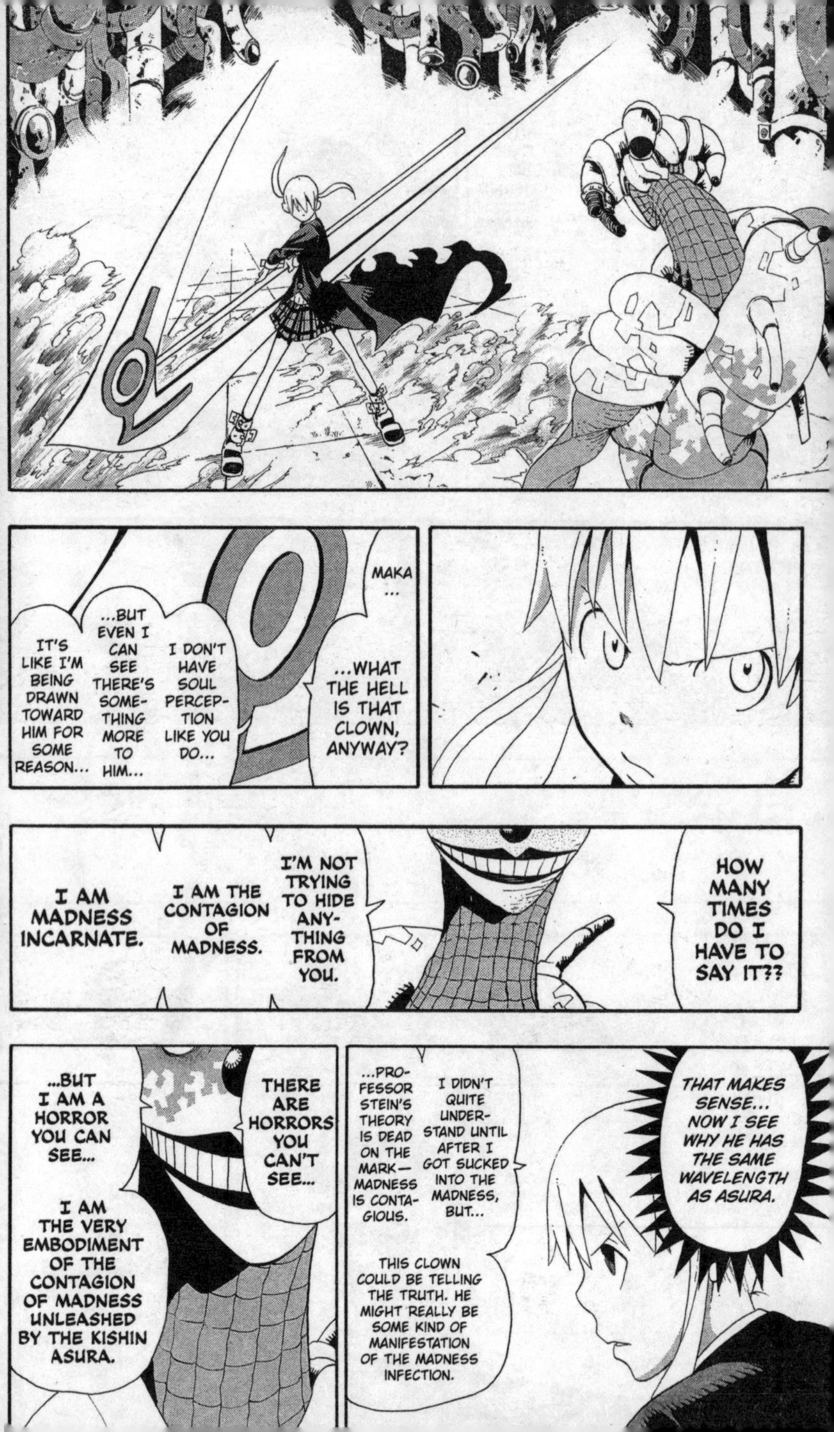
MAKA ...
...WHAT THE HELL IS THAT CLOWN, ANYWAY?
I DON'T HAVE SOUL PERCEPTION LIKE YOU DO...
...BUT EVEN I CAN SEE THERE'S SOMETHING MORE TO HIM...
IT'S LIKE I'M BEING DRAWN TOWARD HIM FOR SOME REASON...
HOW MANY TIMES DO I HAVE TO SAY IT??
I'M NOT TRYING TO HIDE ANYTHING FROM YOU.
I AM THE CONTAGION OF MADNESS.
I AM MADNESS INCARNATE.
THAT MAKES SENSE... NOW I SEE WHY HE HAS THE SAME WAVELENGTH AS ASURA.
I DIDN'T QUITE UNDERSTAND UNTIL AFTER I GOT SUCKED INTO THE MADNESS, BUT...
...PROFESSOR STEIN'S THEORY IS DEAD ON THE MARK—MADNESS IS CONTAGIOUS.
THIS CLOWN COULD BE TELLING THE TRUTH. HE MIGHT REALLY BE SOME KIND OF MANIFESTATION OF THE MADNESS INFECTION.
THERE ARE HORRORS YOU CAN'T SEE...
...BUT I AM A HORROR YOU CAN SEE...
I AM THE VERY EMBODIMENT OF THE CONTAGION OF MADNESS UNLEASHED BY THE KISHIN ASURA.

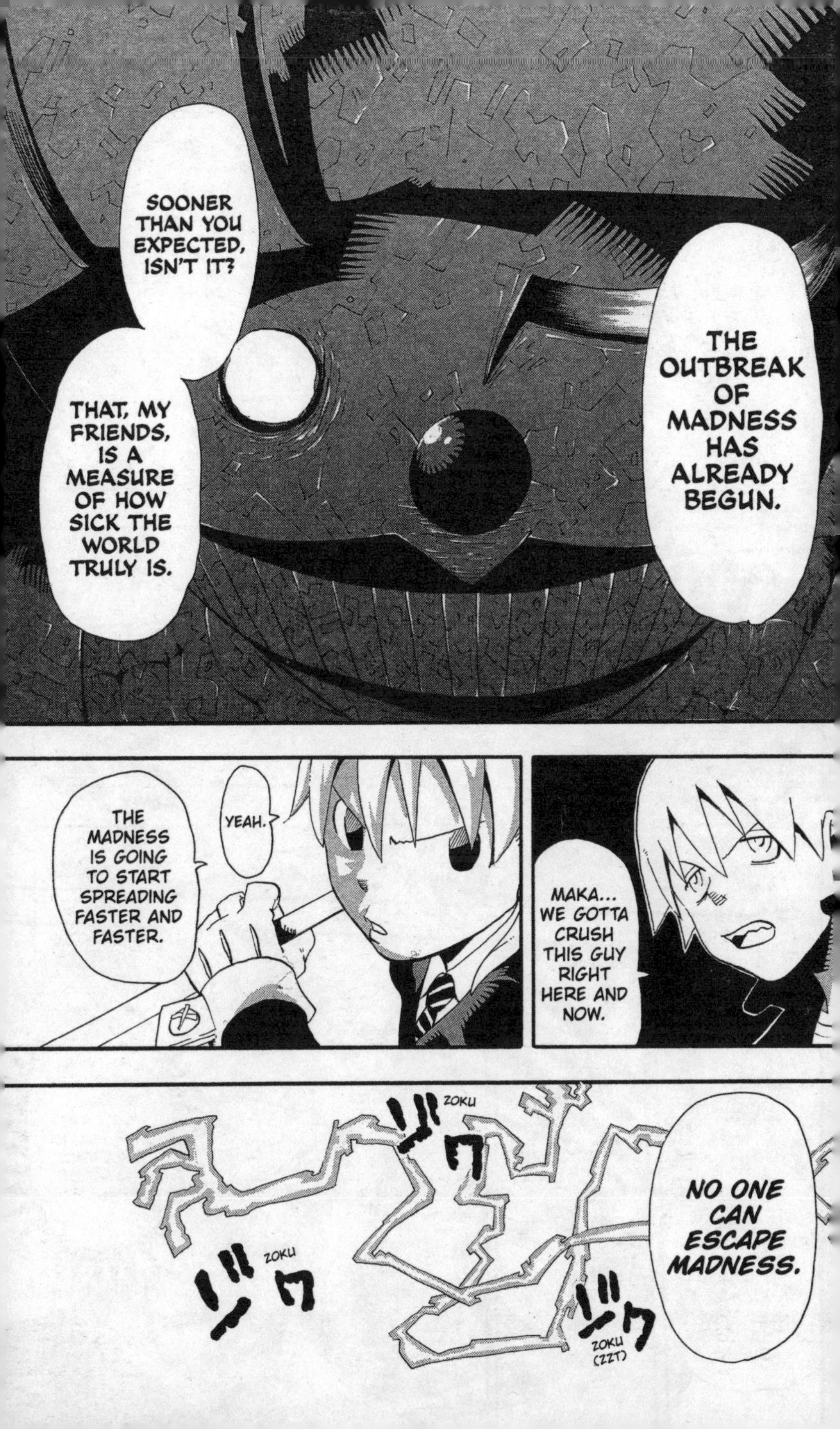
THE OUTBREAK OF MADNESS HAS ALREADY BEGUN.
SOONER THAN YOU EXPECTED, ISN'T IT?
THAT, MY FRIENDS, IS A MEASURE OF HOW SICK THE WORLD TRULY IS.
MAKA... WE GOTTA CRUSH THIS GUY RIGHT HERE AND NOW.
YEAH.
THE MADNESS IS GOING TO START SPREADING FASTER AND FASTER.
ZOKU
NO ONE CAN ESCAPE MADNESS.
ZOKU (ZZT)
ZOKU

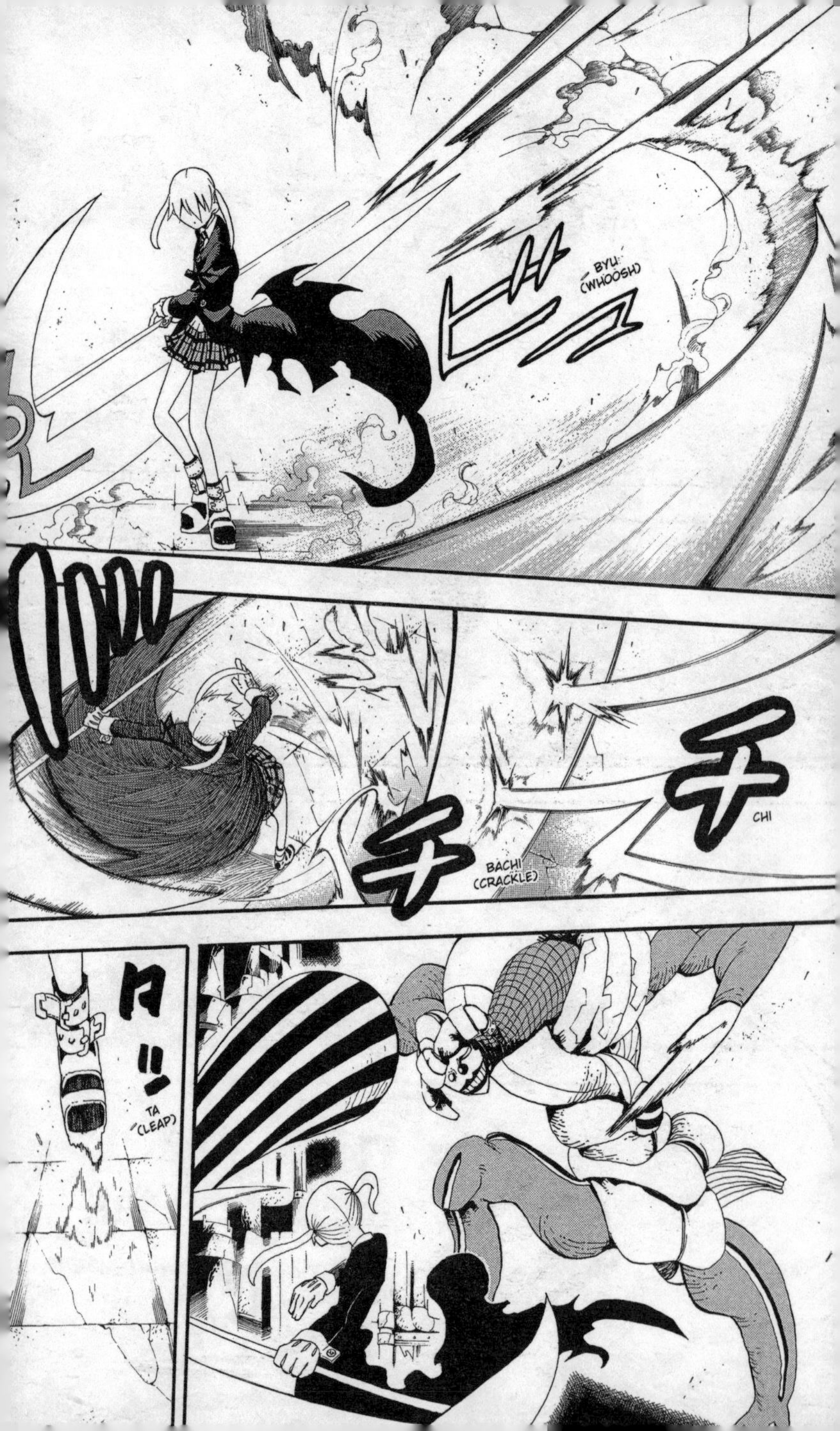
BYU
(WHOOSH)
CHI
BACHI
(CRACKLE)
TA
(LEAP)

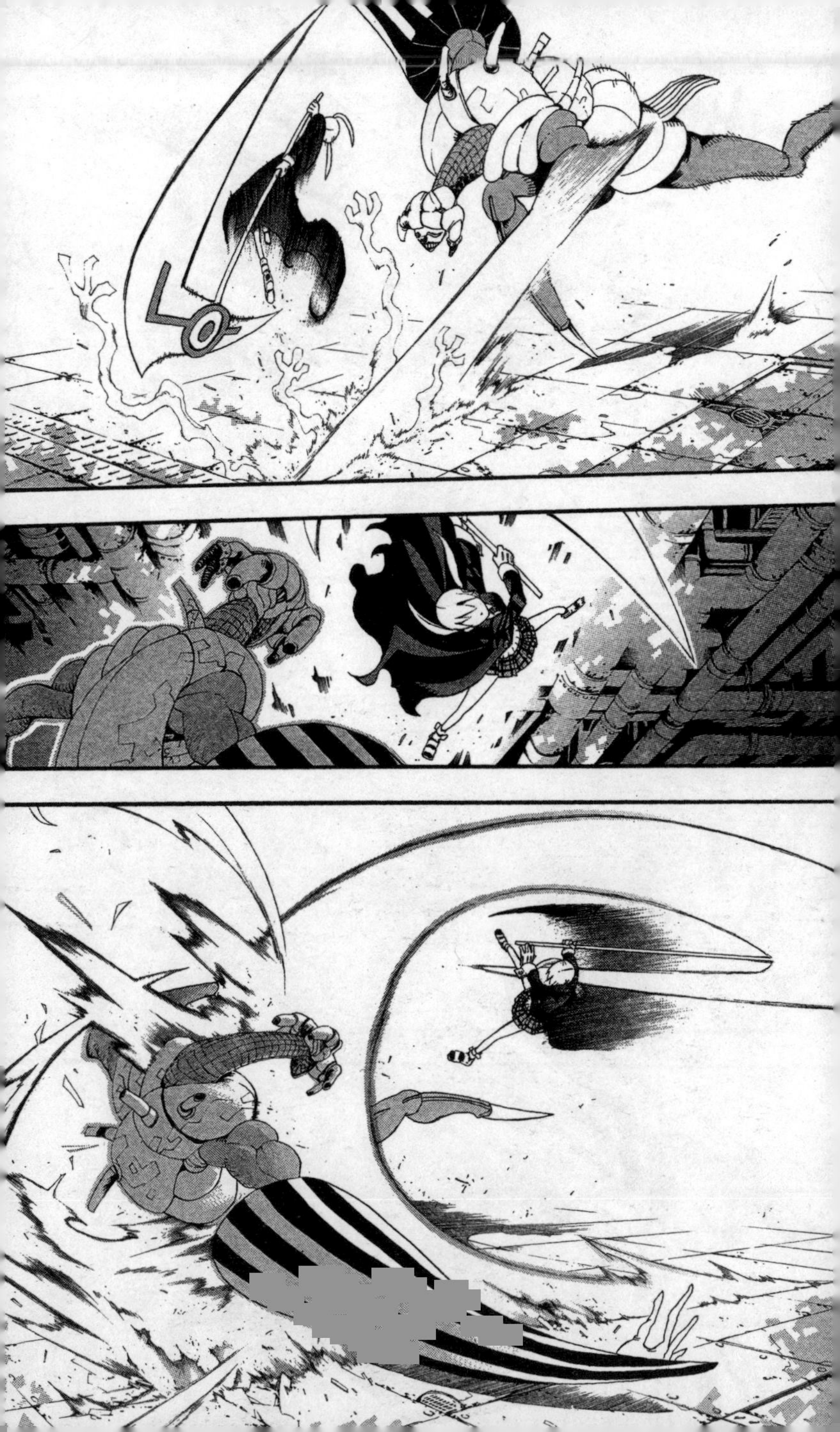

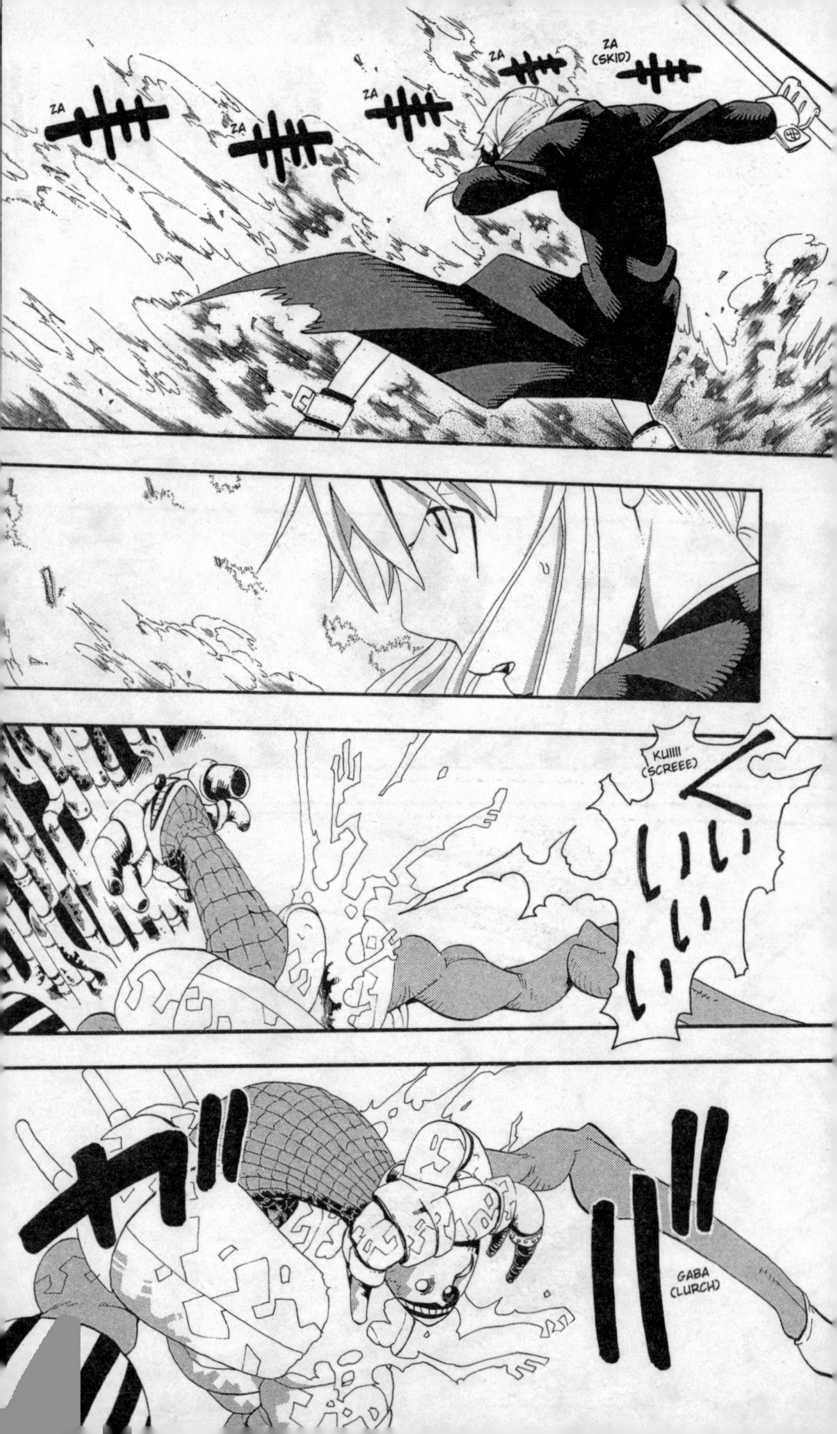
ZA
(SKID)
ZA
ZA
ZA
ZA
KUIIII
(SCREEE)
GABA
(LURCH)

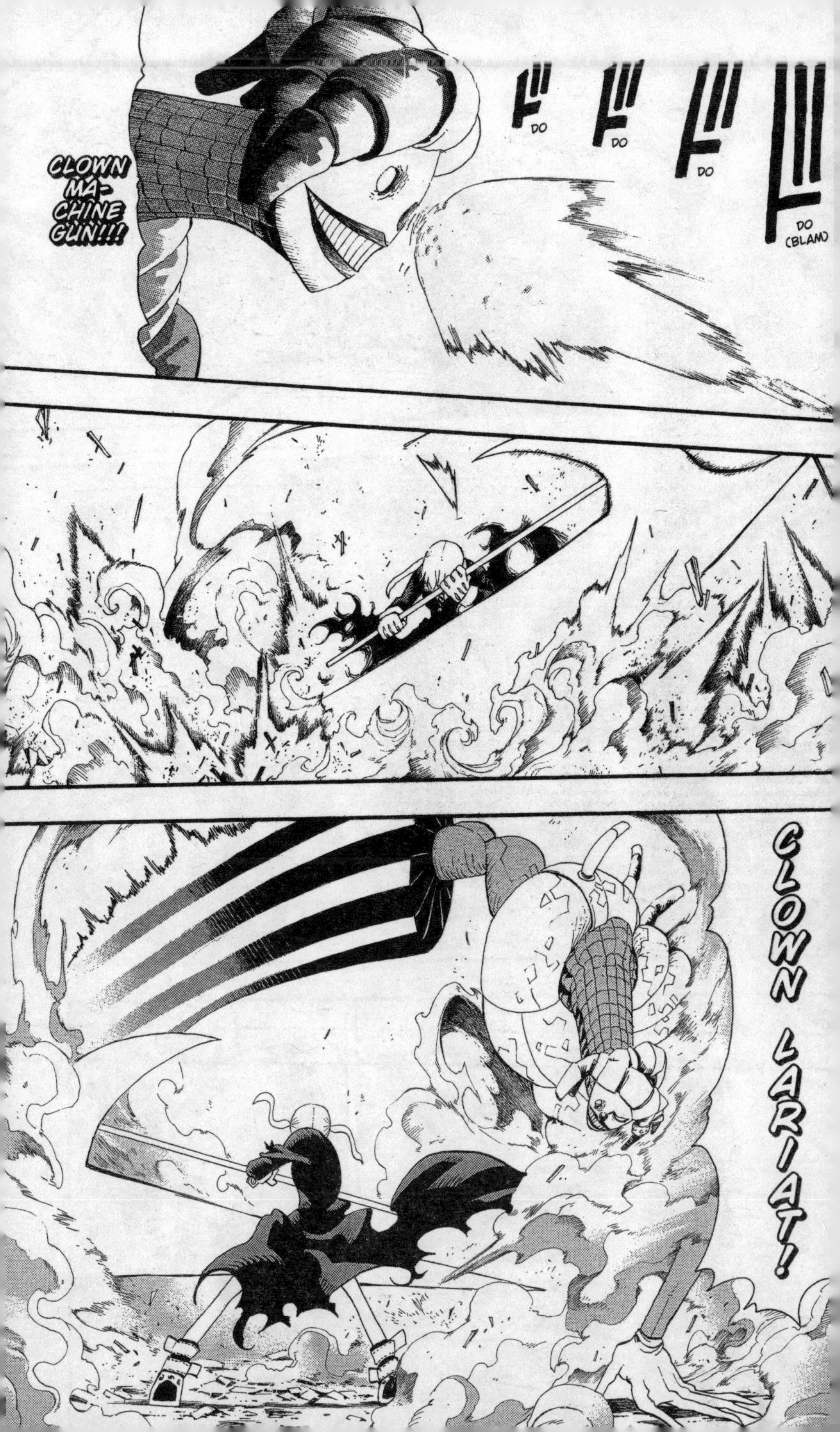

DO DO DO DO (BLAM)
CLOWN MA-CHINE GUN!!!
CLOWN LARIAT!

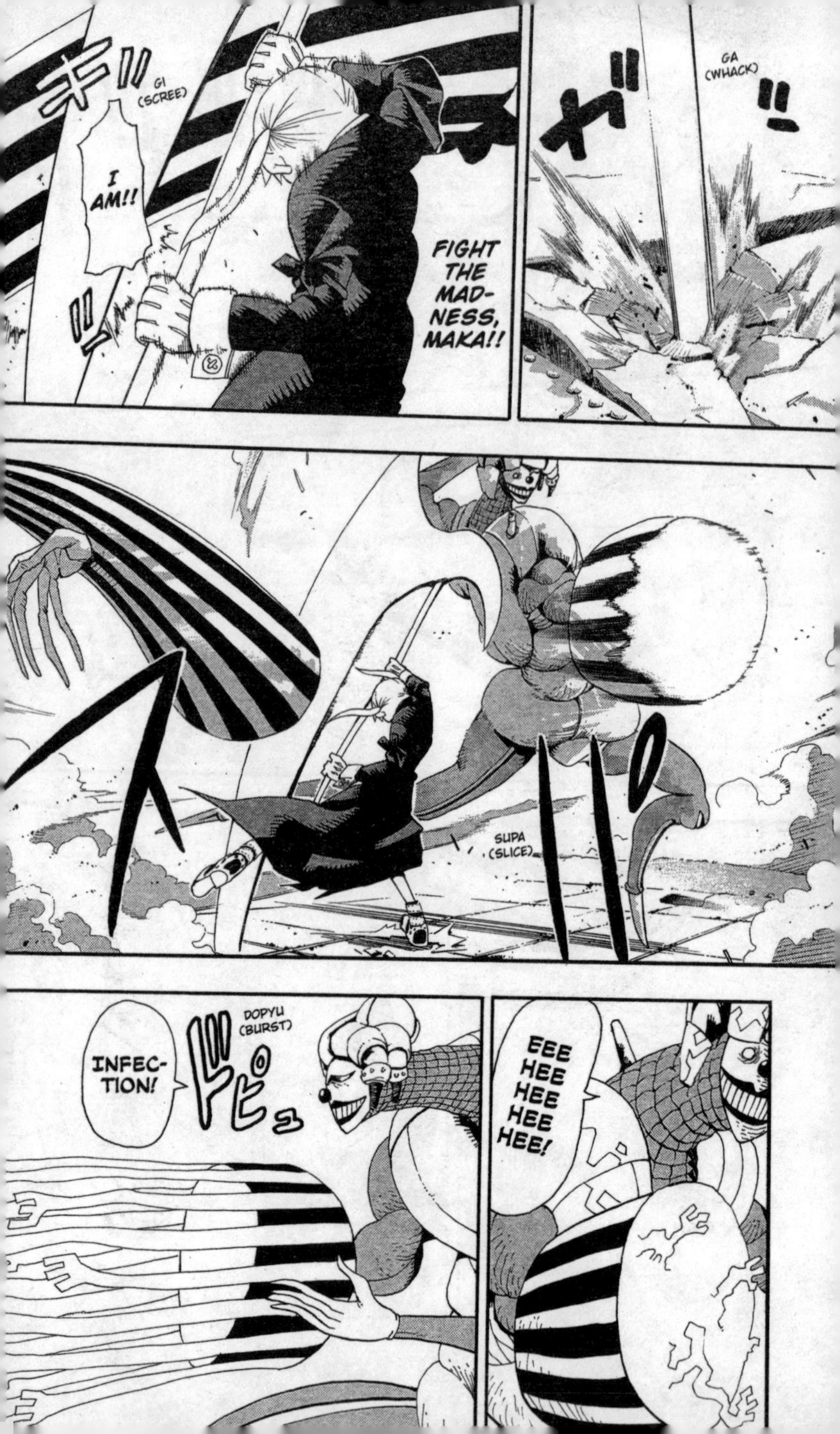
GA (WHACK)
FIGHT THE MAD-NESS, MAKA!!
GI (SCREE)
I AM!!
SUPA (SLICE)
EEE HEE HEE HEE HEE!
DOPYU (BURST)
INFECTION!

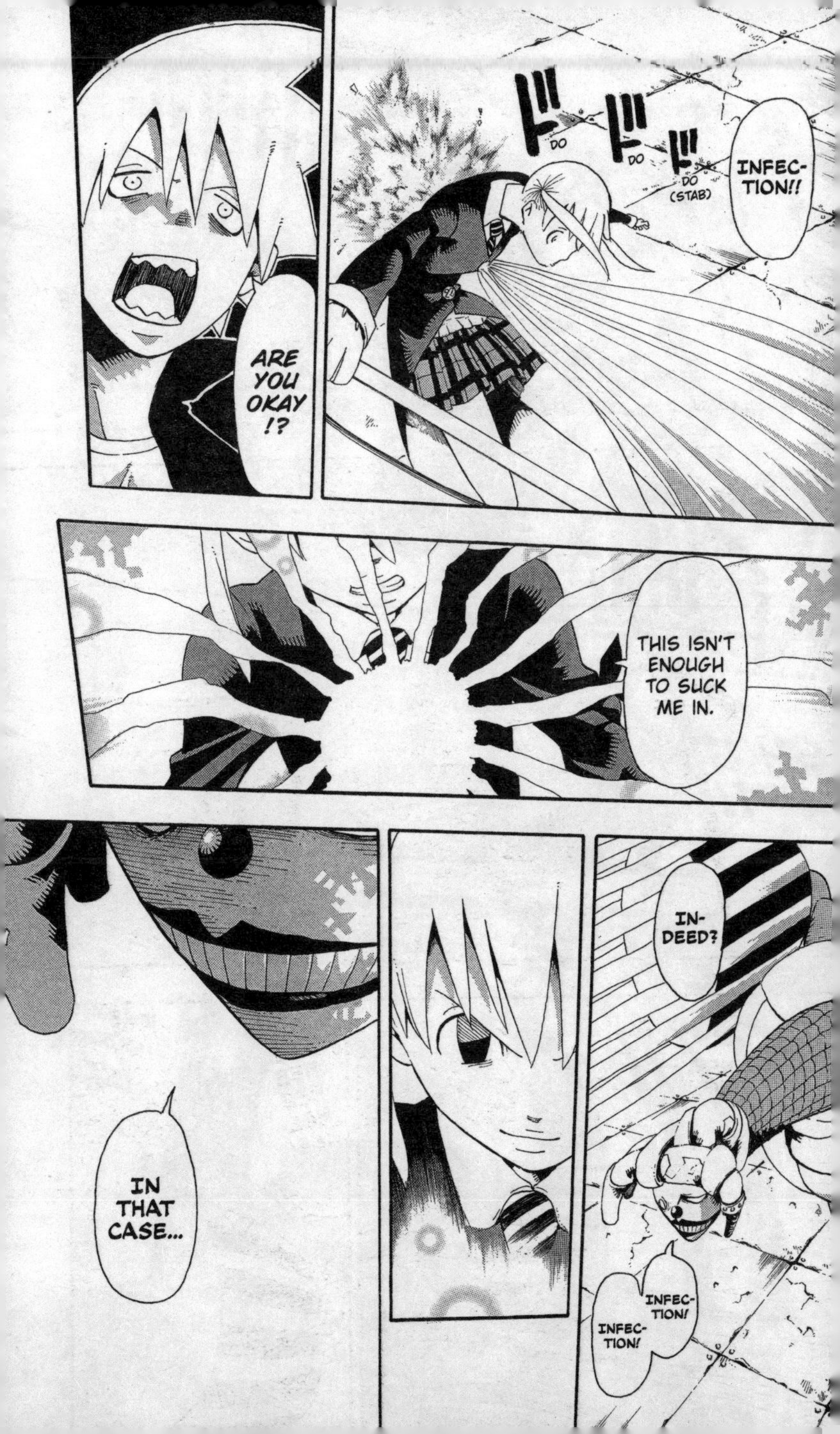

ド DO
ド DO
ド DO (STAB)
INFEC-TION!!
ARE YOU OKAY!?
THIS ISN'T ENOUGH TO SUCK ME IN.
IN-DEED?
INFEC-TION!
INFEC-TION!
IN THAT CASE...

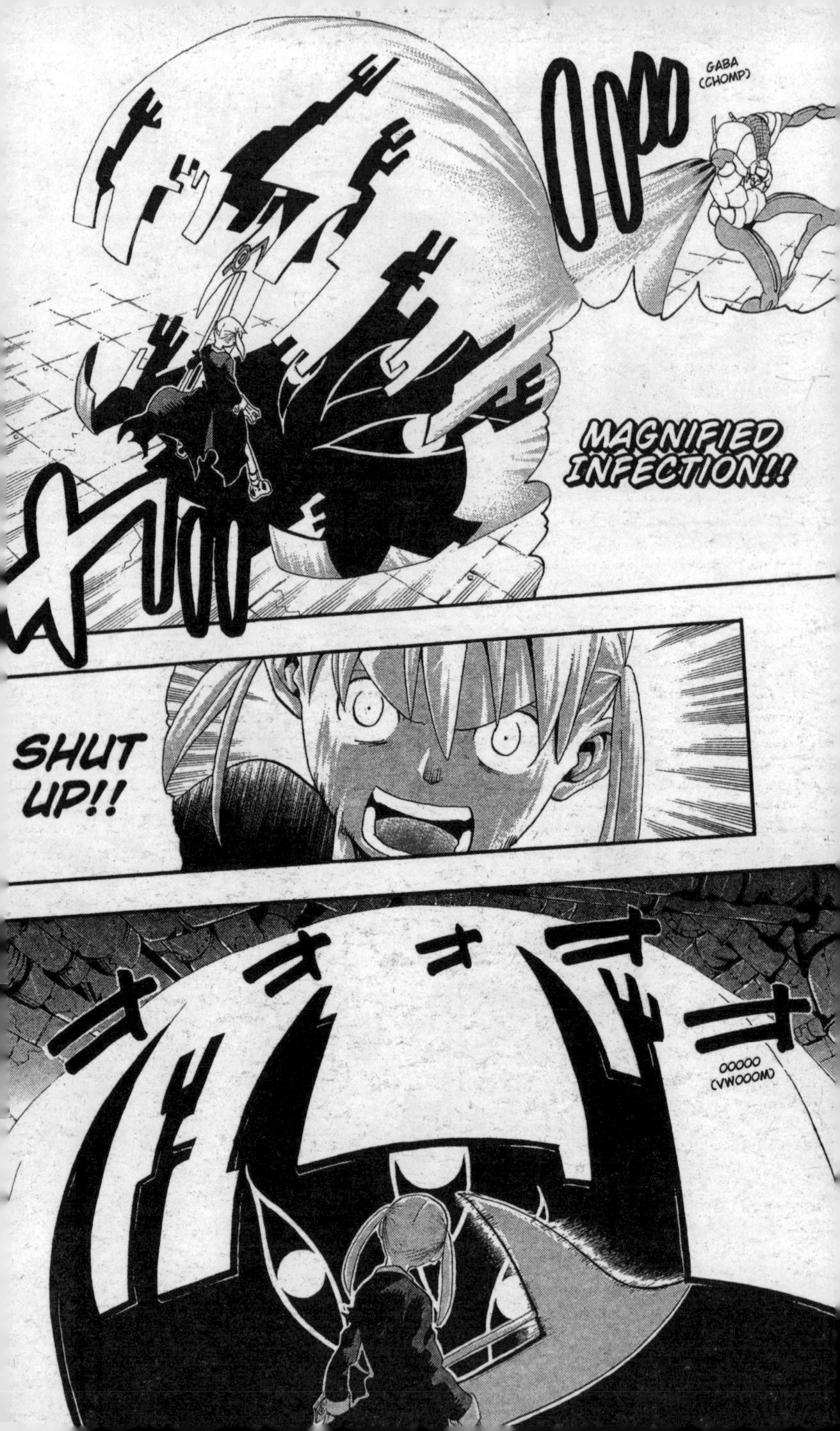
GABA (CHOMP)
MAGNIFIED INFECTION!!
SHUT UP!!
OOOOO (VWOOOM)

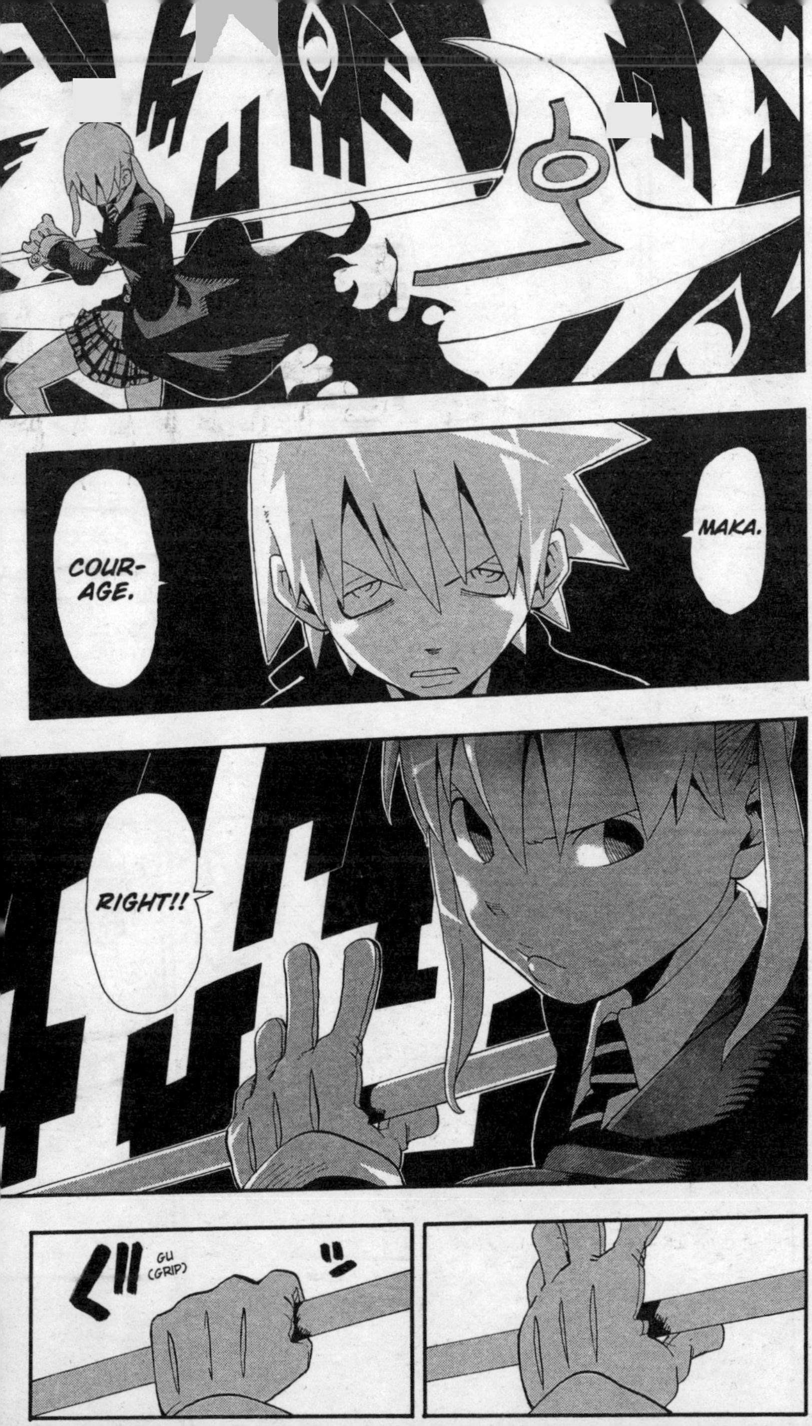
MAKA.
COUR-AGE.
RIGHT!!
ぐッ
GU (GRIP)

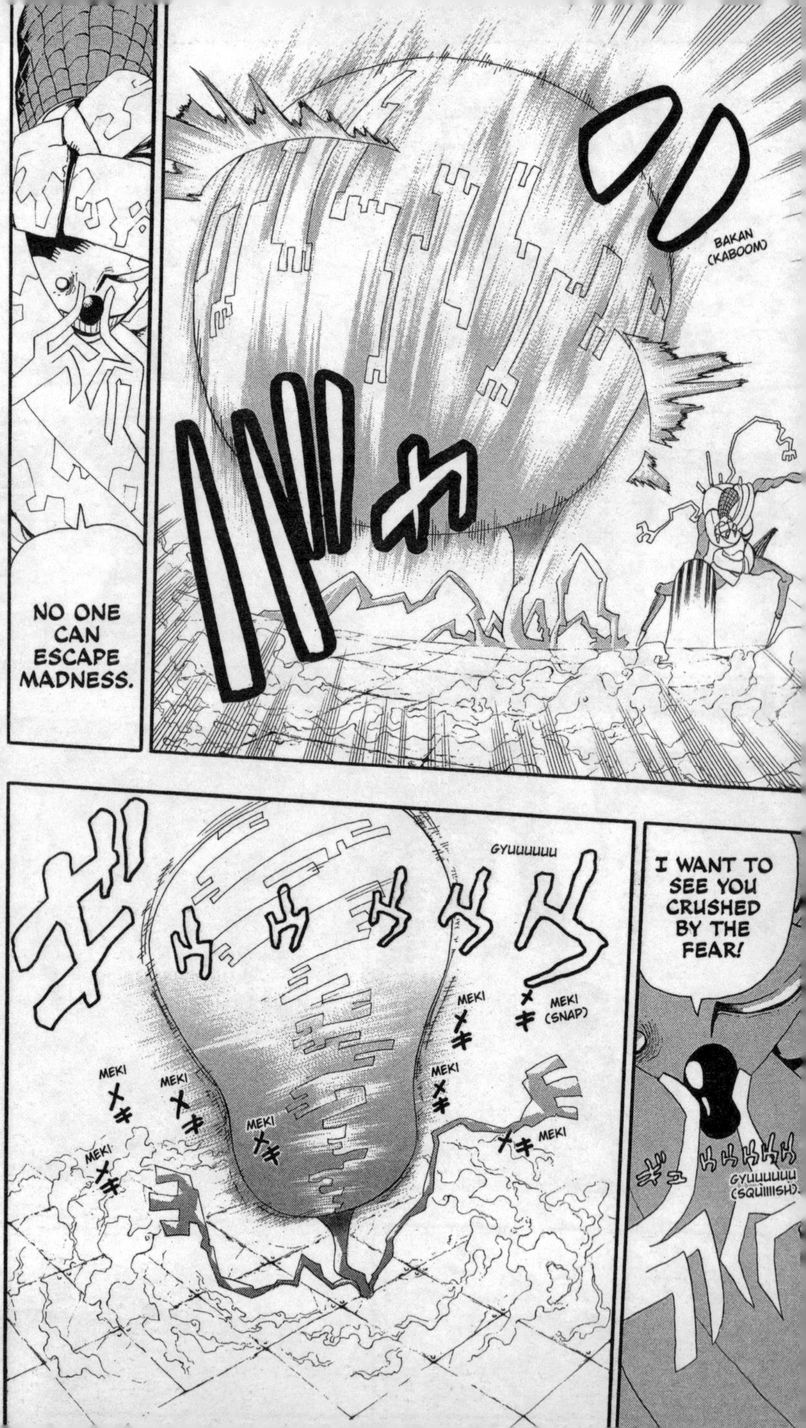
BAKAN (KABOOM)
NO ONE CAN ESCAPE MADNESS.
I WANT TO SEE YOU CRUSHED BY THE FEAR!
GYUUUUUU (SQUIIIISH)
GYUUUUUU
MEKI
MEKI (SNAP)
MEKI
MEKI
MEKI
MEKI
MEKI
MEKI

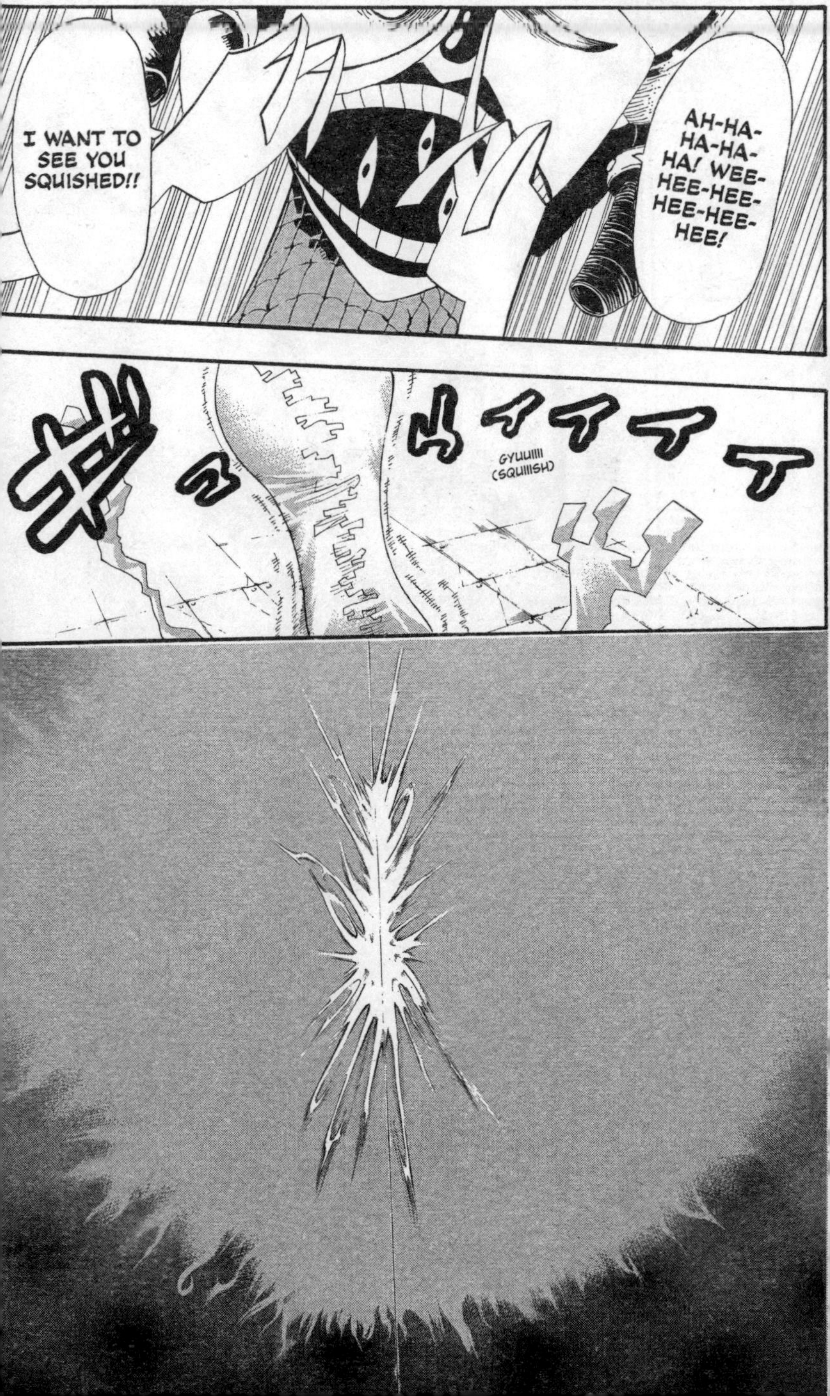
AH-HA-HA-HA-HA! WEE-HEE-HEE-HEE-HEE-HEE!
I WANT TO SEE YOU SQUISHED!!
GYUUIIIII (SQUIIISH)

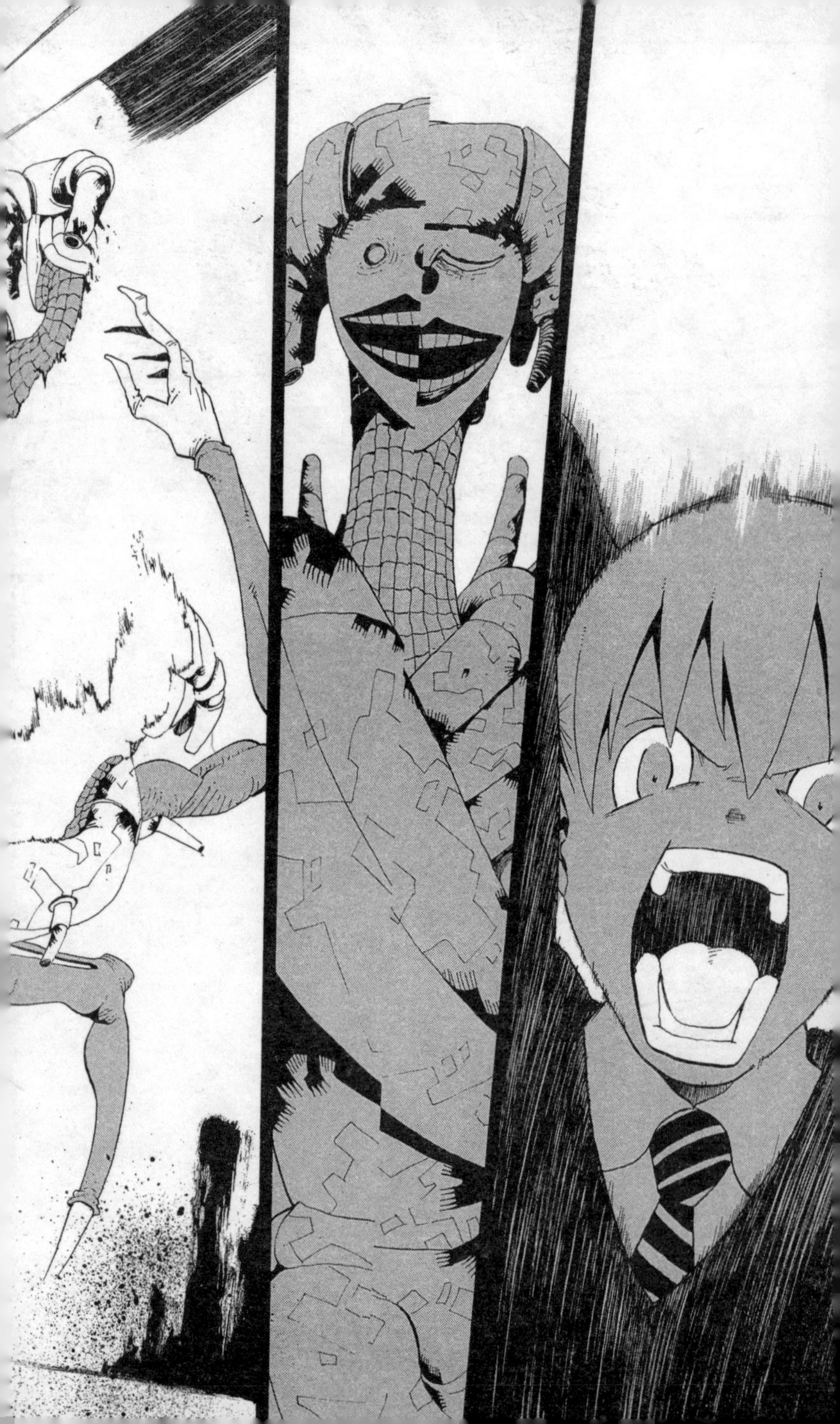

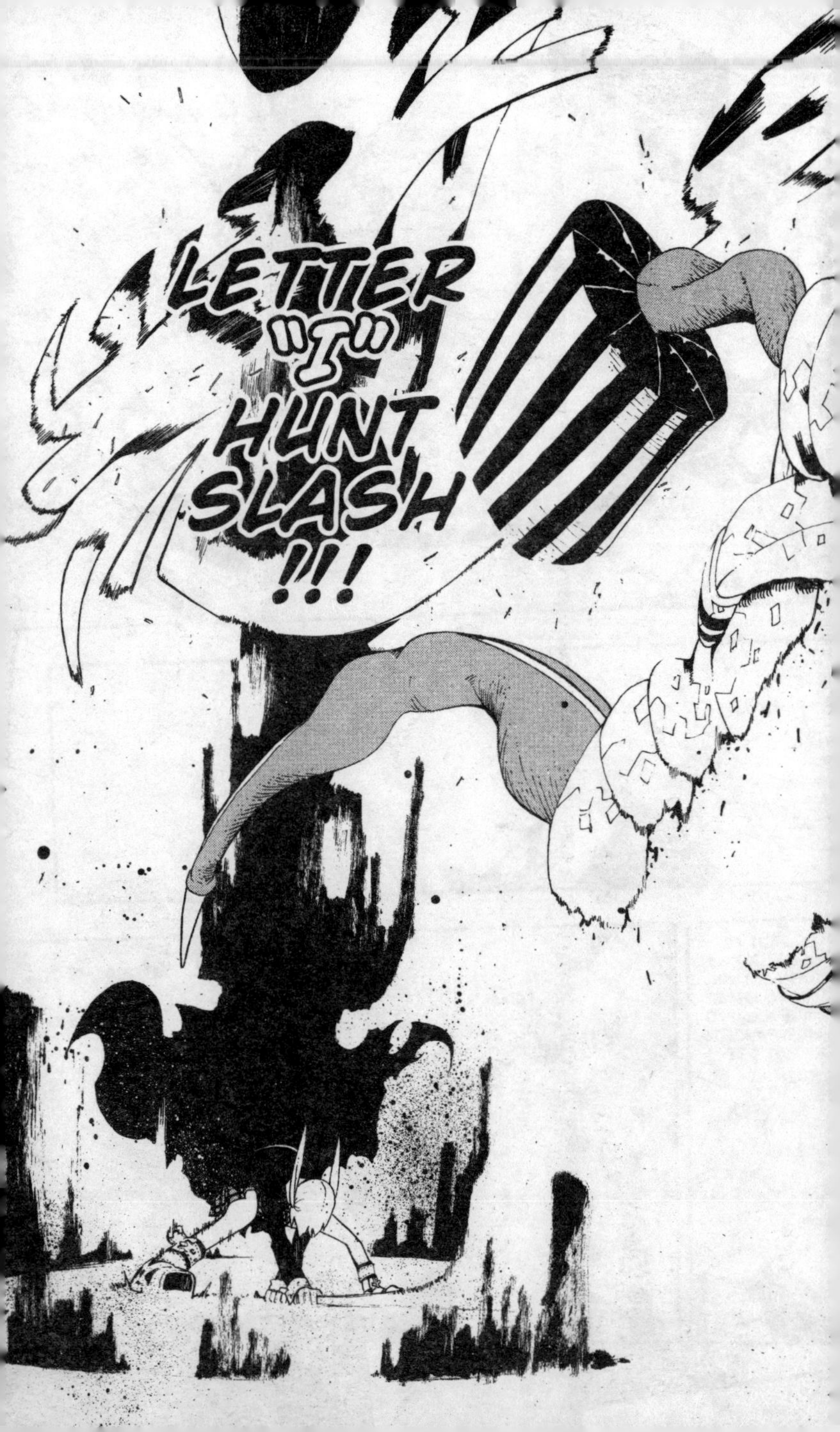
LETTER "I" HUNT SLASH !!!

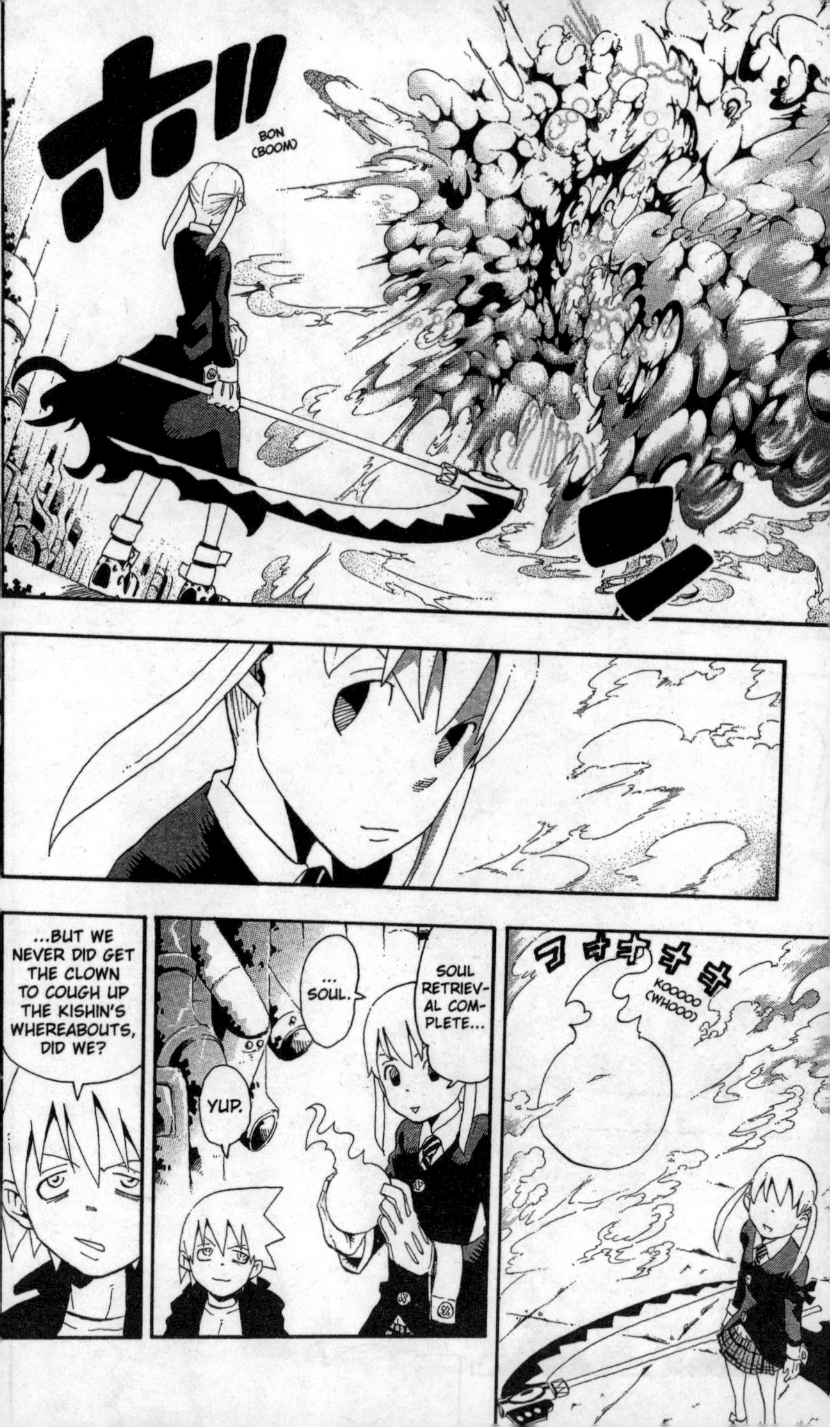
BON (BOOM)
KOOOOO (WHOOO)
SOUL RETRIEV-AL COM-PLETE...
... SOUL.
YUP.
...BUT WE NEVER DID GET THE CLOWN TO COUGH UP THE KISHIN'S WHEREABOUTS, DID WE?

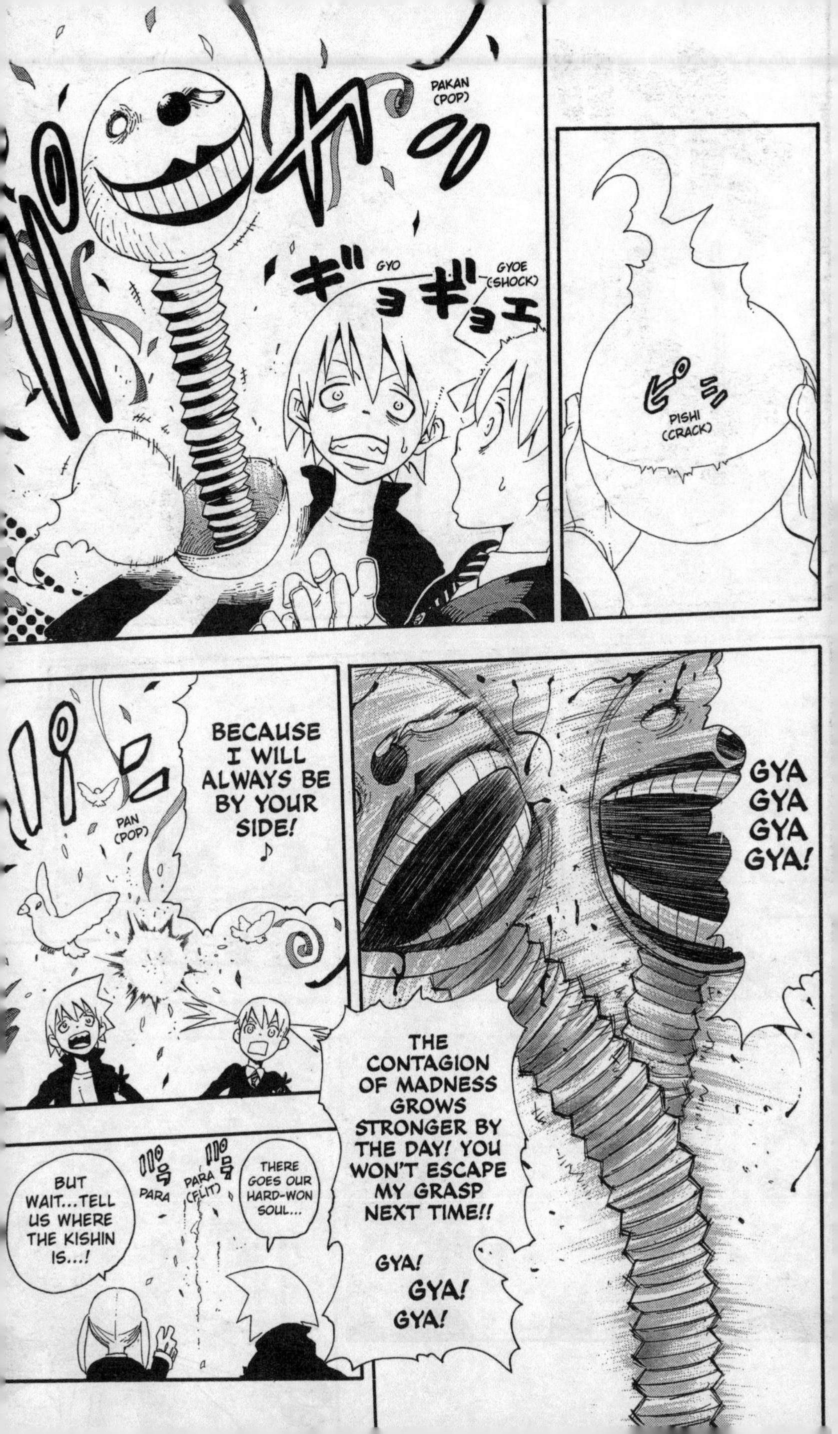
PISHI (CRACK)
PAKAN (POP)
ギョギョエ
GYO GYOE (SHOCK)
GYA GYA GYA GYA!
THE CONTAGION OF MADNESS GROWS STRONGER BY THE DAY! YOU WON'T ESCAPE MY GRASP NEXT TIME!!
GYA! GYA! GYA!
BECAUSE I WILL ALWAYS BE BY YOUR SIDE! ♪
PAN (POP)
THERE GOES OUR HARD-WON SOUL...
PARA PARA (FLIT)
BUT WAIT...TELL US WHERE THE KISHIN IS...!

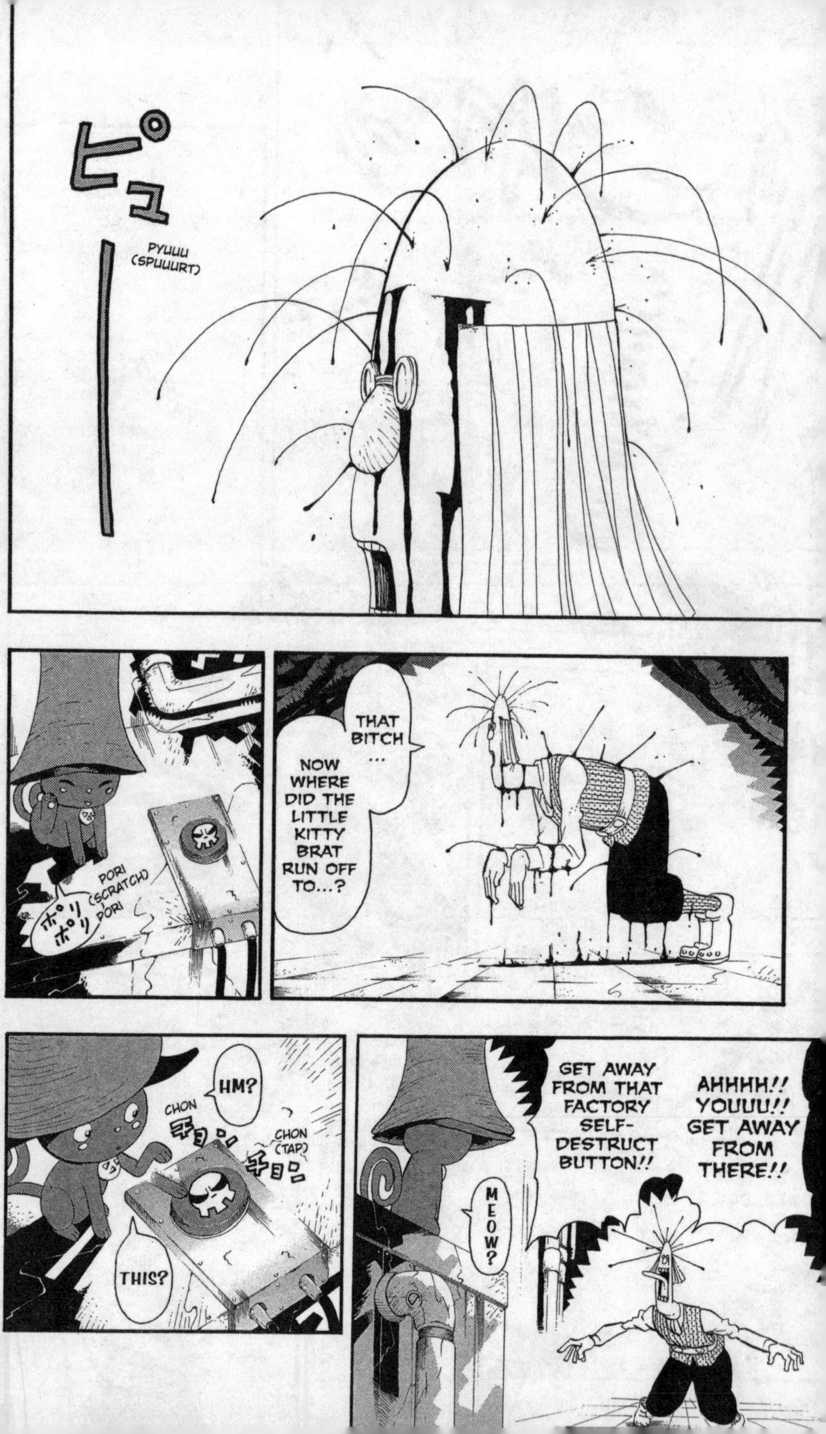
ピュ
PYUUU (SPUUURT)
THAT BITCH...
NOW WHERE DID THE LITTLE KITTY BRAT RUN OFF TO...?
ポリポリ
PORI (SCRATCH) PORI
AHHHH!! YOUUU!! GET AWAY FROM THERE!!
GET AWAY FROM THAT FACTORY SELF-DESTRUCT BUTTON!!
MEOW?
HM?
チョン チョン
CHON CHON (TAP)
THIS?

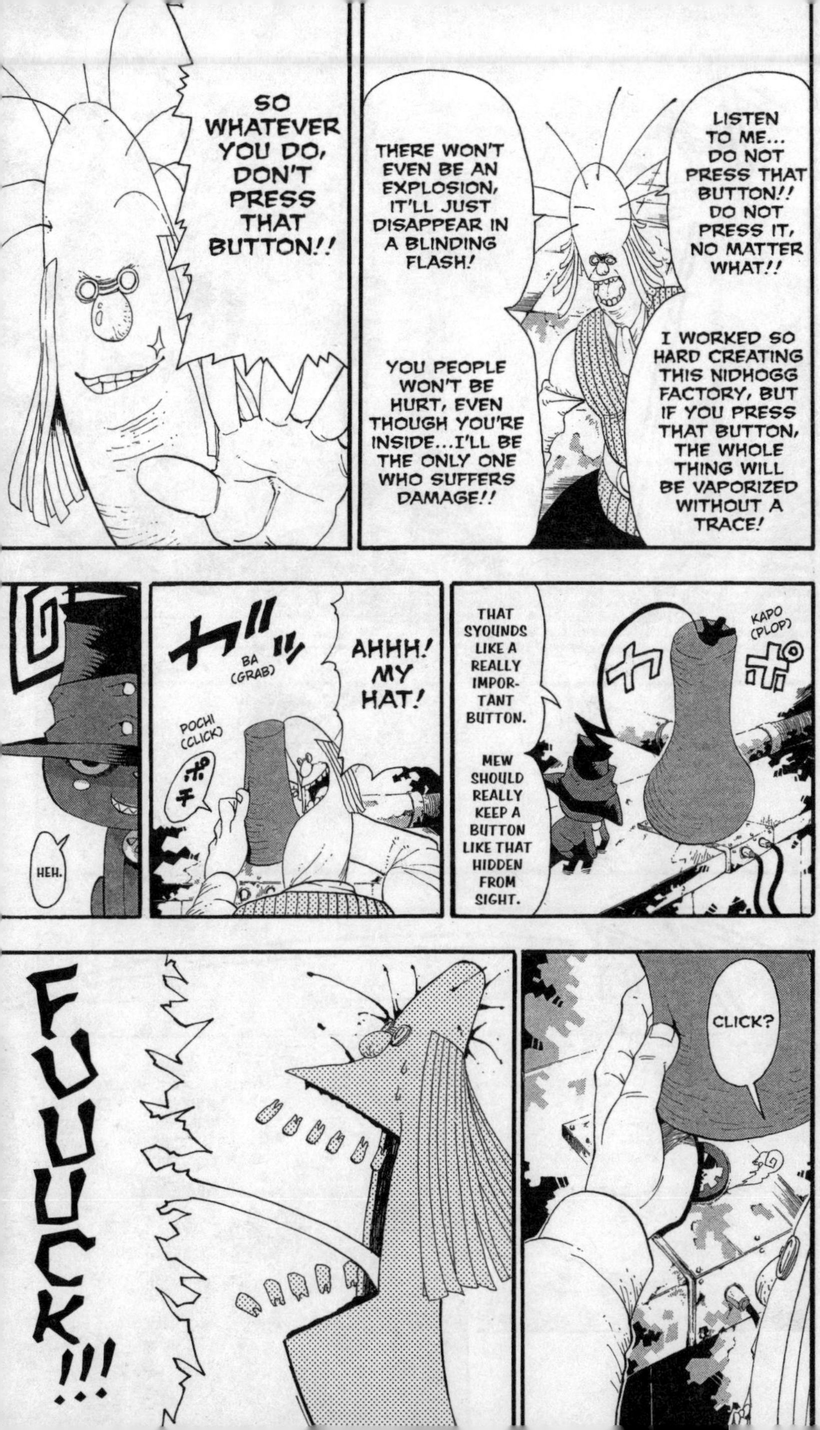
LISTEN TO ME... DO NOT PRESS THAT BUTTON!! DO NOT PRESS IT, NO MATTER WHAT!!
I WORKED SO HARD CREATING THIS NIDHOGG FACTORY, BUT IF YOU PRESS THAT BUTTON, THE WHOLE THING WILL BE VAPORIZED WITHOUT A TRACE!
THERE WON'T EVEN BE AN EXPLOSION, IT'LL JUST DISAPPEAR IN A BLINDING FLASH!
YOU PEOPLE WON'T BE HURT, EVEN THOUGH YOU'RE INSIDE...I'LL BE THE ONLY ONE WHO SUFFERS DAMAGE!!
SO WHATEVER YOU DO, DON'T PRESS THAT BUTTON!!
KAPO (PLOP)
THAT SYOUNDS LIKE A REALLY IMPORTANT BUTTON.
MEW SHOULD REALLY KEEP A BUTTON LIKE THAT HIDDEN FROM SIGHT.
BA (GRAB)
AHHH! MY HAT!
POCHI (CLICK)
HEH.
CLICK?
FUUUCK!!!

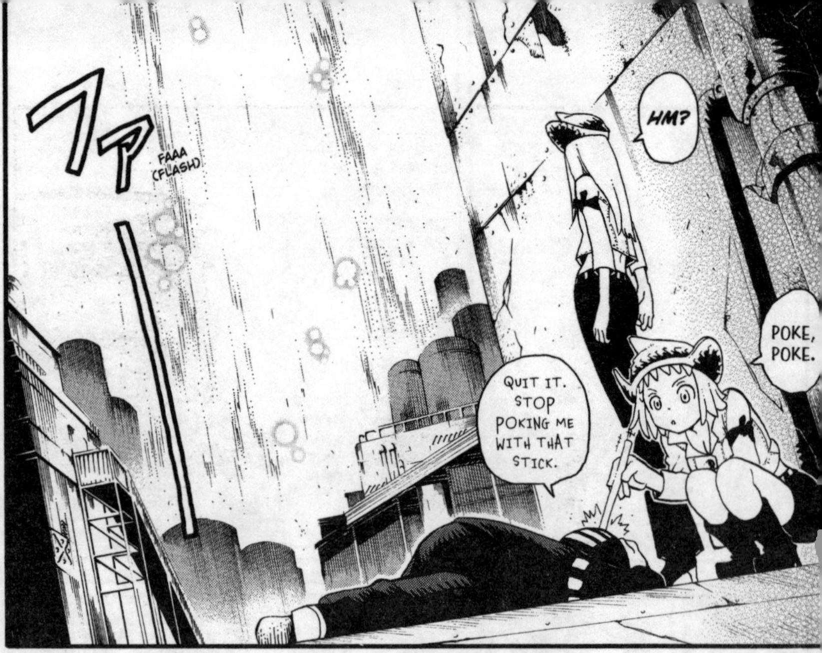
HM?
POKE, POKE.
QUIT IT. STOP POKING ME WITH THAT STICK.
FAAA (FLASH)

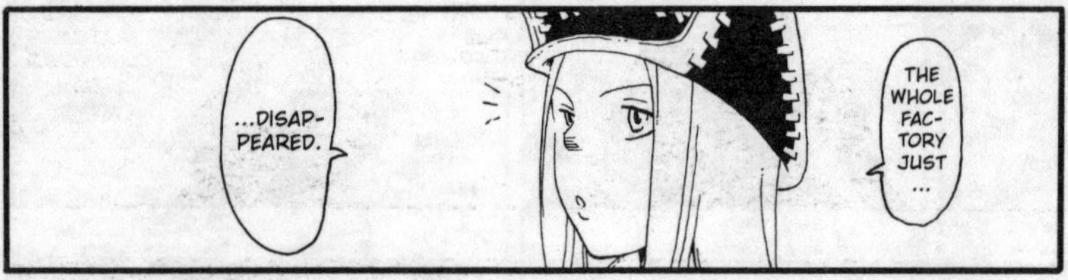
THE WHOLE FACTORY JUST...
...DISAPPEARED.

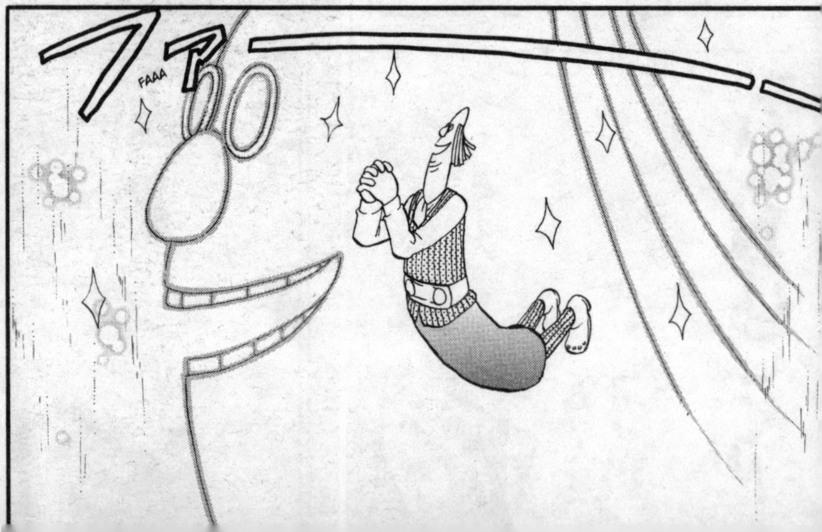
FAAA

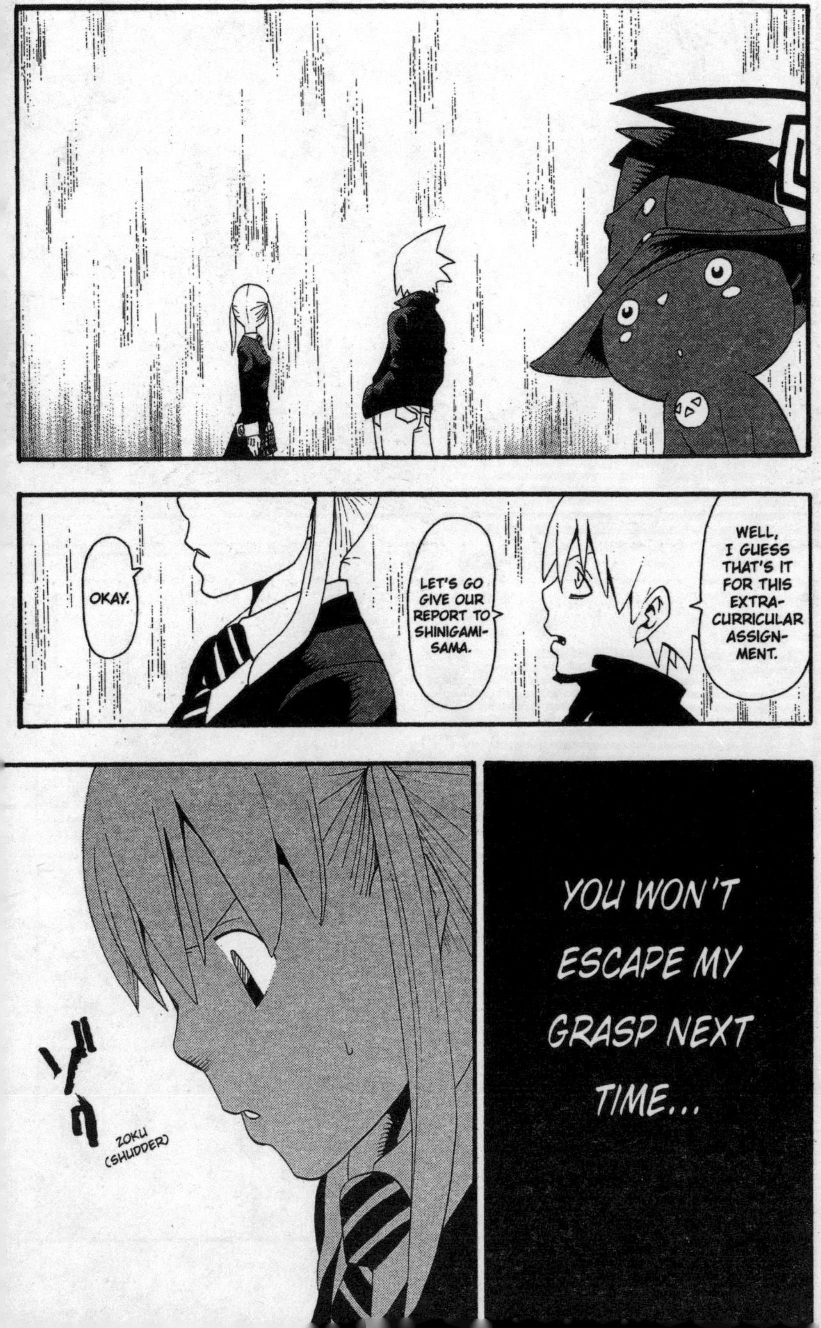
WELL, I GUESS THAT'S IT FOR THIS EXTRA-CURRICULAR ASSIGNMENT.
LET'S GO GIVE OUR REPORT TO SHINIGAMI-SAMA.
OKAY.
YOU WON'T ESCAPE MY GRASP NEXT TIME...
ZOKU (SHUDDER)

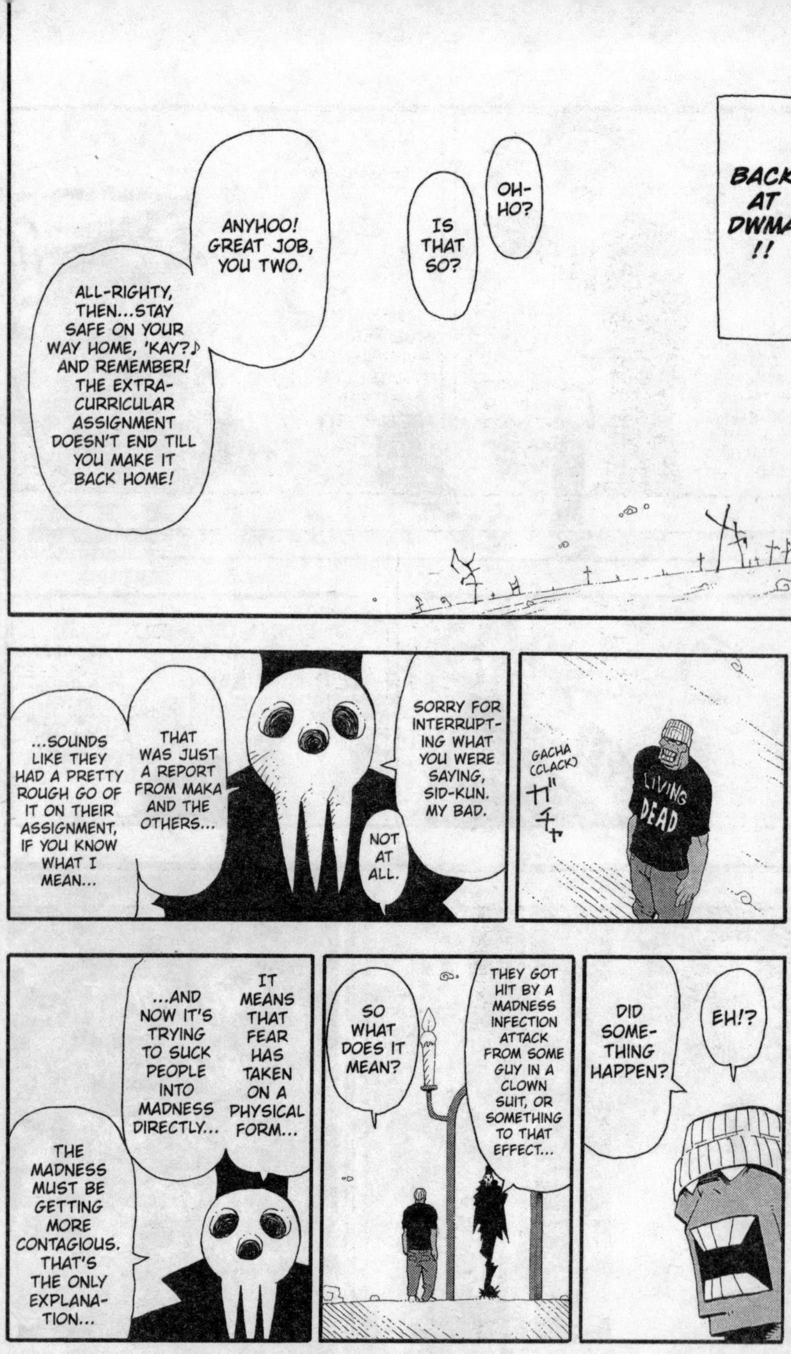
BACK AT DWMA!!
OH-HO?
IS THAT SO?
ANYHOO! GREAT JOB, YOU TWO.
ALL-RIGHTY, THEN...STAY SAFE ON YOUR WAY HOME, 'KAY?♪ AND REMEMBER! THE EXTRA-CURRICULAR ASSIGNMENT DOESN'T END TILL YOU MAKE IT BACK HOME!
GACHA (CLACK)
ガチャ
LIVING DEAD
SORRY FOR INTERRUPTING WHAT YOU WERE SAYING, SID-KUN. MY BAD.
NOT AT ALL.
THAT WAS JUST A REPORT FROM MAKA AND THE OTHERS...
...SOUNDS LIKE THEY HAD A PRETTY ROUGH GO OF IT ON THEIR ASSIGNMENT, IF YOU KNOW WHAT I MEAN...
EH!?
DID SOMETHING HAPPEN?
THEY GOT HIT BY A MADNESS INFECTION ATTACK FROM SOME GUY IN A CLOWN SUIT, OR SOMETHING TO THAT EFFECT...
SO WHAT DOES IT MEAN?
IT MEANS THAT FEAR HAS TAKEN ON A PHYSICAL FORM...
...AND NOW IT'S TRYING TO SUCK PEOPLE INTO MADNESS DIRECTLY...
THE MADNESS MUST BE GETTING MORE CONTAGIOUS. THAT'S THE ONLY EXPLANATION...

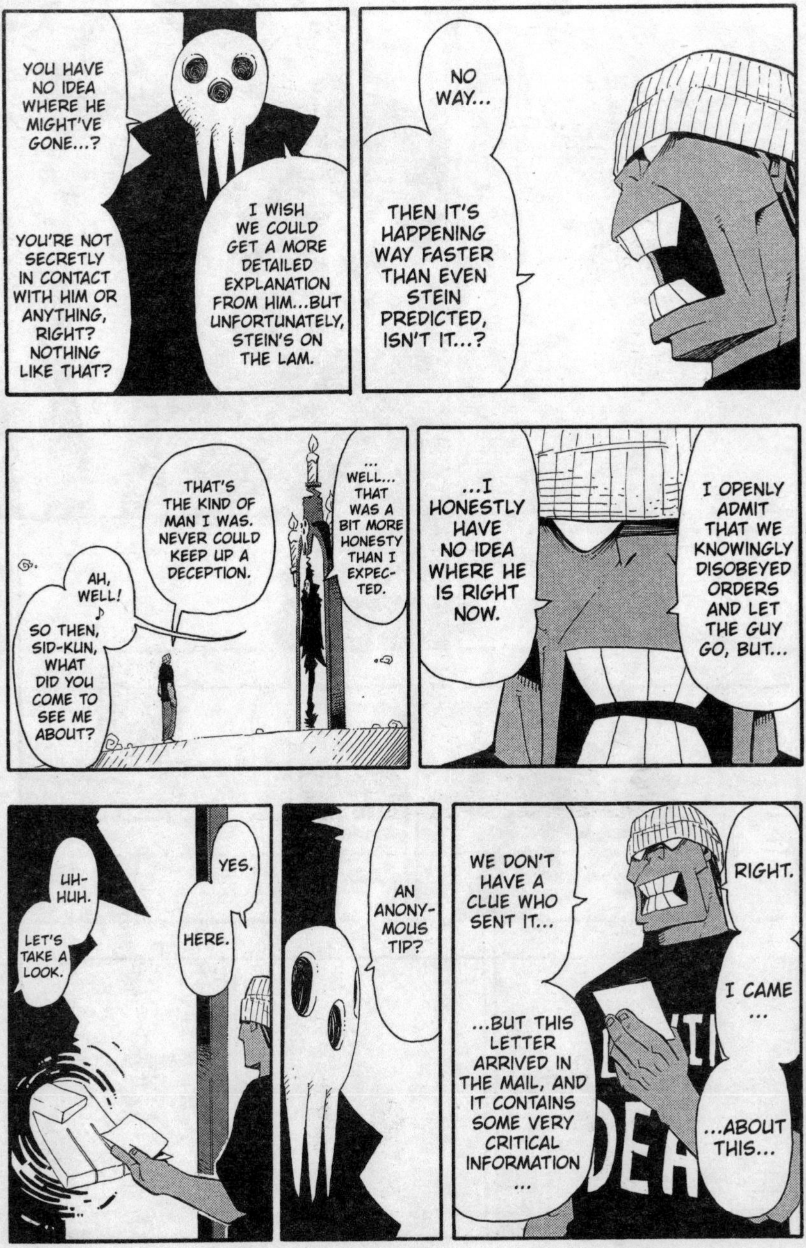
NO WAY...
THEN IT'S HAPPENING WAY FASTER THAN EVEN STEIN PREDICTED, ISN'T IT...?
I WISH WE COULD GET A MORE DETAILED EXPLANATION FROM HIM...BUT UNFORTUNATELY, STEIN'S ON THE LAM.
YOU HAVE NO IDEA WHERE HE MIGHT'VE GONE...?
YOU'RE NOT SECRETLY IN CONTACT WITH HIM OR ANYTHING, RIGHT? NOTHING LIKE THAT?
I OPENLY ADMIT THAT WE KNOWINGLY DISOBEYED ORDERS AND LET THE GUY GO, BUT...
...I HONESTLY HAVE NO IDEA WHERE HE IS RIGHT NOW.
... WELL... THAT WAS A BIT MORE HONESTY THAN I EXPEC-TED.
THAT'S THE KIND OF MAN I WAS. NEVER COULD KEEP UP A DECEPTION.
AH, WELL! ♪
SO THEN, SID-KUN, WHAT DID YOU COME TO SEE ME ABOUT?
RIGHT.
I CAME ...
...ABOUT THIS...
WE DON'T HAVE A CLUE WHO SENT IT...
...BUT THIS LETTER ARRIVED IN THE MAIL, AND IT CONTAINS SOME VERY CRITICAL INFORMATION ...
AN ANONY-MOUS TIP?
YES.
HERE.
UH-HUH.
LET'S TAKE A LOOK.

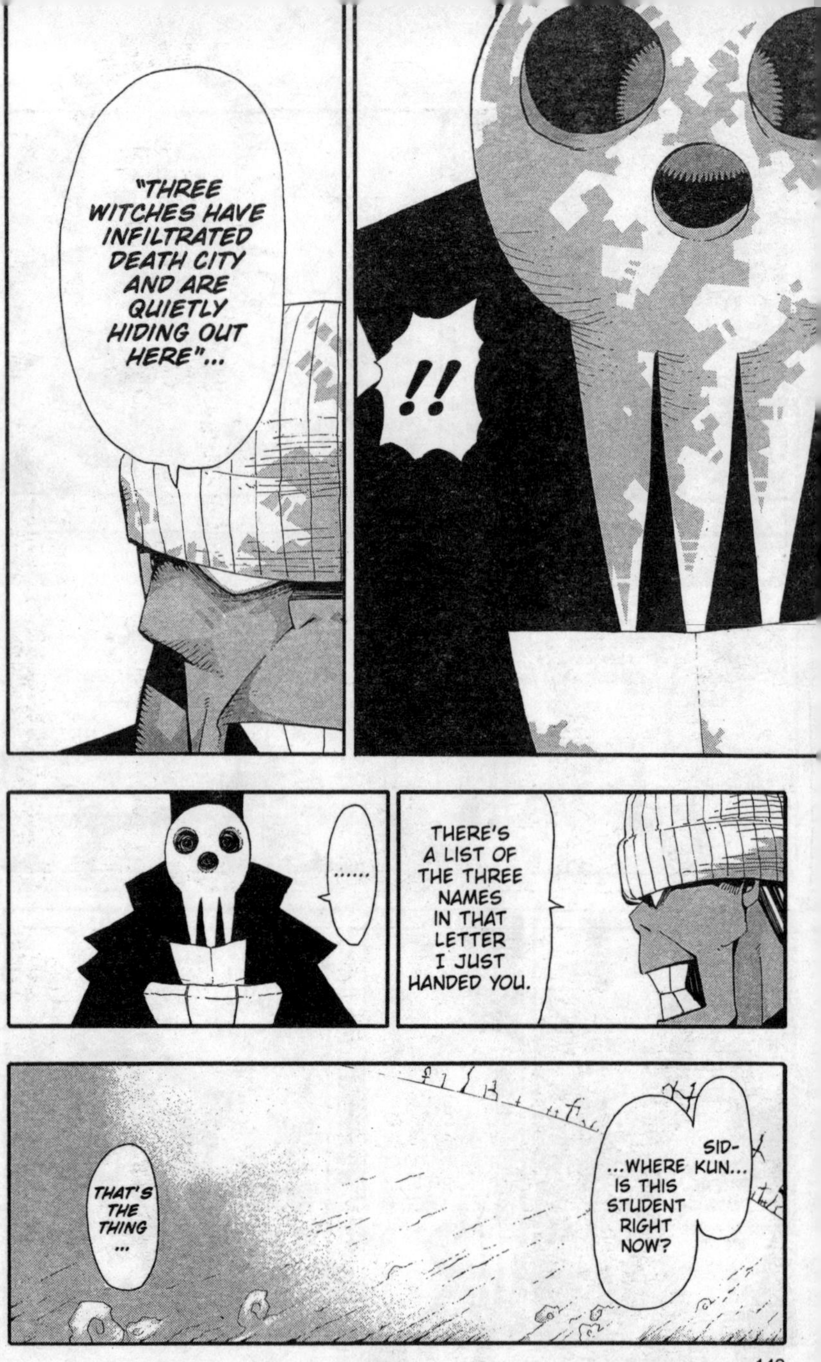
!!
"THREE WITCHES HAVE INFILTRATED DEATH CITY AND ARE QUIETLY HIDING OUT HERE"...
THERE'S A LIST OF THE THREE NAMES IN THAT LETTER I JUST HANDED YOU.
......
SID-KUN... ...WHERE IS THIS STUDENT RIGHT NOW?
THAT'S THE THING...

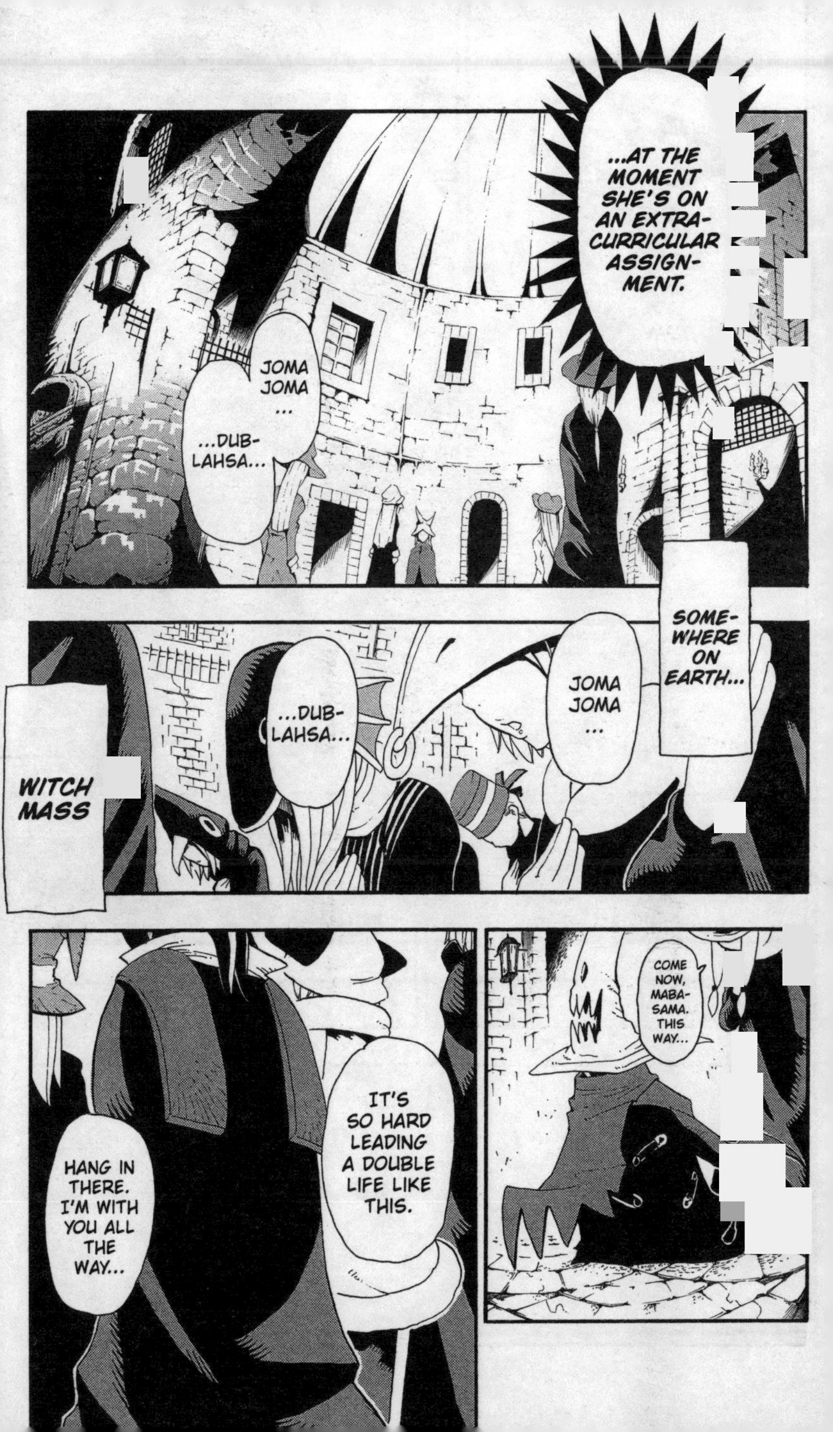
...AT THE MOMENT SHE'S ON AN EXTRA-CURRICULAR ASSIGNMENT.
JOMA JOMA ...
...DUB-LAHSA...
SOME-WHERE ON EARTH...
JOMA JOMA ...
...DUB-LAHSA...
WITCH MASS
COME NOW, MABA-SAMA. THIS WAY...
IT'S SO HARD LEADING A DOUBLE LIFE LIKE THIS.
HANG IN THERE. I'M WITH YOU ALL THE WAY...

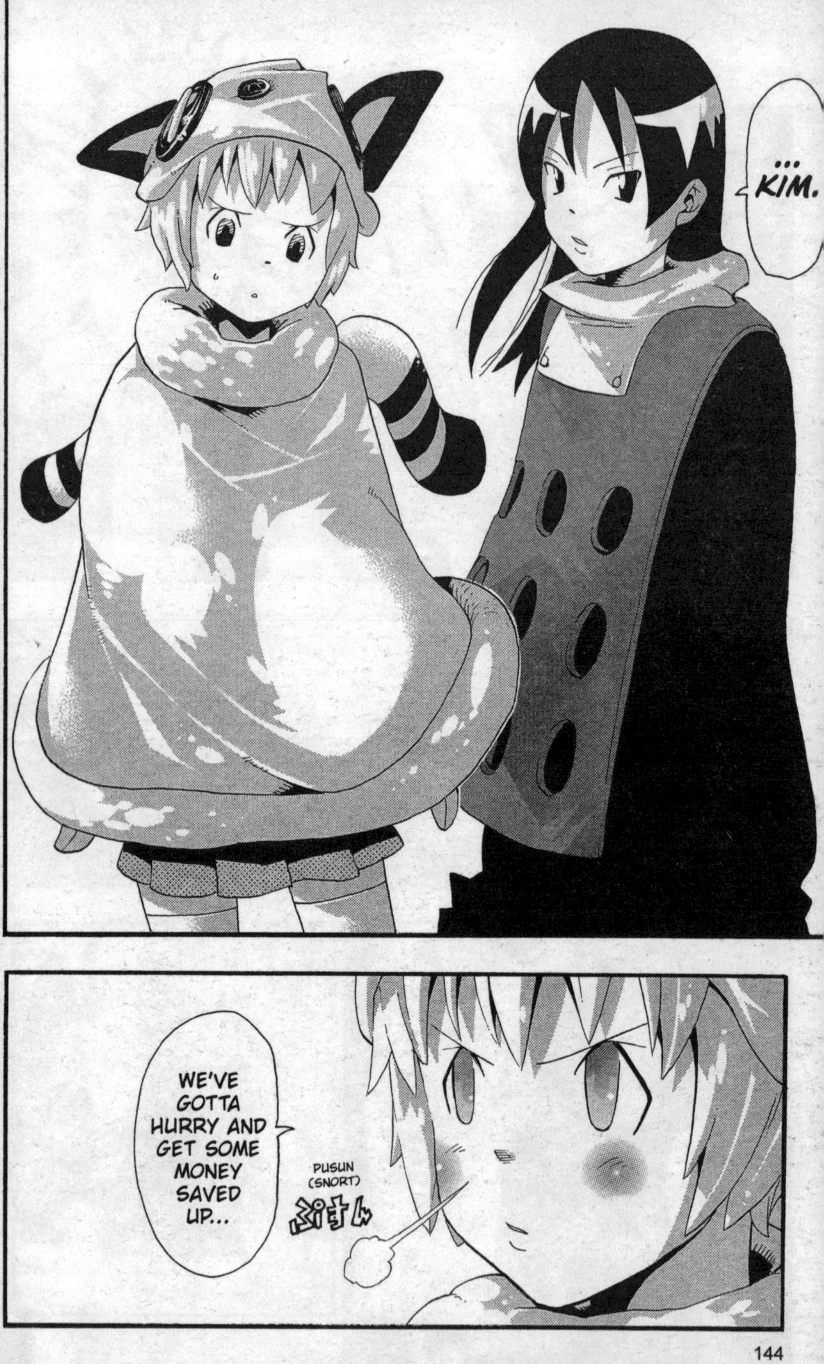
...KIM.
WE'VE GOTTA HURRY AND GET SOME MONEY SAVED UP...
PUSUN (SNORT)
ぷすん

SOUL EATER

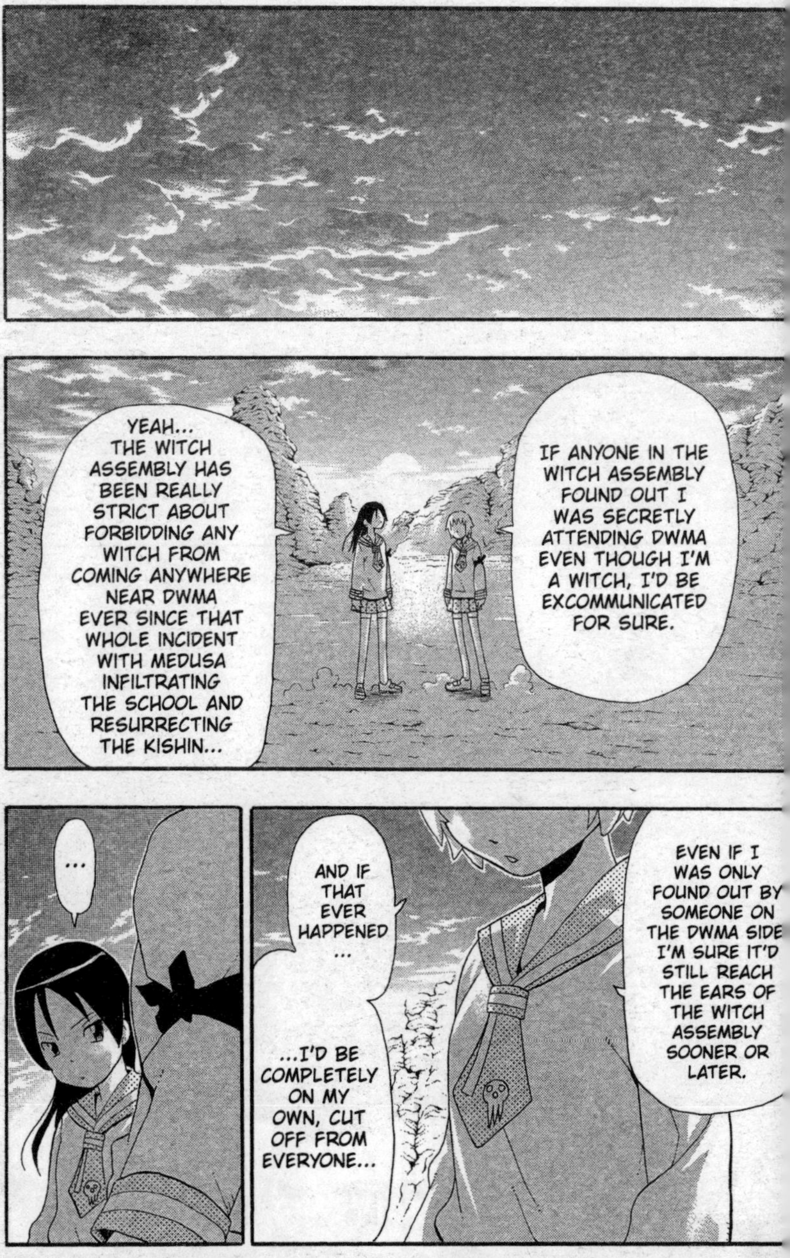
IF ANYONE IN THE WITCH ASSEMBLY FOUND OUT I WAS SECRETLY ATTENDING DWMA EVEN THOUGH I'M A WITCH, I'D BE EXCOMMUNICATED FOR SURE.
YEAH... THE WITCH ASSEMBLY HAS BEEN REALLY STRICT ABOUT FORBIDDING ANY WITCH FROM COMING ANYWHERE NEAR DWMA EVER SINCE THAT WHOLE INCIDENT WITH MEDUSA INFILTRATING THE SCHOOL AND RESURRECTING THE KISHIN...
EVEN IF I WAS ONLY FOUND OUT BY SOMEONE ON THE DWMA SIDE I'M SURE IT'D STILL REACH THE EARS OF THE WITCH ASSEMBLY SOONER OR LATER.
AND IF THAT EVER HAPPENED ...
...I'D BE COMPLETELY ON MY OWN, CUT OFF FROM EVERYONE...
...

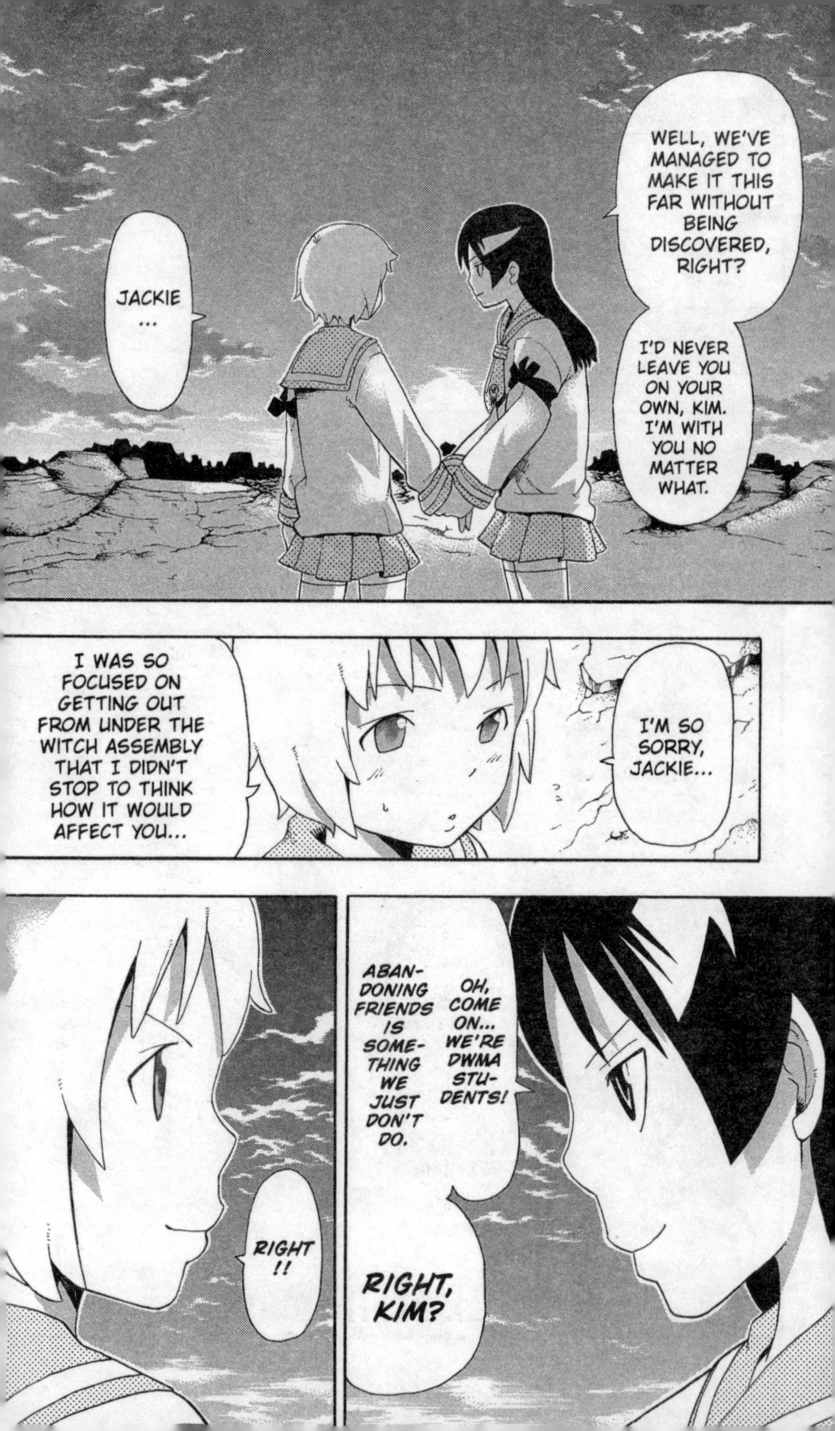
WELL, WE'VE MANAGED TO MAKE IT THIS FAR WITHOUT BEING DISCOVERED, RIGHT?
I'D NEVER LEAVE YOU ON YOUR OWN, KIM. I'M WITH YOU NO MATTER WHAT.
JACKIE ...
I'M SO SORRY, JACKIE...
I WAS SO FOCUSED ON GETTING OUT FROM UNDER THE WITCH ASSEMBLY THAT I DIDN'T STOP TO THINK HOW IT WOULD AFFECT YOU...
OH, COME ON... WE'RE DWMA STU-DENTS!
ABAN-DONING FRIENDS IS SOME-THING WE JUST DON'T DO.
RIGHT, KIM?
RIGHT !!

LET'S HEAD BACK HOME TO DWMA NOW, SHALL WE?

CHAPTER 44: THE CHOICE

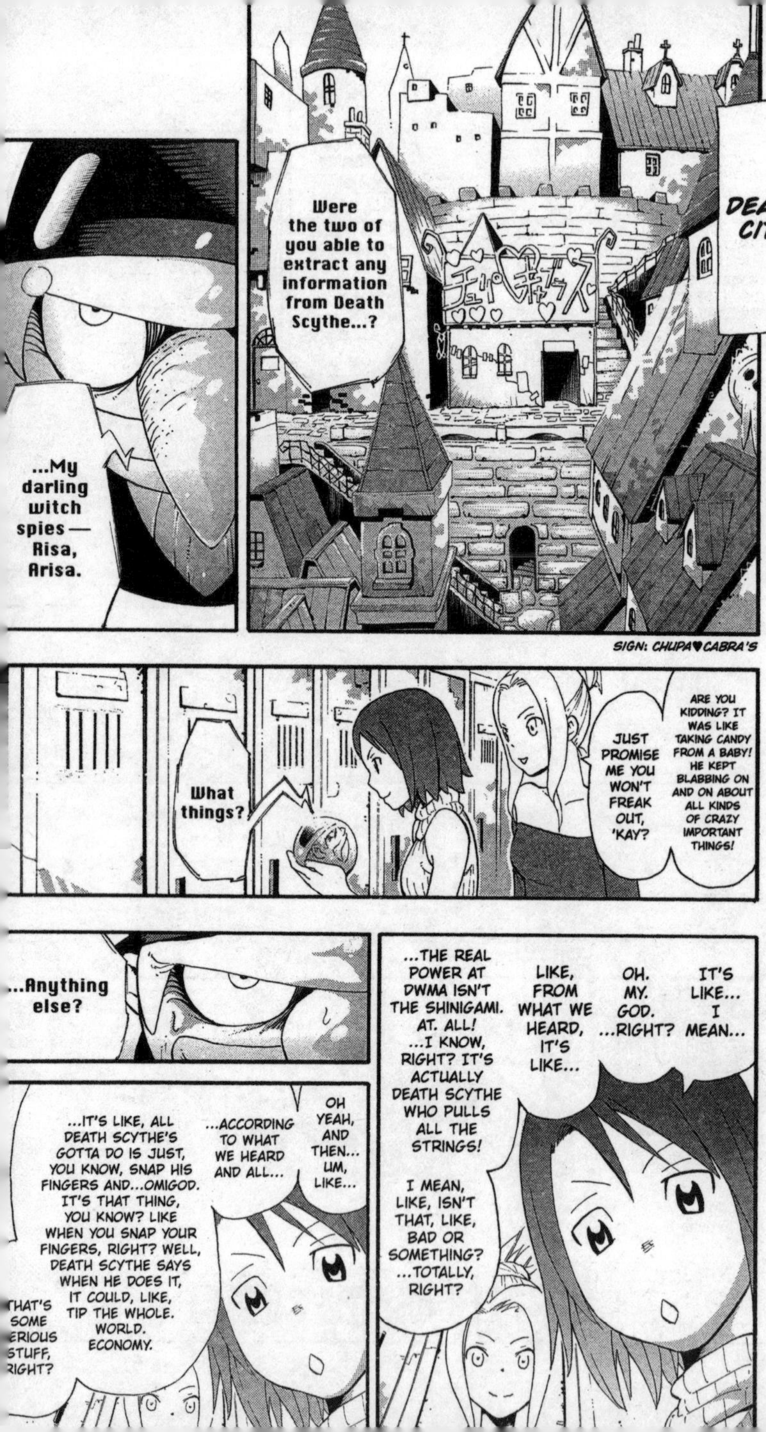
DEATH CITY
Were the two of you able to extract any information from Death Scythe...?
...My darling witch spies— Risa, Arisa.
SIGN: CHUPA♥CABRA'S
ARE YOU KIDDING? IT WAS LIKE TAKING CANDY FROM A BABY! HE KEPT BLABBING ON AND ON ABOUT ALL KINDS OF CRAZY IMPORTANT THINGS!
JUST PROMISE ME YOU WON'T FREAK OUT, 'KAY?
What things?
IT'S LIKE... I MEAN...
OH. MY. GOD. ...RIGHT?
LIKE, FROM WHAT WE HEARD, IT'S LIKE...
...THE REAL POWER AT DWMA ISN'T THE SHINIGAMI. AT. ALL! ...I KNOW, RIGHT? IT'S ACTUALLY DEATH SCYTHE WHO PULLS ALL THE STRINGS!
I MEAN, LIKE, ISN'T THAT, LIKE, BAD OR SOMETHING? ...TOTALLY, RIGHT?
...Anything else?
OH YEAH, AND THEN... UM, LIKE...
...ACCORDING TO WHAT WE HEARD AND ALL...
...IT'S LIKE, ALL DEATH SCYTHE'S GOTTA DO IS JUST, YOU KNOW, SNAP HIS FINGERS AND...OMIGOD. IT'S THAT THING, YOU KNOW? LIKE WHEN YOU SNAP YOUR FINGERS, RIGHT? WELL, DEATH SCYTHE SAYS WHEN HE DOES IT, IT COULD, LIKE, TIP THE WHOLE. WORLD. ECONOMY.
THAT'S SOME ERIOUS STUFF, IGHT?

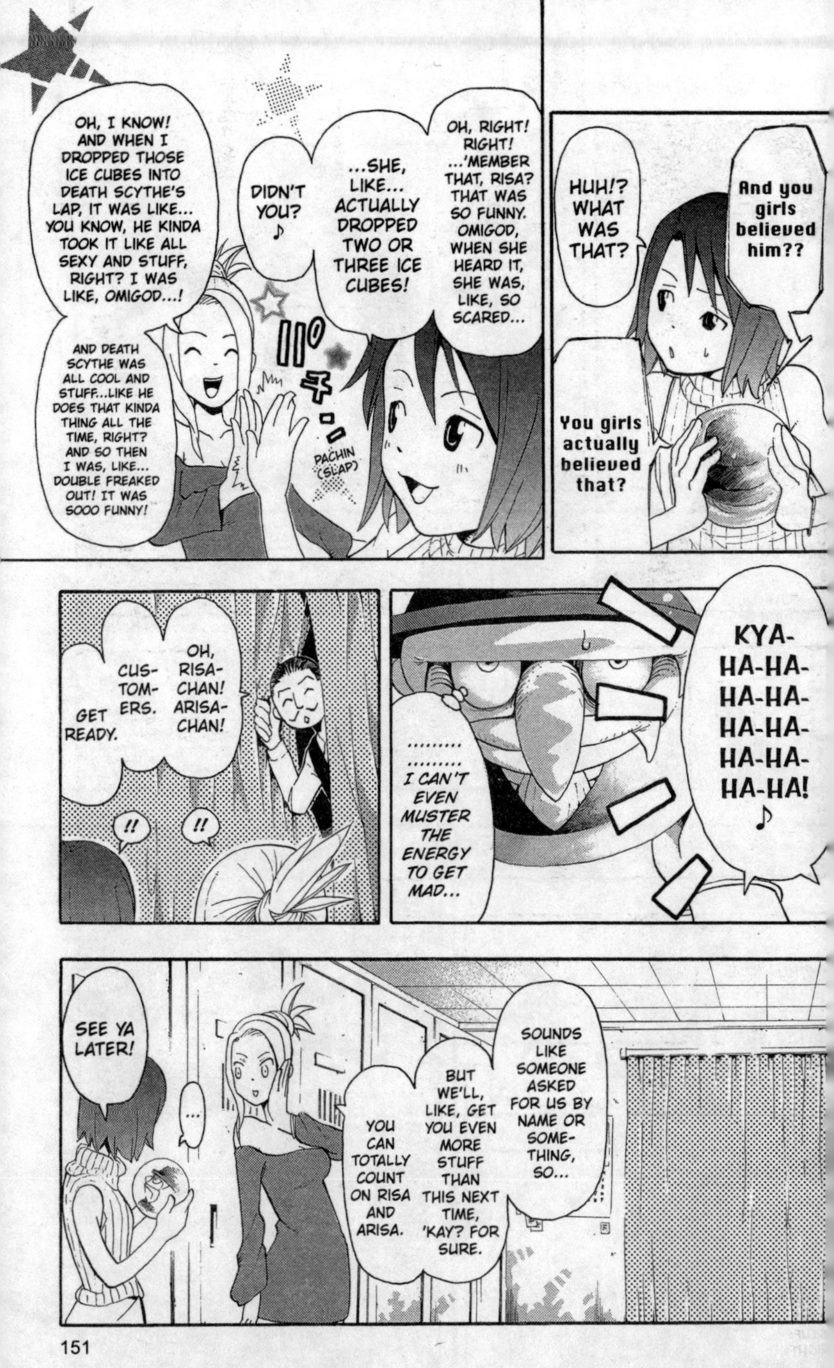
And you girls believed him??
HUH!? WHAT WAS THAT?
You girls actually believed that?
OH, RIGHT! RIGHT! ...'MEMBER THAT, RISA? THAT WAS SO FUNNY. OMIGOD, WHEN SHE HEARD IT, SHE WAS, LIKE, SO SCARED...
...SHE, LIKE... ACTUALLY DROPPED TWO OR THREE ICE CUBES!
DIDN'T YOU? ♪
OH, I KNOW! AND WHEN I DROPPED THOSE ICE CUBES INTO DEATH SCYTHE'S LAP, IT WAS LIKE... YOU KNOW, HE KINDA TOOK IT LIKE ALL SEXY AND STUFF, RIGHT? I WAS LIKE, OMIGOD...!
PACHIN (SLAP)
AND DEATH SCYTHE WAS ALL COOL AND STUFF...LIKE HE DOES THAT KINDA THING ALL THE TIME, RIGHT? AND SO THEN I WAS, LIKE... DOUBLE FREAKED OUT! IT WAS SOOO FUNNY!
KYA-HA-HA-HA-HA-HA-HA-HA-HA-HA-HA! ♪
.... I CAN'T EVEN MUSTER THE ENERGY TO GET MAD...
OH, RISA-CHAN! ARISA-CHAN!
CUS-TOM-ERS. GET READY.
!!
!!
SOUNDS LIKE SOMEONE ASKED FOR US BY NAME OR SOME-THING, SO...
BUT WE'LL, LIKE, GET YOU EVEN MORE STUFF THAN THIS NEXT TIME, 'KAY? FOR SURE.
YOU CAN TOTALLY COUNT ON RISA AND ARISA.
...
SEE YA LATER!

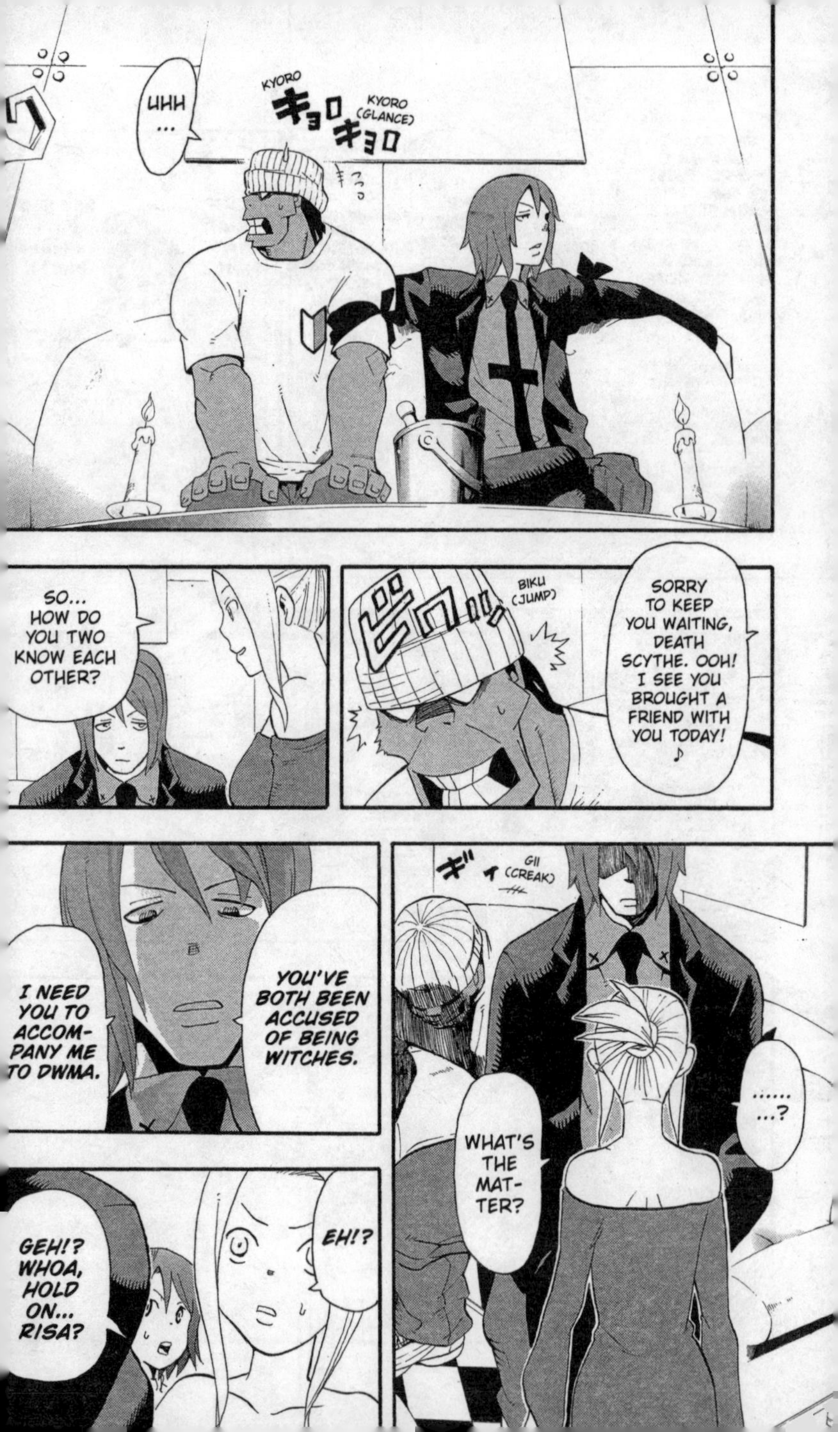
KYORO
KYORO (GLANCE)
UHH ...
SORRY TO KEEP YOU WAITING, DEATH SCYTHE. OOH! I SEE YOU BROUGHT A FRIEND WITH YOU TODAY! ♪
BIKU (JUMP)
SO... HOW DO YOU TWO KNOW EACH OTHER?
GII (CREAK)
......?
WHAT'S THE MAT-TER?
YOU'VE BOTH BEEN ACCUSED OF BEING WITCHES.
I NEED YOU TO ACCOM-PANY ME TO DWMA.
EH!?
GEH!? WHOA, HOLD ON... RISA?

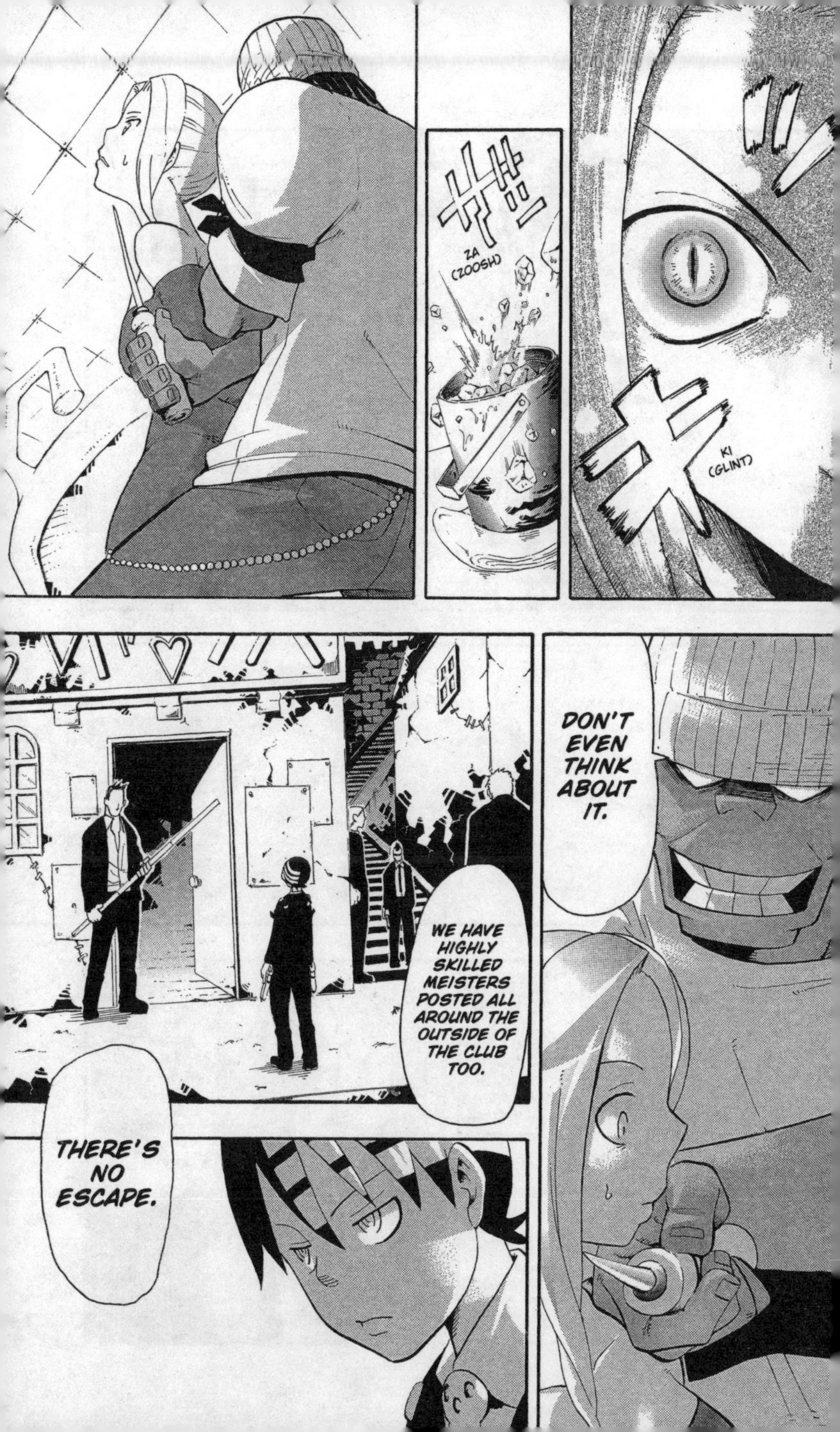
KI (GLINT)
ZA (ZOOSH)
DON'T EVEN THINK ABOUT IT.
WE HAVE HIGHLY SKILLED MEISTERS POSTED ALL AROUND THE OUTSIDE OF THE CLUB TOO.
THERE'S NO ESCAPE.

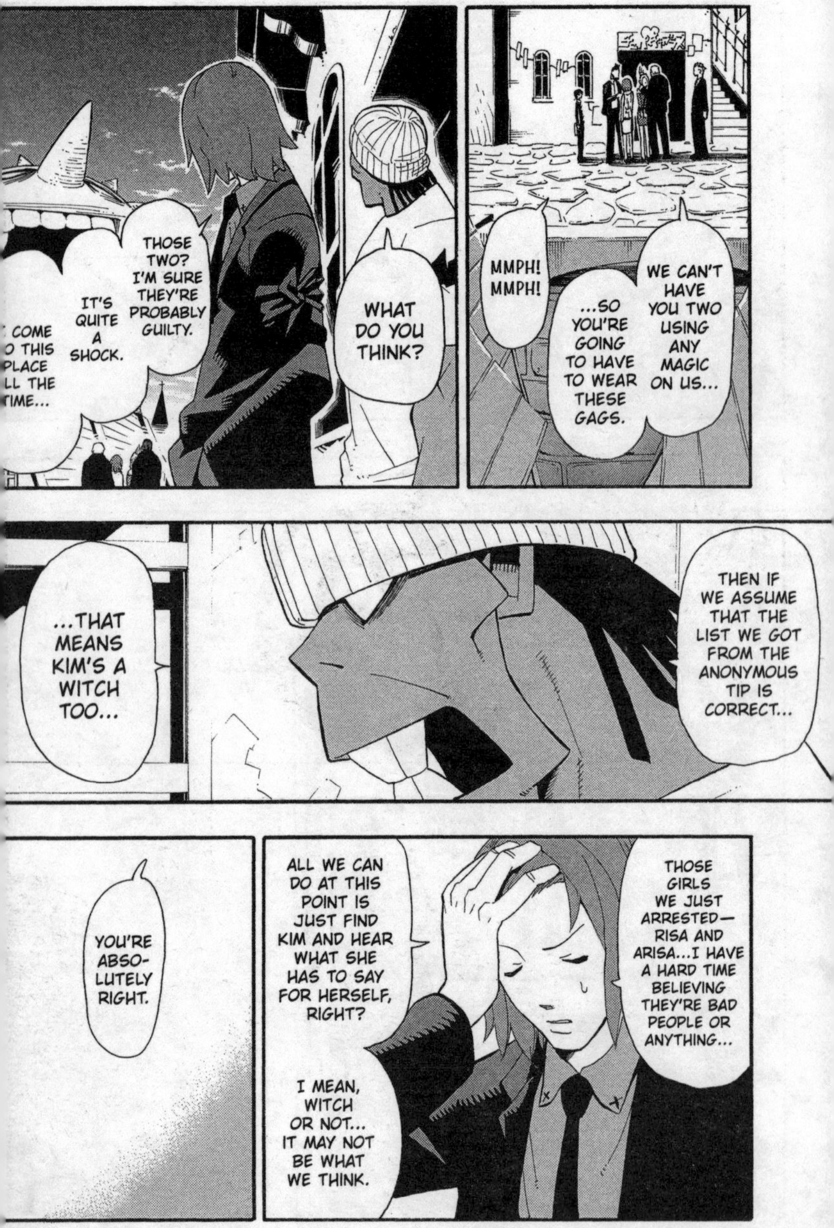
WE CAN'T HAVE YOU TWO USING ANY MAGIC ON US...
...SO YOU'RE GOING TO HAVE TO WEAR THESE GAGS.
MMPH! MMPH!
WHAT DO YOU THINK?
THOSE TWO? I'M SURE THEY'RE PROBABLY GUILTY.
IT'S QUITE A SHOCK.
COME O THIS PLACE LL THE TIME...
THEN IF WE ASSUME THAT THE LIST WE GOT FROM THE ANONYMOUS TIP IS CORRECT...
...THAT MEANS KIM'S A WITCH TOO...
THOSE GIRLS WE JUST ARRESTED—RISA AND ARISA...I HAVE A HARD TIME BELIEVING THEY'RE BAD PEOPLE OR ANYTHING...
ALL WE CAN DO AT THIS POINT IS JUST FIND KIM AND HEAR WHAT SHE HAS TO SAY FOR HERSELF, RIGHT?
I MEAN, WITCH OR NOT... IT MAY NOT BE WHAT WE THINK.
YOU'RE ABSOLUTELY RIGHT.

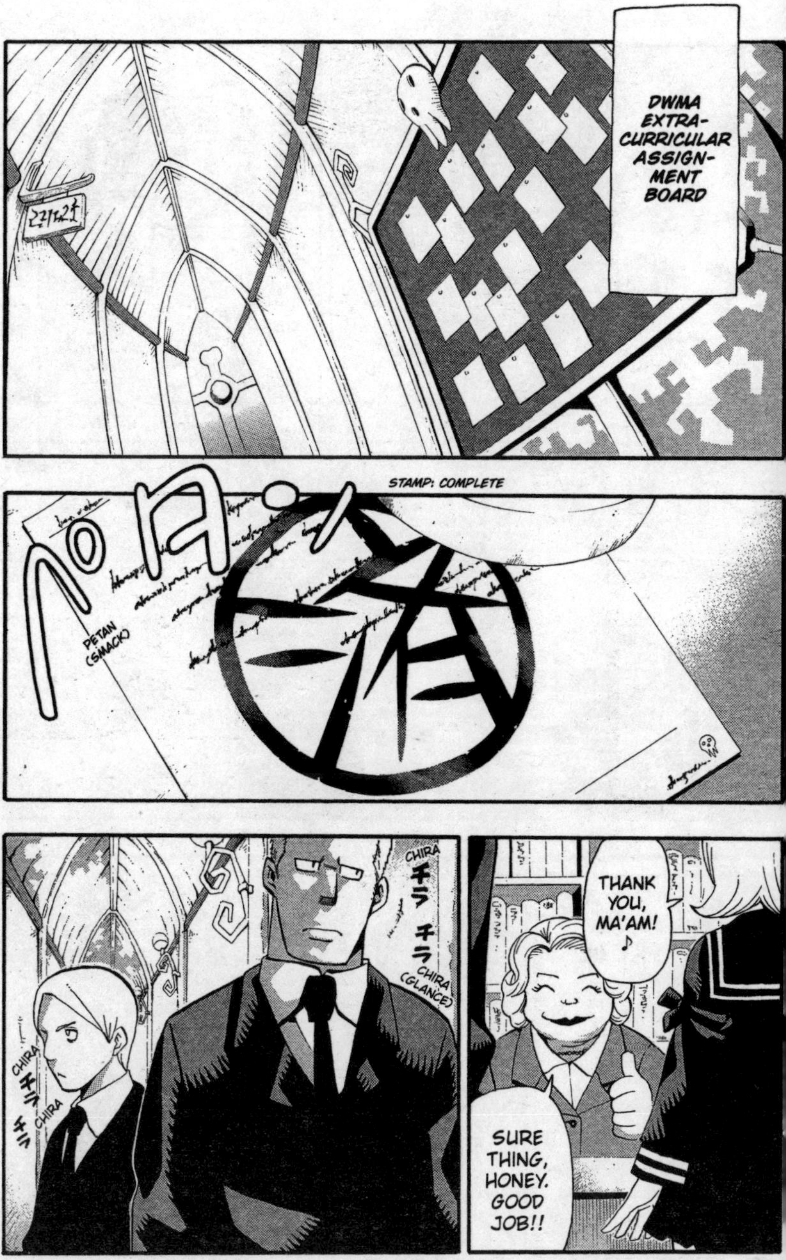
DWMA EXTRA-CURRICULAR ASSIGNMENT BOARD
STAMP: COMPLETE
PETAN (SMACK)
THANK YOU, MA'AM! ♪
SURE THING, HONEY. GOOD JOB!!
CHIRA チラ チラ CHIRA (GLANCE)
CHIRA チラ チラ CHIRA

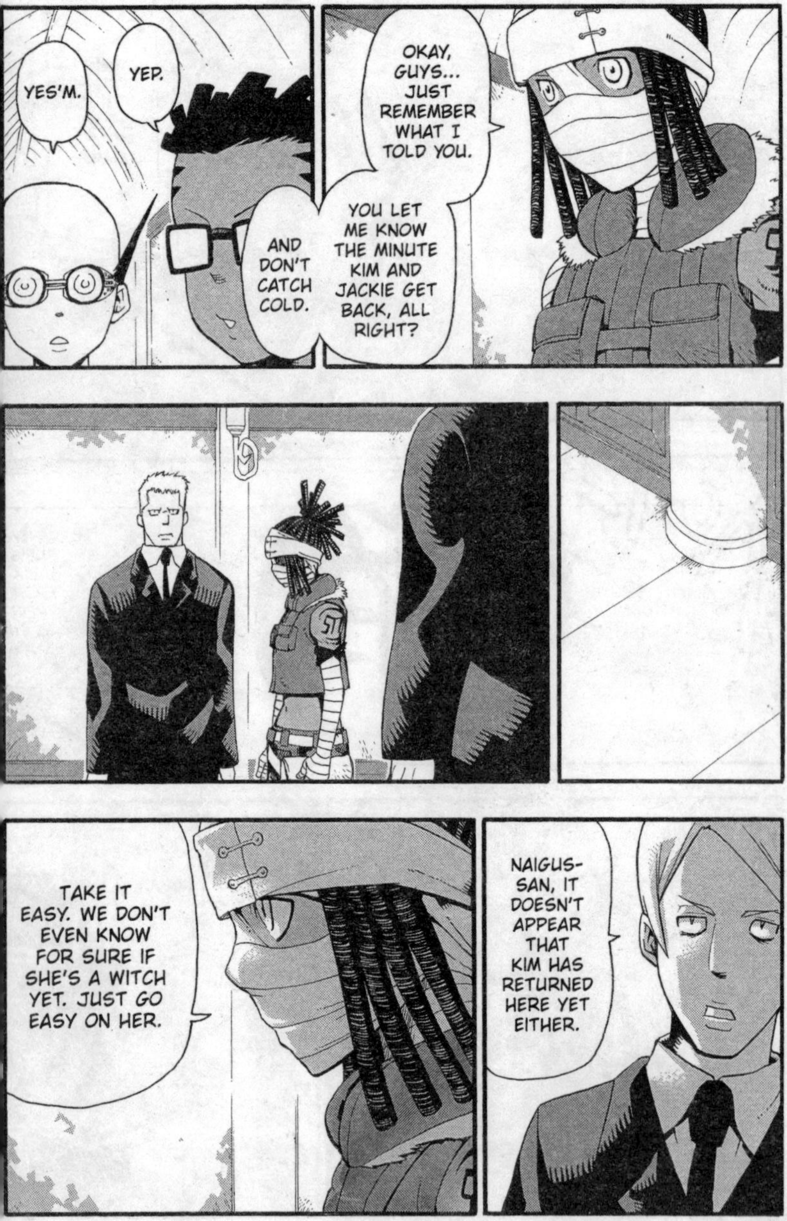
OKAY, GUYS... JUST REMEMBER WHAT I TOLD YOU.
YOU LET ME KNOW THE MINUTE KIM AND JACKIE GET BACK, ALL RIGHT?
AND DON'T CATCH COLD.
YEP.
YES'M.
NAIGUS-SAN, IT DOESN'T APPEAR THAT KIM HAS RETURNED HERE YET EITHER.
TAKE IT EASY. WE DON'T EVEN KNOW FOR SURE IF SHE'S A WITCH YET. JUST GO EASY ON HER.

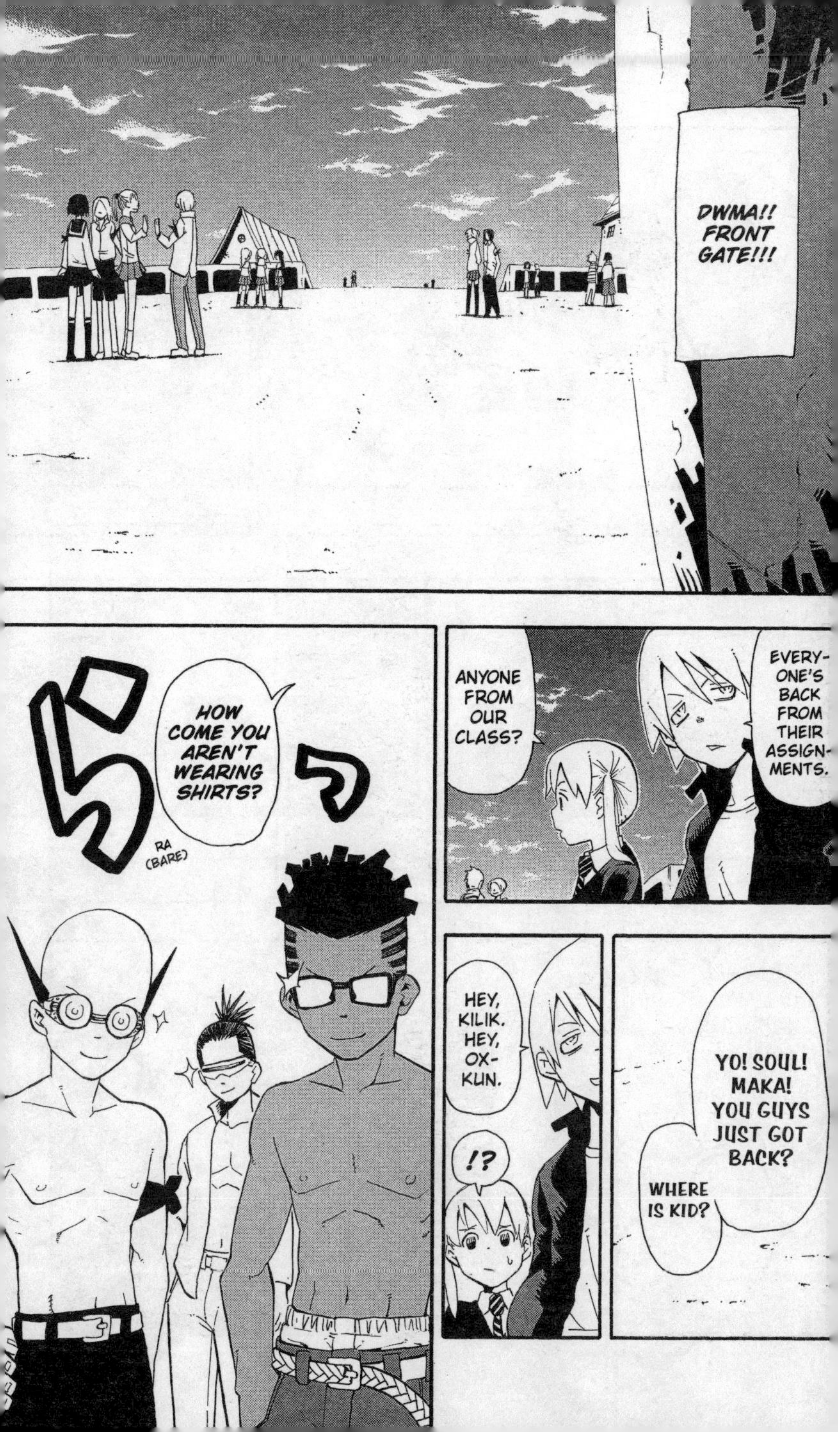
DWMA!! FRONT GATE!!!
EVERY-ONE'S BACK FROM THEIR ASSIGN-MENTS.
ANYONE FROM OUR CLASS?
YO! SOUL! MAKA! YOU GUYS JUST GOT BACK?
WHERE IS KID?
HEY, KILIK. HEY, OX-KUN.
!?
HOW COME YOU AREN'T WEARING SHIRTS?
RA (BARE)

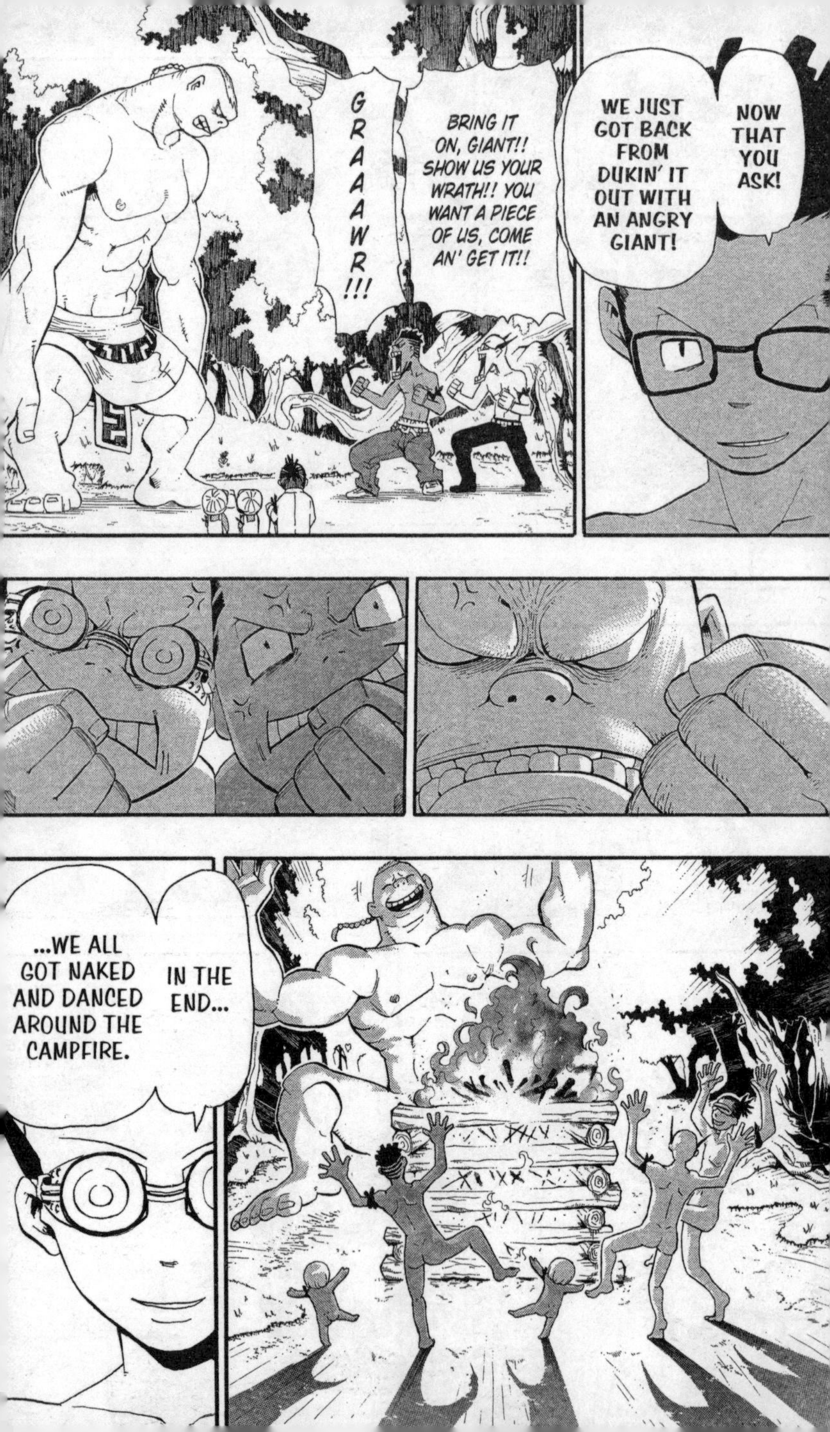
NOW THAT YOU ASK!
WE JUST GOT BACK FROM DUKIN' IT OUT WITH AN ANGRY GIANT!
BRING IT ON, GIANT!! SHOW US YOUR WRATH!! YOU WANT A PIECE OF US, COME AN' GET IT!!
GRAAAAWR!!!
IN THE END...
...WE ALL GOT NAKED AND DANCED AROUND THE CAMPFIRE.

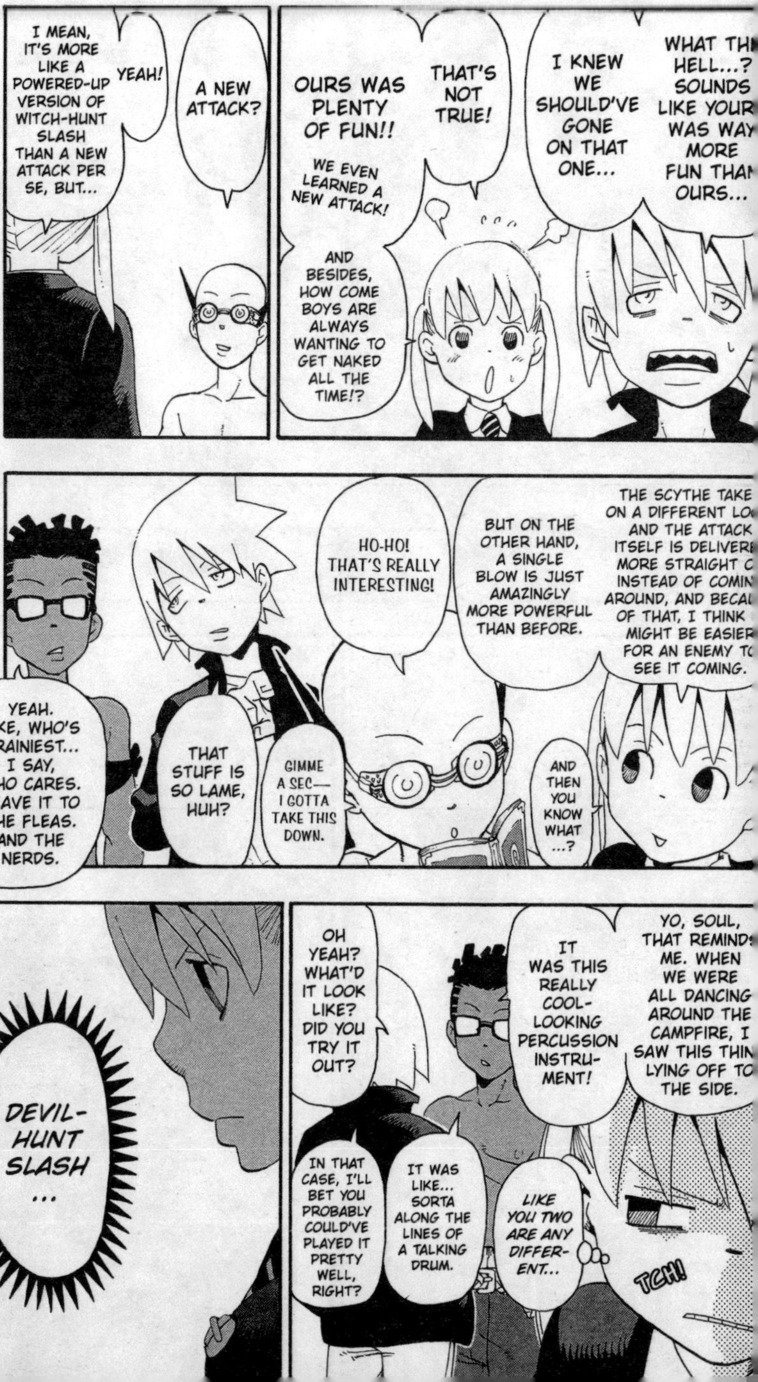
WHAT TH HELL...? SOUNDS LIKE YOUR WAS WAY MORE FUN THAN OURS...
I KNEW WE SHOULD'VE GONE ON THAT ONE...
THAT'S NOT TRUE!
OURS WAS PLENTY OF FUN!!
WE EVEN LEARNED A NEW ATTACK!
AND BESIDES, HOW COME BOYS ARE ALWAYS WANTING TO GET NAKED ALL THE TIME!?
A NEW ATTACK?
YEAH!
I MEAN, IT'S MORE LIKE A POWERED-UP VERSION OF WITCH-HUNT SLASH THAN A NEW ATTACK PER SE, BUT...
THE SCYTHE TAKE ON A DIFFERENT LO AND THE ATTACK ITSELF IS DELIVERE MORE STRAIGHT INSTEAD OF COMIN AROUND, AND BECAU OF THAT, I THINK MIGHT BE EASIER FOR AN ENEMY TO SEE IT COMING.
BUT ON THE OTHER HAND, A SINGLE BLOW IS JUST AMAZINGLY MORE POWERFUL THAN BEFORE.
HO-HO! THAT'S REALLY INTERESTING!
AND THEN YOU KNOW WHAT...?
GIMME A SEC— I GOTTA TAKE THIS DOWN.
THAT STUFF IS SO LAME, HUH?
YEAH. LIKE, WHO'S BRAINIEST... I SAY, WHO CARES. LEAVE IT TO THE FLEAS. AND THE NERDS.
YO, SOUL, THAT REMINDS ME. WHEN WE WERE ALL DANCING AROUND THE CAMPFIRE, I SAW THIS THIN LYING OFF TO THE SIDE.
IT WAS THIS REALLY COOL-LOOKING PERCUSSION INSTRU-MENT!
OH YEAH? WHAT'D IT LOOK LIKE? DID YOU TRY IT OUT?
TCH!
LIKE YOU TWO ARE ANY DIFFER-ENT...
IT WAS LIKE... SORTA ALONG THE LINES OF A TALKING DRUM.
IN THAT CASE, I'LL BET YOU PROBABLY COULD'VE PLAYED IT PRETTY WELL, RIGHT?
DEVIL-HUNT SLASH ...

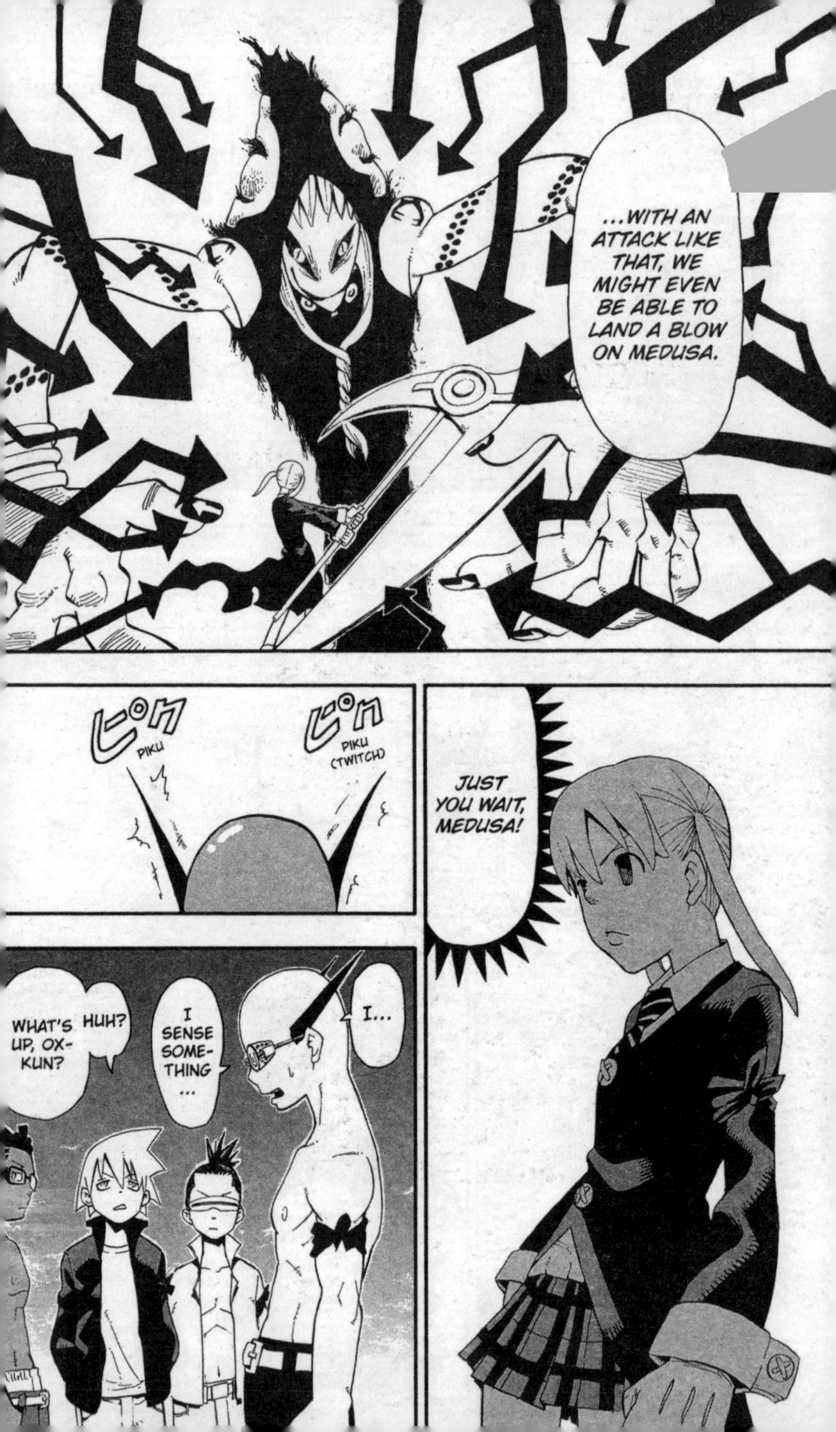
...WITH AN ATTACK LIKE THAT, WE MIGHT EVEN BE ABLE TO LAND A BLOW ON MEDUSA.
JUST YOU WAIT, MEDUSA!
PIKU (TWITCH)
PIKU
I...
I SENSE SOMETHING...
HUH?
WHAT'S UP, OX-KUN?

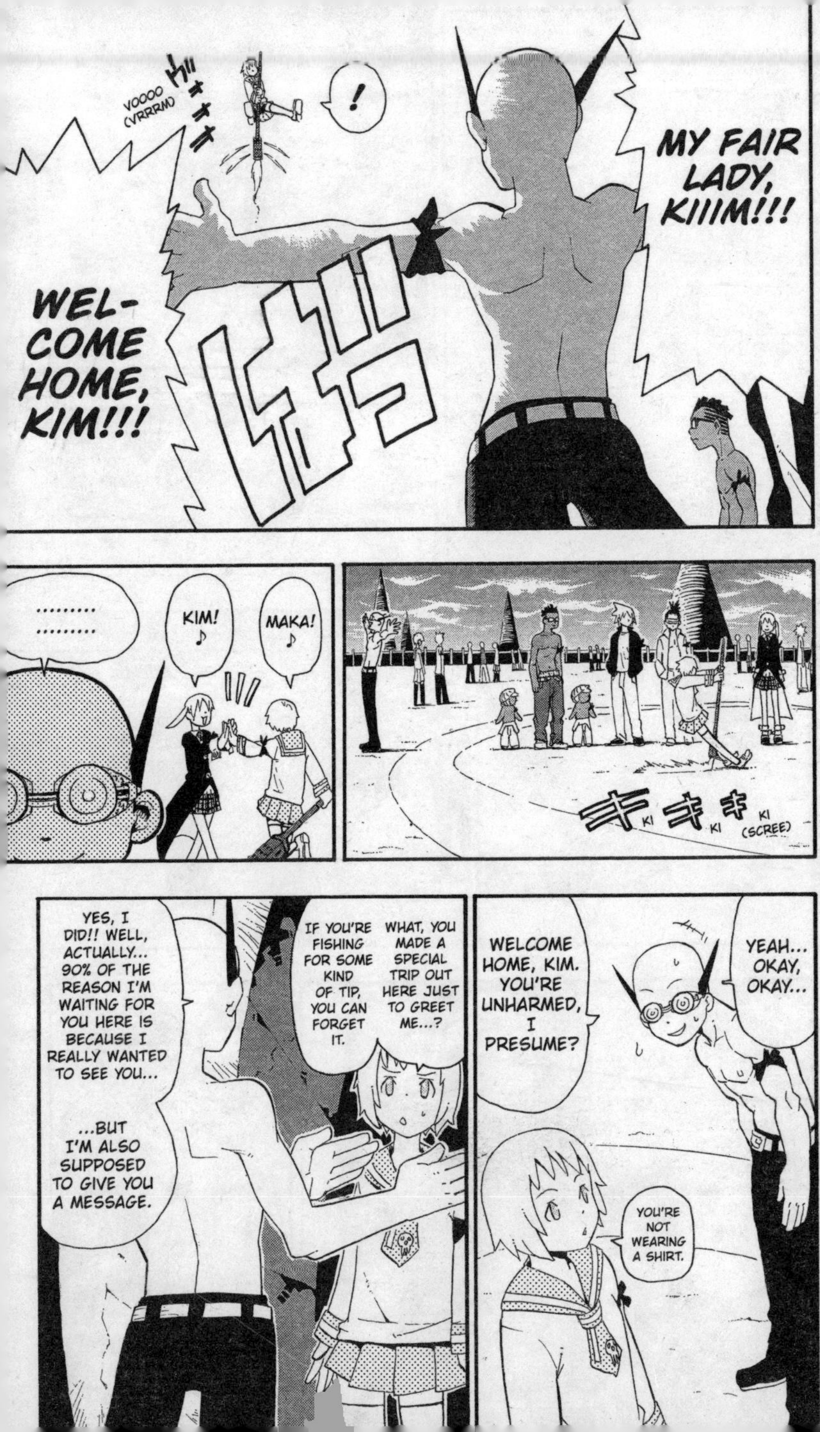
MY FAIR LADY, KIIIM!!!
!
VOOOO (VRRRM)
WEL-COME HOME, KIM!!!
KI KI KI (SCREE)
MAKA! ♪
KIM! ♪
....
....
YEAH... OKAY, OKAY...
WELCOME HOME, KIM. YOU'RE UNHARMED, I PRESUME?
YOU'RE NOT WEARING A SHIRT.
WHAT, YOU MADE A SPECIAL TRIP OUT HERE JUST TO GREET ME...?
IF YOU'RE FISHING FOR SOME KIND OF TIP, YOU CAN FORGET IT.
YES, I DID!! WELL, ACTUALLY... 90% OF THE REASON I'M WAITING FOR YOU HERE IS BECAUSE I REALLY WANTED TO SEE YOU...
...BUT I'M ALSO SUPPOSED TO GIVE YOU A MESSAGE.

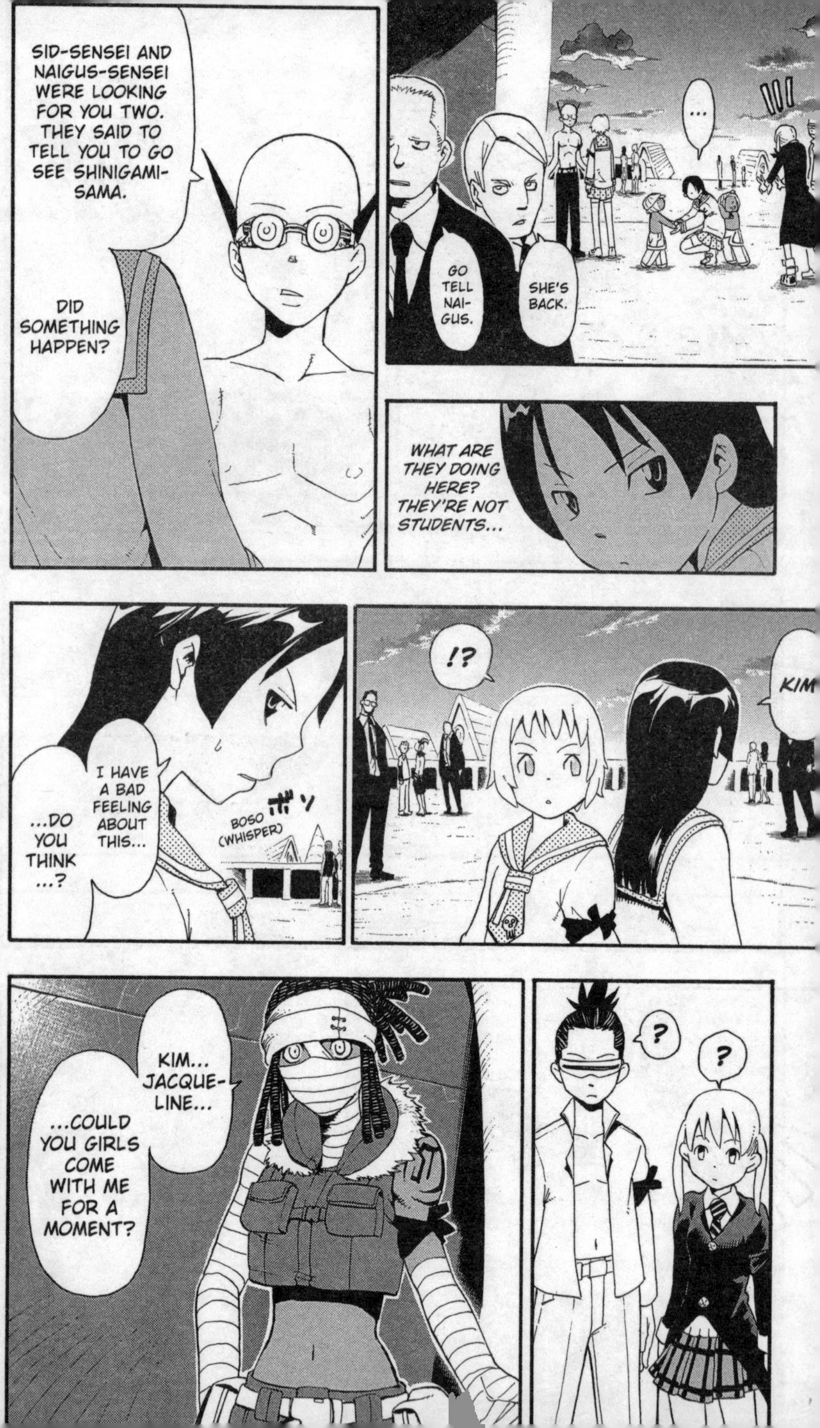
...
SHE'S BACK.
GO TELL NAIGUS.
WHAT ARE THEY DOING HERE? THEY'RE NOT STUDENTS...
SID-SENSEI AND NAIGUS-SENSEI WERE LOOKING FOR YOU TWO. THEY SAID TO TELL YOU TO GO SEE SHINIGAMI-SAMA.
DID SOMETHING HAPPEN?
KIM
!?
I HAVE A BAD FEELING ABOUT THIS...
BOSO (WHISPER)
...DO YOU THINK ...?
?
?
KIM... JACQUELINE...
...COULD YOU GIRLS COME WITH ME FOR A MOMENT?

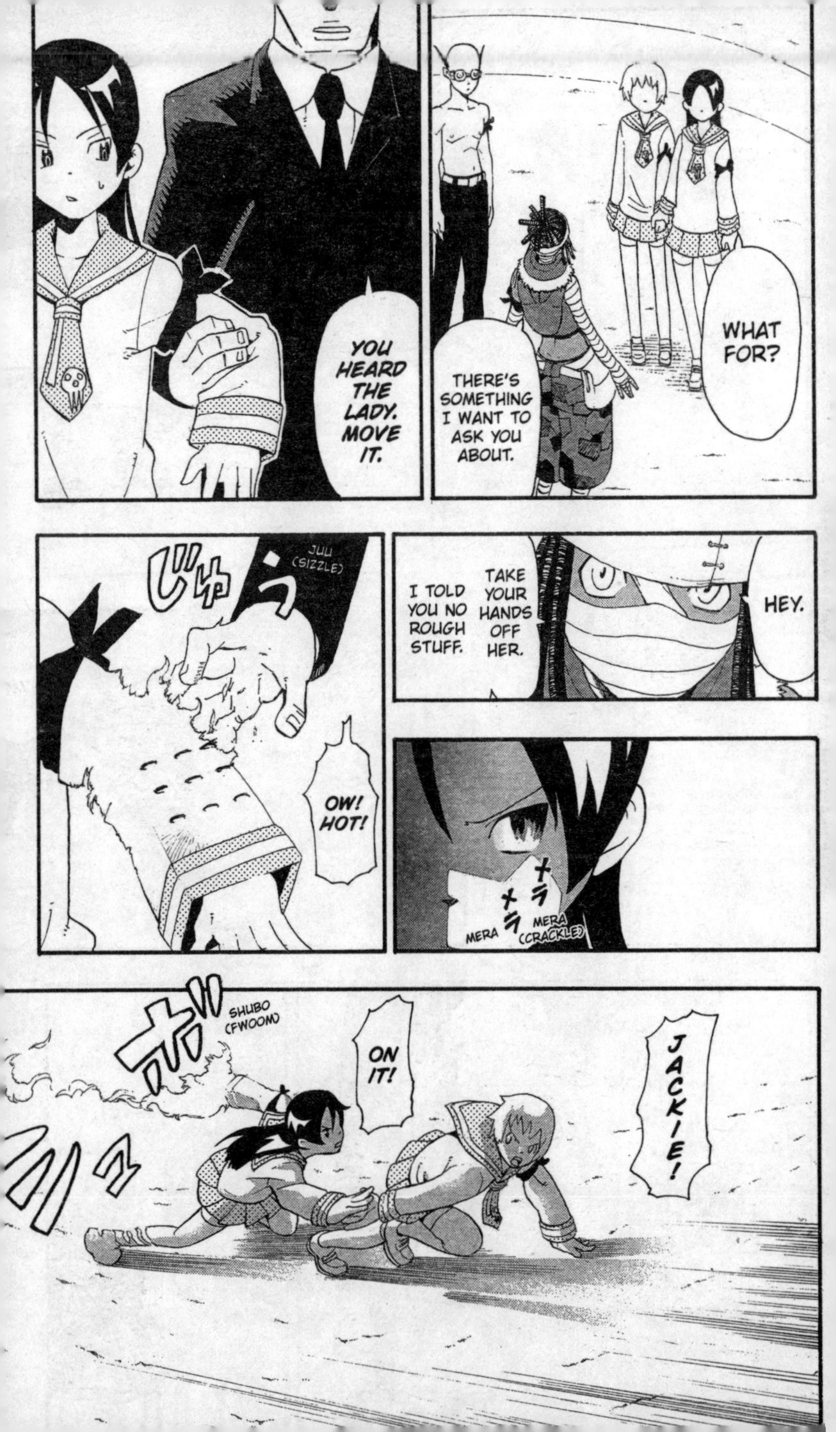
WHAT FOR?
THERE'S SOMETHING I WANT TO ASK YOU ABOUT.
YOU HEARD THE LADY. MOVE IT.
HEY.
TAKE YOUR HANDS OFF HER.
I TOLD YOU NO ROUGH STUFF.
メラ メラ
MERA MERA (CRACKLE)
じゅう
JUU (SIZZLE)
OW! HOT!
JACKIE!
ON IT!
SHUBO (FWOOM)

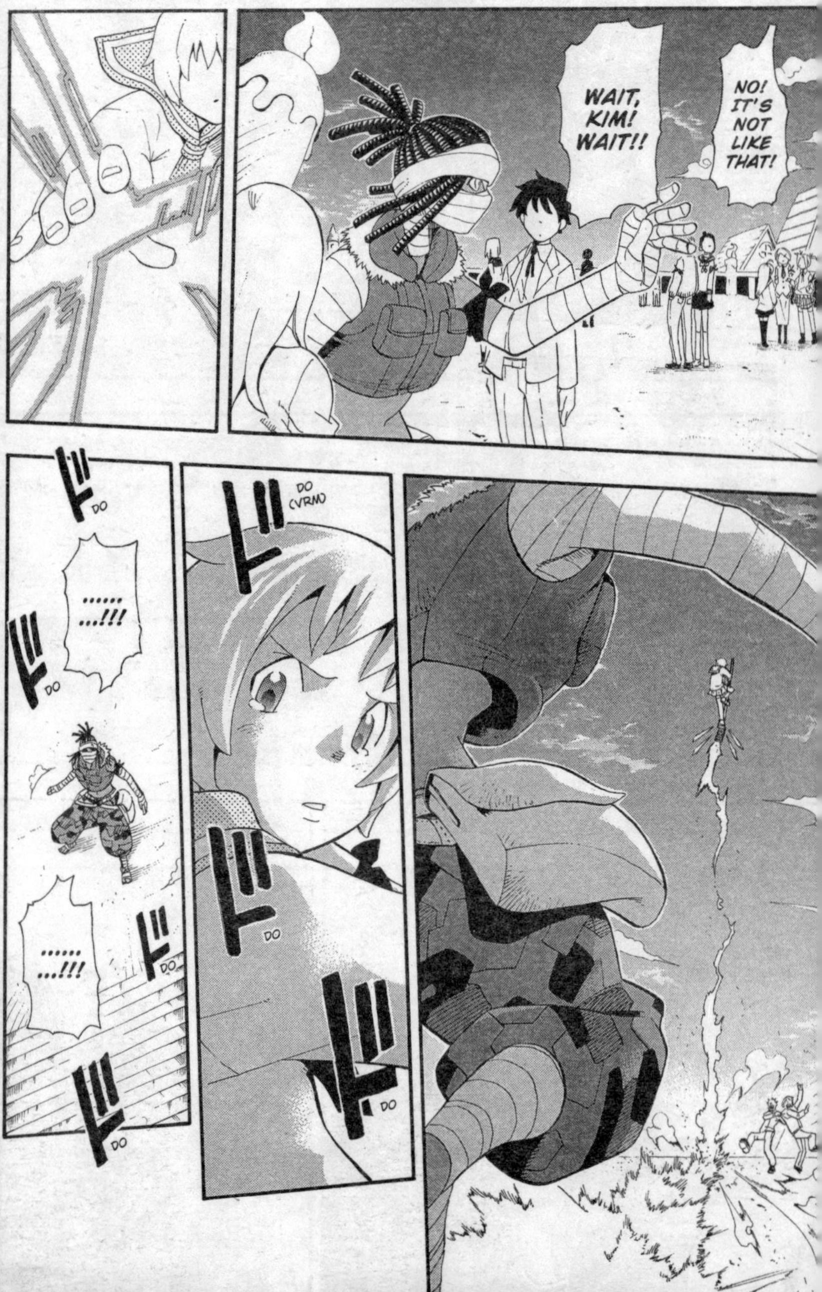

NO! IT'S NOT LIKE THAT!
WAIT, KIM! WAIT!!
ド DO (VRM)
ド DO
ド DO
ド DO
......!!!
ド DO
......!!!
ド DO
ド DO

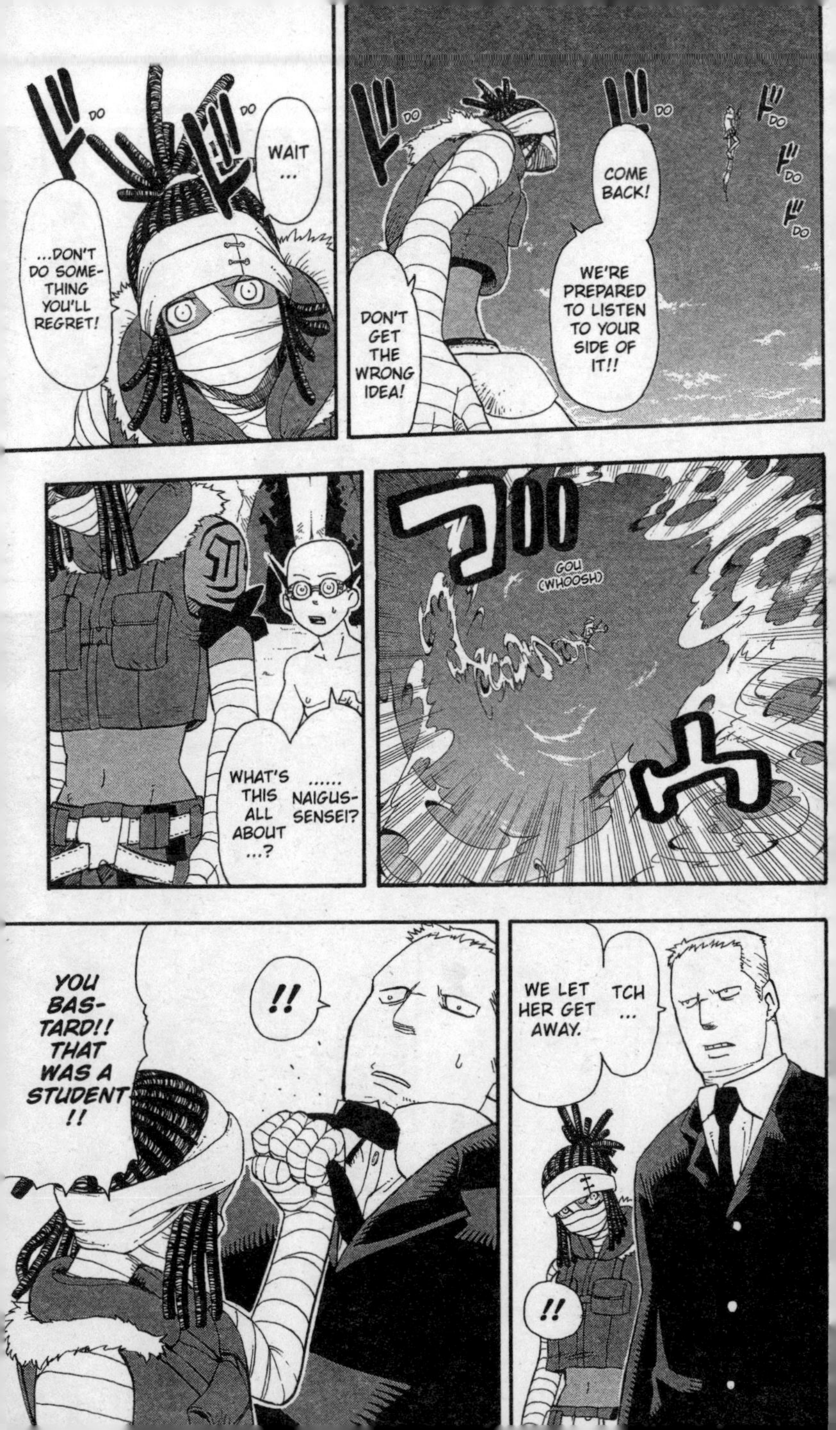
DO
DO
DO
DO
DO
COME BACK!
WE'RE PREPARED TO LISTEN TO YOUR SIDE OF IT!!
DON'T GET THE WRONG IDEA!
DO
DO
WAIT ...
...DON'T DO SOME-THING YOU'LL REGRET!
GOU (WHOOSH)
...... NAIGUS-SENSEI?
WHAT'S THIS ALL ABOUT ...?
TCH ...
WE LET HER GET AWAY.
!!
!!
YOU BAS-TARD!! THAT WAS A STUDENT !!

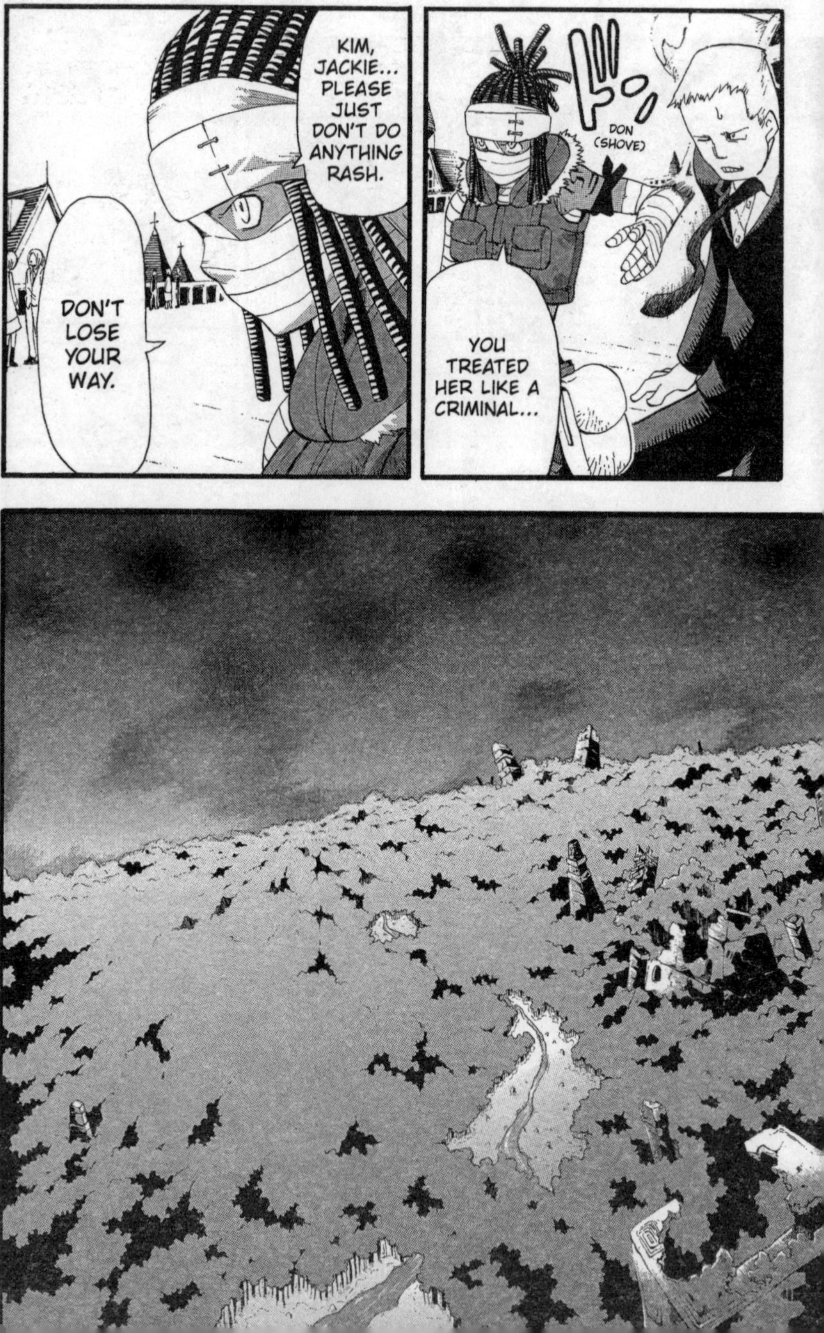
DON (SHOVE)
YOU TREATED HER LIKE A CRIMINAL...
KIM, JACKIE... PLEASE JUST DON'T DO ANYTHING RASH.
DON'T LOSE YOUR WAY.

I CAN'T BE- LIEVE IT...

THEY FOUND OUT...

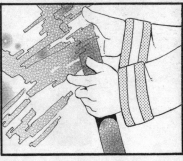

WHAT DO I DO...!?

THEY KNOW I'M A WITCH NOW...I CAN NEVER GO BACK TO DWMA EVER AGAIN ...

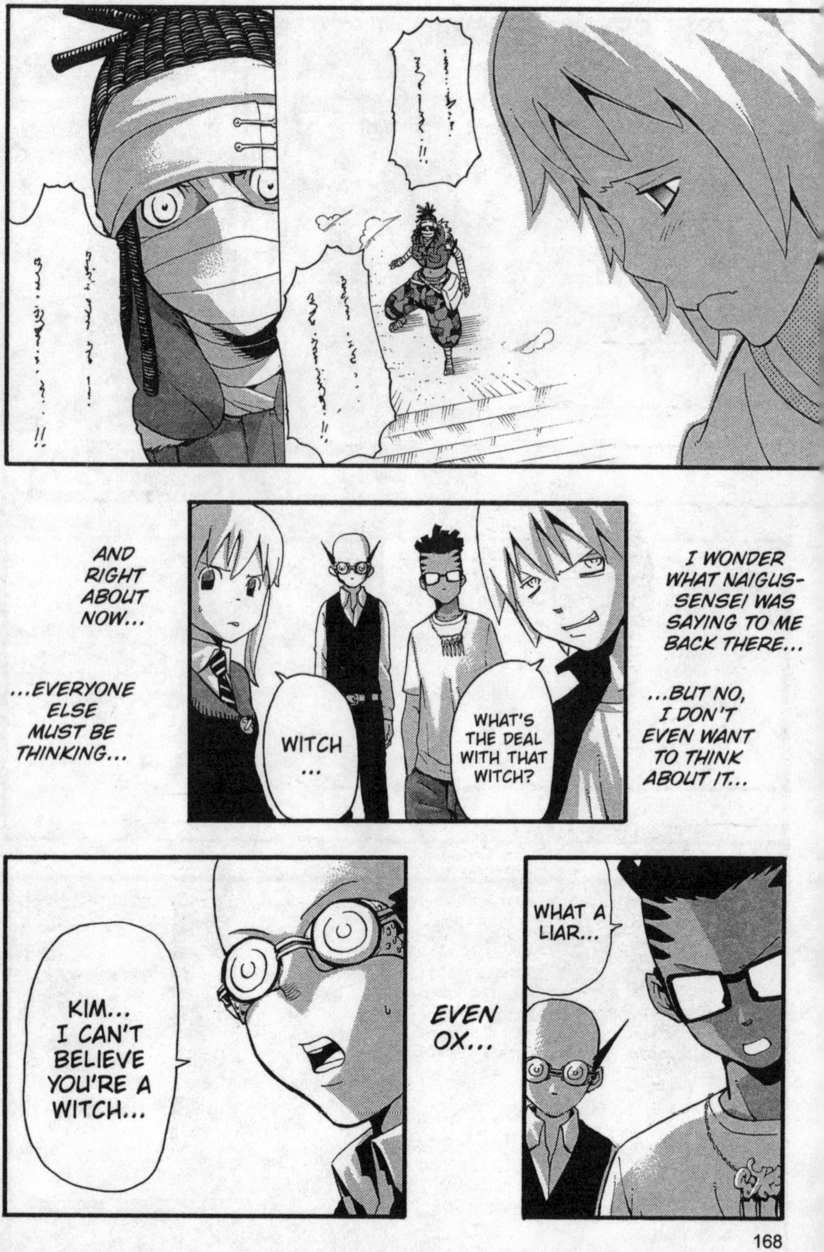
I WONDER WHAT NAIGUS-SENSEI WAS SAYING TO ME BACK THERE...
...BUT NO, I DON'T EVEN WANT TO THINK ABOUT IT...
AND RIGHT ABOUT NOW...
...EVERYONE ELSE MUST BE THINKING...
WHAT'S THE DEAL WITH THAT WITCH?
WITCH ...
WHAT A LIAR...
EVEN OX...
KIM... I CAN'T BELIEVE YOU'RE A WITCH...

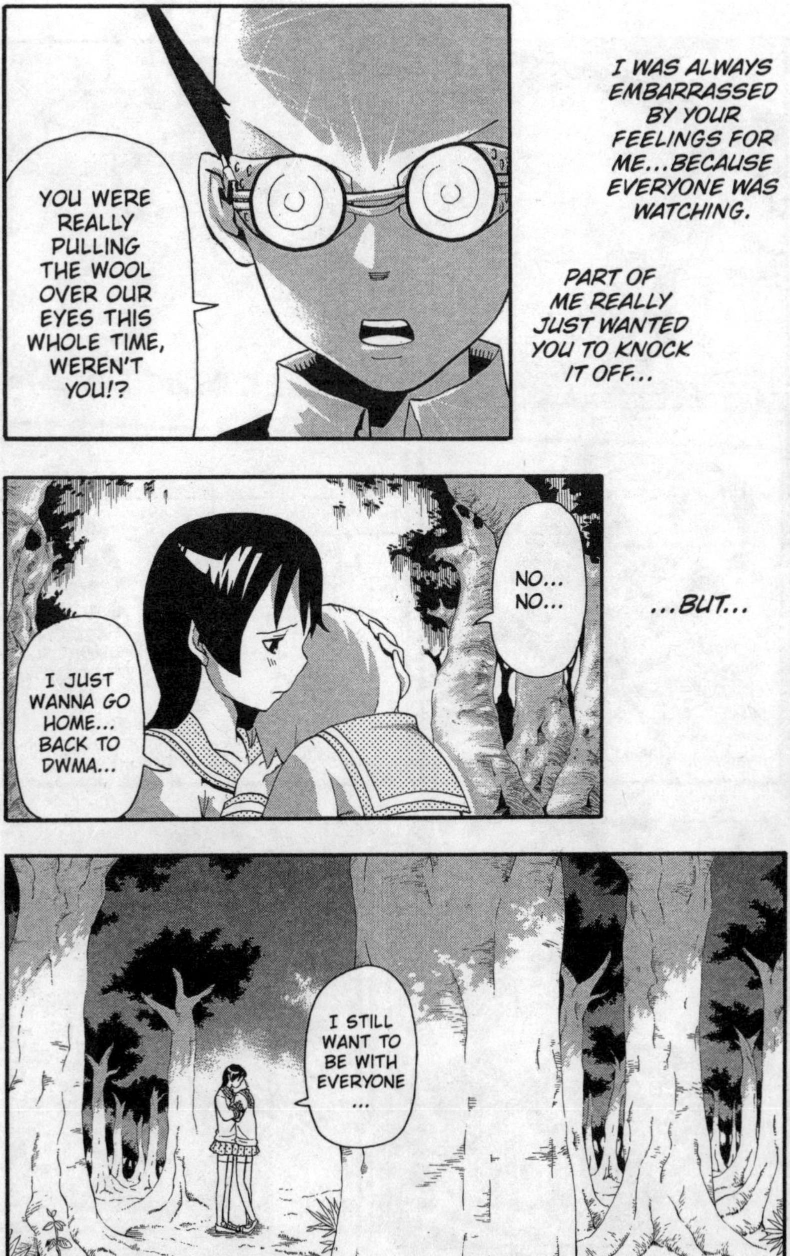
I WAS ALWAYS EMBARRASSED BY YOUR FEELINGS FOR ME...BECAUSE EVERYONE WAS WATCHING.
PART OF ME REALLY JUST WANTED YOU TO KNOCK IT OFF...
YOU WERE REALLY PULLING THE WOOL OVER OUR EYES THIS WHOLE TIME, WEREN'T YOU!?
...BUT...
NO... NO...
I JUST WANNA GO HOME... BACK TO DWMA...
I STILL WANT TO BE WITH EVERYONE ...

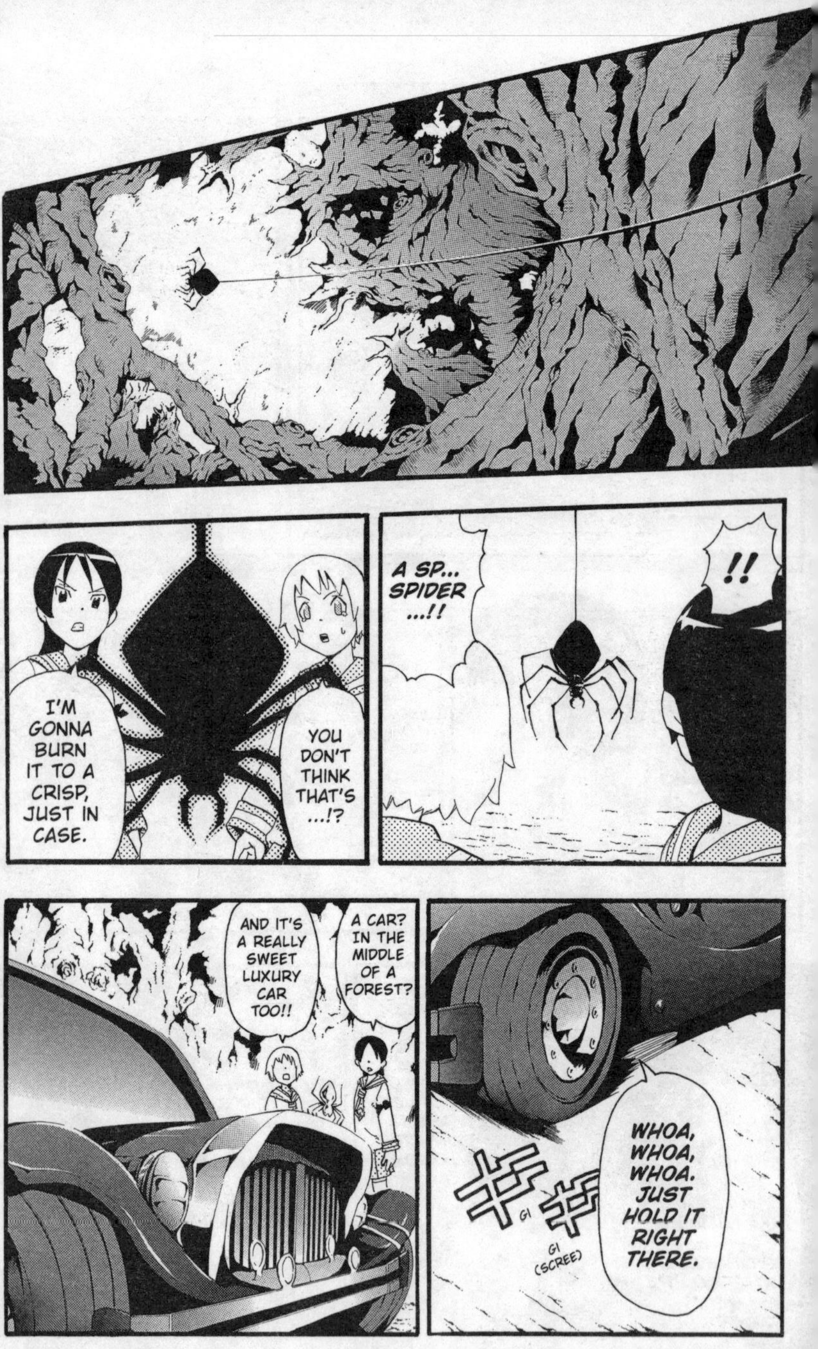
!!
A SP... SPIDER ...!!
YOU DON'T THINK THAT'S ...!?
I'M GONNA BURN IT TO A CRISP, JUST IN CASE.
WHOA, WHOA, WHOA. JUST HOLD IT RIGHT THERE.
GI
GI (SCREE)
A CAR? IN THE MIDDLE OF A FOREST?
AND IT'S A REALLY SWEET LUXURY CAR TOO!!

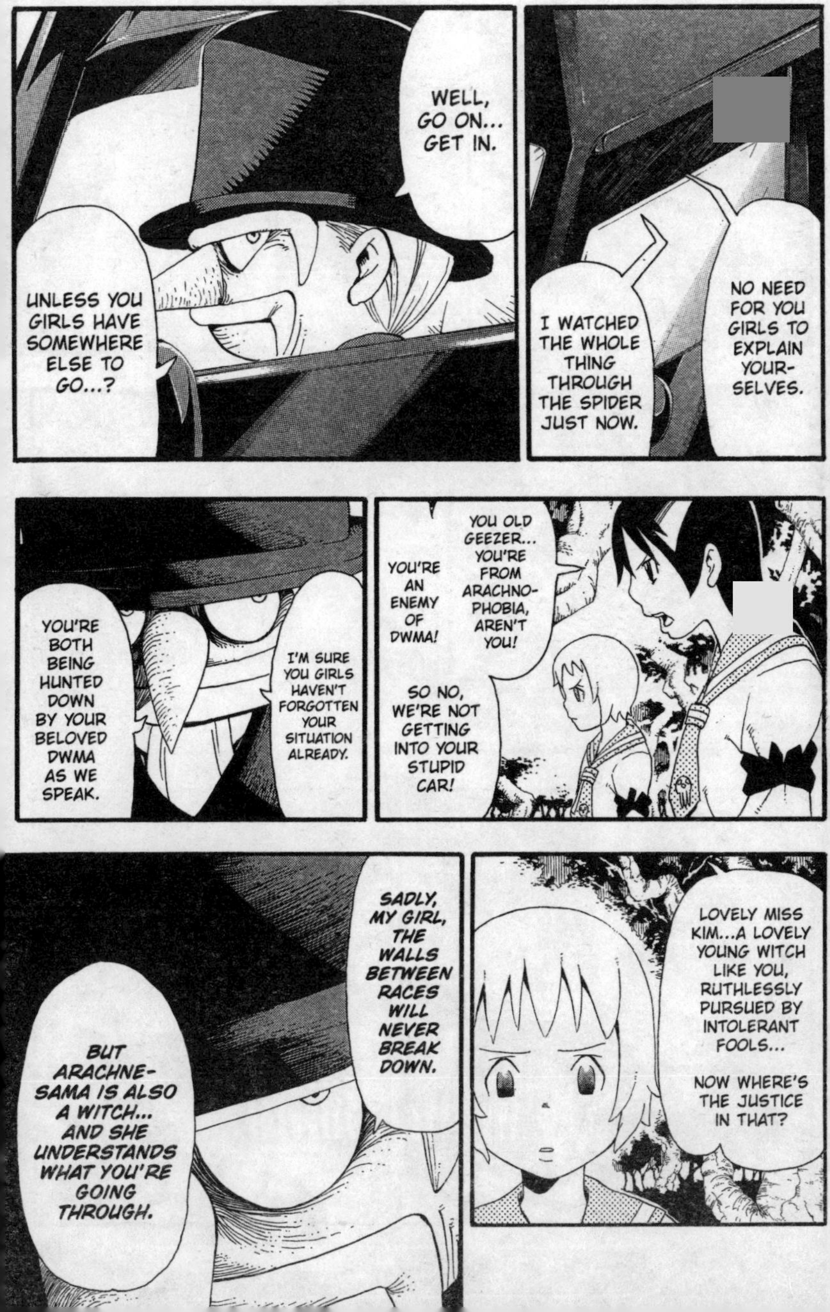
NO NEED FOR YOU GIRLS TO EXPLAIN YOURSELVES.
I WATCHED THE WHOLE THING THROUGH THE SPIDER JUST NOW.
WELL, GO ON... GET IN.
UNLESS YOU GIRLS HAVE SOMEWHERE ELSE TO GO...?
YOU OLD GEEZER... YOU'RE FROM ARACHNOPHOBIA, AREN'T YOU!
YOU'RE AN ENEMY OF DWMA!
SO NO, WE'RE NOT GETTING INTO YOUR STUPID CAR!
I'M SURE YOU GIRLS HAVEN'T FORGOTTEN YOUR SITUATION ALREADY.
YOU'RE BOTH BEING HUNTED DOWN BY YOUR BELOVED DWMA AS WE SPEAK.
LOVELY MISS KIM...A LOVELY YOUNG WITCH LIKE YOU, RUTHLESSLY PURSUED BY INTOLERANT FOOLS...
NOW WHERE'S THE JUSTICE IN THAT?
SADLY, MY GIRL, THE WALLS BETWEEN RACES WILL NEVER BREAK DOWN.
BUT ARACHNE-SAMA IS ALSO A WITCH... AND SHE UNDERSTANDS WHAT YOU'RE GOING THROUGH.

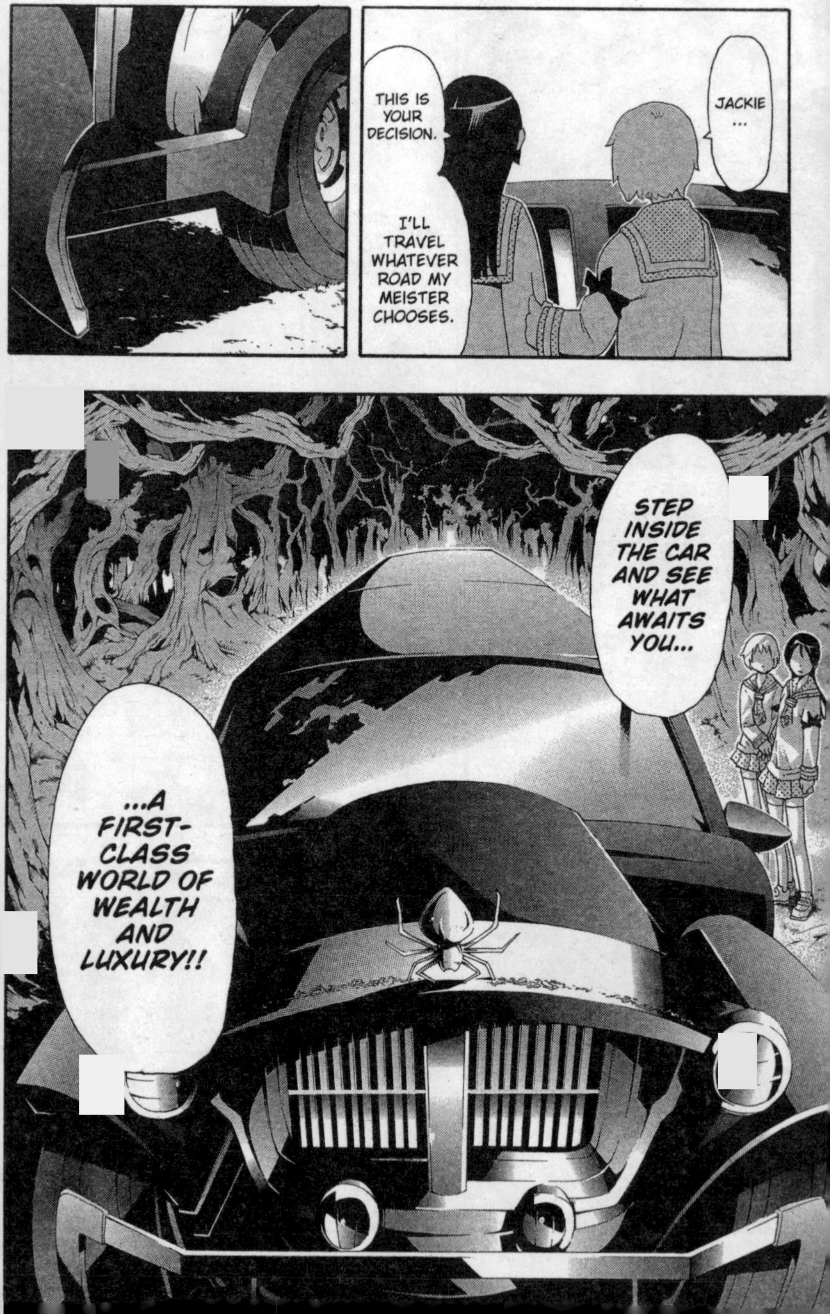
JACKIE ...
THIS IS YOUR DECISION.
I'LL TRAVEL WHATEVER ROAD MY MEISTER CHOOSES.
STEP INSIDE THE CAR AND SEE WHAT AWAITS YOU...
...A FIRST-CLASS WORLD OF WEALTH AND LUXURY!!

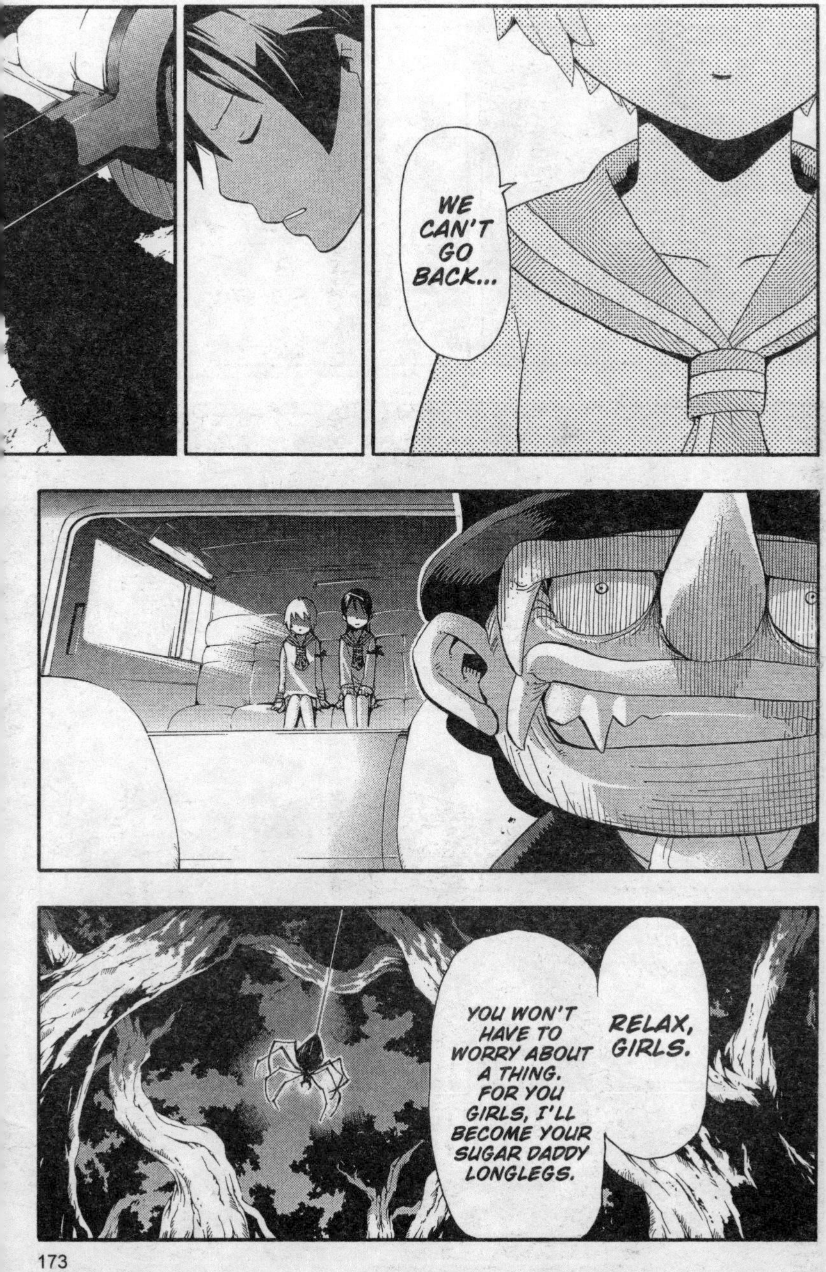
WE CAN'T GO BACK...
RELAX, GIRLS.
YOU WON'T HAVE TO WORRY ABOUT A THING. FOR YOU GIRLS, I'LL BECOME YOUR SUGAR DADDY LONGLEGS.

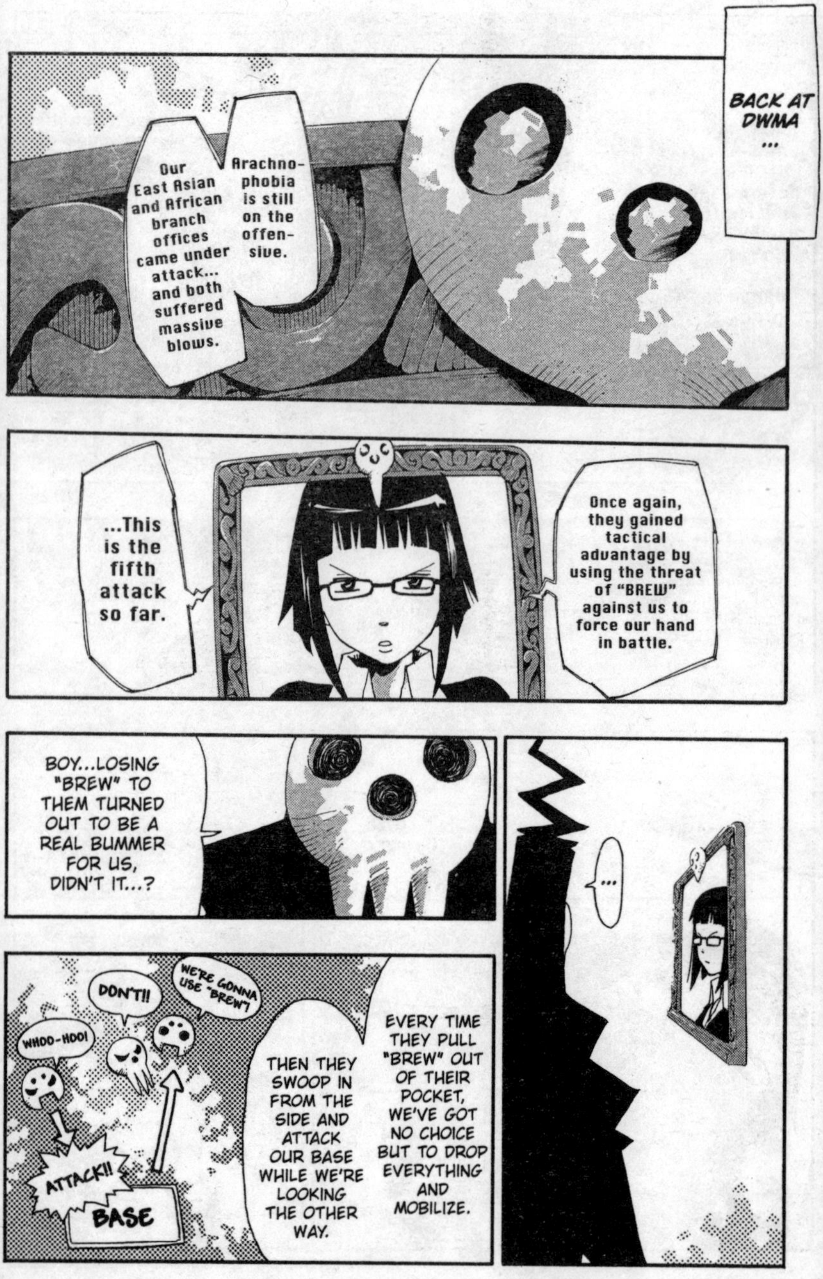
BACK AT DWMA ...
Arachnophobia is still on the offensive.
Our East Asian and African branch offices came under attack... and both suffered massive blows.
Once again, they gained tactical advantage by using the threat of "BREW" against us to force our hand in battle.
...This is the fifth attack so far.
...
BOY...LOSING "BREW" TO THEM TURNED OUT TO BE A REAL BUMMER FOR US, DIDN'T IT...?
EVERY TIME THEY PULL "BREW" OUT OF THEIR POCKET, WE'VE GOT NO CHOICE BUT TO DROP EVERYTHING AND MOBILIZE.
THEN THEY SWOOP IN FROM THE SIDE AND ATTACK OUR BASE WHILE WE'RE LOOKING THE OTHER WAY.
WE'RE GONNA USE "BREW"!
DON'T!!
WHOO-HOO!
ATTACK!!
BASE

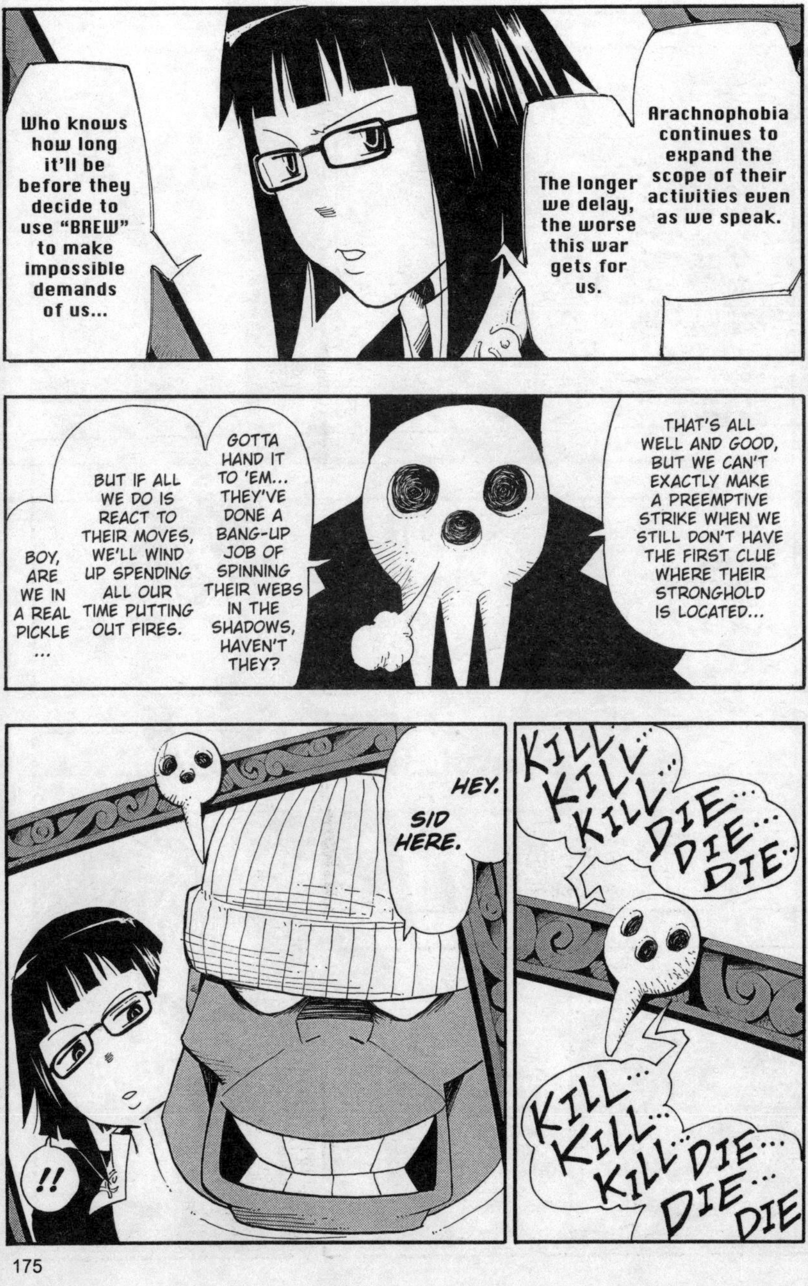
Arachnophobia continues to expand the scope of their activities even as we speak.
The longer we delay, the worse this war gets for us.
Who knows how long it'll be before they decide to use "BREW" to make impossible demands of us...
THAT'S ALL WELL AND GOOD, BUT WE CAN'T EXACTLY MAKE A PREEMPTIVE STRIKE WHEN WE STILL DON'T HAVE THE FIRST CLUE WHERE THEIR STRONGHOLD IS LOCATED...
GOTTA HAND IT TO 'EM... THEY'VE DONE A BANG-UP JOB OF SPINNING THEIR WEBS IN THE SHADOWS, HAVEN'T THEY?
BUT IF ALL WE DO IS REACT TO THEIR MOVES, WE'LL WIND UP SPENDING ALL OUR TIME PUTTING OUT FIRES.
BOY, ARE WE IN A REAL PICKLE...
KILL... KILL... KILL DIE... DIE... DIE...
KILL... KILL... KILL DIE... DIE... DIE
HEY.
SID HERE.
!!

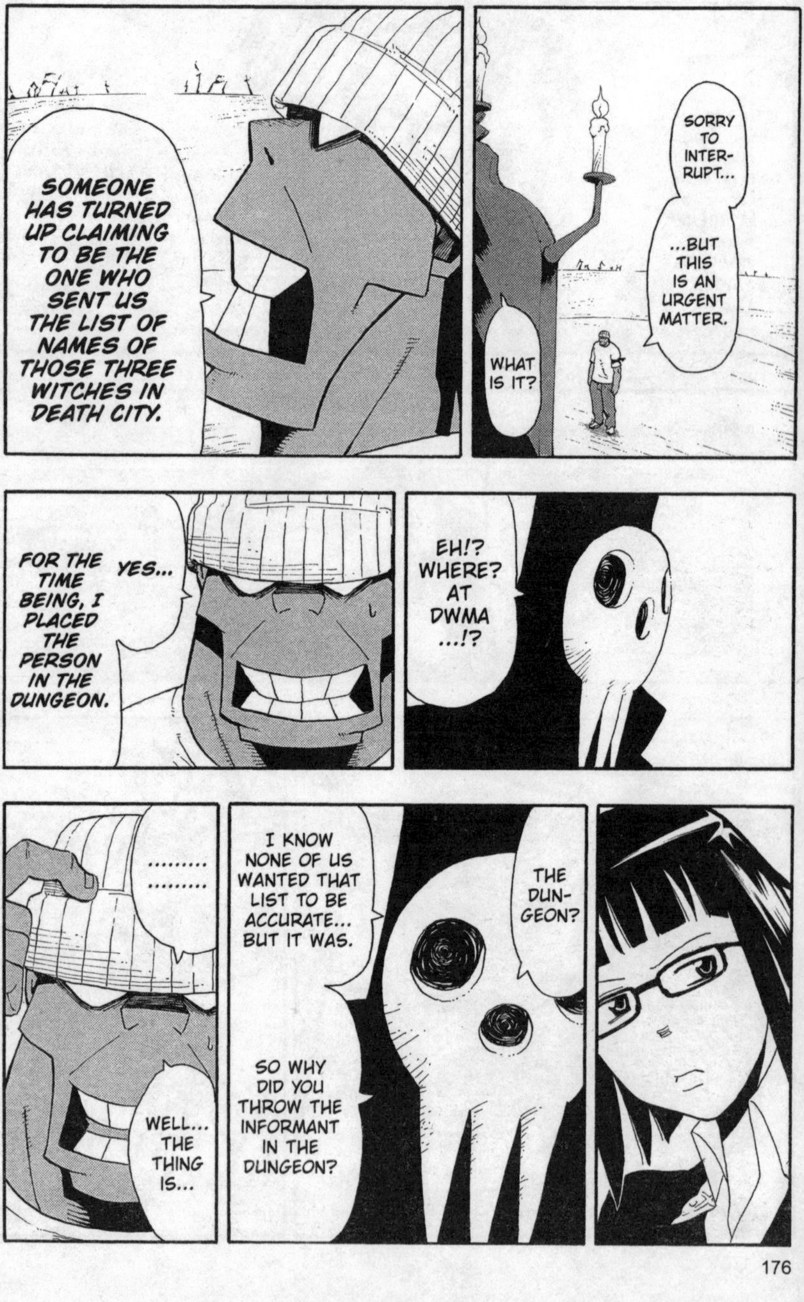
SORRY TO INTER-RUPT...
...BUT THIS IS AN URGENT MATTER.
WHAT IS IT?
SOMEONE HAS TURNED UP CLAIMING TO BE THE ONE WHO SENT US THE LIST OF NAMES OF THOSE THREE WITCHES IN DEATH CITY.
EH!? WHERE? AT DWMA ...!?
YES...
FOR THE TIME BEING, I PLACED THE PERSON IN THE DUNGEON.
THE DUN-GEON?
I KNOW NONE OF US WANTED THAT LIST TO BE ACCURATE... BUT IT WAS.
SO WHY DID YOU THROW THE INFORMANT IN THE DUNGEON?
....
....
WELL... THE THING IS...

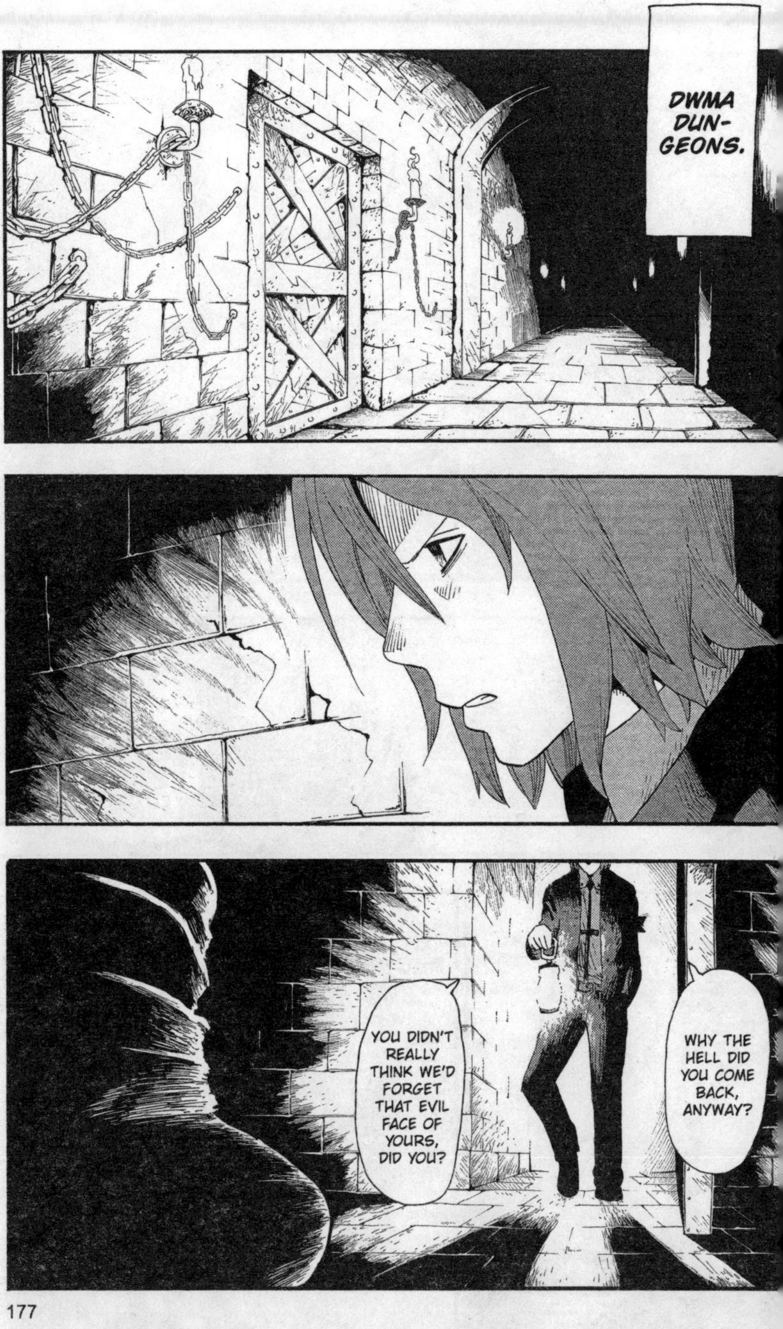
DWMA DUN- GEONS.
WHY THE HELL DID YOU COME BACK, ANYWAY?
YOU DIDN'T REALLY THINK WE'D FORGET THAT EVIL FACE OF YOURS, DID YOU?

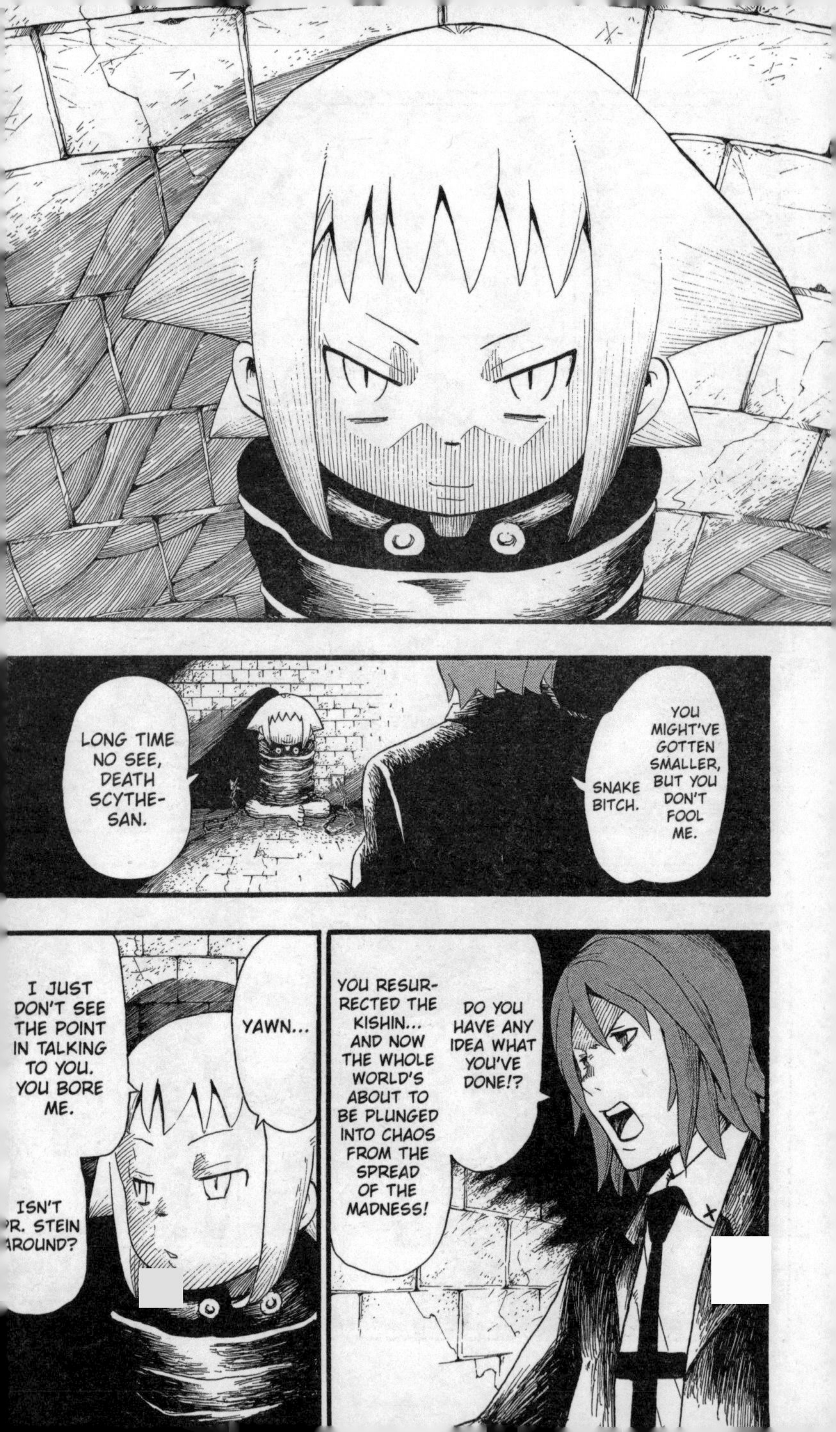
YOU MIGHT'VE GOTTEN SMALLER, BUT YOU DON'T FOOL ME.
SNAKE BITCH.
LONG TIME NO SEE, DEATH SCYTHE-SAN.
DO YOU HAVE ANY IDEA WHAT YOU'VE DONE!?
YOU RESURRECTED THE KISHIN... AND NOW THE WHOLE WORLD'S ABOUT TO BE PLUNGED INTO CHAOS FROM THE SPREAD OF THE MADNESS!
YAWN...
I JUST DON'T SEE THE POINT IN TALKING TO YOU. YOU BORE ME.
ISN'T R. STEIN AROUND?

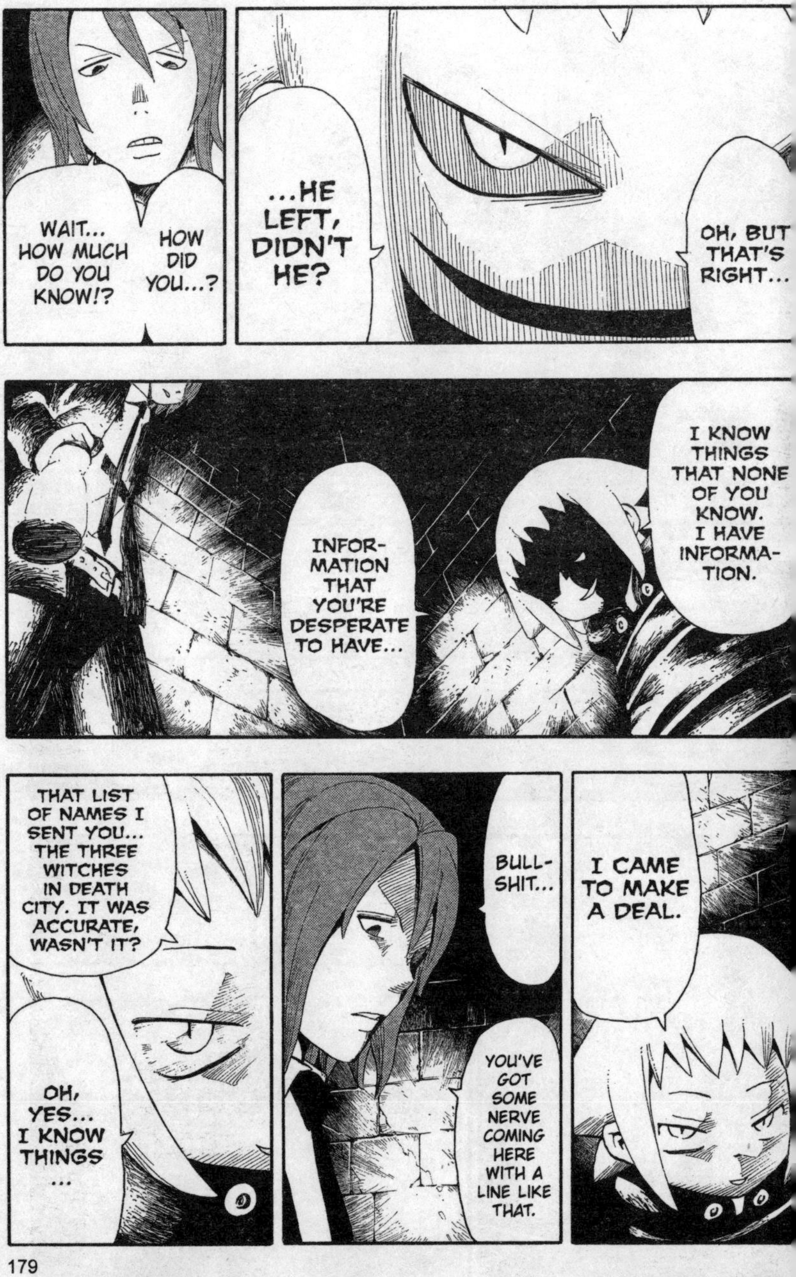
OH, BUT THAT'S RIGHT...
...HE LEFT, DIDN'T HE?
HOW DID YOU...?
WAIT... HOW MUCH DO YOU KNOW!?
I KNOW THINGS THAT NONE OF YOU KNOW. I HAVE INFORMATION.
INFORMATION THAT YOU'RE DESPERATE TO HAVE...
I CAME TO MAKE A DEAL.
BULLSHIT...
YOU'VE GOT SOME NERVE COMING HERE WITH A LINE LIKE THAT.
THAT LIST OF NAMES I SENT YOU... THE THREE WITCHES IN DEATH CITY. IT WAS ACCURATE, WASN'T IT?
OH, YES... I KNOW THINGS...

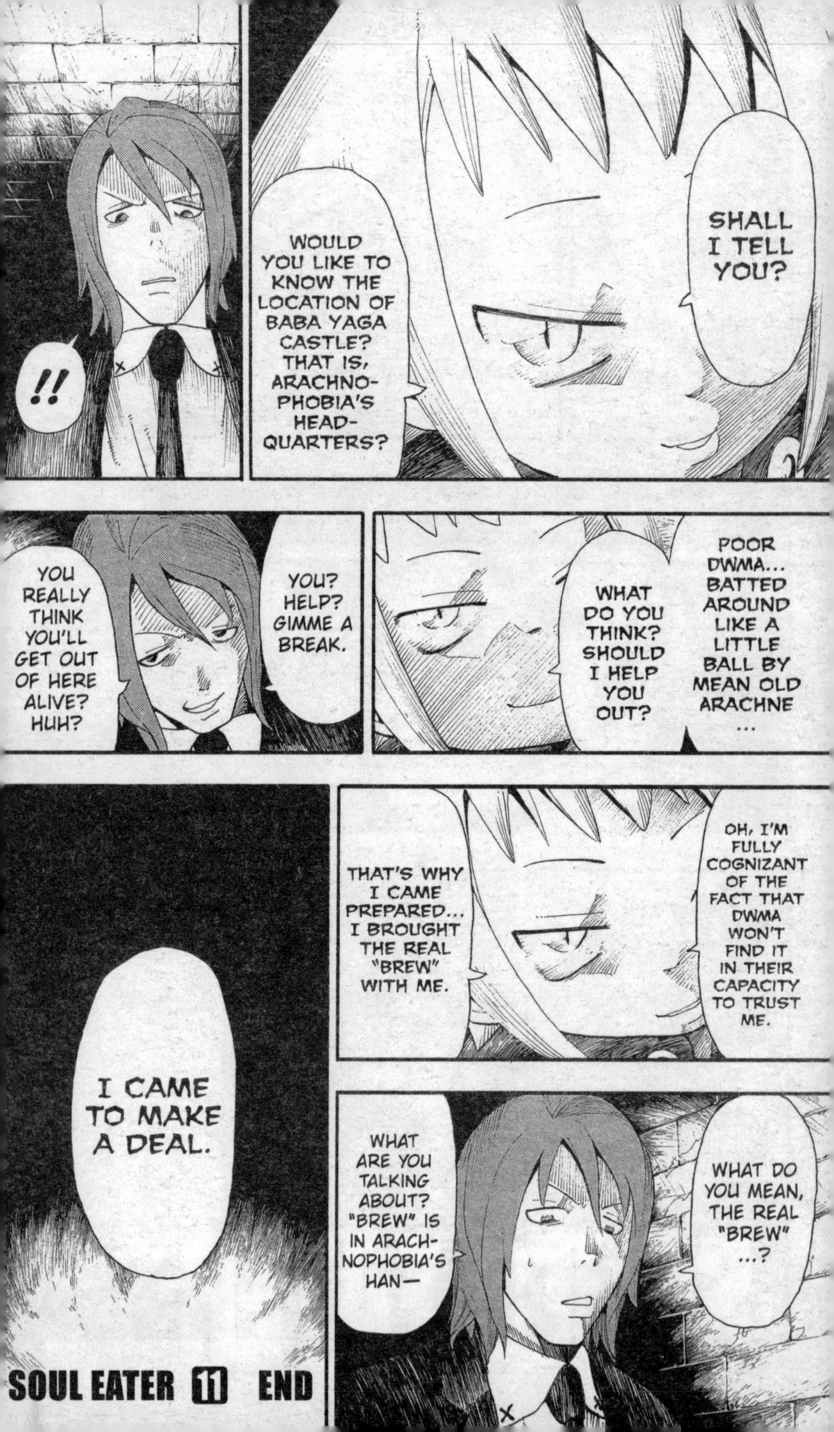
SHALL I TELL YOU?
WOULD YOU LIKE TO KNOW THE LOCATION OF BABA YAGA CASTLE? THAT IS, ARACHNOPHOBIA'S HEADQUARTERS?
!!
POOR DWMA... BATTED AROUND LIKE A LITTLE BALL BY MEAN OLD ARACHNE ...
WHAT DO YOU THINK? SHOULD I HELP YOU OUT?
YOU? HELP? GIMME A BREAK.
YOU REALLY THINK YOU'LL GET OUT OF HERE ALIVE? HUH?
OH, I'M FULLY COGNIZANT OF THE FACT THAT DWMA WON'T FIND IT IN THEIR CAPACITY TO TRUST ME.
THAT'S WHY I CAME PREPARED... I BROUGHT THE REAL "BREW" WITH ME.
WHAT DO YOU MEAN, THE REAL "BREW" ...?
WHAT ARE YOU TALKING ABOUT? "BREW" IS IN ARACHNOPHOBIA'S HAN—
I CAME TO MAKE A DEAL.
SOUL EATER 11 END

SOUL EATER

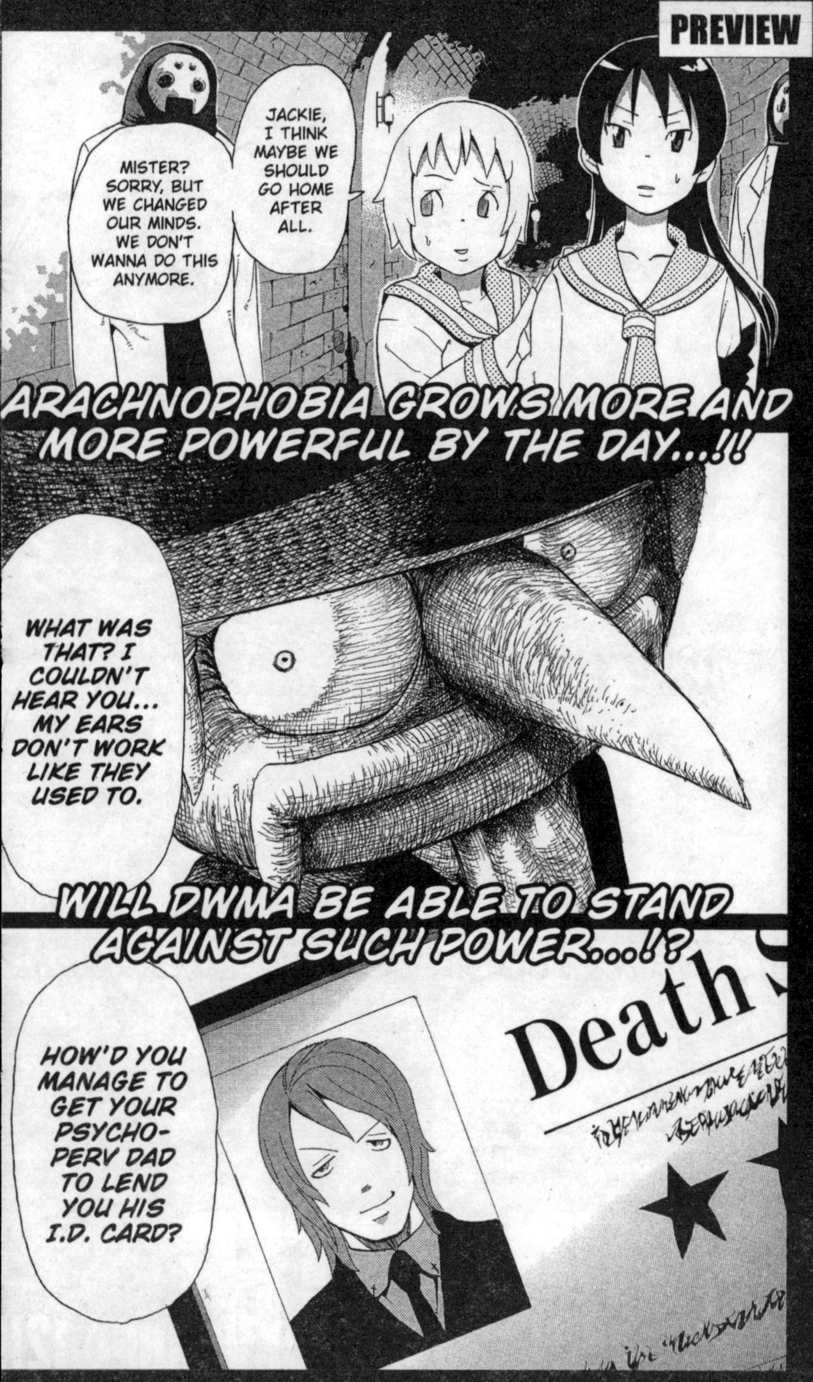
JACKIE, I THINK MAYBE WE SHOULD GO HOME AFTER ALL.
MISTER? SORRY, BUT WE CHANGED OUR MINDS. WE DON'T WANNA DO THIS ANYMORE.
ARACHNOPHOBIA GROWS MORE AND MORE POWERFUL BY THE DAY...!!
WHAT WAS THAT? I COULDN'T HEAR YOU... MY EARS DON'T WORK LIKE THEY USED TO.
WILL DWMA BE ABLE TO STAND AGAINST SUCH POWER...!?
Death
HOW'D YOU MANAGE TO GET YOUR PSYCHO-PERV DAD TO LEND YOU HIS I.D. CARD?

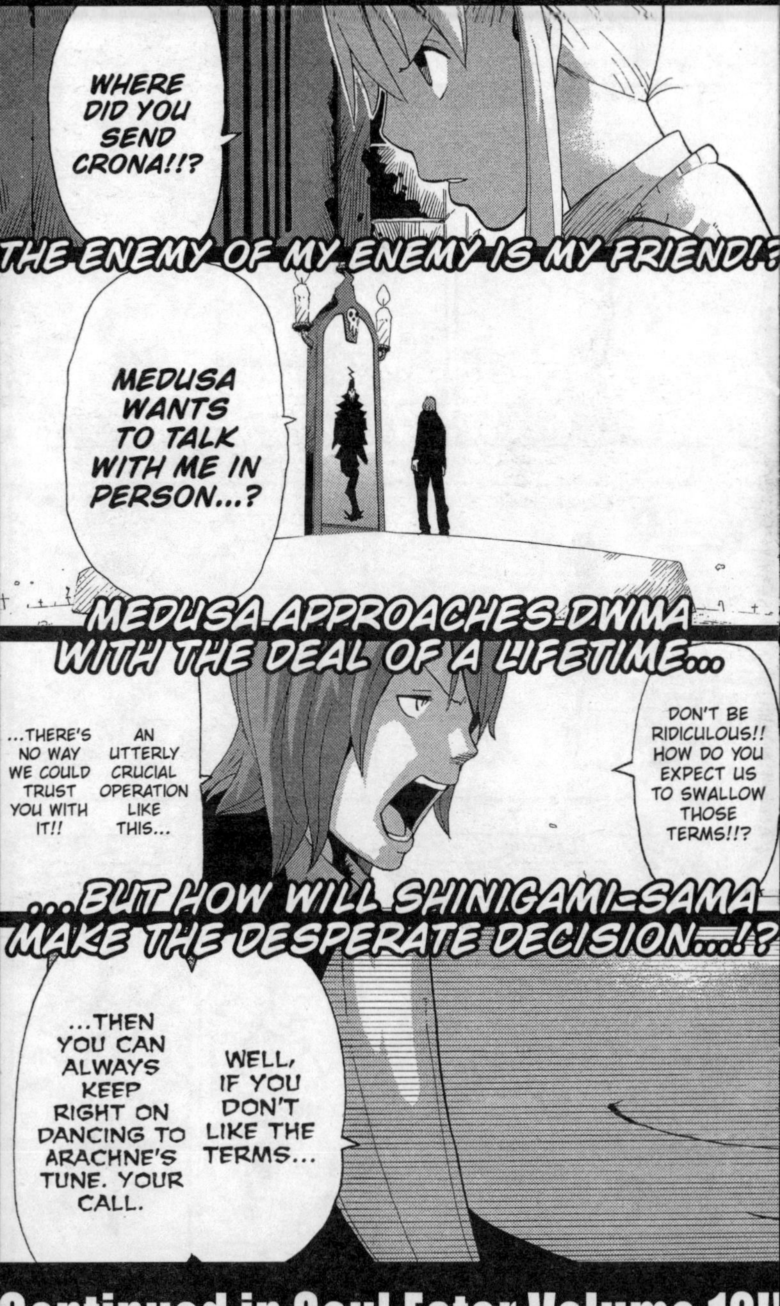
WHERE DID YOU SEND CRONA!!?
THE ENEMY OF MY ENEMY IS MY FRIEND!?
MEDUSA WANTS TO TALK WITH ME IN PERSON...?
MEDUSA APPROACHES DWMA WITH THE DEAL OF A LIFETIME...
DON'T BE RIDICULOUS!! HOW DO YOU EXPECT US TO SWALLOW THOSE TERMS!!?
AN UTTERLY CRUCIAL OPERATION LIKE THIS...
...THERE'S NO WAY WE COULD TRUST YOU WITH IT!!
...BUT HOW WILL SHINIGAMI-SAMA MAKE THE DESPERATE DECISION...!?
WELL, IF YOU DON'T LIKE THE TERMS...
...THEN YOU CAN ALWAYS KEEP RIGHT ON DANCING TO ARACHNE'S TUNE. YOUR CALL.

Continued in Soul Eater Volume 12!!

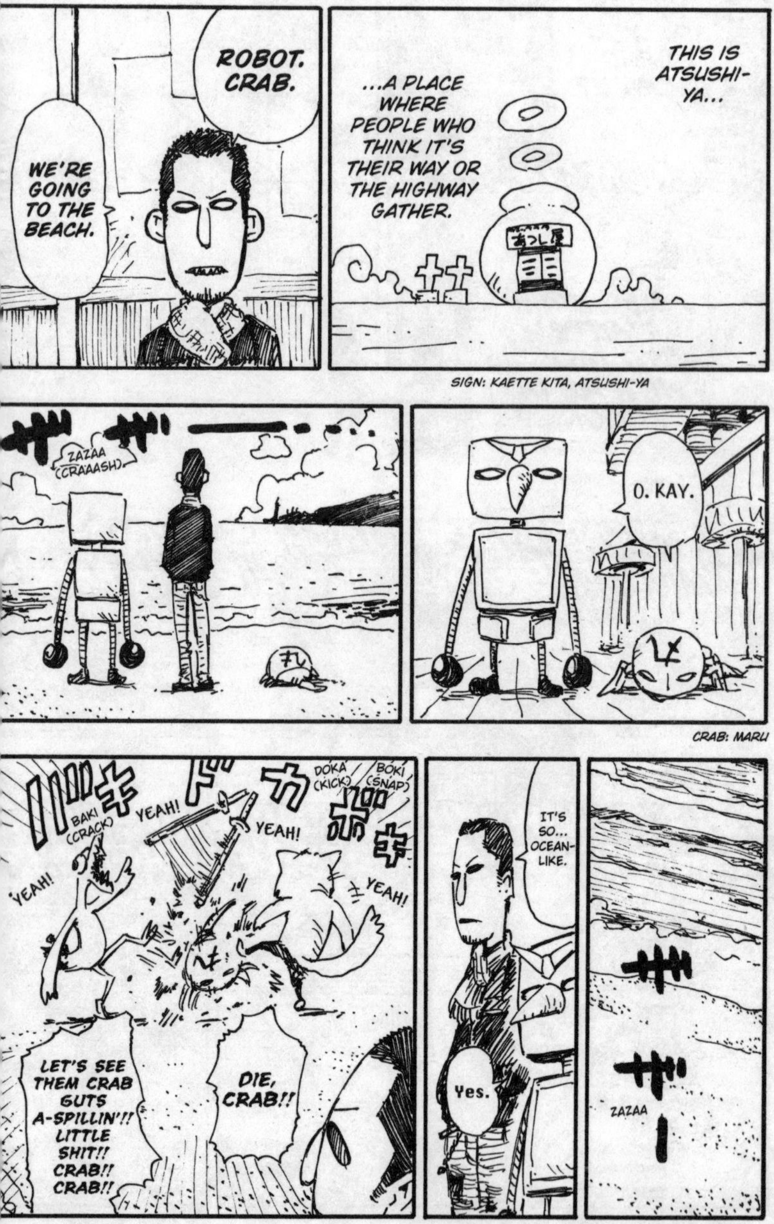
THIS IS ATSUSHI-YA...
...A PLACE WHERE PEOPLE WHO THINK IT'S THEIR WAY OR THE HIGHWAY GATHER.
ROBOT. CRAB.
WE'RE GOING TO THE BEACH.
SIGN: KAETTE KITA, ATSUSHI-YA
O. KAY.
CRAB: MARU
ZAZAA (CRAAASH)
ZAZAA
IT'S SO... OCEAN-LIKE.
Yes.
DOKA (KICK)
BOKI (SNAP)
YEAH!
YEAH!
YEAH!
BAKI (CRACK)
YEAH!
DIE, CRAB!!
LET'S SEE THEM CRAB GUTS A-SPILLIN'!! LITTLE SHIT!! CRAB!! CRAB!!

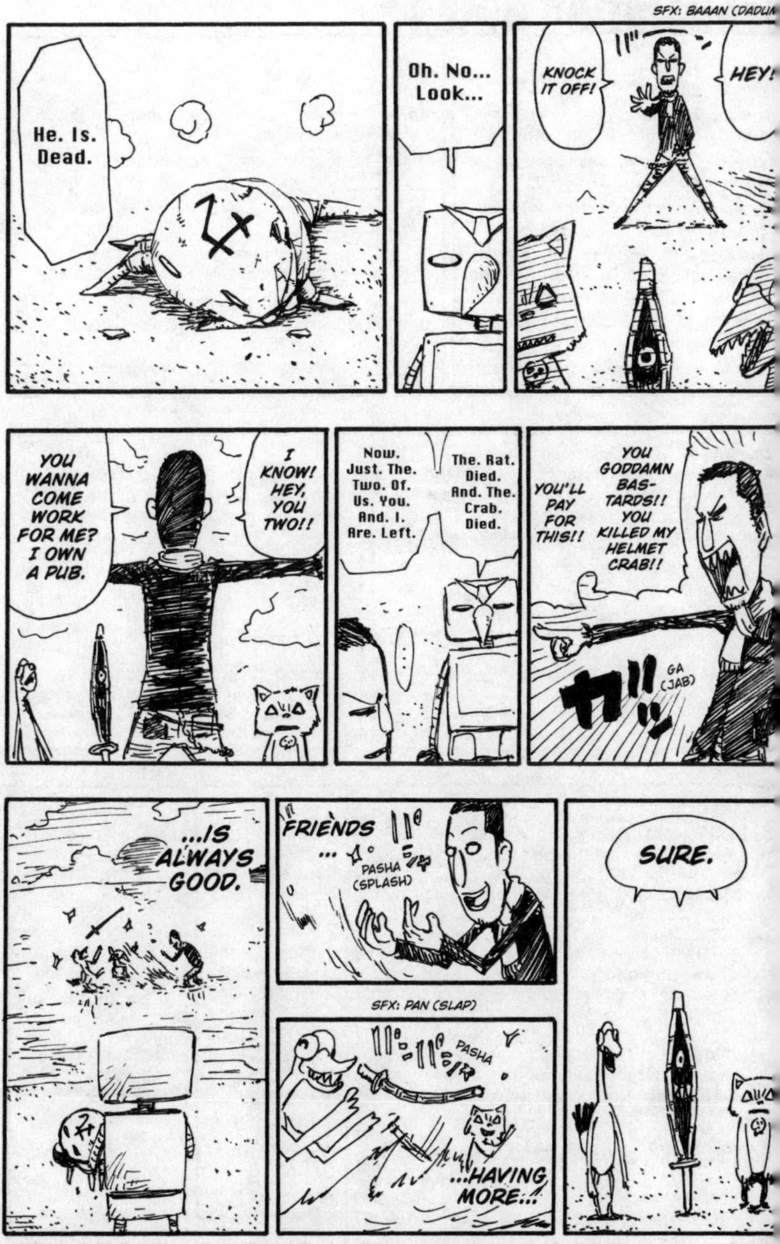
SFX: BAAAN (DADUM
HEY!
KNOCK IT OFF!
Oh. No... Look...
He. Is. Dead.
YOU GODDAMN BASTARDS!! YOU KILLED MY HELMET CRAB!!
YOU'LL PAY FOR THIS!!
GA (JAB)
The. Rat. Died. And. The. Crab. Died.
Now. Just. The. Two. Of. Us. You. And. I. Are. Left.
...
I KNOW! HEY, YOU TWO!!
YOU WANNA COME WORK FOR ME? I OWN A PUB.
SURE.
FRIENDS ...
PASHA (SPLASH)
SFX: PAN (SLAP)
PASHA
...HAVING MORE..!
...IS ALWAYS GOOD.

Translation Notes

Common Honorifics

No honorific: Indicates familiarity or closeness; if used without permission or reason, addressing someone in this manner would constitute an insult.

-san: The Japanese equivalent of Mr./Mrs./Miss. If a situation calls for politeness, this is the fail-safe honorific.

-sama: Conveys great respect; may also indicate that the social status of the speaker is lower than that of the addressee.

-kun: Used most often when referring to boys, this indicates affection or familiarity. Occasionally used by older men among their peers, but it may also be used by anyone referring to a person of lower standing.

-chan: An affectionate honorific indicating familiarity used mostly in reference to girls; also used in reference to cute persons or animals of either gender.

-senpai: A suffix used to address upperclassmen or more experienced coworkers.

-sensei: A respectful term for teachers, artists, or high-level professionals.

Page 44
The name **Borscht 7 Factory** is a pun on the Japanese pronunciation of borscht: *borushichi*, which sounds like "ball 7" to Japanese ears. In this manga, it's spelled "Boru 7" but meant to evoke "borscht" (also because of the Russia connection, obviously), thus "Borscht 7" captures a little of both parts of the pun.

Page 49
The suffix *–tan* is a cutesy form of *–chan*, and the name "Blair" can be shortened to "Bu" in Japanese, so **Bu-tan** is just a cutesy form of Blair-chan.

Page 61
The name "The **Flying Dutchman**" comes from a legend about a ghost ship doomed to sail the sea forever, never to return home. In some versions of the tale, "The Flying Dutchman" refers to the ship itself, and in others it refers to the ship's captain. Some retellings have it that the captain is only allowed to go to port every certain number of years (the number varies in each version) to seek out a woman to share his fate. Seeing the ship is considered a bad omen.

Page 64
The **kamaitachi** (demon weasel; literally "scythe-weasel") is a fearsome mythological Japanese monster taking the form of a weasel with scythe-like claws. Maka's attack uses a homophonous kanji spelling that translates to "Scythe-Threat Cut," but the image of the kamaitachi monster is meant to be invoked by the name.

Page 83
In Norse mythology, Niðhöggr (often anglicized as "**Nidhogg**") is the name of the dragon who gnaws at the roots of Yggdrasil, a great tree known as the "world tree." In this series, Nidhogg is also the name of the Flying Dutchman's ghost ship.

Page 85
The various sound words describing the Flying Dutchman's slobbering and smacking his lips and fingering his temple include "**gripper**" and "**crystal**" among them because they are made from the sounds in *guri* and *chuppa*. The whole sequence is just playing with words and doesn't mean anything in particular.

The Dutchman's gasp of *hatto* (sudden realization) is also obviously a pun for "hat."

Page 86
Liz's motto is a nod to Dostoyevsky's acerbic unnamed narrator's famous line in *Notes from Underground*: "I say let the world go to hell, so long as I can have my tea whenever I want it."

Page 125
The Japanese names of the Clown's attacks—**Clown Machine Gun, Clown Lariat**—are portmanteau words based on Japanese sound similarities. "Clown Machine Gun" is *dokeshin gan*, where the first word is a blend of *dokeshi* (clown) and *mashin* (machine), and "Clown Lariat" is *pieriatto*, a blend of *piero* (also clown, from the French word *pierrot* of the same meaning) and *rariatto* (lariat, which in this case refers to a kind of pro wrestling move similar to a clothesline).

Page 132
The Japanese pronunciation of **Letter-"I"-Hunt Slash** is *ichi-monji-gari* (literally "letter-one-hunt"), which suggests that the "Letter 'I'" part is meant to be interpreted as the Roman numeral I (for "1").

Page 143
The **witch mass chant** is actually *majo, majo, saraba da* (witch, witch, this is farewell) backward by syllable.

Page 159
A **talking drum** is an hourglass-shaped West African percussion instrument that can be played in such a way as to mimic the rhythms of speech. Traditionally, talking drums were even used to pass complex messages across long distances.

Page 173
When Mosquito says he will become Kim and Jackie's **sugar daddy longlegs**, what he actually says in Japanese is *nagaashi-ojisan* ("Daddy Longlegs"), a term that specifically refers to someone who provides financial support to college students, especially girls. Of course, Mosquito chooses this particular phrase because of the connection to spiders. The usage of the Japanese phrase itself stems from an early 20th-century American popular novel titled *Daddy-Long-Legs*, about an orphan girl whose college fees are paid by a generous rich man whom she has never met.

Can't wait for the next volume? You don't have to!

Keep up with the latest chapters of some of your favorite manga every month online in the pages of YEN PLUS!

READ IT THE SAME DAY AS JAPAN!

SOUL EATER NOT!

MAXIMUM RIDE

SOULLESS

WITCH & WIZARD

THE INFERNAL DEVICES
CLOCKWORK ANGEL

Visit us at
www.yenplus.com
for details!

YEN + Plus

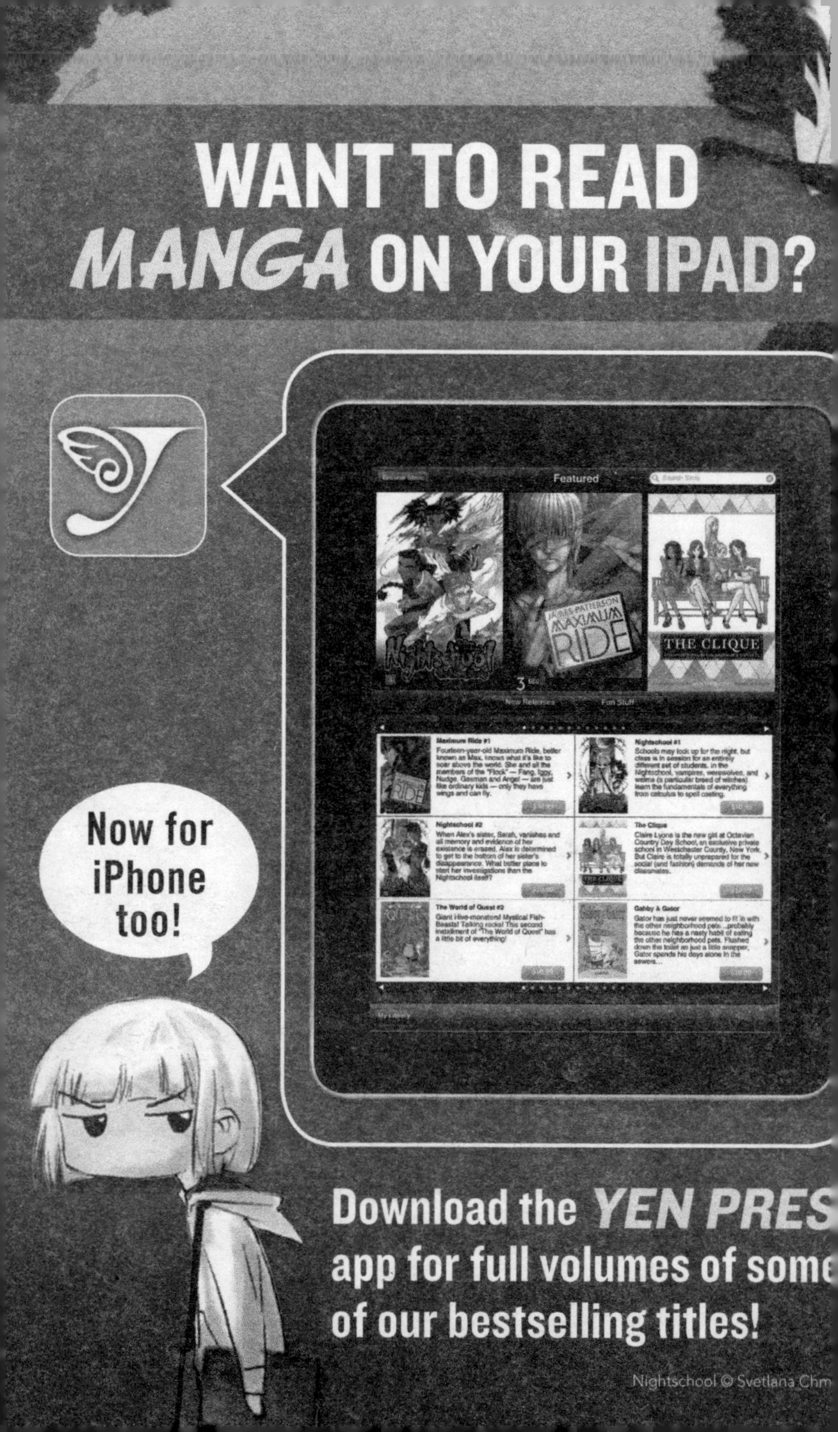
WANT TO READ
MANGA ON YOUR IPAD?
Featured
THE CLIQUE
Now for iPhone too!
Download the YEN PRES
app for full volumes of some
of our bestselling titles!
Nightschool © Svetlana Chm

DING-DONG!

DEAD-DONG!

DON'T BE LATE FOR THE "NOT" CLASS AT DEATH WEAPON MEISTER ACADEMY!

OLDER TEEN
OT

Yen Press

SOUL EATER NOT!

ATSUSHI OHKUBO

WELCOME TO IKEBUKURO, WHERE TOKYO'S WILDES CHARACTERS GATHER!!

AS THEIR PATHS CROSS, THIS ECCENTRIC CAST WEAVES A TWISTED, CRACKED LOVE STORY...

AVAILABLE NOW!!

SOUL EATER ⑪

Atsushi Ohkubo

Translation: Jack Wiedrick

Lettering: Alexis Eckerman

SOUL EATER Vol. 11 ©2008 Atsushi Ohkubo/SQUARE ENIX CO., LTD. First published in Japan in 2008 by SQUARE ENIX CO., LTD. English translation rights arranged with SQUARE ENIX CO., LTD. and Hachette Book Group through Tuttle-Mori Agency, Inc.

English translation ©2012 by SQUARE ENIX CO., LTD.

Yen Press
150 West 30th Street, 19th floor
New York, NY 10001

Visit us at yenpress.com
facebook.com/yenpress
twitter.com/yenpress
yenpress.tumblr.com
instagram.com/yenpress

First Yen Press Edition: November 2012

Yen Press is an imprint of Yen Press, LLC.
The Yen Press name and logo are trademarks of Yen Press, LLC.

ISBN: 978-0-316-07115-4

10

OPM

Printed in the United States of America